D1520691

FOREIGN POLICY RESTRUCTURING AS ADAPTIVE BEHAVIOR

China's Independent Foreign Policy 1982-1989

Sanqiang Jian

University Press of America, Inc.
Lanham • New York • London

Copyright © 1996 by
University Press of America,® Inc.
4720 Boston Way
Lanham, Maryland 20706

3 Henrietta Street
London, WC2E 8LU England

Library of Congress Cataloging-in-Publication Data

Jian, Sanqiang.
Foreign policy restructuring as adaptive behavior : China's
independent foreign policy, 1982-1989 / Sanqiang Jian.
p.   cm.
Includes index.
1. China--Foreign relations--1976- 2. International relations.   I.
Title.
DS779.27.J53   1996   327.51 --dc20   96-17905   CIP

ISBN 0-7618-0419-6 (cloth: alk. ppr.)

To Peng
and
To My Parents

Contents

List of Figures and Tables

Figures

Tables

PREFACE

Foreign policy restructuring as a particular type of foreign policy behavior has long received little attention in the literature of foreign policy study. In this book, foreign policy restructuring is defined as the dramatic wholesale alteration of a state's previous pattern of external relations within a region or in the global system. It is operationalized as the major change in the pattern of foreign partnership and the type of activities in which it engages. It includes a class of actions through which the state copes with external and/or internal changes affecting its national interest so that it can continue to function well.

According to the conceptual framework developed in this book, the case of China's foreign policy restructuring in the 1980s under the name of "independent foreign policy of peace" is systematically examined. It is not a simple chronicle study of China's foreign policy in the 1980s. Rather, it is an in depth analysis of China's foreign policy from a conceptual point of view. The purpose of the analysis is to address five issues: (1) the driving forces behind China's foreign policy restructuring, (2) the interaction of these forces in generating such a restructuring, (3) the reasons for China to choose an "independent foreign policy of peace" as opposed to others, (4) restructuring activities, and (5) the effectiveness of China's foreign policy restructuring.

Through a comprehensive examination, the book finds: (1) China's foreign policy restructuring started in the early 1980s when its united front foreign policy had become increasingly unproductive in the face of the dramatic changes at home and abroad; (2) the reform leadership under Deng Xiaoping played a decisive role in reshaping China's policies under the new circumstances; (3) independence, peace and development became the themes of China's new foreign policy; (4) restructuring occurred in four aspects of China's foreign policy (i.e., strategic/military posture, foreign economic relations, major diplomatic activities and efforts to reunify the country); (5) the new policy enhanced China's security environment and greatly promoted its economic growth. Such a policy continues even following the 1989 Tiananmen Incident and in the immediate post-Cold War era.

In contributing to the literature, this book not only provides a systematic analysis of Beijing's foreign policy in the 1980s, but also uses the analysis to develop more general propositions about foreign policy restructuring. They are: (1) Foreign policy restructuring is likely to occur when a country's existing foreign policy increasingly becomes unproductive in the core issue areas (i.e., national security, economic development, major foreign contacts, and domestic political control) and no longer serves the basic needs of the country. (2) Major external and/or internal events affecting a country's basic interests often exercise pressures on the country's existing foreign policy and may trigger foreign policy restructuring. (3) Foreign policy restructuring happens only when the decision-makers of the country recognize the pressures and the inadequacy of their existing foreign policy and define the need for a change under the new circumstances. (4) The interplay of external environment, domestic politics and political leadership in the process of foreign policy restructuring is linked by the self-preservation goal of the country. (5) Foreign policy restructuring is measured by the change in its basic attitudes towards its major foreign partnerships and the way it manages its major foreign policy sectors over time. (6) The effectiveness of foreign policy restructuring is judged by whether the new policy can remedy the problems of the previous policy and enhance the country's basic interests under the new circumstances.

In the final analysis, foreign policy restructuring is a response made by a state in face of change. As a matter of fact, we are now living in an era of constant change and no governments are immune to changes. Undoubtedly, China like many other countries must often adjust its foreign policy accordingly. The question is not whether a country should change its foreign policy. Rather, it is a question whether a country can change it in a correct manner.

Finally, the author wishes to thank Boleslaw A. Boczek, Frank K. Klink, Yeh-chieh Wang and Donald A. White for giving their time and attention to helping improve this book.

February 1996
Sanqiang Jian

Chapter 1

Foreign Policy Restructuring:
An Introduction

China's Foreign Policy was
Restructured in the 1980s

At the Twelfth National Congress of the Chinese Communist Party (CCP) in September 1982, the Chinese leadership announced that the People's Republic of China (PRC) would adopt a new foreign policy known as "independent foreign policy of peace." This announcement marked an official shift in the PRC's anti-Soviet foreign policy which had been implemented throughout the 1970s. Very soon five major changes took place in Beijing's foreign policy.

The first change was that China adjusted its foreign strategic arrangement by formally disavowing too close a relationship with either the United States or the Soviet Union. Beijing publicly declared that it would not enter into an alliance or establish strategic relations with any superpower or groups of countries; it would independently decide its positions and policies on international issues.[1] Soon China restructured its relations with the two superpowers by moving away from the anti-Russian and pro-American position to a more independent one.

In the 1970s, China's foreign policy was grounded on persistent growth of the Soviet military threat to China's security. In order to resist the primary threat from Moscow, the PRC reopened relations in 1972 with its former enemy, the United States. On the basis of their common strategic concern over the Soviet threat, Beijing and Washington established a de facto alliance, aiming at increasing Soviet strategic vulnerability by forcing Moscow to confront a multifront conflict with both the West and China. This strategic arrangement significantly strengthened China's national security and enhanced Beijing's importance in world affairs.

However, in the early 1980s big changes occurred in the international balance of power which seriously challenged the basic assumptions of Beijing's anti-Soviet and pro-American strategy. Under President Reagan, the United States adopted a policy of "all around confrontation" with Moscow as a means of reversing U.S. strategic setbacks of the past decade.[2] Washington actively engaged in a new round of the arms race by building up its military forces. The Soviet Union at the same time was struggling with tremendous problems including domestic economic failure, leadership successions, and the quagmire in Afghanistan. As a result, Soviet influence started to decline and a certain strategic parity emerged between the superpowers. In the face of this development, the Reagan administration publicly downgraded China's importance in the anti-Soviet strategic cooperation. Problems soon appeared in Sino-American relations because of U.S. arms sales to Taiwan and difficulties in technology transfers to China. Obviously, Beijing's overreliance upon the West for the security arrangement reduced China's leverage in dealing with Washington. In the meantime, Moscow deliberately made conciliatory gestures towards Beijing. In March 1982, Leonid Brezhnev, for the first time, publicly expressed Moscow's willingness to improve relations with China and signaled to end the ideological disputes between the two countries.[3] China's response was very cautious and demanded the removal of "three obstacles" (i.e., withdrawal of Soviet troops from Afghanistan, the end of Soviet support for the Vietnamese occupation of Cambodia, and a substantial reduction of Soviet military buildup along the Chinese border) before the normalization of bilateral ties.

The strained Sino-American relationship and the declining Soviet threat to China made Beijing rethink its relations with the superpowers. After the internal debate on China's foreign policy and on the changed international balance of power, Beijing concluded that by not entering into an alliance with either superpower the Chinese would gain more leverage and freedom to maneuver in the strategic triangle.

Thus, China began to distance itself from the United States and bargain with Moscow for improved relations. By doing so, Beijing was successful in pressing Washington to ease China's complaints. In August 1982, Washington agreed to "eventually" stop selling arms to Taiwan; in May 1983, the White House liberalized technology transfers to Beijing. Gradually, Beijing and Washington refocused their relations from solely strategic areas to more functional ones. In Sino-Soviet relations, the normalization process between the two countries was slow but steady. They were quick to restore economic collaboration. On the political front, China resolutely continued to push Moscow to make concessions toward removing the obstacles. In maneuvering between the two superpowers, Beijing deliberately kept relations with Washington one step ahead of its relations with Moscow. Chinese patience finally paid off. By the end of the 1980s, the Soviet Union under Gorbachev's "new thinking" removed the "three obstacles" as China had long demanded. On May 15, 1989, Gorbachev made his historic visit to Beijing officially ending twenty years of hostility between the two giants. In stabilizing its relations with the superpowers, the PRC had obtained its most favorable security environment at any time since 1949.

The second major change in China's foreign policy was Beijing's greater emphasis on creating a stable international environment favorable to China's economic modernization drive. The rise of a reform-minded leadership under Deng Xiaoping fundamentally shifted China's domestic top priority from Mao's emphasis on revolutionary values and political movements to the stress of economic modernization. Accordingly, the primary concern of Beijing's foreign policy became the establishment of a peaceful external environment, especially around China's periphery. Chinese leaders were realistic enough to see that the military threat to its security from the Soviet Union was not immanent due to the fact that Soviet influence had declined. In the mid-1980s, Beijing even concluded that, because of the difficulties that the superpowers faced, both Moscow and Washington would resume serious efforts to reach arms control agreements and reduce regional conflicts. Under such a détente, there would be no major threat to China for quite a while. The 1987 Intermediate Nuclear Forces Treaty (INF) and the cooling down of regional rivalry largely supported this judgement. The Chinese definition of global reality became more optimistic resulting in a decision to engage in major military reductions by substantially cutting down one million service personnel, one-fourth of its armed forces. A large portion of the defense industry was also converted to civilian-oriented functions.

In order to create a peaceful external environment in support of the country's economic reform, China advocated international peace efforts under the slogan of opposing international hegemony.[4] After reevaluating the role of the United Nations (UN) in maintaining world peace, China abandoned its past policy of nonparticipation in UN peace-keeping activities. On the international arms control and disarmament issue, China changed its past evaluative attitude. In the 1970s, Beijing had criticized all the West-East arms control and disarmament efforts as an appeasement policy in the West that could only encourage the Soviets to move more forces to East Asia. But in the 1980s, China turned to highlight the dangers of the buildup of nuclear forces. Believing that dialogue was better than confrontation,

Chinese leaders called for reductions in superpower nuclear arsenals. In 1986, Beijing also announced plans to cease aboveground nuclear tests.

The third major change in Beijing's foreign behavior was China's pragmatic attitudes in developing cooperative relations with all countries on the basis of the Five Principles of Peaceful Coexistence, irrespective of the differences in their social or ideological systems.[5] As a part of its efforts to establish a favorable international environment, Beijing vigorously cultivated good relations with various countries. In the Asia-Pacific region, China made efforts to play a major role in maintaining regional stability and actively developed good-neighborly relations. It supported political settlement of both the Cambodian and Afghan issues and welcomed relaxations of tension on the Korean Peninsula. While keeping friendly ties with North Korea, Beijing pragmatically developed economic cooperation with South Korea. Sino-Japanese economic cooperation became an integral part of China's modernization program. In South Asia, China improved its relations with India and continued its friendly ties with Pakistan. In Southeast Asia, China strengthened ties with Thailand, Malaysia and the Philippines, and move to reopen relations with Indonesia and Singapore. Sino-Vietnamese ties were also slowly improved.

China also adjusted its policy towards developing countries and started to improve its tarnished image in the Third World. In the 1970s Beijing had aligned itself too closely with the West and developed its relations with third world countries depending too much upon their reactions toward Moscow. As a result, China had lost a wide range of third world support. In 1982 Beijing changed this policy and took a more realistic approach to regain this support. China became more critical of both superpowers' policies in the Third World and raised more concern over third world issues such as the North-South dialogue and South-South cooperation. Meanwhile, Beijing reduced relations with most national liberation movements and significantly cut its support to revolutionary parties. While deemphasizing ideology in its relations with the Third World, China rapidly expanded ties with many right-wing developing countries, especially in the Middle East and in South America. In adopting a more pragmatic approach, Beijing encouraged cooperation and negotiations between various third world nations and placed strong emphasis on expanding economic ties between China and the Third World.

China's relations with Europe also changed in the 1980s. In the past, China had paid more attention to strategic cooperation with Western Europe and firmly supported armament of the North Atlantic Treaty Organization (NATO) to counter-balance the Soviet threat. After 1982, Beijing began to support peace initiatives in Europe and focused more on developing commercial relations with Western Europe. The change in China's perception of the international balance of power and the incentive to obtain capital and technology from the West were the reasons for this shift. Consequently, China established diplomatic relations with all the major Western European countries including the European Community. Economic and technological cooperation between them grew rapidly. China's relations with Eastern European countries had been cool in the 1970s (except for Yugoslavia and Romania). But, along with the reduction of tensions between China and the Soviet Union, Beijing was very careful to take pragmatic steps to restore commercial, cultural, diplomatic, and political contacts with Eastern European countries.

The fourth major change in China's foreign policy was an unprecedented expansion of China's foreign economic relations and the opening of the country to the outside world. During the 1980s, China significantly increased its participation in the world economy. The open door policy was the most fundamental restructuring in China's foreign policy. For centuries, China has been a closed society with a self-sufficient economy. In the 1970s, while putting much emphasis on the strategic cooperation with the United States against the Soviet military threat, Mao Zedong had allowed only limited economic and cultural cooperation with the West for the fear that the Western influence would damage the revolutionary values he had preferred in China. But after Mao, under the leadership of Deng Xiaoping, China resolutely abandoned the "self-reliance" policy and opened up to the outside world, including not only the West, but also all other countries. China was determined to integrate itself into the modern international system. For the purpose of introducing foreign capital, technology and management into China, Beijing downplayed the role of ideology and actively developed economic relations with any possible partners. Beijing offered many preferential policies to foreign investors. As a result, numerous foreign investments were attracted and joint ventures set up across the country in the 1980s. China also established Special Economic Zones (SEZs) in the nation where capitalist market practices were allowed. Not only that, China also reversed its previous practice of not borrowing money in the international market and obtained a large amount of loans and credits from abroad. Meanwhile, large numbers of Chinese visiting scholars and students were sent to work or study in the West. Foreign experts and technicians also came to China. By integrating itself into the world economy, China achieved significant economic growth in the 1980s. Despite a virtually worldwide economic recession, Chinese exports quintupled, growing far faster than aggregate world trade.[6] Besides, China joined a wide range of international organizations during the 1980s, including the International Monetary Fund (IMF), the World Bank, the Asian Development Bank, the international Atomic Energy Agency and over 200 international science and technology agencies.

Last but not least, in changing China's foreign policy, its government took a realistic step towards reunification with Hong Kong, Macao and Taiwan. By applying Deng Xiaoping's "one country, two systems" model,[7] Beijing was successful in signing agreements with Great Britain and Portugal to regain China's sovereignty over Hong Kong in 1997 and Macao in 1999. Meanwhile, Beijing also made conciliatory gestures toward Taiwan. Tensions between the two deadly enemies were sharply reduced and the economic and cultural relations between them greatly expanded.

All the above descriptions of China's foreign policy in the 1980s have shown that Beijing adopted a completely new foreign policy emphasizing independence, peace and economic development. With this policy, China stabilized its relations with the superpowers, improved relations with almost all of its traditional rival neighbors and dramatically expanded its economic ties with the rest of the world. In conducting this "omni-directional" diplomacy, Beijing had become less radical and less ideological, and more realistic, pragmatic and sophisticated in handling its foreign relations.[8]

A Systematic Analysis

There are numerous studies on Chinese foreign policy in the 1980s.[9] Most of them are either event-driven analyses, such as disputes between China and the United States on the issue of Taiwan, reconciliatory developments between Beijing and Moscow, Chinese arms sales to the Middle East, and Sino-British negotiations on the future of Hong Kong; or concentrate only on specific aspects of

China's foreign policy like the strategic triangular relations, economic opening-up, and China's third world policy. There has been little systematic study of China's unique overall foreign policy during this period. As a result, most scholarly study of Chinese foreign policy in the 1980s is fragmented and lacking in overall coherence. The underlying themes which ran through Beijing's foreign policy activities during this period have not been well studied. One reason for this situation is the time-lag effect. When most studies were conducted, many events were still under way or unfolding. This is particularly true for the studies which concentrate on China's foreign policy in the first half of the 1980s. At that time Beijing had just started restructuring its foreign policy. Many of the studies did describe the events in Beijing's foreign relations and might have sensed the change in Beijing's foreign policy. But they were not clear about what China's "independent foreign policy of peace" really meant to China's overall foreign policy. Still following the traditional strategic triangle perspective (i.e., Beijing sought a position of equidistance between Moscow and Washington or sought to occupy the advantageous "swing" position among the three nuclear powers in East Asia), they believed that China's new initiative was just another round of strategic maneuvering.[10] So most conclusions reached by these studies failed to catch the true meaning of the development of China's foreign policy.

In fact, the reality of China's foreign policy in the 1980s was much more than just strategic restructuring. Since the mid-1980s, Beijing had made a series of foreign policy reform efforts ranging from an independent strategic stance to a comprehensive open door policy, and from a conciliatory attitudes towards its neighboring countries to pragmatic dealings with all countries on the basis of peaceful coexistence. With the accumulative account of these specific foreign policy actions taken by Beijing, people gradually came to realize that the independent position represented a wholesale reorientation in China's foreign policy. The major themes behind the "independent foreign policy" were threading through all of China's foreign policy activities in the 1980s. Clearly, without grasping these themes, it will be impossible to fully understand Chinese foreign behavior at that time.

This book is a comprehensive examination of China's foreign policy restructuring in the 1980s. It traces themes behind the major events in Beijing's foreign policy during this period, providing a descriptive and analytic account of China's foreign policy restructuring from the rigid and unidimensional anti-Soviet orientation to the flexible and omni-directional "independent" one. The following chapters will answer such questions as: What were the driving forces which promoted the Chinese leadership to recognize that its pre-1982 foreign policy was seriously inadequate and in need of restructuring? How did these forces interact with one another to generate such a restructuring? Why did China choose an independent foreign policy strategy as opposed to others? What specific plans did China have and what concrete actions did it take under the new policy? And what consequences has the new strategy produced for China?

In answering these questions, this author develops a theoretical framework to analyze the behaviors involved in foreign policy restructuring. This framework includes both definition and operationalization of foreign policy restructuring, and general propositions about it. Only in this way can the case of China's foreign policy restructuring in the 1980s be explained in a systemic and logical manner. Moreover, China is one example of foreign policy restructuring which may generate some relevant findings for the larger universe of similar restructurings.

Foreign Policy Restructuring
As a Theoretical Problem

Foreign policy restructuring *in the form of either a reversal or a redirection of a nation's foreign policy course,* as exemplified by the Chinese case, is of special interest in international studies. It is vital for international peace and security in today's interdependent world because the changing course of a nation's foreign policy not only poses new demands for the country in question, but also produces potentially significant consequences for other related countries. This is especially true in cases of important countries restructuring their foreign policies. China's "independent foreign policy of peace" in 1982 is just one example. Richard Nixon's visit to Beijing in 1972 is another, in that it eventually reshaped the international balance of power and brought about a series of changes in international politics. Still another example is Great Britain's discarding its previous anti-Common Market policy and joining the European Economic Community in 1973. The world was shocked when President Sadat of Egypt announced his trip to Jerusalem in 1977 after a long period of hostility and war with Israel.

The trip was a turning point in the Middle East politics which not only brought peace to Egypt, but also caused realignments among other Arab countries. The "new thinking" under Gorbachev in the former Soviet Union which fundamentally changed international politics and eventually brought the Cold War to an end. Clearly, foreign policy restructuring is an important topic in the study of international relations.

The study of foreign policy restructuring also has theoretical significance since it requires an explanation of what factors under what circumstances cause a state to realize that there is a need to restructure its current foreign policy course. A variety of factors may determine whether or not a state's foreign policy strategy is likely to endure or to change. Regime change, state transformation and revolution are obviously important ways for a state to change its foreign policy course. The disintegration of the Soviet Union is one of the recent examples in this regard. But in most cases, foreign policy redirection is a self-correcting change by the incumbent government. *This book is concerned only with the latter type of foreign policy restructuring.* Of course, the latter type is less easy to explain as an existing government may choose different foreign policy courses even under similar conditions. But it is not impossible to develop some general propositions about this type of foreign policy restructuring through empirical studies. As noted by one student of foreign policy, "any country is both different from all others and similar to some of them, the differences stemming from its unique circumstances and the similarities being the result either of structural requirements inherent in polities, economies and societies at comparable stages of development or of forces at work on a transnational scale in a particular era."[11] Hence, any single country has both its uniqueness and the dynamics it shares with other countries.

How Well Do We Know Foreign Policy Restructuring?

Although foreign policy restructuring, as a special type of foreign policy behavior, is an important topic in the study of foreign policy, there is a shortage of literature which systematically studies this specific phenomenon.[12] A review of current foreign policy writings reveals that foreign policy research is concerned with identifying the internal and external determinants of a state's foreign policy behavior. The sources of foreign policy, such as international power structures, economic conditions, public opinion, misperceptions, the personality drives of key policy-makers, and bureaucratic struggles in the decision-making process, have received more attention than the actual policies.[13] Even where policy is reviewed, rather static pictures are described without the aim of analyzing a type of foreign policy behavior. For example, dramatic changes, such as China's realignment with the United States or Egypt's break from the Soviet Union in the 1970s, were often studied in a static fashion by explaining ad hoc policy determinants. They were not analyzed as a type of foreign policy behavior. Therefore, the purpose of a specific type of foreign policy behavior, such as foreign policy restructuring, and the relationship between that behavior and its "sources" are neglected.

It is true that no sources of foreign policy remain static; foreign policy determinants change over time, resulting in foreign policy adjustments. Different changes (e.g., extent, scope, speed, importance, etc.) in determinants may bring about different types of foreign policy changes. All states must carry out minor adjustments or modifications in their daily foreign activities which may include changes of specific ways, methods or programs to handle their foreign relations. Usually such a type of change does not involve a shift in the basic objectives of foreign policy. On the contrary, it helps improve the realization of the basic objectives and the change itself is still largely conditioned by the basic objectives. On some occasions, however, another type of foreign policy change--foreign policy restructuring which involves dramatic redirection of a state's basic foreign policy objectives--may take place. *The focus of this book is on such a type of foreign policy change rather than minor adjustments in a given country's foreign policy.*

Unfortunately, the foreign policy literature lacks an adequate description or explanation of foreign policy restructuring. In fact, foreign policy restructuring involves the relationship between change and foreign policy making. This relationship has long been a neglected area in the study of foreign policy. Since the 1980s, some works about the relationship between change and foreign policy making begin to explain the phenomenon of foreign policy restructuring. But the questions regarding the sources, process, purpose, and even consequences of this type of foreign policy behavior have not been thoroughly answered.

Change and the Study of International Relations: The Evaded Dimension (1981), edited by Barry Buzan and R.J. Barry Jones, seeks primarily to "produce a set of concise critical essays that [reveal] the inadequacies of the way in which change is conceptualized in much of international relations literature, and to contribute to the refinement of the concept."[14] The argument is in large measure concerned with epistemology. Contributors to that book discuss many aspects of change in international relations and provide a variety of views on how to study change in international relations. Their conclusion is that change is still a dimension that has not been well studied in international political studies.

Change in the International System (1980), edited by Ole R. Holsti, Randolph M. Siverson and Alexander L. George, explores the relationship between two levels of change in international politics: international system transformation and foreign policy change.[15] The book demonstrates an obvious truth that systemic transformation alters the conditions for foreign policy making. At the same time, systemic change is triggered by changes in units. Just as the structure affects the units, changes in systems originate in their parts. Systemic change which leads to foreign policy changes is emphasized only in a general sense.

Robert Gilpin's *War and Change in World Politics* (1981) argues that international political change is the result of efforts of political actors "to change the international system in order to advance their own interests."[16] Based on five assumptions, Gilpin argues that states engage in cost-benefit calculations about alternative courses of action.[17] To him, the key factor to account for change in the international system is "the tendency in an international system for the powers of member states to change at different rates because of political, economic, and technological developments."[18] The differential growth in power of the various states indicate the redistribution of power in the system that eventually will cause international political changes and foreign policy changes too.

Political Change and Foreign Policies (1987), edited by Gavin Boyd and Gerald Hopple, is a collection of policy analyses on changing global actors, especially some major countries (e.g., the United States, the Soviet Union, China, Japan, Britain, France, and Germany) in the world today.[19] The book also discusses changing behavior in such issue areas as political cooperation, foreign economic policies, international security policies, and systemic change. The collection is not theoretically and conceptually oriented but basically refers to practical policy considerations for decision-makers.

In his book *Change and Stability in Foreign Policy* (1988), Kjell Goldmann studies the relationship between change and foreign policy stability. He hypothesizes that in any given foreign policy, there exist some factors in the governmental decision-making process which have the function of resisting policy change. Goldmann calls these factors policy stabilizers which "may (1) block policy change unless removed, (2) reduce the scope of policy change, or (3) delay policy change."[20] In his study, Goldmann identifies four categories of policy stabilizers. They are international, cognitive, political and administrative stabilizers.[21] He uses détente policy in the 1970s as an empirical case to test the hypothesis of policy stabilizers. The findings of his research support his hypothesis.

The work which specifically focuses on foreign policy restructuring is *Why Nations Realign: Foreign Policy Restructuring in the Postwar World* (1982) edited by Kalevi J. Holsti. In this study, Holsti defines foreign policy restructuring as "the dramatic, wholesale alteration of a nation's pattern of external relations...within a region or in the global system."[22] Holsti explains that foreign policy restructuring takes place when a country has the need to respond to a threat. This threat can be military, cultural, or economic. Six cases of foreign policy restructuring are studied in the book. Holsti's book represents a preliminary effort to systematically study the phenomenon of foreign policy restructuring.

In his article "Changing Course: When Governments Choose to Redirect Foreign Policy" (1990), Charles Hermann argues that major policy change is not a simply determined by forces operating at home and abroad, but by decision-makers' perceptions.[23] Although major changes in the international political and economic systems may result in modification of foreign policy, policy-makers can either anticipate such changes, respond just in time, or react only after suffering dramatic consequences. To Hermann, major policy shifts sometimes occur as a result of the leader's initiative rather than resulting from international changes. Hermann develops a model which identifies the conditions under which a government is likely to redirect its foreign policy course. This model gives much attention to variables such as primary change agents (e.g., leader-driven, bureaucratic advocacy, domestic restructuring, external shock, political learning), government decision to change course, and extent of foreign policy change.

James N. Rosenau's adaptive behavior model also attempts to explain the relationship between change and foreign policy making. Published in 1981, *The Study of Political Adaptation* is a collection of Rosenau's works on the adaptive behavior in foreign policy since 1970.[24] The adaptive behavior model uses an organic metaphor to explain changes in foreign policy. His basic assumption is that, like any organism, a state in international relations must constantly protect its basic interests and adjust itself to cope with pressures caused by the changes in its external and/or internal environments. To Rosenau, foreign policy is viewed as an adaptive behavior which involves not only objective forces operative at home and abroad, but also subjective responses made by decision-makers on behalf of the state for the purpose of protecting its basic interests. In a sense, the linkage between objective changes and subjective responses is provided by the state's basic need to survive and prosper in competitive international politics. Because of this, any questions regarding the state's physical safety, economic well-being, international environment, and national cohesion are likely to lead the state to adjust its foreign policy behavior so as to satisfy the state's basic demands.

Since Rosenau first introduced the concept of adaptation in 1970, his model has been heavily criticized.[25] Although the model is not suited for empirical use in its original form, it nevertheless consists of a number of interesting ideas which could be fruitfully developed. For this reason, numerous studies have been published on the subject.[26] While there are some empirical studies based on this model, no research on foreign policy restructuring has been conducted.[27]

To sum up, the literature review above indicates the fact that the relationship between change and foreign policy making is not well studied. As a special type of foreign policy behavior, foreign policy restructuring "has been largely neglected in international theory" as well.[28] There is a need to further explore the relationship between change and foreign policy making and develop general propositions about foreign policy restructuring.

The Analytical Framework

This book develops an analytical framework based on Rosenau's adaptive behavior approach to explain why China restructured its foreign policy in the 1980s. According to the adaptation model, a country's foreign policy restructuring is considered an adaptive behavior in which the country adjusts itself to changing circumstances. Adaptation refers to a class of activities through which a state copes with convergence of challenges to its vital interests from at home and/or abroad so that it can continue to function well as a state.[29] The vital interests usually include the basic conditions allowing a state to exist such as its physical safety, economic well-being, internal stability (i.e., national cohesion), and appropriate status in international relations.[30] It is thus evident that the adaptive behavior model regards foreign policy restructuring as a state's self-preserving function to ease pressures (as a result of internal and/or external changes) on its basic conditions. In this sense, foreign policy restructuring is a stimulus-response process linked by the self-preservation goals of states. Therefore, the theoretical substance underlying the model reflects the *raison d'état* concerns of *realpolitik* in international politics.[31]

Four reasons have made the adaptive behavior model appealing to this writer. First, the units of analysis in the adaptation model are nation-states, the principal actors in international relations. The model assumes that all units have similar functions (i.e., self-preservation) in international politics. Survival and prosperity are the basic goals of states. Thus, satisfying national interests is the fundamental mission of states. Second, changes in a state's external and/or internal environments often constitute pressures on the state's existing foreign policy and affect its national interest. As a result, the state must adjust itself to cope with and accommodate the changed circumstances. The purpose of adaptation in the form of foreign policy restructuring is to re-ensure the state's basic interests. In this sense, the independent variables leading a state to engage in foreign policy restructuring are pressures upon national security, economic demand, internal stability, and proper international environment for the state. Third, the task of foreign policy restructuring is undertaken not automatically by the state itself but by decision-makers on behalf of the state through their authoritative actions. They evaluate the effectiveness of the existing foreign policy and interpret pressures on it. Once they believe that the existing foreign policy is no longer productive and there is a need for policy restructuring, they will choose what they consider as the best policy to re-satisfy the state's national interest. Fourth, the adaptive behavior model gives much emphasis on the interaction among domestic politics, the external environment, and political leadership in foreign policy restructuring. Such an interaction centers on the self-preserving goal of a state. Therefore, the model does not over-emphasize the international constraints as the fundamental independent variable determining the state's foreign policy restructuring. Nor does the model focus on domestic factors as the sole source affecting foreign policy making. Nor does it look only at foreign policy decision-makers in the process. The model stresses that all the activities among the three factors in foreign policy restructuring are linked by the state's basic goal of self-preservation. Domestic, international, or individual factors are relevant only when they are related to this goal. Otherwise, policy failure will eventually take place. Clearly, foreign policy restructuring is a purposeful action by the state to ease pressures on its basic conditions. It is because of this that the model makes it possible to study and explain foreign policy restructuring. The adaptation model provides the explanation of why and under what conditions a country engages in foreign policy restructuring. But to show how this country restructures its foreign policy, if at all, requires an explanation of the differences in the country's foreign policy behavior (i.e., dependent variable) between one time and another. Clearly, continuity or discontinuity of behavior based on a specific foreign policy over a period of time provides a basis for determining whether or not the country has restructured its foreign policy. The official announcement of "independent foreign policy of peace" by the Chinese leadership in 1982 indicated that Beijing had started to abandon its previous anti-Soviet foreign policy and adopt a new one. In demonstrating China's foreign policy restructuring in the 1980s, this book uses a comparative method[32] to show in which ways China's "independent foreign policy of peace" in the 1980s were different from its previous "anti-Soviet united front foreign policy" in the 1970s. In doing so, this research first proves that China has restructured its foreign policy by indicating the degree of change in China's foreign behavior. Second, it also shows how the restructuring is proceeding. Third, such a comparison leads to the examination of the different assumptions underlying the two foreign policy patterns. The next logical step is to further explain what prompted formation of each of the two different sets of foreign policy assumptions. The focus is thus on changes in both independent variables (e.g., security concerns, economic demands, major foreign relations, and national cohesion) and intervening variables (e.g., role of decision-makers) at different periods. Because of the different performance of the independent variables at the two periods, China's safety, prosperity, internal stability, and appropriate status in international politics were affected differently. And the Chinese government had different interpretations. As a result, Beijing had to adjust its foreign policy and choose what it believed to be the best policy to satisfy the country's self-interest. It is at this point that the adaptation model explains why China restructured its foreign policy in the 1980s. To sum up, the research method used in this book addresses well issues of the process, sources, purpose and consequences of foreign policy restructuring as a special type of foreign policy behavior.

Finally, the year 1989 provides a climactic end for this book. First, in May 1989, Soviet President Gorbachev made his historic visit to Beijing, formally ending the twenty-year confrontation between the two countries; one of the major objectives of China's "independent foreign policy of peace" was met. Second, China was plunged into a deep domestic political crisis because of the Tiananmen Square Incident in June 1989. The brutality of the Chinese government in cracking down upon the pro-democracy movement caused indignation and protest the world over. Facing political condemnation and economic sanctions, China faced the most serious setbacks in its foreign policy since 1982. Third, after the fall of the Berlin Wall in late 1989, Communism collapsed first in Eastern Europe and two years later in the former Soviet Union. The Cold War came to an end and a "new world order" was taking a shape. As a result of these developments, China again faced new challenges from abroad and at home and had to adapt itself to the new circumstances. The period between 1982 and 1989 provides a relatively complete pattern in China's foreign behavior under the name of "independent foreign policy of peace." It is appropriate and reasonable to systematically examine the whole process of China's foreign policy restructuring during this eight-year period.

How is This Book Organized?

The adaptive behavior model provides the conceptual foundation for an analysis of foreign policy restructuring and explains why a state engages in foreign policy restructuring. Chapter 2 examines the definitional aspects of foreign policy restructuring. Questions concerning what foreign policy restructuring is and how the concept of foreign policy restructuring is empirically operationalized are addressed. This is followed by a discussion of foreign policy restructuring as adaptive behavior. Based on the adaptation model, a framework for the analysis of foreign policy restructuring is formulated. The framework regards foreign policy restructuring as an adaptive process including such basic stages as (1) pressures (e.g., external and/or internal) on the existing foreign policy; (2) decision-makers' interpretation activities; (3) foreign policy reorientation and its applications in specific actions; (4) and evaluation of restructuring effectiveness. The analysis of China's foreign policy restructuring in the 1980s in the following chapters is arranged according to this analytical framework.

One crucial task in applying a general framework to the study of a particular country is to identify the specific performance of the country's basic conditions and the specific way its decision-makers behave in foreign policy restructuring. This is due to the unique national attributes of each country in terms of geography, economic structure, history and political culture. Chapter 3 examines the sources of Chinese foreign policy restructuring by looking at the particular context of Chinese diplomacy. Several major aspects which are likely to cause China to redirect its foreign policy course are discussed in detail and the combined impact of these factors on China's foreign policy direction is summarized at the end of the chapter.

Because continuity or discontinuity of a country's certain foreign policy behavior constitutes the basis for the study of a country's foreign policy restructuring, Chapter 4 reviews China's pre-independence foreign policy pattern in the 1970s. Not only the basic assumptions of such a rigid policy and Mao's "three worlds" theory are analyzed, but also major international and domestic events which had made Beijing adopt the anti-Soviet united front policy are carefully presented.

Chapter 5 examines limitations of Beijing's anti-Soviet united front foreign policy under both the internal and external pressures of the late 1970s and the early 1980s. Domestically, it focuses on how China adapted to the post-Mao era. Political, economic and social crises at the time of Mao's death and the rise of reformers led by Deng Xiaoping in the Beijing government are reviewed, and shown to explain in large part how China changed its top priority from Mao's emphases of revolutionary values and political mass mobilizations to Deng's economic modernization drive. Emphasis is on the implications of domestic changes for China's foreign policy. Apart from analyzing domestic pressures for change, this chapter also examines international pressures for restructuring China's foreign policy in the early 1980s. They include difficulties in Sino-American ties, new developments in the relations between Beijing and Moscow, and the unproductive results of the united front strategy.

Chapter 6 explains how Beijing under Deng Xiaoping reshaped its foreign policy and developed an independent stance. It traces criticisms of the strong anti-Soviet and pro-West posture within the Chinese leadership. This is followed by an analysis of changed perceptions on the part of Chinese leaders of the international environment. These perceptions included a reassessment and downgrading of any immediate Soviet threat to China, the view that a new strategic parity was emerging between the superpowers, and the realization that international peace was actually possible. In line with China's new domestic policy priorities and the changed views on the international balance of power, the Chinese reform leadership put forward new foreign policy objectives. The principles of the "independent foreign policy of peace" are presented in the discussion. In the end, this chapter describes the preliminary initiatives under Beijing's new foreign policy orientation which include: (1) how China started to keep its distance without going to extremes in its relations with the United States; (2) how Beijing bargained for Sino-Soviet reconciliation; and (3) how China adopted new policies toward the Third World.

Chapter 7 and 8, respectively, examine how the new orientation of "independent foreign policy of peace" was translated into the major aspects of China's foreign policy and how Beijing changed its ways of conducting foreign activities. In the military/strategic aspect, China showed much confidence in its security environment and developed a new defense thinking. Beijing not only engaged in a big defense reduction, but also actively participated in international peace efforts. In China's foreign economic relations, Beijing adopted an open door policy substantially changing China's economic development strategy. Remarkable economic progress was made through "economic diplomacy" in the 1980s. As for China's relations with major foreign countries, Beijing and Washington refocused their relations on a functional basis. Sino-Soviet relations were finally normalized and Sino-Japanese ties constituted one of important components of China's modernization plan. By following the principle of peaceful coexistence, China established good-neighborly relations. Finally, Beijing also successfully regained its sovereignty over Hong Kong (1997) and Macao (1999) through negotiations with Great Britain and Portugal respectively. Relations between Beijing and Taipei also substantially improved. In sum, the themes of independence, peace and economic development in China's foreign policy were embodied in all these achievements.

The conclusion of this book is Chapter 9 which comprehensively evaluates the effectiveness of China's "independent foreign policy of peace," sums up the driving forces behind China's foreign policy restructuring in the 1980s. It also presents theoretical implications of the Chinese case in the study of foreign policy restructuring. Finally, it discusses some basic developments of China's foreign policy after the Tiananmen Square Incident in June 1989.

Chapter 2

Studying Foreign Policy Restructuring

What is Foreign Policy Restructuring?

Foreign policy restructuring is the core concept of this book. However, it is only one type of foreign policy behavior. Hence, before foreign policy restructuring is defined, it is necessary to elaborate on the general concept of foreign policy.

Conceptual Distinctions

Foreign policy is generally defined as "the authoritative actions which governments take--or are committed to take--in order either to preserve the desirable aspects of the international environment or to alter its undesirable aspects."[1] Clearly, foreign policy includes "goal-oriented or problem-oriented" governmental activities involving: (1) the selection of national needs beyond its border, (2) the choice of means to achieve the goals, and (3) the actual implementation in the pursuit of selected goals.[2]

James N. Rosenau, one of the most influential scholars in the study of foreign policy, points out that since foreign policy involves many aspects of activities, its study should avoid imprecise use of the term "foreign policy." Without more precise conceptual distinctions of the term, there will be much ambiguity and failure of communication because of the considerable confusion which stems from the loose use of the term.[3] According to Rosenau, the term *foreign policy* has at least three meanings: foreign policy "as a cluster of orientations, as a set of commitments to and plans for action, and as a form of behavior."[4]

First, foreign policy as a cluster of orientations means generalized intentions on which officials draw for guidance when confronted with external conditions that require decisions and action. Orientation means a state's basic attitudes, values, perceptions, and goals toward its salient external environment.[5] A state's foreign policy orientation is derived from the state's historical experiences, basic domestic structures, and the strategic circumstances which mark the state's place in world politics; and it allows for diverse applications when translated into specific actions. In this sense, a state's foreign policy orientation involves the general tendencies and principles that guide and underline the state's conduct in international affairs.

The second meaning of foreign policy refers to concrete plans and commitments which decision-makers develop for achieving certain objectives abroad that are consistent with their basic orientation. Rosenau points out that "the plans and commitments are, in effect, both translations of generalized orientations and reactions to the immediate context."[6] In this sense, foreign policy as a set of commitments to and plans for action involves specific strategies vis-à-vis particular countries, regions, or specific issues. It is usually reflected in a state's "policy statements," such as formal pronouncements, press conference remarks, and diplomatic communications.

The third meaning of foreign policy involves specific activities, "the concrete steps that officials of a nation take with respect to events and situations abroad."[7] If foreign policy is viewed in this way, it consists of actual behavior and concrete actions by which a state implements its foreign policy orientation, fulfills its plans, and seeks its goals abroad.

The analysis of foreign-policy-as-orientation involves problems and phenomena other than the investigation of foreign-policy-as-plans, and both encompass issues different from those involved in the study of foreign-policy-as-behavior. Furthermore, the three meanings of foreign policy are closely related to one another in terms of sequence. Any change in foreign policy orientation will certainly bring about a series of changes in foreign policy plans and foreign policy behavior. This point is extremely crucial in understanding the concept of foreign policy restructuring.

Foreign Policy Restructuring

In international relations, a nation's foreign policy is "not randomly directed toward the outside world."[8] Virtually all accounts of nations' external ties assume certain patterns. (To be sure, random acts may occur, but most governmental actions in international relations are patterned.) In other words, nations follow certain courses of actions while participating in international economic activities, engaging in cultural exchanges, or undertaking military commitments. If we can demonstrate that an action fits into the pattern of a nation's behavior, we can not only describe, but also explain the action. If we know the pattern, sometimes we may even anticipate with a high degree of probability the nation's future policy actions.[9] But no nation's foreign policy pattern can remain unchanged forever. As changes take place in international relations, in the nation's domestic politics, or even in its political leadership, every nation, from time to time, has to adjust its foreign policy accordingly. As one student of foreign policy says, "change is a pervasive quality of governmental foreign policy."[10] Minor adjustments or modifications often occur in the implementation of foreign policy plans, in selecting means, and in handling routine work. Such changes are normal in terms of natural adjustments to changing conditions. But they do not represent a fundamental redirection. The basic foreign policy pattern remains unchanged. However, sometimes a situation occurs in which a country redirects the whole course of its external relations. The country may change its strategic alignment; it may close its door and choose an isolationist foreign policy; or it may avoid economic dependence by diversifying its trade relations. All these changes involve a profound transformation of the country's foreign policy pattern. K.J. Holsti defines such a behavior as "foreign policy restructuring," meaning "the dramatic wholesale alteration of a nation's pattern of external relations" within a region or in the global system.[11] In other words, foreign policy restructuring is a type of foreign policy behavior in which a government abandons its existing foreign policy pattern and adopts a new one.

According to the three meanings of foreign policy given by Rosenau above, the total pattern of a nation's foreign relations consists of three elements: foreign policy orientation, plans, and concrete actions. Clearly, the restructuring of a nation's total foreign policy pattern is, first of all, a foreign policy reorientation, a profound shift in the nation's basic foreign policy goals and guideline. Reorientation is followed by a series of corresponding changes in the nation's specific foreign policy plans and concrete actions.[12] Foreign policy restructuring, therefore, is a process in which a country's government decides to reshape its foreign policy orientation and translates the new orientation into its actual foreign activities. The study of foreign policy restructuring traces the process and explains why a government engages in such a behavior.

The Operationalization of Foreign Policy Restructuring

The discontinuity of a state's foreign policy pattern over a period of time constitutes the basis for the examination of foreign policy restructuring. To assess such a discontinuity, one must find out whether the state has shifted its general foreign policy orientation and taken different actions in its major foreign policy sectors (i.e., military-security, economic-developmental, and political-diplomatic.)[13] As a state's foreign policy orientation (i.e., a state's basic goals with respect to its external environment) determines both the direction and types of its external involvement,[14] the state's total foreign policy pattern can be appraised by examining with whom the state engages in its foreign relations (i.e., the direction of foreign involvement); and how well its major foreign policy sectors are managed (i.e., the types of foreign activities and the level of involvement). In other words, foreign policy restructuring can be operationalized as "wholesale changes in the pattern of partnerships for the state, and the type of activity in which it engages."[15] That is to say that changes in the way a state deals with its major foreign partnerships (It may be carried out either in the form of isolation, self-reliance, non-alignment, diversification, dependence or alliance) and the types of activities in its major foreign policy sectors are the two indicators by which to judge whether the state is restructuring its foreign policy.[16]

Foreign Policy Restructuring as Adaptive Behavior

Generally speaking, foreign policy restructuring occurs under three interrelated conditions. First, changes, external and/or internal, make a state's current foreign policy pattern unproductive in serving its vital national interest. Second, the government of the state realizes such a policy's inadequacy and intends to respond to it. Third, the government comes up with a new foreign policy alternative to cope with problems and puts it into effect. This process of policy restructuring indicates that a state pursues self-preservation. This essence of foreign policy restructuring is well explained by the adaptive behavior model.

The concept of adaptation is central either explicitly or implicitly to much writing about foreign policy. James N. Rosenau is the pioneer in applying this concept to the study of foreign policy.[17] The central concern of the adaptation model is to view states as analogous to organisms having to adapt to their changing external and/or internal environments so as to ensure their survival and prosperity. In the face of a new situation, does a state need to adjust itself to the changes? Can it take advantage of changes and prosper or will it face danger? What price will it have to pay to make adjustments? Are radical alterations necessary to meet the new demands generated by the changes? All these questions are concerned with how states can continue to function well in the face of external and/or internal changes. But why do states need to adapt themselves to changes?

According to the adaptation model, the fundamental task facing any state in a competitive international system is the continuation and prosperity of a society. All national societies can be identified by having some "essential structures" which constitute the existence of these societies. Rosenau defines "essential structures" as:

> The interaction patterns among those who comprise the political entity that have become so highly valued as to be considered necessary to its persistence as an autonomous, identifiable entity, distinguished from its environment and relating to its environment in more or less regularized ways. Any political entity is composed of many interaction patterns, but only relatively few of these are "essential" in the sense that without them the entity would no longer be recognizable.[18]

In Rosenau's opinion, at least four "essential structures" must be present in all societies. They are the physical, political, economic, and social bases of societies and represent:

> The patterns whereby the life and property of societies are preserved and protected, their policy decisions made and implemented, their goods and services acquired and distributed, [and] their member's cooperation achieved and maintained.[19]

Each structure may vary in its level of performance, but each is an essential precondition for the continued existence of the unit. Hence it is imperative that a state keep variations in its essential structures caused by external and/or internal changes within the acceptable limits of the state's survivability and prosperity. Otherwise, the state will face difficulties or even dangers in terms of physical safety, economic well-being, major foreign relations, or national cohesion.

Foreign policy restructuring happens when a state's existing foreign policy cannot satisfy its essential structures in the face of the changed situation. The very purpose of foreign policy restructuring is to re-ensure the state's continuation, stability, prosperity and appropriate status in the competitive international system by introducing a new foreign policy. It is in this sense that foreign policy restructuring is an adaptive behavior. As summarized by one scholar, an adaptive system is generally thought of as one which responds to pressure on its existence and produces outputs in such a way as to attain its self-preserving purpose.[20]

Clearly, change is a central dimension of foreign policy restructuring. "When there is no change, there is nothing to which a society must adapt."[21] Since changes constantly take place in a society's external and/or internal environments, some salient changes will eventually impose pressures on the society's essential structures. Once such pressures emerge in the foreign policy domain and the current foreign policy cannot effectively cope with them, the government of that society is likely to look for new policy arrangements to ensure the basic interests of the society. As concluded by Rosenau, "when developments at home give rise to new needs and wants with respect to their environments, or when developments abroad give rise to potential threats to their essential structures," they will also give rise to demands for "new arrangements."[22] Indeed, the relationship between changes (international and/or domestic) and policy responses linked to the state's self-serving need to survive and prosper in international politics is at the heart of the phenomenon of foreign policy restructuring.

Given the demands for "new arrangements," the function of meeting these demands is not automatically undertaken by the state itself but by "those persons [in the government] who are authorized to act on behalf of the state, i.e. the decision-makers."[23] On the one hand, constant changes (international and/or domestic) may lead to significant pressures (in terms of high stakes) on the country's essential structures; whereas, on the other hand, these pressures "have to be interpreted, assessed, and managed" by the decision-makers of the country in question.[24] The interaction between objective pressures on the country's essential structures and subjective perception of them leads decision-makers to make choices. Rosenau identifies four fundamental choices for decision-makers to follow.[25] They can adopt a strategy which responds only to external factors; one that responds only to internal factors; one that responds to both external and internal factors; or finally a strategy which is responsive to neither external nor internal factors. According to Rosenau, if decision-makers abandon their current strategy and adopt a new one, an adaptive transformation in foreign policy will occur.[26] This is exactly what is here referred to as foreign policy restructuring.

In sum, foreign policy restructuring is an adaptive behavior in which a government transforms its foreign policy from one pattern to another when its decision-makers realize that the existing policy pattern cannot adequately satisfy the country's basic interests. Motivated by the need to satisfy the country's basic interests, the government chooses what it believes to be the best policy to cope with threats to its essential structures. Through foreign policy restructuring, the country's goal is to re-ensure its continuation, stability, prosperity and appropriate status in international politics.

A Framework for Analysis of Foreign Policy Restructuring

As indicated earlier, foreign policy restructuring is an adaptive process including three basic stages in sequence. First, domestic and/or international changes cause pressures upon a country's vital interests and the current foreign policy fails to cope with the pressures. Second, governmental decision-makers realize the inadequacy of the exiting foreign policy, assess the changes and come up with new policy perceptions. And third, foreign policy reorientation (i.e., new policy goals) is introduced and translated into actual foreign activities. In tracing these three stages, one can not only describe how a country restructures its foreign policy pattern, but also explain why it does so.

Essential Structures, Vital National Interests and Threats

Changes, external and/or internal, may lead to enormous pressures upon a country's essential structures. As defined by Rosenau, essential structures are those interaction patterns that constitute the basic conditions of a national society and are preconditions for the society's survival.[27] In order to survive and, further, to prosper, any country must keep its essential structures within acceptable limits. In this sense, a country's essential structures are its vital national interests defined as those basic needs and desires which satisfy matters of importance to its existence. Dr. Donald E. Nuechterlein has identified four matters of material importance to a nation's survival.[28] The first one is its *Physical Safety* (i.e., defense interest), which refers to protection of the country and its citizens from the threat of physical violence by another country, and/or protection from an externally inspired threat to the national political system. *Material Well-being* (i.e., economic interest) is the second matter of importance to a country. It involves the enhancement of the country's economic well-being in relations with other countries. The third, involves the *Political-Diplomatic Order* (i.e., world-order interest), which relates to the maintenance of a favorable external environment in which the country feels secure and can conduct functional activities peacefully with other countries. Finally, *Basic Social Values* (i.e., ideological interest of national cohesion) which assure the protection and furtherance of a set of principles the citizens of the country share and believe to be good. Not surprisingly, the four vital national interests given by Nuechterlein are highly correlated with Rosenau's four essential structures: physical, economic, political and social.[29] In a sense, essential structures represent a country's vital national interests.

Any perceived threat related to a country's vital national interests will as a rule precipitate policy adjustments. To a great extent, foreign policy restructuring is dictated by security considerations.[30] Historically, military threats have been the most important factors in determining the behavior of foreign policy restructuring. But more and more foreign policy restructurings in modern times have also been responses to complex domestic circumstances, economic vulnerability, ideological disputes, xenophobia, or nationalism.

Obviously, the assessment of the intensity of a threat to a country's vital national interests plays a crucial role in foreign policy restructuring. When a national government feels a threat and realizes that its current foreign policy is unable to protect the country's vital interests, it is likely to redirect its foreign policy course. How a country interprets threats to its national interest is closely related to the sensitivity and vulnerability of a given state's essential structures. Sensitivity involves "degrees of responsiveness within a policy framework--how quickly do changes in one country bring costly changes in another, and how great are the costly effects?" Vulnerability can be defined as "an actor's liability to suffer costs imposed by external events even after policies have been altered."[31] A nation can be sensitive to events in that it will face various costs and difficulties if it fails to do something; it is vulnerable to events when it will face those costs and difficulties because it cannot do anything about them. Every country has its own sensitive and vulnerable issue areas. However, because of differences in geography, economic structure, history, and political culture, sensitive and vulnerable issue areas are country-specific in terms of unique circumstances. Thus, when focusing on a particular country, one must identify its sensitive and vulnerable areas according to the country's national attributes. In this sense, foreign policy restructuring can also be seen as a class of foreign activities through which a country deals with those issues that render it sensitive and/or vulnerable.

In his analysis of sensitive and vulnerable interest areas, Nuechterlein points out four degrees of intensity of interest for a country in the face of external and/or internal threats.[32] (1) *Survival issues* involve immediate and credible threats of massive physical harm by another country. The very existence of the country is in jeopardy as a result of either overt military attack on its own territory or the imminent threat of attack should an enemy's demands be rejected. Usually military-security issues belong to this category. (2) *Vital issues* refer to the events which can result in serious harm to the country unless some critical measures are taken to counter the events. A vital issue may, in the long run, be as serious a threat to a country's political and economic well-being as a survival issue. Time is the essential difference. A vital issue usually provides the government of the country with sufficient time to take countermeasures to reverse the unfavorable situation. A vital issue many involve not only defense interests but also economic, world-order and even ideological interests. (3) *Major issues* mean that the country's political, economic and ideological well-being may be adversely affected if some events and trends at home and abroad are not properly dealt with. Most issues in international relations fall into this category and are usually resolved through diplomatic negotiation. It is when diplomacy fails to resolve such disputes that they may become vital issues. (4) *Peripheral issues* are events or trends at home and abroad which do not adversely affect the well-being of the country--although some of them may endanger the interests of its private citizens and companies. Clearly enough, a country's sensitivity and vulnerability are closely related both to the survival and vital issues it faces. If the country meets difficulties in these issue areas and its current foreign policy cannot effectively deal with the problems, this country is likely to look for new solutions and engage in foreign policy restructuring as a way of satisfying its own self-serving need.

The Role of Decision-Makers

A country's adaptation in the form of foreign policy restructuring, however, does not happen automatically. It is realized, instead, through the authoritative action of the government on behalf of that country. In other words, decision-makers, the responsible persons within the government, play a decisive role and carry out foreign policy restructuring for the country. Decision-makers, therefore, represent the country's interests and serve as the mechanics of national adaptation.[33] It is the decision-makers who assess threats to the country's vital interests (i.e., national security, economic prosperity, diplomatic environment, and basic social values). Once they find that serious problems regarding the country's basic needs have occurred and that the country's current policy is inadequate to cope with the new circumstances, they will raise the question of policy restructuring so as to ease the country's sensitivity and vulnerability. For this purpose, possible alternatives are formulated whereupon the decision-makers choose what they believe to be the most appropriate foreign policy strategy with respect to satisfying the country's essential structures. In this sense, foreign policy restructuring results more directly from the determined authoritative efforts by decision-makers, than from the actual threats themselves.

Clearly, the composition of political leadership (i.e., key decision-makers) and the perceptions of this political leadership are the two intervening variables in deciding (1) whether a country needs to restructure its current foreign policy, and (2) what a new policy should be if there is a need for restructuring. In reality, either the change in political leadership or the change in leadership's perceptions often result in different interpretations of the world as well as different policy choices. Thus, it is important to take a close a look at the influence of particular political leaders and their perceptions in examining foreign policy restructuring. In doing so, much emphasis should be given to the ways they came to power, their policy platforms, their composition, their power bases, and their major competitors. In a word, power struggle within a political system and its influence on foreign policy making deserve close attention.[34] In studying the perceptions of the power elite, it is necessary to focus on the factors shaping such perceptions, including personalities, value preferences, experiences, national history, and culture.[35]

The Implementation of New Foreign Policy

Once a country's government recognizes the unproductive results of the current foreign policy, defines the country's basic interests under the new circumstances, and decides to restructure that policy, the next step involves actual restructuring activities. It includes foreign policy reorientation and the translation of the new orientation into major functional sectors (i.e., strategic/military, economic/developmental, political/diplomatic, etc.). As discussed above, foreign policy reorientation involves a profound shift in the country's basic attitudes towards its immediate international environment in terms of its fundamental strategy for accomplishing domestic and external objectives. This translation of the new foreign policy orientation into specific foreign policy sectors is seen in changes in the country's foreign partnerships and adjustments in types of functional engagement.

The restructuring activities may be carried out either in a sudden, quick and unexpected manner or in an incremental fashion. The former type involves a quick shift in a country's foreign alignments and massive activity changes in its major foreign functional sectors (e.g., political, economic, or military). The latter is characterized by a series of cumulative and/or piecemeal changes in the translation of the new foreign policy into actions.

No matter which type it is, the goal for a country engaging in foreign policy restructuring is to re-ensure its national interest under pressure. But in reality, all foreign policy restructurings are not bound to produce desired results. Some foreign policy restructurings do and others do not. Because of misperceptions of the reality or unrealistic policy choices made by decision-makers, maladaptive restructurings do happen resulting in policy ineffectiveness or even failure.[36] Successful foreign policy restructuring requires the enhancement of a given country's national interest while a maladaptation further weakens the country's basic needs. The effectiveness of the new policy with respect to satisfying the country's basic needs is actually the quintessence of the adaptation model.

To sum up, foreign policy restructuring is an adaptive process including such elements as (1) changes in a country's external and/or internal conditions which produce pressures on the country's vital interests; (2) leadership interpretation (i.e., the recognition of the inadequacy of the exiting foreign policy), (3) foreign policy reorientation (i.e., new policy goals) and its applications in specific foreign activities; and (4) evaluation of the effectiveness of the new foreign policy. Figure 1 is the graphic summary of the research framework for analyzing foreign policy restructuring.

Using the Adaptation
Model for the Chinese Case

There are three major schools in the study of Chinese foreign policy. The first one explains Chinese foreign policy in terms of domestic determinants. It believes that, unlike the other major powers' foreign policies, Chinese foreign policy is basically driven by domestic factors such as Chinese culture, tradition, leadership, ideology, politics, and economic development. No matter how the international environment changes, Chinese leaders would form and pursue their foreign policy mainly according to their own preferences and perceptions of the world. Chinese foreign policy is simply an extension of the country's domestic developments. This school argues that "China is relatively insulated from international pressures" and "domestic factors have tended to dominate in the shaping of Chinese foreign policy."[37]

The second school believes that China's international behavior is determined by its position in the international system and is a reaction against events in its international environment. It argues that "Chinese foreign policy behavior can best be understood in terms of the constraints imposed upon it by the structure of the international system."[38] According to this school, all other variables--including decision-makers, domestic politics and so on--are relevant only if they cause changes in Chinese capabilities, leading to changes in the distribution of power or to structural transformation in international politics.

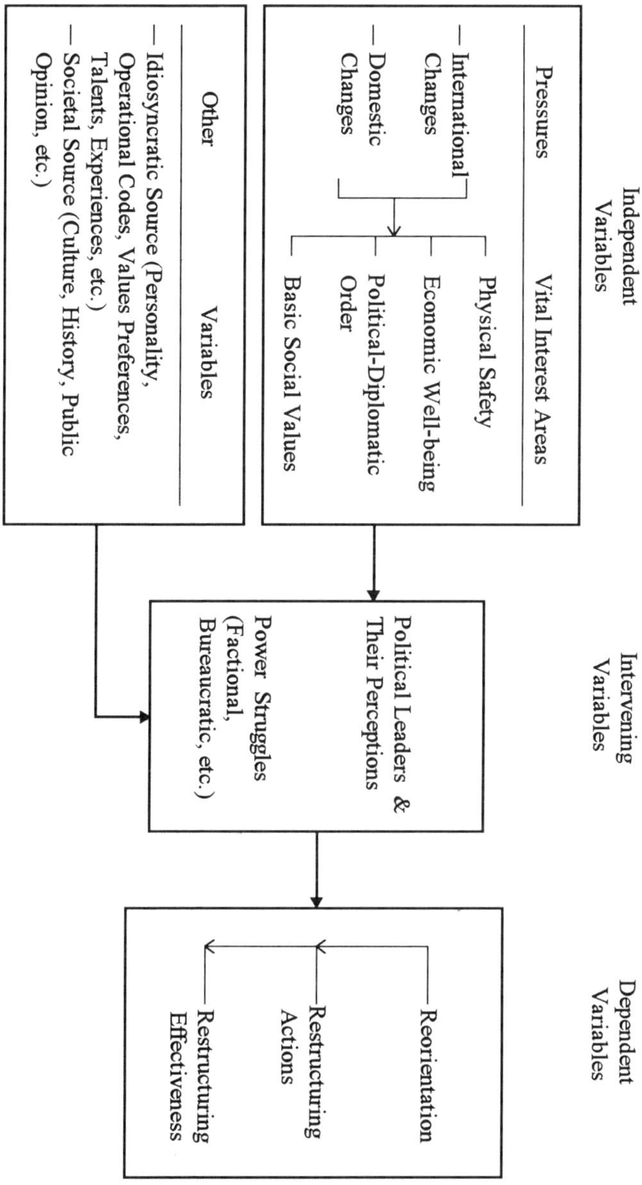

Figure 1: The Framework for Analysis of Foreign Policy Restructuring

The third school of Chinese foreign policy combines the first two schools. In its view Chinese foreign policy is determined by both internal and external developments. While carefully analyzing China's culture, tradition, politics, social development, and economics, it is important to look at the dynamics of the international system within which China has to act. As a nation-state, China cannot ignore the nature of the contemporary international system. To pursue its national interest, China should act according to its position in the international system. Meanwhile, due to its specific internal structure and conditions, Chinese leaders have to balance their foreign policy with China's domestic developments.[39]

All three schools in the study of Chinese foreign policy have their merits. But each of them has its limitations. How can the first school explain the triangular relations between the United States, the Soviet Union and China over the past several decades? The second school obviously neglects China's internal constraints in its foreign policy making. Actually, Chinese internal politics plays an extremely important role in China's foreign policy making. The third school seems to be very comprehensive and includes all the possible aspects of Chinese foreign policy making. However, it fails to explain what links the interaction among domestic politics, the external environment and political leadership. Therefore, it cannot isolate and identify "some of the crucial variables that determine...responses to concrete situations" in such behavior as foreign policy restructuring.[40]

According to the adaptation model, China's foreign policy, especially its foreign policy restructuring, is determined by China's fundamental interests in terms of its national security, its economic well-being, its basic values, and its salient international environment. None of the three factors--domestic politics, international constraints and Chinese decision-makers--operates by and for itself, in isolation from the others. Their relative weights in shaping foreign policy may vary in different situations or at different times. But they should be linked by China's self-preservation goals. In order to ensure the country's continuation, stability, prosperity and appropriate status in international relations, the Chinese leadership has to choose what it perceives to be the best means to adapt to the external environment as well as accommodate domestic developments. Thus, in the adaptation model, internal and external determinants are relevant only when they constitute pressures upon China's essential conditions and such pressures are deeply felt by Beijing's leadership.

As a matter of fact, the adaptation model does not exclude any of the three aforementioned schools of thought. On the contrary, this book investigates China's foreign policy restructuring in the 1980s from three perspectives. First, how China's vital interests were affected by specific conditions, external and/or internal during this period. Second, how the Chinese leadership responded to those pressures. And third, whether the response better served China's basic needs. In this way, the adaptation model enables us not only to analyze what has led China to engage in a foreign policy restructuring in the 1980s and examine the restructuring process systematically, but also to judge the effectiveness of Beijing's "independent foreign policy of peace" in terms whether it has enhanced the country's basic interests. In addition, centered on the assumption that adaptation results from a country's self-serving need in the face of changes, we may also construct some generalizations about foreign policy restructuring. The following chapters will develop these generalizations.

Chapter 3

Sources of Chinese Foreign Policy Restructuring

The main purpose of studying a country's foreign policy restructuring behavior is to examine the driving forces that make the country change its foreign partnership pattern and how it deals with issues sensitive to the country's basic interests. Every country has its own sensitive issue areas. But due to different national attributes, sensitive issue areas are country-specific in terms of unique circumstances. Thus, in examining the driving forces behind China's foreign policy restructuring in the 1980s, there is a need to identify "Chinese" factors that have shaped Beijing's foreign policy formulation.

Since the founding of the People's Republic in 1949, some major factors specific to China have played vital roles in shaping Beijing's foreign policy making. The interplay of these factors has conditioned the course of China's foreign behavior over the past several decades, including the period under examination in this book. While the relative weights of these factors varied during different periods of time and under different circumstances, they have worked collectively in shaping Chinese foreign policy. Today these factors are still influencing Beijing's present foreign behavior, and they will surely continue to govern China's foreign policy making in the future. Without taking them into account, one could scarcely understand the dynamics of China's foreign behavior.

Factor One: China's Historical Legacy

China has the longest history of any nation on earth. The longevity of Chinese history and the richness of Chinese culture have shaped the unique Chinese world view. Historic experiences with foreign countries, especially since the 19th century, have given a profound nationalistic character to China's external behavior.

A Sense of Greatness

Chinese society has retained a high degree of historical consciousness. Its long and rich history as a grand civilization has made the Chinese aware and proud of their nation's greatness. For centuries, the Chinese were convinced that they possessed a culture superior to all others, and they stubbornly remained aloof from and ignorant of the rest of the world. Until the nineteenth century, China saw itself as the cultural center of the universe, a view reflected in the concept of the Middle Kingdom (*Zhongguo*, the Chinese word for China). For the most part, it viewed non-Chinese peoples as uncivilized barbarians. A sinocentric perception of the world associated with the tribute system influenced the Chinese way of conducting foreign relations.[1] Because of this, the Chinese tend to have a strong sense of national greatness and to pay more attention to what is called "face diplomacy" in which requires China to behave as a great power.

A Century of Shame and Humiliation

But their stubborn resistance to commercial demands from the "Western barbarians" in the nineteenth century cost China severely. In the period between the Opium War of 1839-42 and the end of World War II, China became a target of foreign imperialist domination. Through numerous wars, Western powers like Britain, France, Russia, Germany, the United States, and even Japan defeated China and forced it to sign a series of unequal treaties in which China ceded territory, paid indemnities and gave many political and economic privileges to foreign countries.[2] Much of China was divided into competing spheres of foreign influence. Within these spheres of interest foreign powers had complete jurisdiction over economic resources and the establishment of military bases. Although China did not become a colony of a single foreign power, its people suffered the worst type of humiliation and exploitation. China was known as an "opium-eating nation" or the "sick man in East Asia."[3] The Chinese call this situation a "semicolonial" status. As Sun Yat-sen, the founding father of Republican China (1911), once commented:

> We are the poorest and the weakest country in the world, occupying the lowest position in world affairs; people of other countries are the carving knife and the serving dish while we are the fish and the meat.[4]

The history of suffering, humiliation, and aggression continued until 1945 when China together with other allies finally defeated Japan.

During this period, the Chinese sense of greatness had been replaced by shame and humiliation. The bitter recollection of suffering in the minds of the Chinese created a extremely strong nationalist desire to get the foreigners out of their country and restore China's former glory through modernization. Together with the popular demand for land redistribution, strong anti-imperialist sentiment and the desire to rebuild China's greatness were the driving forces in China in the first half of this century making the Communist revolutionary ideology appealing both in practical and emotional terms. In 1949, with popular support, Chinese Communists finally took power after several years of the Civil War with the corrupt *Kuomintang* (KMT) under Chiang Kai-shek. The founding of the People's Republic unified the country and Mao Zedong proclaimed proudly to the world in 1949:

> Ours will no longer be a nation subject to insult and humiliation. We have stood up.... The era in which the Chinese people were regarded as uncivilized is now over.[5]

An Overemphasis on Absolute Sovereignty

Drawing on their historical experience as victims of foreign imperialism since the last century, the Chinese people and their leaders alike have particularly treasured national sovereignty and independence the highest value in preserving China because sovereignty and independence were won at tremendous costs paid by several generations. The belief that is popularly supported by the general public in China is that anything can be sacrificed but national sovereignty. It is politically incorrect for the Chinese leadership to be soft on an issue related to national sovereignty and independence. As a result, China has a tendency to overemphasize national sovereignty in its foreign relations. Absolute sovereignty seems to be the only condition that Chinese leaders would like to accept. The excuse that internal affairs should not be interfered with by other countries is China's shield to block foreign influence and to legitimate its rejection of foreign demands.

Apparently, the wounds left by foreign imperialism are still fresh in the minds of Chinese leaders, making them believe that "foreign imperialists are bent on subjugating China."[6] Thus, in the conduct of foreign relations, Beijing tends to be suspicious of the intentions of foreign powers and sensitive to any implications of inferior status. Any notion of limited sovereignty is often rejected by the Chinese government. This strong nationalistic sentiment was vividly exemplified by Deng Xiaoping's 1982 pronouncement that "no foreign country can expect China to be its vassal or expect it to swallow any bitter fruit detrimental to its interests."[7] Criticism on China's human rights record has been seen by the Chinese as the conspiracy of some foreign powers to intervene in China's internal affairs. As a matter of fact, no Chinese leader can afford to face the domestic repercussions for appearing soft on the sovereignty issue. The five principles that highlight the Chinese government stand in foreign relations--mutual respect for each other's territorial integrity and sovereignty, nonaggression, non-interference in each other's internal affairs, equality and mutual benefit, and peaceful coexistence--is, to a large extent, the Chinese demand to be treated as an equal in international affairs. Chinese handling of the Taiwan issue, and of the future of Hong Kong as well as its assertiveness in territorial disputes along its borders have all proved that China will choose to put national sovereignty and independence above everything else in its relations with other countries. In his speech in New York on September 29, 1995, Chinese foreign ministry Qian Qichen said that "China has its own dignity. For the Chinese people who suffered tremendously from the invasion and bully of foreign powers in modern Chinese history, the nation's independence was hard-won, and national sovereignty as well as territorial integrity are the supreme value. The Chinese government will react vehemently to any violation of China's sovereignty."[8]

Factor Two: Security Environment and Relations with Key Countries

The central concern of a country's national security is how it can survive, politically and physically, in terms of creating international conditions "favorable to the protection or extension of its vital values against existing and potential adversaries."[9] Any country must pay attention to its international environment, either actions by other states or international developments which affect its position in the international system. As the principal architect of Chinese security strategy, Mao Zedong clearly understood that his preeminent foreign policy objective was to manage China's national capabilities, political, economic and military, in response to international balances of power and diminish China's vulnerability to external threats of any kinds.

Clearly, establishing a relatively stable strategic environment around the nation's periphery in Asia has long been Beijing's primary foreign policy objective. But since 1949 China has actually experienced military threats to its security from almost all directions in geographic terms: from the United States (e.g., the Korean War and the Vietnam War) and Taiwan to the east and southeast, the Soviet Union to the North and northwest, Vietnam to the southeast, and India to the south. One student of Chinese foreign policy says that "Few other major powers have felt as threatened, for such a long period of time, and by such powerful adversaries, as China has."[10]

China's geo-demographic features (i.e., location, size, natural resources, vast population, ethnic composition, long record of history and rich cultural tradition) are enormous and have made China an important country in the Asian-Pacific region. But for a long time, China's influence on its external environment has been limited due to its economic underdevelopment. So during the Cold War era, China's environment was largely controlled by the superpowers and their allies. Chinese leaders had to assess their surroundings constantly and adjust foreign policy accordingly because any substantial changes in the Asian-Pacific region could affect Chinese security and development interests. In other words, China's security concerns are largely determined by its relations with states capable of influencing Chinese domestic developments.[11]

As two superpowers during the Cold War, the United States and the Soviet Union, by any reasonable measure--economic capabilities, conventional military strength and reach, or their enormous nuclear arsenals--had the capability to affect war and peace in the world. There was no escape for China from this reality. Indeed, China experienced directly threats from the United States and/or the Soviet Union during the Cold War era. China's relationship with the two superpowers constituted the central question for China's security concerns. The so-called Sino-Soviet-American strategic triangle played a key role in determining Chinese foreign policy. For years, relations between China and the rest of the world have largely depended upon Beijing's attitudes toward the superpowers.[12]

At its periphery, countries, such as Japan, Korea, Vietnam, and India, are of importance to China for geo-political reasons. Japan is central to China because of its economic strength, its alliance with the

United States, and its military potential. The Chinese had military conflicts with India over territorial issues in 1962. Moreover, Beijing is quite concerned with India's nuclear capability. The stability of the Korean Peninsula has also been closely related to Beijing's security concern over its industrial center in the Northeast. In Southeast Asia, relations between China and Vietnam have long been divorced from ideological considerations but carry a heavy historical legacy.[13] China has territorial disputes with Vietnam and other Southeast Asian countries. From a geo-political perspective, "China historically has sought to keep regional powers weak, divided, or deferential and to exclude competitors in order to minimize threat [from its neighboring countries]."[14]

Interestingly enough, as this century draws to a close, China is no longer in the shadow of strategic threat from other countries. The collapse of the former Soviet Union and the end of the Cold War took place coincidentally as China achieved a tremendous success in its economic reform. The reduction of superpower influence in the Asian-Pacific region and the dramatic economic growth in China have provided a historic opportunity for China to rise as a new major power playing a key role, politically, economically and militarily, in determining courses of action of other countries in the region. For the first time since 1949, China is in a favorable position without facing any major military threat to its security from other countries. Although Beijing is happy with this situation, China's foreign behavior is still conditioned by the international balance of power. Relations with some key countries, especially with the United States, still dominate China's foreign policy making. In the post-Cold War era, the United States is the sole remaining superpower. China's relationship to the United States has become the most important element of Beijing's foreign policy. To a large extent, it is also a leading factor in influencing China's domestic policy. On the American side, Washington gives its relations with Beijing high priority. But with superpower status and more interests elsewhere in the world, the United States is less dependent on smooth ties with China than China is with it.[15] Next to the United States, relations with China's neighbors, including Japan, Russia, India, Southeast Asian countries all carry significant weight in China's foreign policy making. Although it is an "internal matter", the Taiwan issue is a very sensitive one for the Chinese leadership. It could have a major impact on Beijing's foreign relations as the Taiwan authorities attempt to win international recognition. Last but not least, economic relations with major industrial countries also occupy an important position in Beijing's foreign policy making as China continues to attract foreign investors in its economic reform.

Factor Three: Modernization

Aware of the humiliating treatment by foreign powers since last century, Chinese leaders have concluded that economic and technological power is essential for the country if China is to enjoy security and prestige in the world. Without the modernization of agriculture, industry, national defense, science, and technology, China could only remain weak and vulnerable.[16] The quest for wealth and power which the Chinese have been struggling for over past 150 years has a strong nationalistic appeal in China, representing a traditional realist attitude towards world affairs shared by the Chinese leadership.[17]

Different Approaches

Despite a consensus among Chinese leaders over the general goal of modernization, the methods to be used in order to achieve this goal have varied in the face of the country's backward economic conditions (e.g., a large population, the impossibility of increasing arable land area, high illiteracy rate, and lack of surplus capital for industrialization) and the complexities of the international environment. How can China modernize without losing the Chinese essence? Like their predecessors, China's Communist leaders have also been divided in their responses to the question of how to preserve the Chinese essence while adopting foreign technologies on China's road to modernity.

Three attitudes can be found within the Chinese leadership.[18] The first attitude toward economic development is shared by those who see power, both internationally and domestically, more in political and moral than in material and economic terms. They stress the importance of maintaining the Chinese essence, and thus encourage an isolationist foreign policy in order to prevent contamination by Western culture and values. They believe that only by excluding foreign influence can China become powerful.

The second stand is to strengthen China by using foreign

technology while at the same time shielding the country from the cultural influences that accompany these technological imports. This view is well expressed in the slogan: "Chinese learning for the essence; Western learning for the application."[19] As claimed by a commentary in *Beijing Review*, China wanted to master advanced science and technology from capitalist countries but at the same time to discard "the capitalist ideology and social system which safeguards exploitation and oppression, as well as its evil and corrupt aspects."[20]

The third group consists of all-around modernizers. While they do not seek westernization uncritically, they, more than the others, would like to integrate China into rest of the world.

Shifting Strategies

Since 1949, the balance has been shifting among the above-mentioned positions. In the 1950s, Chinese leaders carried out a modernization program under the sponsorship of the Soviet Union. Having copied the Soviet model and received economic, technological, and military aid from Moscow, China became heavily dependent on the Soviet Union politically, economically, and strategically.

By the mid-fifties, Mao began to worry about this position of dependency. In the late 1950s, a more nativist approach prevailed, as reflected in the Great Leap Forward Movement (1958-1960). As a result of the split between Beijing and Moscow in the early 1960s, the Soviets terminated all their economic and technological aid programs in China. This experience made the Chinese leaders very cautious about foreign assistance. Even those who had advocated such assistance warned that China might become economically dependent on its foreign patron. The nativist position under the name of "self-reliance" reached its climax during the Cultural Revolution in the years of 1966-1969.

In the early 1970s China had to turn to Washington for strategic cooperation against the Soviet military threat. But China was quite cautious and kept its economic ties with the West within limits because of the fear of Western ideological influence.

After Deng Xiaoping came to power, circumstances shifted in favor of the country's opening-up. The reform-minded leaders placed modernization as the nation's top priority and believed that "opening to the outside world" was the only way to make modernization a success in China. They argued that in today's more interdependent world it was impossible to modernize China relying on the close-door policy of "self-reliance." On the contrary, China could narrow the gap with the industrial nations and get access to foreign capital, advanced science and technology, and modern management only through an "open-door" policy.[21] As a result, China's foreign policy was reshaped according to this line of thinking.

National Capabilities

The purpose of national modernization for the Chinese leadership is to enhance China's national capabilities in the international arena. Drawing lessons from the last century of being dominated by foreign powers, the Chinese firmly believe that economic and military weaknesses of their country can only invite bullying from other more powerful countries. They also clearly understand that China's international status in the world will largely depend on its own national capabilities in terms of economic and technological development and in terms of a powerful national defense. Therefore, China has made tremendous efforts to build up a nuclear arsenal and develop ballistic delivery capabilities. Meanwhile, China maintains the world's largest military forces. In fact, China's foreign behavior is closely related to the capabilities the country has in response to international events. It also relates to how Chinese leaders perceive and use these capabilities in international affairs.

Factor Four: Ideological Influence

Ideology is a set of values, ideas and beliefs that guides and justifies behavior. China is a Communist country led by the Communist Party and guided by the Marxist ideology. By combining the Marxist ideology with Chinese reality, the Chinese Communist Party created the Chinese version of Marxism, the "Mao Zedong Thought" or "Maoism." China's foreign policy has been influenced by this thought.

Anti-Hegemony

Opposition to imperialist hegemony is a major ideological component of Chinese foreign policy. During different periods of time, it might be termed differently as "anti-power politics," "anti-imperialism," "anti-bullying," "anti-intervention in one's internal affairs," "anti-sanctions," and "anti-spheres of influence." In fact, the Chinese mindset of anti-hegemony is the most important code of conduct in China's foreign policy. The Chinese particularly appreciate the Leninist emphasis on the struggle against imperialism because of China's semi-colonial experiences.

In association with the anti-hegemony theme, China looks at itself as a champion of opposition to exploitation of developing countries by the developed world. Since the Bandung Conference in 1955[22], China has long regarded developing countries as its allies. China's third world policy is one of the important components of Beijing's overall foreign policy. In the 1950s and 1960s, China actively supported national liberation movements in some Asian, African and Latin American countries by providing weapons and introducing Mao's guerilla strategy. Militancy and support for worldwide revolution peaked during the Cultural Revolution. Since the 1970s, China has lessened or discontinued its support for most of the revolutionary movements around the world and begun cultivating state-to-state relations in the Third World. In 1982, China even admitted that "revolution cannot be exported but can occur only by the choice of the people of the country concerned."[23] However, Beijing has never dropped the claim that "the Third World constitutes a powerful force against imperialism, colonialism and hegemonism" and that "China is part of the Third World."[24] Upholding its image as a major defender of the interest of the Third World in international relations, China has persistently claimed that "it is our sacred duty to support other third world countries and people in their struggles to win and uphold their national rights."[25]

Contradiction Theory

According to Marxist dialectical materialism, Chinese Communists believe that the international situation can best be understood in terms of the "principal contradictions" of the time. Once these contradictions are understood, they can be exploited in order to, as Mao once said, "win over the many, oppose the few, and crush our enemies one by one."[26] By using the Leninist policy of uniting with some forces in order to oppose others more effectively, Mao adopted Stalin's "Two

Camps" Theory in support of China's anti-American and pro-Soviet foreign policy in the 1950s. In the 1970s, Mao developed his famous "Three Worlds" Doctrine justifying China's anti-Soviet and pro-American foreign policy. As one student of China's foreign policy notes, "Chinese foreign policy has consistently been based on consciously held and carefully articulated theoretical propositions derived from an analysis of the international order."[27]

Because of its belief in the necessity of struggle on the road to progress, China has often described world events as a struggle between opposing forces. For a long time, Chinese leaders maintained international wars were inevitable as a result of international struggles, especially those between the two superpowers. They argued that international peace was only a temporary phenomenon and competition between the two superpowers was the major source of international war. In order to prevent war, the "people" of the world must unite and form a united front against the "hegemonic policies" of the most dangerous superpower. In the 1980s, the post-Mao leaders began to assert that forces for peace in the world had become greater than the forces for war. War was no longer "inevitable," peace was not only "desirable" but "possible."[28] The growing world stability was furthered by "multipolarization," that is, the growth of additional forces, such as the Third World, Japan and Europe, which could counterbalance the tensions between the two superpowers. This line of reasoning justified Beijing's "independent foreign policy of peace."

Principle, Flexibility and the Party's General Line

One of the major characteristics of Chinese foreign policy since 1949 has been its claim of consistently adhering to principles while particular interpretations and policies were changing dramatically. A statement by Mao summarizes this as follows: "We should be firm in principle; we should also have all flexibility permissible and necessary for carrying out our principles."[29]

On the one hand, Marxism-Leninism-Mao Zedong Thought remains a central mode of discourse in China. Policy debates are frequently framed in terms of Marxist-Leninist categories of analysis and terminology to justify the reality. For the Party to retain its legitimacy, theoretical justification has to be found for its claim to the leading role in government. This means continuing to uphold the idea that Marxism embodies fundamental truth, and that only the Party can correctly interpret and apply those truths.[30]

But on the other hand, the Chinese leadership has made major shifts in foreign policy based on their practical assessment of domestic goals and international events. As found to be the case in the former Soviet Union, one must distinguish between "pure" and "practical" ideology.[31] The former refers to the corpus of Marxist-Leninist doctrine as applied to international affairs while the latter is more a theoretical justification for substantial policy choices. This is also true in the case of China's foreign policy making. In the 1980s, China made modernization the country's priority. This "practical" ideology dominated the Party's "general line." The ideas of "building socialism with Chinese characteristics" and "practice being the sole criterion of truth" justified China's "independent foreign policy of peace" and allowed Beijing to take flexible stands in its foreign activities. In fact, the Chinese Communist leaders can always find ideological bases for the Party's "general line" to justify policy changes. Each new "general line" of the Party certainly "lends inspiration, shape and legitimacy to Chinese diplomacy."[32]

Factor Five: Chinese Leaders and Their Foreign Policy Perceptions

One fundamental aspect of Chinese foreign policy which has remained relatively constant since 1949 is that the decision-making power for the most important decisions has been concentrated in the hands of a few key individuals at the top of the leadership hierarchy. In the past, Mao Zedong, Zhou Enlai, and other senior leaders exerted overriding control over foreign policy. After Mao, Deng Xiaoping and his associates played such a role. Although there has been an increase of institutionalization and more and more professionals have participated in Chinese foreign policy making since 1989, major decisions remain controlled by a small group of leaders. Clearly, not only the Chinese view of the external environment is filtered through lenses colored by the nation's history, culture, and ideology,[33] but also the top leaders' personal experiences, value preferences and talents have a profound impact on China's foreign policy direction. How the top Chinese leaders see the world and how they define China's interests in international relations directly affect the course of Chinese foreign policy.

In fact, leadership personality (especially that of a paramount leader) has played a crucial role in Beijing's foreign policy making. In some countries, institutional checks and balances and bureaucratic politics tend to dilute the paramount leader's power. But in China the ultimate policy-making process has remained highly centralized and personalized rather than institutionalized.[34] The dictates of a paramount leader carry extraordinary weight in decision-making. Mao Zedong and Deng Xiaoping vividly exemplified this phenomenon. During the Maoist period, almost all the major foreign policy initiatives originated with Mao himself. China's break with the Soviet Union and rapprochement with the United States were principally of Mao's doing. Deng also placed his imprimatur on Sino-American and Sino-Soviet normalization as well as on China's open-door policy in the 1980s.

Factor Six: Bureaucratic Interests And Foreign Policy Making

Factional Politics

The extent of strength and unity of the Chinese leadership as a whole can also influence the nation's foreign policy direction. To be sure, top leaders need political support from their subordinates and sometimes their decisions are also influenced by the internal political struggles within the leadership. That political differences do exist within the elite is almost a truism in any political system. In the Chinese context, these differences are articulated and channelled through factional struggles. Factionalism is endemic in Chinese politics. It plays a significant role in China's domestic and foreign policy formation and no policy sphere is immune to its intrigues.[35] As argued by one scholar, "changes in the relationships between contending groups in the Chinese hierarchy" often affect "the regime's external activity."[36]

Conflicting views among the top Chinese leaders on issues concerning the country's vital interests often cause policy debates with respect to defining the nature of an issue, assessing policy priority, setting goals, and choosing means. Debates on the issues at stake are often "the putative policy alternatives or the power positions of the factions or some combination of these."[37] They usually evolve into factional struggles and realignments within the Chinese ruling elite. The dominant groups and their leaders tend to determine the country's domestic and foreign policy direction. Since 1949, China's foreign policy has been repeatedly affected by Beijing's high-level politics. For example, the Lin Biao affair in 1971 helped remove the major obstacle within Beijing's leadership to the opening of Sino-American ties. Hu Yaobang's over-promotion of the Sino-Japanese relationship was one of the excuses raised by the Party's conservative elements to push him out of power in 1987. The ascendance of Li Peng and other Soviet-trained elites in the late 1980s provided impetus for a restoration of Sino-Soviet relations. The dismissal of Zhao Ziyang in the wake of the Tiananmen Square Incident limited Beijing's ties to the West as he was the leading proponent of those relations.

Generally speaking, factional politics affect Chinese foreign policy in four principal ways. First, even though the Chinese Communist Party Constitution prohibits any factional activities within the Party, in reality "groupings of officials are scattered within the hierarchy of Chinese politics."[38] Factional networks are characterized by strong personal patronage relationships starting from the top level of leadership all the way down to the lower levels of the bureaucracies. In the past, the Zhou Enlai's network dominated the Foreign Ministry for years. Hu Yaobang worked hard to place his Communist Youth League cronies in the foreign ministry and succeeded in naming Wu Xueqian as Foreign Minister. Qian Qichen, the present Foreign Minister, is also thought to have ties to Premier Li Peng and General Secretary Jiang Zemin.

Second, there is a close linkage between domestic and foreign policy choices. Major policy changes often have a strong influence on the distribution of power, status, and wealth among different institutions, leaders, and regions. The groups and individuals that prosper under one policy priority may suffer under the others.[39] In the early and mid-1950s, for example, the strategy of leaning toward the Soviet Union placed enormous power in the hands of a central planning apparatus and the heavy industry ministries that it served. Mao's shift to a self-reliance policy stripped power from these ministries and shifted it to the army and interior areas. Under Deng's open-door policy in the 1980s, enormous wealth was pumped into coastal areas while the power and prestige of party cadres and the military were severely damaged.

Third, factional struggles in China are often issue-oriented. In China, issues--and hence policies--are resolved by the ruling elite within the Party. This situation is quite different from polities where policy-making authority is dispersed among numerous legislative bodies, functional bureaucracies, and regulatory agencies. Therefore, factional struggles in China have been "more than contests over position; substantive issues have continually been at stake as well."[40] For any factions, maneuvering on foreign policy issues serves as one of the aspects in enhancing their particular interests and especially their leadership standing. Sometimes issues are routine enough for bureaucratic mechanisms to handle. But at other times, some issues may dominate the leadership's agenda and become embroiled in factional struggling. These issues usually involve sensitive nationalistic problems, national security concerns, economic development strategies or ideological differences. In fact, major issue debates can be seen as a battleground for various factions to compete for power.

Finally, factionalism requires coalition-building. As found by a scholar of Chinese politics, "policymaking in China normally involves the formation and realignment of coalitions built around common or compatible stands on a number of policy issues."[41] A successful preeminent leader must have a factional power base. Both Mao and Deng can be seen as the masters of manipulating their subordinates and building factional coalitions. Any settled policy in Beijing cannot be made without consensus among factions. Otherwise, opposition factions are very good at blunting policy initiatives they do not agree with or from which they stand to lose power or prestige. Differences at the *Zhongyang*, the power center of the regime,[42] often lead to heated debates and factional tensions. As a result, factional strife and personality clashes will be involved. Personnel purging at the top is likely to take place, indicating the end of one round of power struggle within the Chinese leadership. Once the problem of personnel purging is resolved, there may be widespread compulsive support for the winner's policy programs as cadres seek to identify with the new consensus. Thus, the new factional alignment with the Chinese ruling elite will determine Beijing's general posture, including its foreign policy direction.

Policy Coordination

In addition to foreign policy decision-making, policy implementation involves the participation of various functional departments within the government. The effectiveness and integrated foreign policy, to a large extent, is determined by good coordination between different policy agendas and various institutional interests within the Chinese government. This is particularly true as China foreign policy concerns are now no longer dominated only by strategic issues. Although sensitive and strategically important issues are still handled by a small group of top leaders, policy recommendations and policy implementations have become much more bureaucratic, diffused, and complex as foreign policy agendas have significantly increased and as policy operations are enhanced by the participation of various interests. Several institutions, like Foreign Ministry, the People's Liberation Army, and the Ministry of Foreign Economic Relations and Trade, all have their own agendas under China's broad foreign policy guidelines. In addition to the factor of factional politics as analyzed earlier, compartmentalization and the lack of good communications and information-sharing among different ministries within the Chinese government have sometimes made China awkward in foreign policy making. Policy coordination is, in fact, a management issue which requires an effective organizational structure and cooperation among different divisions of labor. Unlike the United States, China does not have a National Security Council system, responsible to the President, to command the foreign policy community. Instead, policy coordination in Beijing is conducted in a horizontal manner through a "concord system" ("*Huiqian Zhidu*"). In this collective management system, policy coordination is organized on the basis of issue areas in which a government department with the corresponding responsibilities plays the role as a convener and the lead in formulating policy options, organizing operations and coordinating different government agencies. As a result, different issue areas may have different entities guiding them. This kind of concord system works well if the organizer is politically powerful enough within the Chinese government or if paramount leaders interfere. Otherwise, it will cause difficulties in policy coordination among departments with different agendas and interests within the Chinese government. Sometimes, it involves inconsistent voices or even actions in China's foreign policy implementation.

Summary: Combined Impact

As it is in other countries, China's foreign policy is goal-oriented and consists of a number of objectives ranging from securing China's national security and political independence to guiding economic development. However, at different periods of time, Beijing's primary foreign policy objective was modified leading to changing policy patterns. Those modifications in foreign policy objectives came from interactions among the above-analyzed factors.

Of these factors, the Chinese leadership's perception of international and domestic developments and its assessment of the country's need under any given circumstance play a defining role in China's foreign policy making. At different times, Chinese leaders may have different interpretations of internal and external situations. According to their perceptions, the Chinese leaders would give different rankings to political, economic, and defense priorities in China's foreign policy. Accordingly, China would pursue different foreign policy objectives.

In the early 1950s, Beijing perceived the United States as the pressing threat to China's security as Washington followed a containment policy and the two countries engaged in the Korean War. As a result, China had to align with the Soviet Union for security and economic assistance. But later, as domestic ambitions (e.g., the Great Leap Forward Movement), Mao's ideological concerns (e.g., the Cultural Revolution), and the power struggle within the Chinese leadership dominated the scene in the 1960s, China followed a self-righteous and isolationist foreign policy. This pattern of foreign behavior was abandoned as Beijing faced a growing military threat from the Soviet Union. Mao turned to the United States for strategic cooperation to resist the Soviet threat in the 1970s. After he came to power, Deng Xiaoping shifted China's top priority from Mao's revolutionary movements to economic modernization. This shift was reinforced by the positive changes in the international strategic balance of power at the time. Eventually, it brought China to an "independent foreign policy." In general, when Chinese leaders judge that their international surroundings are relatively stable, they tend to stress domestic considerations in their foreign policy making. But when the environment is perceived as unfavorable, Beijing would put other objectives aside and let the strategic factor dominate Chinese foreign policy making.[43]

In interpreting situations and assessing the country's need, Chinese leaders are obsessed with the country's experiences in modern Chinese history. The mix of realist and nationalistic mindset often dominates political alignment within the Party leading to severe power struggles within the government. The sensitive issues regarding China's national security, nationalistic feelings, economic development strategy or ideological concerns often trigger policy debates. For example, there is a consensus among Chinese leaders that economic modernization is in China's interests to make the country prosperous and powerful. But the leadership is often divided over the appropriate actions to gain access to foreign advanced technology and know-how without generating dependence and without causing the country to be flooded by foreign ideologies and institutions that could undermine the Chinese socialist identity.[44] Indeed, policy debates may easily result in factional struggles within the government. Chinese foreign policy, therefore, is made by the winning faction of the Party with its interpretations of the country's interests as well as with its own parochial concerns.

Chapter 4

Foreign Policy before the 1982 Restructuring

Before it adopted an "independent foreign policy" in 1982, China had consistently followed an anti-Soviet foreign policy since the early 1970s. This strategy was the Chinese response to the massive military buildup of Soviet conventional and nuclear forces along the Sino-Soviet border and to the Soviet search for greater political influence around China's periphery. The perceived Soviet threat to China's security was the strategic center of gravity for China's entire foreign policy and defense at the time.

The Increasing Soviet Military Threat

Isolationist Foreign Policy

In the late 1960s, Chinese foreign affairs were marked by acute isolation, stemming from the negative impact of the Cultural Revolution on the conduct of foreign policy.[1] Troubled by internal disunity and civil strife, Beijing failed to pay close attention to foreign affairs and adopted an attitude of self-righteous hostility and disdain toward other countries. The Chinese leadership openly encouraged the export of revolution to other nations and took an uncompromising approach to superpowers. China not only condemned the American containment policy and its invasion of Vietnam, but also severely criticized the Soviets as "revisionists." All these radical foreign activities severely weakened China's international image and isolated it from most of its few foreign friends.

The Escalation of the Sino-Soviet Conflict

The relationship between Beijing and Moscow has been rooted in a complex of historical, territorial, racial, geo-political, ideological, and psychological factors.[2] As China's biggest neighbor, the Soviet Union had tremendous influence on Chinese domestic as well as foreign policies. Since the Sino-Soviet split in the early 1960s, the bilateral ideological dispute between China and the Soviet Union had deepened.

Meanwhile, after the Cuban missile crisis in 1962, the Soviets were engaged in a steady buildup of their military power. Soon the Sino-Soviet dispute spread to other issue areas. In 1963 the boundary dispute came into the open when China explicitly raised the issue of territory lost through "unequal treaties" with Tsarist Russia.[3] After unsuccessful border consultations in 1964, Moscow began a military buildup along the border with China and in Mongolia, which continued into the 1970s.[4] The Sino-Soviet dispute was also intensified by increasing competition between Beijing and Moscow for influence in the Third World and in the international Communist movement. Beijing's support for worldwide revolution became increasingly militant although in most cases it lacked the resources needed for large amounts of economic and military aid. Besides, Beijing accused the Soviet Union of signing the Partial Nuclear Test Ban Treaty with the United States in 1963 and regarded the treaty as a Soviet sellout of the interests of international Communism and, furthermore, as showing Soviet collaboration with the United States against China.

The removal of Khrushchev in 1964 brought a brief lull in Sino-Soviet polemics, but since the new Soviet leadership continued Khrushchev's foreign policy, Beijing soon resumed its intense polemics and continued to charge the new Soviet leaders with revisionism and collaboration with the United States to manipulate the world. The dispute later expanded to party relations. In 1966, the Chinese Communist Party broke off ties with the Communist Party of the Soviet Union.[5]

During the Chinese Cultural Revolution, Sino-Soviet relations further deteriorated. Any relations that had survived up to the middle of 1966 were broken off. The Soviet Union was labeled by the Red Guards as "Communist traitor." Then came the Soviet invasion of Czechoslovakia in August 1968 and the enunciation of the Brezhnev Doctrine of "limited sovereignty." Beijing accused the Soviets of becoming a "social-imperialist" power which intended to establish its hegemony by threatening other countries with war.[6]

The watershed of Sino-Soviet relations was the armed clashes on their common frontier between March and August 1969 which escalated the Sino-Soviet dispute from ideological and political differences into a military confrontation. A new phase in Sino-Soviet relations thus began.

Military Confrontation

The Chinese-Soviet border dispute is leftover from history. The border was established on the basis of the Russo-Chinese treaties of Aigun (1858), Beijing (1860), and Ili (1881).[7] Through these treaties, China lost over 380,000 square miles of territory to Russia. The Chinese call these treaties "unequal" because the imperial court of China was forced to sign the treaties at bayonet's point by the Tsarist Government at a time when China had been weakened by a war with Britain and France, 1856-58, and the Taiping Rebellion.[8]

Until 1949, the boundary question between the two countries remained dormant. For nearly a decade after the formation of the People's Republic, friendly relations ostensibly existed between the two countries. Border relations were dealt with amicably. The two states by and large lived up to the commitment to respect the status quo according to their alliance treaty of 1950, as well as agreements concerning civil aviation, mineral resources, shipping and railroads.[9] But as relations between the two countries deteriorated in the late 1950s and the early 1960s, border problems came to the fore. Incidents along the border occurred as early as 1959 and matched step-by-step the general decline in Sino-Soviet relations. Starting in the mid-1960s, both China and the Soviet Union reinforced the military forces deployed along their common frontier and incidents took place from time to time. The main challenge came at the Amur and Ussuri River Areas.

The Russians had long claimed that the border ran along the bank on the Chinese side of the two rivers and that their entire waterways and more than 700 islands which they contained belonged exclusively to Russia. The Chinese disputed the Russian claim and contended under international law that the central line of the main channel of the rivers formed the boundary line. Thus, about 600 islands belonged to China. The problem was complicated by the fact that after the breaking up of the ice in spring, the rivers regularly flooded their banks and frequently shifted their channels. The winter of 1968/69 saw heavy Soviet vehicles being used on the ice-bound islands to evict or otherwise interfere with Chinese occupants and Chinese patrols.[10]

Ultimately, the two sides engaged in serious armed clashes over several small islands in the Ussuri River. The major clashes first occurred on the Zhenbao (or Damansky in Russian) Island in the Ussuri River on March 2 and March 15 in 1969. Several hundred military personnel from both sides participated in the battle on March 2 and even artillery and armored vehicles were used. The entire battle lasted about two hours. Both sides had several dozens killed and wounded. Further fighting involving several thousand soldiers from both sides occurred on March 15, and was on a even larger scale, continuing for hours.[11] Tanks, infantry, armed troop carriers and artillery were used by both sides. The casualties were heavy with several hundred killed and wounded.

Immediately after the armed clashes on the Zhenbao Island, Moscow conducted a well-orchestrated diplomatic-military campaign to force the Chinese to reopen negotiations on the border question which had been terminated by China in 1964. Secondly, throughout the spring and summer of 1969, the Soviets engaged in a number of increasingly severe bold actions against the Chinese. In May, border incidents took place near the town of Blagoveshchensk and in various areas in Kazakhstan. From the beginning of June to the middle of August 1969, the Soviet border authorities registered no fewer than 488 border violations and armed incidents.[12] In mid-August, Soviet forces badly mauled Chinese units in the largest border clash ever along the Western frontier. Soviet troops were given orders to open massive missile and artillery fire on Chinese territory up to a depth of 10 kilometers. Large numbers of troops and heavy weapons such as tanks, combat planes, artillery, and missiles were used. One battle lasted a whole day.[13]

The extreme tension in Sino-Soviet relations was climaxed by Moscow's moves and signals of an preemptive Soviet military attack deep into Xinjiang to destroy China's nuclear weapon installations. Brezhnev even discussed with U.S. President Nixon and Henry Kissinger the possibility of Western support in the event of war with China. By using its overwhelming military superiority, the Soviet Union attempted to engage in a brinkmanship policy to force a less belligerent posture from Beijing.[14]

The military clashes between China and the Soviet Union attracted worldwide attention raising the possibility of a major war in East Asia. But hopes of reducing the confrontation came in September 1969 when the Soviet Premier Alexei N. Kosygin, on his way home from the funeral of Ho Chi-minh, stopped briefly in Beijing and had a meeting with his Chinese counterpart Zhou Enlai. They agreed to reopen discussions on the border issue in October 1969.[15]

Besides, the Soviets accelerated buildup of military forces east of Lake Baikal, resulting in increasing the number of divisions from fifteen to around forty-five. The Soviet forces also occupied Mongolia, laid the infrastructure for the presence of a Siberian force three or four times the level reached in 1972, and raised the total number of military personnel from 300,000 to over 750,000.[16] This buildup and the accompanying campaign of threats upset the balance of power between the two countries. From late 1969 forward, China was no longer able to defend itself against any reasonably large Soviet military incursion anywhere along its border with the Soviet Union and Mongolia. The situation was made worse by the unprepared state of the Chinese military whose major task during the previous several years had been to maintain internal order in the Cultural Revolution. The upshot was that China was neither militarily defensible nor economically stable. Having deliberately isolated itself from contact with potential allies, Beijing was now facing a severe threat which it could not counter by its own efforts.

Crisis Management

The Sino-Soviet border clashes created a war scare in China. The clashes and the precedent of the Soviet intervention in Czechoslovakia in August 1968, raised the possibility of a large-scale Soviet attack against China. Mao was reportedly worried that the continued chaos at home might give the Soviets a pretext to apply the Brezhnev Doctrine to China.[17] In this context, Beijing concluded that the international isolation and internal chaos produced by the Cultural Revolution were becoming increasingly dangerous to China's security and possibly even to its survival. Thus, the Chinese leadership had little option but to completely to revamp its domestic and foreign policies.

Domestic Efforts and Leadership Debate

Domestically, Beijing intensified its efforts to stop the chaos caused by the Red Guards and started to restore a certain degree of order while continuing the revolution. As a result, the most violent phase of the Cultural Revolution was over and government agencies, including the foreign policy apparatus, were gradually returning to normal modes of functioning.[18]

Besides, the Chinese leadership conducted major campaigns to convince the citizens of the imminence of war and to encourage them to make whatever preparations they could. A huge campaign was launched throughout China to "prepare for war." *Renmin Ribao* (*People's Daily*) claimed that war with Moscow was inevitable because of "irreconcilable differences of principle between China and the Soviet Union."[19] Meanwhile, Beijing also praised the doctrine of People's War: a militia, tens of millions strong; an enormous air-raid shelter program; and verbal taunts at the Russians, daring them to come ahead and be swallowed by the sea of popular resistance.

These were weak reeds and the leadership knew it. Faced with the continued unfavorable change in the balance of forces around China, the top level Chinese leaders of whatever background or ideological inclination were forced to focus on how to deal effectively with the Soviet military threat and political intimidation. The implications of the new situation affected, and in turn were influenced by, differing political, economic, and defense priorities of competing groups in the Chinese leadership. Initially they came up with strikingly different approaches, leading to the most serious leadership debate over foreign and security policy since 1949.[20]

Defense Minister Lin Biao, the second most powerful person in the Party at the time, and other radicals who had come to prominence during the Cultural Revolution, were opposed to moderation in foreign policy. They argued that both Moscow and Washington were implacably hostile to China and were determined to cooperate to contain China. A moderate diplomacy designed to split the two powers, using one against the other, would only reveal Chinese weakness and encourage them to pressure China even harder. Therefore, China must rely on its own efforts, spending more on defense and preparing the masses for a protracted people's war.

But Premier Zhou Enlai favored diplomatic maneuvers to offset the Soviet threat. He argued that such maneuvers could be undertaken by a well-executed, pragmatic foreign policy designed to end China's isolation and create a new international alignment to restore international balance of power.[21] He maintained that the common interests against the Soviet threat might lead to a Sino-American rapprochement which could provide China with the needed leverage to check the threat posed by Moscow.[22]

Initially, Mao did little to show distinct policy preferences and appeared receptive to diverse recommendations.[23] Later Lin Biao was killed in a plane crash on his way to flee the country after a failed coup attempt against Mao in September 1971.[24] Following this event, many of Lin Biao's military and political lieutenants were purged and Mao started to endorse the opening to the United States. As a result, the differences of opinion within the Chinese leadership on China's foreign policy became markedly reduced. From that time on, China developed a fairly consistent strategy, at first under the leadership of Mao Zedong and Zhou Enlai, and later under Hua Guofeng and Deng Xiaoping. It attempted to use superpower confrontation pragmatically to China's advantage. Believing that the United States had viewed China as a counterweight to the Soviet power and that the United States was about to drop the containment policy against China, Beijing began to move toward a collaborative relationship with the United States. This change of policy was based on a realistic assessment of the international environment in the early 1970s.

International Environment Assessment

Having ignored the world for the previous several years, Beijing now discovered that China's external environment had changed immensely. Shortly after the border clashes with the Soviet Union, senior Chinese leaders began to reassess China's external environment and seek fundamental changes in China's foreign policy in order to offset the overwhelming threat from the north.[25] The Chinese evaluated the Soviet threat both in terms of the Sino-Soviet bilateral military balance and in the context of Moscow's global strategy. By the end of 1971, a new view regarding world politics had become clear for Beijing.[26]

First, the Soviet buildup in Asia and its invasion of Czechoslovakia had demonstrated that the expanding power of Moscow represented the most dangerous threat to China. The escalating Sino-Soviet border clashes of March-August 1969 appeared to support this view. Globally, the Soviet military power was increasing rapidly while the United States was preoccupied in Vietnam, shifting the international balance of power from the United States toward the Soviet Union. Therefore, the Soviet military pressure and political intimidation, especially around China's periphery, would be the predominant Chinese foreign policy concern.

Second, the United States was about to disengage from the Vietnam conflict following the Tet offensive and the American presidential election of 1968. The United States might begin at least a tactical withdrawal from its long-standing military containment of China in Asia. Thus, the United States represented less of a military threat to China as it pulled back forces from around China's eastern and southern borders.

Third, Japan had become a principal economic power by virtue of its enormous industrial and technological growth in Asia. Western Europe had reemerged as a major international player in world politics. In addition, developing countries had also been an important force which could not be ignored any longer in the international arena. But the sad reality was that China had no reliable friends among any of them.

In these circumstances, China's interests would be well served by an active diplomacy plus a gradual buildup of its own defense forces. For this purpose, China needed to abandon its self-righteous ideological approach to foreign affairs which left Beijing diplomatically isolated and weak in the face of the Soviet pressure.

Soon Beijing took two initiatives. First, on the basis of the assessment of American intentions and capabilities, the Chinese began to explore the possibility of improved relations with the United States. Second, pulling back from the extremism of Cultural Revolution diplomacy, Beijing was more willing to overlook past grievances, ideological disputes, and other difficulties, for the purpose of improving, resuming or establishing relations with a number of countries, such as Romania, Yugoslavia, Japan, West European countries, and most of the Third World nations.[27] In only two years (1971-72), China opened or resumed diplomatic relations with thirty-two countries. In 1971 the Beijing government replaced Taiwan and became represented at the United Nations.[28]

Sino-American Rapprochement

The rapidly changing international balance of power and the substitution of the Soviet Union for the United States as China's principal enemy paved the way for a possible cooperative relationship with the United States. Prospects for better ties between Beijing and Washington were further enhanced by the United States' policy of reducing American military role in East Asia under terms of the Nixon Doctrine, thereby corroborating China's international assessment.[29]

On the American side, Washington was also alarmed by the

unprecedented expansion of the Soviet Union. After redefining the international balance of power, Nixon changed the 2½ war strategy to 1½ wars and attempted to side with Beijing as a means to make the Soviet Union more accommodating in negotiations over strategic arms limitation and European disarmament. According to Kissinger, the opening to China was a policy instrument designed to attract Beijing, impose constraints on Moscow, and increase the United States' freedom of maneuver in Vietnam. In his own words, "China needed us precisely because it did not have the strength to balance the Soviet Union by itself," and the United States should play the power game to "give each Communist power a stake in better relations with us."[30] Moreover, the Nixon administration apparently judged that its new move with regard to China would also assist the United States in finding a compromise solution to the Vietnam conflict.

The common ground shared by the two countries concerning the Soviet threat finally led to Nixon's landmark visit to China in February 1972. The Shanghai Communiqué signed at the end of the visit formally solidified the shift in China's foreign policy from opposing both superpowers to opposing the Soviet Union while treating the United States as an implicit ally. The Shanghai Communiqué had two major features. First, it noted that the two countries had reached general agreement about the international order in East Asia. In particular, they pledged to cooperate to ensure that the region would not become subject to international "hegemony," a code word used especially by China to denote Soviet expansion. Second, it also noted that the Taiwan issue was the major stumbling block in the normalization of Sino-American relations. Both sides expressed respectively their positions on the Taiwan issue in the communiqué and pledged to continue negotiations on the normalization of relations.[31] The communiqué clearly indicated that the United States and China were willing to defer the problems of formal diplomatic relations and Taiwan in order to work together on the basis of their common strategic interests in East Asia.[32]

Anti-Soviet United Front

Mao's Three Worlds Theory

After the initial focus on the Sino-American rapprochement, Mao's attention was turned to the task of creating a more systematic and theoretical basis for the new policy. The result was the famous "three worlds theory" which was first spelled out by Mao in his talk with the visiting president of Zambia, Dr. K.D. Kaunda, in February 1974. Mao said:

> In my view, the United States and the Soviet Union form the First World, Japan, Europe, and Canada, the middle section, belong to the Second World. We are the Third World.... The Third World has a huge population. With the exception of Japan, Asia belongs to the Third World. The whole of Africa belongs to the Third World, and Latin America, too.[33]

Two months later the theory was formally presented by Deng Xiaoping, Chinese vice-premier, in his speech at the Sixth Special Session of the United Nations General Assembly. According to Deng, "all the political forces in the world have undergone drastic division and realignment" since the 1950s and the early 1960s. The Soviet Union had degenerated into "social-imperialism," and, as a result, the socialist camp was "no longer in existence." The global influence of the United States had peaked, and the "Western imperialist bloc" had begun to disintegrate. Moreover, decolonization had produced a large number of new nations in Asia, Africa, and Latin America, which were "playing an ever greater role in international affairs." This process of division and realignment had produced a world divided into three parts: a "First World," consisting of the United States and the Soviet Union: a "Second World," comprising Japan, Australia, New Zealand, and the developed countries of Eastern and Western Europe; and a "third world," including all developing countries, among them China itself. The growing resistance of both the third and second worlds against the economic and political hegemony of the two superpowers had become the major feature of contemporary world politics. China should join this trend and unite with the Second and the Third World to oppose hegemonism.[34]

In China's view, the Soviet Union and the United States were the major sources of conflict and the contention between the superpowers caused tensions in the world. Beijing argued that any "détente" between them was only temporary and in the long run, Moscow and Washington would contend for global dominance because of their imperialist nature. Mao made it clear that the superpowers "may reach some agreement, but I wouldn't take it as something solid. It's transitory, and deceptive too. In essence, rivalry is primary."[35] The continuing competition between the superpowers in the Third World and Europe demonstrated this point. Because the Soviet Union was on the offensive and making substantial gains in the world, while the West in general and the United States in particular were on the defensive and ineffective in the face of the Soviet expansion, of the two superpowers the Soviet Union had become the more "ferocious, the more reckless...and the more dangerous source of world war."[36]

China's devastating view on Moscow was not solely because the Soviet Union threatened China's security. It was also "determined by a whole set of historical conditions under which the Soviet Union has grown and become an imperialist superpower." Namely, as a latecomer following on the heels of the United States, Moscow had to be more aggressive and adventurous since it was trying to expand whereas Washington was merely protecting its position. In addition, as the Soviet Union was economically inferior, it needed to place a greater reliance on military power, while its centralized economy made it easier to put the country on a war footing. Finally, the Soviet Union was more deceptive because it could "flaunt the banner of 'socialism' to bluff and deceive people everywhere."[37] The Soviet Union was, according to the Chinese, a socialist in name but an imperialist in action and had become "an imperialist superpower that threatened the world," just as American imperialism had done, but the latter was in decline.[38] The concept of Soviet social-imperialism enabled Beijing to portray the Soviet Union as guilty of territorial expansion, economic encroachment, military intervention, and political infiltration and subversion.

Based on the "three worlds" conception, China called for a united front of "all the forces in the world that can be allied with,"[39] presumably including right-wing third world governments and Western capitalist regimes and even the United States, in opposition to the Soviet expansionism. Beijing argued that "World war, though inevitable, can be postponed.... The key to putting off war lies not in holding talks and concluding agreements, as is vociferously suggested by some people, but in the united struggle of the people of all countries against hegemonism."[40]

There were three policy implications of Mao's theory. First, the United States presented less of a threat than the Soviet Union and compromises could be made to gain Washington's participation in a united front against Moscow as the confrontation between Moscow and Washington could be used. Theoretically, China still put both the United States and the Soviet Union into the same category. But Beijing subtly incorporated its partial alignment with the United States into its formal foreign policy doctrine. China justified this differentiated approach on November 1, 1977 by stating the Leninist principle of dealing blows at the most dangerous enemy.[41] Secondly, all third world countries, regardless of their social or political systems, could be a part of the same united front and China would be more interested in mobilizing their opposition to Soviet hegemonic behavior than in promoting revolution in the Third World. Thirdly, The Second World consisted of industrialized countries. On the one hand, they had economic and political contradictions with the Third World. But at the same time, they also faced the Soviet threat. Therefore, they could be an important ally of China in opposing Moscow.

Mao's three worlds theory was, first of all, introduced as a theoretical preparation for the major turn in China's foreign policy. It was also used to offset some of the negative feelings that certain third world countries had with regard to the rapprochement and the subsequent close ties between China and the United States. Quickly the theory became a handy device used primarily to support China's foreign policy priorities for a united front against Soviet expansionism. The gist of the "three worlds" conception was that the Soviet Union represented the greatest threat both to China and to world peace. This claim legitimized Beijing's close relations with the West and placed China among third world nations.[42]

Building An Anti-Soviet United Front

The central work of Beijing's foreign policy in the 1970s was to form the "broadest united front" to counter Soviet expansionism which would entail closer relations with the United States, Western Europe, Japan, and the Third World. The cornerstone of this united front was strategic cooperation between China and the United States. Since the 1972 Sino-American rapprochement, Beijing had reduced its previous criticism of American military presence and influence in Asia, and given unusually favorable notice to Washington's statements of resolve to retain strong ties with Japan and other non-Communist Asian states, and to maintain a strong naval presence in the western Pacific and the

Indian Ocean. Beijing also reported favorably on the strengthening of the American nuclear arsenal, of the North Atlantic Treaty Organization (NATO) and of American forces in Europe and the Middle East as a means to counteract Soviet power in these areas. The Chinese understood the implications of American strength for China, asserting that American power served to preoccupy the Soviet Union so that Moscow could not easily increase its military pressure on China. Despite bilateral differences over the Taiwan issue and sometimes conflicting conceptions of the most effective means of countering Soviet power, Beijing stressed that convergence of strategic views constituted the foundation of the Sino-American relationship.[43]

The Sino-American rapprochement cleared the road for China to establish good relations with advanced capitalist countries. From 1970 to 1973, Beijing established or upgraded diplomatic relations with major industrialized nations including Japan, Britain, West Germany, Italy, Canada, Australia, Spain, Greece, Belgium, and the Netherlands. In 1974, formal relations were established with the European Economic Community (EEC). By the mid-1970s, China had formal relations with all the advanced countries in the Second World.[44] In almost all cases, those countries broke ties with Taiwan as Beijing demanded.

China began also to pay more attention to right-wing governments of developing countries and assigned virtually no role to revolutionary forces and national liberation movements. In terms of relations with individual developing countries, China now took a black-or-white approach to value these relations primarily according to the degree of a country's "Soviet connections." Those who allied with or supported the Soviet Union were automatically considered as adversaries and those who did not were regarded as friends. In the meantime, China used almost every available occasion to show its strong opposition to any moves that might help the Soviet Union gain ground in the Third World. China reacted strongly against India's intervention in Bangladesh in 1971, warning that such moves would ultimately benefit the Soviet Union. Beijing was quite critical of a series of Soviet actions in Africa and Asia during the mid-1970s, such as the Soviet-Cuban involvement in Angola in 1975 and the Soviet-backed coup in South Yemen in 1977. Besides, the Chinese were noticeably receptive to events undermining the Soviets' global influence, sometimes at the risk of contradicting some of Beijing's long-valued principles or practices. For example, contrary to its long-time practice of standing with the majority of the Arab countries, China welcomed the Egyptian-Israeli peace treaty of 1979, a move that was condemned by most Arab nations at that time. The main reason was that with a strong American initiative, the move helped keep Soviet influence out of the Middle East. China responded similarly to events in Somalia, Zaire, and the two Yemens in the late seventies.[45]

The Chinese View of Détente

Throughout the 1970s, Beijing actively followed an anti-Soviet united front policy. At the same time, it kept criticizing the West's détente policy with Moscow and considered it as an appeasement toward the Soviet Union. Two themes were often used by China to build an anti-Soviet united front as the effective means to check the Soviets. One was the conviction that because of the weakening of the United States, Moscow had become the only rising and therefore more immediately threatening hegemonist. To target anything other than Soviet hegemonic behavior would do a disservice to world stability. The other was the assertion that because the Soviet Union was the most dangerous source of a world war, nations should firmly resist Soviet expansion instead of engaging in détente with Moscow.

In his report to the Tenth Party Congress in 1973, Zhou Enlai analyzed the Soviet threat to China both in terms of bilateral relations and in global terms. He argued that China was one target of the Asian aspect of Moscow's global strategy for dominance. The rivalry with the United States was the primary concern of Moscow. Zhou cited Europe as "strategically the key point" in the superpower contention.[46] Since the two sides were essentially at a stalemate there, Moscow had begun to carry out a strategy to outflank Western Europe by enlarging its sphere of influence and pushing out the influence of the United States from other parts of the world. In this process, there would be severe struggles between the United States and the Soviet Union worldwide, and the peace and security of other countries, including China, would be threatened. Zhou Enlai concluded that the expansion of Soviet influence was the source of world conflict and the effective way to counter the Soviet threat was to adopt a hardline position vis-à-vis Moscow. He particularly pointed out that in the context of the weakening position of the United States, it was impossible to restrict Soviet behavior by seeking a détente with Moscow as some people in the West expected. On the contrary, under the cover of détente, the

Soviet Union would gain even more ground from the West. Zhou pointedly stated that a détente with Moscow in Europe could only divert the "Soviet peril" toward China. He warned that Moscow had adopted a policy of feinting to the east while thrusting toward the west. In the end, Zhou predicted that the détente between the East and West was a "temporary and superficial phenomenon" and soon would be replaced by further tensions. So the most effective way to restrict Soviet behavior was Beijing's united front strategy rather than any efforts toward détente with Moscow.[47]

In late 1975 the Chinese showed new alarm over signs concerning what they viewed as a less resolute Western posture vis-à-vis the Soviet Union. In particular, the 1975 East-West summit meeting of the European Security Conference in Helsinki was considered by China as evidence of a growing trend in the West to "appease" the Soviet Union in order to direct the Soviet menace away from Europe and toward China. Beijing responded with warnings to the West that détente gave the Soviets more opportunities to further their expansion. In stepping up its propaganda concerning the dangers of détente, China depicted détente as a Western attempt to capitulate to Moscow. Meanwhile, Beijing portrayed the Soviet Union as rapidly building up its armed strength to a point where it was equal to, and in some respects surpassed, the power of the United States. The United States was said to have been weakened as a result of the 1974-1975 economic recession, the political disruption caused by the Watergate scandal, and the collapse of the U.S.-supported governments in Indochina. Not only was the United States seen as failing to keep pace with Soviet power, but it was said to have shown an alarming tendency to "appease" Moscow over such issues as strategic arms limitation, détente in Europe, East-West trade, and Soviet involvement in conflicts in Africa. China deliberately reminded people of the historical case of British Prime Minister Neville Chamberlain during negotiations with Adolf Hitler at Munich in 1938.[48] The Chinese were really frank in hoping that the United States would be less accommodating to the Soviet Union in the Strategic Arms Limitation Talks (SALT) and elsewhere. Beijing was well aware that if the United States did not offset Soviet strength in areas away from China, Moscow might be more inclined to focus greater force against Beijing. The Chinese criticism of American appeasement and their encouragement of a more resolute American position against Moscow received an authoritative endorsement from Deng Xiaoping in his remarks at a banquet for President Ford at

Beijing in December 1975. Deng labeled the Soviet Union as the "most dangerous source of war" and asked the United States to be firmer toward the Soviet Union on SALT and other issues.[49]

Limited Commercial Relations

After 1972, China began to resume some commercial transactions with the rest of the world, particularly with the West. For example, it imported some 170 complete industrial plants from the West at the value of $2.6 billion between 1972 and 1975.[50] But largely because of the concern of Mao and his radical supporters with the danger of economic dependence on foreigners and western ideological penetration in China, both the types and levels of economic, cultural and intellectual exchanges with the West remained quite limited. Beijing provided a rather restrictive account of its commercial transactions with the rest of the world. It would not allow foreigners to "dump" their consumer goods on its domestic market, would not accept foreign loans, would not "mortgage its natural resources" for foreign technology, would never allow foreign investment in China, and would not permit foreigners to "meddle in the management" of Chinese enterprises.[51] For most of the time in the 1970s, China was mainly interested in establishing strategic relationship with the West which provided China with an adequate leverage against the Soviet threat while economic and cultural exchanges with the West were proportionally limited.

United Front After Mao

Following the death of Mao Zedong and the arrest of the "Gang of Four"[52] in late 1976, China's leaders faced a host of domestic problems. Though divided on many issues at the time, they were able to achieve a consensus in continuing the anti-Soviet united front foreign policy to secure the country's interest in the unsteady international balance of power threatened by the further growth of the Soviet expansion. Because of this and the initial economic modernization efforts inside China, Beijing, in the late 1970s, further strengthened the anti-Soviet foreign policy and began to add more economic contacts to its strategic relations with the West, particularly the United States.

Broader Anti-Soviet Efforts

The Soviet external expansion reached its peak in the late 1970s. In Asia, the most striking development that China was so concerned about was Vietnam's alliance with the Soviet Union and its open rift with China. Following the collapse of the United States-supported governments in South Vietnam and Cambodia in 1975, Beijing began to worry about the Soviet move to fulfill the vacuum following the United States withdrawal and China's inability to influence Hanoi to follow policies more consistent with Chinese interests. Vietnam's relations with Moscow, its efforts in Cambodia which conflicted Chinese interests in Indochina, and the dispute over the Sino-Vietnamese border presented serious security problems to China.

China's objective in Asia then was to reverse the trend toward an unfavorable balance of power and attempt to stop the alliance between the Soviet Union and Vietnam. But Beijing failed and in December 1978 Moscow and Hanoi signed a friendship and alliance treaty. Only one month after signing the treaty, Vietnam invaded Cambodia and ousted the Chinese-backed Khmer Rouge government in Phnom Penh. The Soviet-Vietnamese alliance and the Vietnamese invasion of Cambodia were interpreted as a direct threat to China as well as to other countries in Southeast Asia.

In order to block the possible spread of Soviet influence in the region, Beijing responded swiftly. In February 1979, China started a short punitive war against Vietnam in the name of "self-defense" of Chinese territory. The purpose of the war was very clear that China was determined to contain the Vietnamese and minimize its collaboration with Moscow. In teaching Hanoi a lesson, the Chinese troops entered into Vietnam's territory and captured the most important strategic stronghold on the way to Hanoi. After the "lesson" was delivered, the Chinese troops pulled back and withdrew from Vietnam in four weeks.

The results of China's military "lesson" to Vietnam were mixed. Chinese armies seriously damaged Vietnamese border areas, diverted Vietnamese forces from Cambodia to northern Vietnam, further complicated Vietnam's economic planning, and demonstrated China's willingness to use force if necessary to halt Soviet-backed Vietnamese expansion in Southeast Asia. But Vietnam managed to return tit for tat and received ample support from its Soviet ally. Most notably, the

Chinese assault resulted in a reported 20,000 Chinese casualties and a large increase in Chinese defense spending at a time when China just started its economic reform programs. Besides, the Vietnamese were able to end Chinese influence in Laos, and to drive the Chinese-supported Pol Pot to the border area between Cambodia and Thailand. Meanwhile, over 250,000 refugees were expelled from Vietnam to China which created severe burdens on China.[53]

Apart from the Soviet-Vietnamese collaboration, Beijing also noticed that by the late 1970s the Soviet Union had greatly augmented its military deployments in Siberia, Mongolia and the Kurile Islands. Making a visible challenge to China, Japan and the United States, the Soviets deployed more modern air and naval forces and some weapons of mass destruction, including SS-20 missiles and the Backfire bomber, in East Asia. Through its cooperation with Vietnam, Moscow had obtained important strategic port facilities at Cam Ranh Bay and Da Nang in Vietnam which allowed the Soviet Pacific fleet to further project is power in the region.[54]

The impressive Soviet military buildup in Asia clearly challenged the interests of China, Japan and the United States. The common strategic interest gave Beijing and Washington greater incentive to establish closer ties. On the eve of China's war against Vietnam, Beijing and Washington normalized their diplomatic relations and Chinese leader Deng Xiaoping visited Washington discussing the possibility of further strategic cooperation between the two countries.

In December 1979, the Soviets invaded Afghanistan. Like the United States, Beijing reacted to the event with extreme concern. Beijing stated that the Soviet invasion of a China's neighbor was a direct threat to China's security and China warned that Moscow had extended the Brezhnev Doctrine to nonaligned and Islamic countries.[55] It described the event as a major step in Moscow's southward thrust (also called "south-bound strategy") to outflank Europe through dominance over the world's energy sources and supply routes. The Soviet "hegemonistic action" posed a "grave threat to peace and security in Asia and the whole world."[56]

In light of the new threat posed by Moscow, China doubled its efforts to form a broader international anti-Soviet united front and appealed for a strong international response, particularly from the United States. It pledged that "the Chinese Government and people will work tirelessly with all countries and people who love peace and uphold justice to frustrate Soviet acts of aggression and expansion." World peace could be maintained only if the people of the world "exert pressure on those hegemonists who stop at nothing to engage in aggression and expansion." In order to "stop" the Soviets "from committing aggression" and "force them to observe the most rudimentary principles" of international behavior, Beijing was looking to Washington for a strong response to the Soviet actions.[57]

Satisfied with the Carter administration's strong responses to the Soviet adventure in Afghanistan, Beijing welcomed Washington's "new and uncompromising stand" in its relations with the Soviet Union.[58] Meanwhile, Beijing frankly pointed out that the tension in the world exacerbated by the Soviet invasion of Afghanistan was the direct result of appeasement tendency in the West on such issues as the Strategic Arms Limitation Talks (SALT) and the Soviet-Cuban adventure in Africa. While charging that Moscow was exploiting the cover of "détente" in its drive for "world hegemony," China complained that "certain friends in the world have indulged in the illusion of making certain concessions to the aggressors."[59] To Beijing, the effective tactics for checking Soviet expansion were not those of détente, but rather, the formation of an international anti-hegemony united front to stop Soviet expansion anywhere in the world.

As an effort to foster a broader international front, the Chinese leaders worked hard to seek closer cooperation among the anti-Soviet countries. They repeatedly highlighted "anti-hegemonism" as the centerpiece of Beijing's developing relations with the West, especially the United States and Japan. This was most notable in Chinese treatment of the conclusion of the Sino-Japanese peace treaty in August 1978 and in the Sino-American communiqué announcing the normalization of diplomatic relations in December 1978. In the two documents, the anti-hegemonism clause was the "nucleus."[60] At the same time, Beijing voiced greater support than in the past for Western and pro-Western international groupings and the need for continued unity in countering Moscow, both among the European governments and with the United States in the NATO.

Besides, the Chinese leaders gave stronger endorsement of the Association of Southeast Asian Nations (ASEAN) in its efforts against the Soviet-Vietnamese expansion in Indochina. Political and military ties between China and Thailand in particular were strengthened. China also enhanced ties with Japan, supported Japanese defense efforts against the Soviet Union and expressed understanding of the American-Japanese security treaty. Meanwhile, Beijing sharply condemned Cuba and Vietnam as proxies of Soviet expansion. In addition, China aligned itself with strong anti-Soviet governments such as those of Zaire, Chile, Egypt, and Somalia. Beijing publicly encouraged third world nations to cooperate more with the West in order to preclude the opening of opportunities for Soviet expansion. Chinese officials even put aside past ideological concerns and identified closely even with extreme right-wing regimes as long as they were appropriately anti-Soviet. Hua Guofeng's visit to Iran just a few days before the fall of the Shah at the beginning of 1979 was such an example.

Closer Ties with the West

Moscow's continuing expansion rapidly changed the international balance of power and further moved Beijing to get closer to the West. The diplomatic normalization between Washington and Beijing in 1979 seemed, at least temporarily, to put aside the Taiwan issue as an obstacle to the strategic cooperation between the two countries. The incident proved that Chinese leaders were pragmatic enough to balance the country's interests in face of enormous danger posed by the Soviet Union.

The diplomatic normalization of Sino-American relations created momentum to expand the relationship between the two countries in a number of dimensions. Beijing and Washington started to consult on a wide range of regional and global issues of common concern and began to devise parallel or coordinated policies on such issues as Indochina and Afghanistan. Washington relaxed its restrictions on the export of military technology to China and Beijing agreed to establish a joint intelligence surveillance facility in West China to monitor Soviet missile tests.[61] Washington publicly stated that it was in the interest of the United States to have a "secure and strong" China,[62] while Chinese leader Deng Xiaoping called for a strong anti-Soviet partnership among China, the United States, Japan, and Western Europe.[63]

However, neither side publicly described their cooperation as a formal military alliance comparable to the Sino-Soviet alliance of 1950. Instead, they seemed satisfied to remain, in the words of the Carter administration, "friends, rather than allies."[64] Even so, the two countries began increasingly to speak of their parallel international objectives and common foreign policy interests and worked to narrow their remaining points of disagreement. All this amounted, if not to an alliance, at least to a reasonably close alignment between the two countries.

Closer ties between China and the West also spread swiftly into the economic sphere. Inside China, the purge of the Gang of Four removed the leaders of the opposition not only to alignment with the United States, but also to greater economic relations with the West. As the reform-minded pushed to make economic modernization top priority in China, cooperation with the West was seen as the most important source of financial, technical and managerial support for China's modernization drive. Soon China significantly relaxed its previous restrictions on its commercial relations with the West and concluded that its economic and scientific modernization could be promoted better by opening to the outside world than by pure self-reliance. The open-door conclusion later became the core reform program in the 1980s.

China's anti-Soviet and pro-American foreign policy reached its peak in 1980. But after that the factors that made such a strategy attractive began to show their fundamental limitations as drastic changes occurred both on the Chinese domestic scene and in the international environment. The basic assumptions of Beijing's anti-Soviet united front strategy increasingly faced severe challenges. In the end, the Chinese leaders had to reassess the country's basic interests under the new circumstances and soon they resolutely moved toward a new direction.

Chapter 5

Pressures for Foreign Policy Restructuring

One hypothesis for foreign policy restructuring as adaptive behavior assumes that when a country's basic interests are confronted with heavy pressures and its current foreign policy cannot effectively ease such pressures, it will be likely to engage in foreign policy change. In the early 1980s, China was in just that kind of situation. Both domestic and international developments exerted pressures on Beijing to drop its decade-long anti-Soviet united front foreign policy and develop a new one.

Domestic Pressures for Change

Internal Chinese Complications

Mao Zedong, the founding father of the People's Republic of China, died on September 9, 1976 at the age of eighty-two. His death marked the end of an era in modern Chinese history. Because of the complexity of his life, the popular reaction to Mao's death was quite ambivalent. As noted by a student of Chinese politics, most Chinese still revered Mao for founding the People's Republic. He sponsored the greatest program of land reform, launched the country on the path of industrialization, ended foreign privileges in China, and presided over the development of China's nuclear capability. And yet, as the years passed, Mao acted in an increasingly arbitrary manner, and the social and economic costs of his mistakes assumed apocalyptic proportions. The Great Leap Forward, Mao's great economic campaign of the late 1950s, plunged the country into depression, and the Cultural Revolution, the political movement Mao launched in 1966, produced a decade of turmoil and violence.[1] Millions of people suffered miserably from those mass campaigns. The failures in the latter part of Mao's life left China with a host of serious problems. At the time of Mao's death in 1976, China was facing severe economic and political crises that threatened the stability of the regime itself.

Economically, China had indeed made notable achievements in

economic development through several five-year plans since 1949. The central government tightly controlled all the country's economic resources and activities determining prices, plans, allocation, and distribution of goods. It was easier for the state to concentrate enough resources to develop a particular economic sector. Besides, ideological concerns and social objectives often played important part in influencing economic decisions.

This rigid and highly centralized economic structure ignored market factors like profits, quality and efficiency, and favored heavy industry to consumer goods. To manage economy, the government relied totally on administrative methods conducted by a large number of bureaucrats who were typically not competent in running a modern economy. Irrational economic decisions, waste and inefficiency often occurred and nobody would be held responsible for such wrongdoings. Because of the egalitarian emphasis in income distribution and full employment, employees did not have economic incentives to work hard and efficiently. All these chronic problems became acute in 1976 when China was experiencing declining rates of growth, stagnant levels of consumption, persistent inefficiency, and growing technological obsolescence. These economic difficulties were largely the result of the inefficiencies inherent in a Soviet-style centrally planned economy, including irrational prices, isolation from foreign competition, lack of contact between supplier and consumer, and a pervasive emphasis on quantity rather than quality of output. Many problems were further exacerbated by the Maoist biases against material incentives, markets, and the division of labor. Additional investment made by the government did not result in the expected growth. The rate of investment had been rising rather steadily from about one-quarter of national output in the mid-1950s to one-third in the 1970s, but rates of growth were declining sharply over the same period.[2] On the one hand, the centrally planned economy allowed the government to make enormous investment in certain high-priority areas in which China could make impressive achievements. But on the other hand, Chinese technology in general during the late 1970s lagged decades behind world levels. Most of the technology employed in the country's industry was completely obsolete and much of the rest was in dire need of upgrading. Furthermore, China also faced tremendous population pressure (around one billion in 1976). As far as the people's living standards were concerned, the situation became worse at that time. Urban residents faced serious shortages of housing, services, and consumer goods. The living space available for each urban resident amounted to only a few square feet. Other urban services, such as public transportation, parks, stores, and restaurants, were in short supply. The availability of foodstuffs and clothing depended on increasing imports of grain, cotton, sugar, and vegetable oils from abroad. And increasing numbers of agricultural and manufactured goods were subject to rationing and queuing and delivery delays.[3] Indeed, China's economy was verging on complete collapse in 1976.

Politically, the Cultural Revolution had produced a severe crisis of confidence among large sectors of Chinese society. The years between 1966 and 1976 were characterized by unremitting intrigue, betrayal, and violence. Millions of officials were branded capitalist roaders, placed under house arrest, imprisoned, sent to labor camps or put into internal exile. Intellectuals, as a group, were the principal targets of the Cultural Revolution and experienced a virtual reign of terror throughout the decade. They were physically tortured and psychologically intimidated. Some were killed and others committed suicide. Millions of high school and college students had originally joined the movement with great enthusiasm. But when the Red Guard movement had produced division and chaos, they were disbanded by the People's Liberation Army (PLA) and later sent to the countryside. The sudden change of their destiny caused many of the former Red Guards to reassess their role in the movement. They were shocked by the Lin Biao Incident and disillusioned to watch that their country degenerate into chaos. Urban workers also suffered a lot and their wages were frozen throughout the Cultural Revolution. The bonus system was totally suspended. They were also the principal victims of cramped housing, inadequate city services, and shortages of consumer goods. In short, the turmoil and hypocrisy of the Cultural Revolution alienated and angered millions of urban Chinese, especially the younger generation and intellectuals. There was a widespread public dissatisfaction with the political and economic trends that had emerged in the latter years of Mao's life. People were sick of continuous political mass mobilization and ideological indoctrination. As victimized officials formed a powerful constituency to fight against the beneficiaries of the movement; intellectuals were angered at the persecution they had suffered at the hands of radicals; young people resented the way they were treated in the movement; and workers were tired of stagnant living conditions, domestic pressure for change gradually joined forces.[4]

In themselves, China's domestic political and economic conditions were powerful forces for change as the country entered the post-Mao era at the end of 1976. These pressures were intensified further by the unfavorable comparison between China's economic performance and that of the rest of East Asia. At the time when China was plunged into domestic chaos during the Cultural Revolution, most of China's Asian neighbors were enjoying rapid economic growth. Japan, which had been regarded by China as sharing a similar economic level of development in the 1950s, had become an economic giant in the world by the late 1970s. Following Japan's economic take-off, South Korea, Singapore, Taiwan, and Hong Kong soon became "four tigers" in Asia and entered into the rank of newly industrializing countries, while China was galled by its own economic stagnation.[5]

Viewing both political and economic crises, many intellectuals and political elite in China could not help but look for policy change that could halt the decline in economic growth rates, increase consumption levels, and thus help restore political confidence. But during the late Maoist period, expressions of dissent were quite risky. Even under such circumstances, China's crisis was manifested in a series of dramatic protests against the regime's radical policies. The massive demonstration in the Tiananmen Square in April 1976 was one outstanding example.

At the time of Mao's death, Chinese domestic difficulties were so huge that they constituted powerful pressures for change. In fact, the situation was too explosive for the status quo to remain intact. Within the Chinese leadership, an intense succession struggle for power between radicals who supported the continuation of Mao's policies and reformers who wanted to look for new ways to govern the country erupted soon after Mao's death. In fact, divisions within the leadership were so deep that compromise and coexistence were impossible. Thus, a decisive political battle within the government became crucial to the destiny of the country.

The Rise of Reformers

At the time of Mao's death in 1976, the Chinese leadership was deeply divided into three broad groups. On the left of the political spectrum were the leftists headed by Mao's widow, Jiang Qing, and three other Politburo members, Zhang Chunqiao, Yao Wenyuan and Wang Hongwen (the so-called "Gang of Four"). Their followers were largely the activists and beneficiaries of the Cultural Revolution. They wished to preserve the policies of the Cultural Revolution, continue Mao's revolutionary values, and oppose any revisionist tendency.

The second group of leaders was those represented by Premier Hua Guofeng, who seemed to be convinced that the crisis of confidence and the wounds of the Cultural Revolution could be healed by fairly modest changes to restore political order and promote economic growth. They were mainly bureaucrats. Before the Cultural Revolution, they had already been second-echelon party and state officials, primarily in provinces. During the Revolution, they were promoted to the power center when their superiors were swept aside. These people preferred stability and harmony under the party leadership to radical policies as supported by the leftists. They placed much higher priority than did the leftists upon resuming economic growth and raising popular living standards. They were even willing to look abroad for some foreign assistance. But they did not want to criticize Mao explicitly for the disastrous consequences of the Cultural Revolution. Rather they blamed the leftists.

The third group of leaders were the so-called reformers represented by Deng Xiaoping. Whereas Hua and his group sought simply to blame the Gang of Four for the tragedy of the Cultural Revolution, the reformers were determined to repudiate the movement and attempted to significantly restructure the party's social, political and economic policies. Most members of this group were principal victims of the Cultural Revolution. They were condemned as "capitalist roaders" and sent to labor camps or imprisoned during the movement. Some of them, like Deng Xiaoping himself and Hu Yaobang, were rehabilitated and returned to their original posts in the early 1970s. But at the beginning of 1976, Deng Xiaoping and some of his associates were again demoted when their protector Premier Zhou Enlai died and they lost to the leftists. But Mao did not assign a leftist to the position of premier but rather appointed Hua. Before his death, Mao personally hand-picked Hua as his successor. Thus, at the time of Mao's death, the succession struggle was mainly between the leftists and Hua Guofeng.

Immediately after the death of Mao, the leftists intensified their action and fabricated what they described as Mao's final behest--"act according to the principles laid down"--and presented it as his final endorsement of the principles, programs, and leaders of the Cultural Revolution.[6] With this as justification, the leftists attempted to mobilize support for the notion that Jiang Qing, and not Hua, should succeed Mao as party chairman. Realizing that the Gang of Four was not about to accept Hua's leadership, Hua and his associates decided to strike first. With the support of Ye Jianying, a veteran military leader who had survived the Cultural Revolution, and other Politburo members who controlled the military and the public security forces, Hua launched a preemptive coup to arrest the Gang of Four on October 6, 1976. The following day, a Politburo meeting confirmed Hua's position as the top leader with the title of chairman of the party and of the party's Military Affairs Commission, as well as his continuing position as premier of the government.

Hua Guofeng thus emerged as the most powerful person in China. Although he had a reputation for sincerity and modesty, Hua did not earn distinction for innovative leadership. Since he had spent most of his career at the provincial level and had only seven years' membership on the Central Committee, Hua did not forge a national network of political supporters. He remained the protégé of Mao. Because of this, he lacked the political power bases that count for more than official titles in the relatively personalized and uninstitutionalized Chinese political process.[7]

After his appointment as party chief, Hua tried to enlarge his power base by defining national policies that could attract and maintain a broad coalition of national leaders and political institutions.[8] His overall strategy was to maintain some continuity with the recent past while redefining some of the Maoist legacy to promote faster economic modernization and greater political stability. In so doing, Hua was responding to the contradiction between his own path to power and the political and economic crises that China faced in 1976. Hua's rise to national prominence was the direct result of the Cultural Revolution. His selection as Mao's heir was the immediate consequence of Mao's personal intervention. In such a situation, for Hua to repudiate either the man or the movement risked fatally undermining his own position. Accordingly, Hua continued to revere Mao and his doctrines. Yet he also seemed to recognize the country's need for political order and economic development to heal the wounds of the Cultural Revolution.

With this contradictory nature, Hua formally announced the end of the Cultural Revolution and acknowledged the country's need for unity and stability. But he still continued to describe the doctrines that had justified Mao's decision to launch the Cultural Revolution--the theories of permanent class struggle and continuous revolution under socialism--as fundamental concepts. He also promised more such movements in the future when needed to prevent the reemergence of revisionism in the party.[9] By stressing the need for loyalty to Mao's doctrines, Hua sought to link his own legitimacy to the charismatic authority of Mao. Although Hua took credit for the arrest of the Gang of Four, he tried to restrict further purges of the leftist associates across the board and protect other leaders who, like himself, had also seen their careers flourish as a result of the Cultural Revolution. Besides, Hua sponsored the rehabilitation of many of the intellectuals persecuted during the Cultural Revolution and hefty increases in urban wages, but he resisted the reinstatement of the most prominent veteran officials purged in the movement, including Deng Xiaoping.

In running the national economy, Hua announced an ambitious "new leap forward" program intended to transform China into a powerful nation by the year of 2000. As set out in his ten-year development program introduced in 1978, Hua's strategy assumed that higher rates of growth could be stimulated by political stability, higher investment, larger technology imports and foreign loans, and greater incentives, without any basic structural reforms. Hua's strategy, which retained some aspects of the Maoist legacy while rejecting others, was meant to build and expand a political coalition that would be strong enough to keep him in power. The institutions from which Hua sought to secure support included the military, the planning apparatus, and the machine-building industry.

Unfortunately for Hua, his strategy met increasing difficulties throughout 1977 and 1978. His economic program did yield relatively high rates of growth nearly 11 percent in 1977 and more than 12 percent in 1978.[10] But the cost of these achievements was too high. The rapid growth of imports was not fully matched by the concurrent increase in exports, and in 1978 China ran its largest trade deficit since the First Five-Year Plan in the 1950s.[11] The expansion of capital investment far exceeded what the state's industrial resources could sustain and created acute bottlenecks in both construction materials and capital goods. These inflationary pressures were exacerbated by increasing wages faster than expanding the production of consumer goods. Accordingly, Hua's plan was shelved only a year after it had been announced.[12]

By the end of 1978, Hua's overall program had encountered serious setbacks without alleviating the crisis of confidence that plagued China. Dissatisfied with the economic "leap forward" which went too fast and a political program which proceeded too slowly, Hua's leadership faced tremendous challenges. Hua's defense of the Cultural Revolution became unacceptable to the victims of the movement who wanted a decisive repudiation of the events during the Cultural Revolution. Hua's leniency toward those officials who had collaborated with the Cultural Revolution was resisted by the individuals who advocated a thoroughgoing purge of the movement collaborators within the party. Finally, Hua's attitude toward Mao, summarized by himself in an ill-chosen formula known as the "two whatevers," that China should "resolutely defend whatever policies Chairman Mao has formulated and unswervingly adhere to whatever instructions Chairman Mao has issued,"[13] made him vulnerable to his political opponents. This rigid policy was opposed by those who sought an objective evaluation of the decisions of the late chairman, especially during the latter years of his life. In short, Hua proved to be unable or unwilling fully to confront and resolve the deeper crises that China faced at the time of Mao's death.

At this point, it was clear that China needed much more sweeping political and economic reforms than Hua was willing to undertake. The party had to offer a new alternative to resolve the political and economic crises. This mission was finally put on the shoulder of Deng Xiaoping, a person who could launch a fundamental restructuring of the Chinese political and economic order. With his seniority in the party, his political skill and his fate during the Cultural Revolution, Deng gained much support both within the party and from the general public for his program.[14] In the political realm, he sought to resolve China's political crisis by repudiating the Cultural Revolution, rehabilitating its victims, and conducting a thorough reassessment of Mao's career as China's paramount leader. He wanted to abandon Mao's doctrine of continuous class struggle and engage in reforms in China. In economics, Deng was strongly committed to a substantial reform of the Soviet economic planning model. He believed in a greater use of market mechanism in running the economy, a larger role for individual entrepreneurship, and more stress on profitability. He also strongly favored opening China to the rest of the world, particularly to the West, as a way of promoting China's economic development. At the time of Mao's death, however, Deng was in internal exile.

Under severe pressure within the party (especially from veteran leaders who survived the Cultural Revolution) and from the general public, Hua Guofeng finally agreed to rehabilitate Deng and restore his previously held position as vice-Chairman of the party, vice-premier, and chief of staff of the People's Liberation Army (PLA). Soon after he returned to power, Deng launched a series of skillful political attacks on Hua's leadership. Initially, Deng and his supporters criticized the Cultural Revolution and argued that class struggle was no longer appropriate as the principal feature of Chinese social life. Then Deng and his associates challenged Hua's position of "two whatevers." Deng argued philosophically that the truth was judged only in practice rather than according to anyone's subjective preferences.[15] He suggested that the correct approach in policy making was to "seek truth from facts" and to apply Marxism pragmatically to China's present conditions. Deng and his followers complained that if whatever Mao did and said must always determine the current policy making, it would lead the party nowhere.[16] The debate on the criterion of the truth (i.e., the truth is measured by objective reality rather than by subjective preference) significantly cleared the way to reassess Mao, to end the cult of personality, and to reevaluate the Cultural Revolution. Finally, Deng successfully built up his coalition by reinstating the veteran leaders purged during the Cultural Revolution.

The breakthrough for Deng to ease Hua out of the power center was made at the Third Plenum of the Eleventh Party Central Committee in December 1978. In a historic sense, this plenum was a watershed in Chinese politics. It marked the formal consolidation of Deng's authority in the party. First, the plenum explicitly endorsed several key elements of Deng's program. The party decisively shifted the focus of its work toward economic modernization and away from class struggle. The party also publicly announced that the era of mass movements, whether in political or economic affairs, had come to an end. Second, the plenum seriously questioned the ideological thinking of the "two whatevers" and "highly evaluated the discussion of whether reality is the only norm of truth." The plenum pointed out that "reality is the only norm of truth" had "given the party a new, lively guideline" and promised a full reassessment of Mao and the Cultural Revolution in the near future. Third, several victims of the purges during the Cultural Revolution returned to the Central Committee and reform-minded leaders entered the Politburo.[17] Obviously, all these decisions explicitly changed Hua's previous policies and weakened his position. In fact, the plenum set the stage for further victories for

Deng's "reform" faction over Hua's "whatever" faction in the following years.

Immediately after the plenum, Deng and his associates expanded their rural reform in the form of "household responsibility system" which dramatically raised agricultural production and laid the foundation for the later abandonment of the People's Commune.[18] Meanwhile, Deng made vigorous efforts to strengthen his own power base and remove "the whatever" leaders associated with Hua from power. At first, he secured the appointment of his own supporters to influential administrative positions in the party, army and government. Then at the Fifth Plenum of the Eleventh Party Central Committee in February 1980, Deng won a substantial success on personnel matters by isolating Hua and removing Hua's closest supporters from the Politburo on the grounds that they had supported the theory of the "two whatevers." At this meeting Deng's associates such as Hu Yaobang and Zhao Ziyang were elevated to the Standing Committee of the Politburo and other leaders sympathetic to reform were also added to the inner leadership core.[19] The coalition around Deng further strengthened its control over the party machine by the official reestablishment of the Secretariat of the Central Committee headed by Hu Yaobang. The Secretariat gradually assumed the responsibility for national policy making that had previously rested in the Politburo under Hua's chairmanship.

Although isolated in the inner leadership core, Hua still kept his positions as chairman of the party and the Military Commission of the Party Central Committee, as well as premier of the government after the Fifth plenum. However, Deng moved close to his final confrontation against Hua himself. In the name of fostering a clearer division of functions between the party and state administration machines, Deng persuaded the Central Committee to limit the practice of holding concurrent positions in the two bureaucracies. This enabled Deng to exchange his own resignation as vice-premier for Hua's removal from the premiership. In September 1980, Deng did this along with many other veteran leaders. In this situation, Hua was forced to resign as premier and Deng's loyal follower Zhao Ziyang assumed the position.[20] Between November and December 1980, during a series of intense meetings of the Politburo now under control of Deng, Hua was subjected to direct and full attack. Finally, he presented his self-criticism, admitting his mistakes in promoting "two whatevers" policy, in launching the "new leap forward," in blocking the rehabilitation of the victims of the Cultural Revolution, and in fostering the personality cult around himself.

Soon the Party Central Committee adopted an authoritative resolution on certain questions in the history of the party since 1949. This document marked the party's formal acceptance of Deng's political and economic program. It repudiated the Cultural Revolution and the ideological tenets connected with the later years of Mao Zedong. It called for a reform of the economy and for the development of "methods other than class struggle" to resolve the political problems in the Chinese society. More importantly, Mao's role in the Chinese revolution and in the People's Republic was also critically assessed in the document.[21]

Under such circumstances, Hua was finally forced to step down as party boss in June 1981. His position as party chairman was given to Hu Yaobang, one of Deng's key followers. Deng Xiaoping himself assumed Hua's position as chairman of the Military Commission. Hua remained as vice-chairman of the party and on the Politburo until the Twelfth Party Congress in September 1982. But he was barely able to get elected to membership to the Central Committee at that Congress. Within six years, Hua Guofeng, Mao's choice of his own successor, was thus displaced by Deng.

With the removal of Hua from the party chairmanship in 1981 and from the Politburo in 1982, Deng and his reformer group made further progress in the reconstitution of national leadership. At the Twelfth Party Congress in 1982, and at the National Party Conference in September 1985, they almost completely reshuffled the highest organs of the party and state with younger and reform-minded persons. Hu Yaobang and Zhao Ziyang consolidated their positions as the Party General Secretary and the Premier of the State Council respectively. Although publicly he only held the position as Chairman of the Military Affairs Commission of the Party Central Committee, Deng Xiaoping was the real person in charge and kept that position of power throughout the 1980s. Even after he resigned from this last official post in the wake of the Tiananmen Incident in 1989, Deng Xiaoping remained the nation's supreme leader behind the scenes. Zhao Ziyang in public confirmed this so-called "party secret" in 1989 and indicated that all major decisions within the Chinese Communist Party were ultimately determined by Deng Xiaoping.[22] Indeed, Deng Xiaoping has been China's preeminent leader and the principal architect of China's reform since the beginning of the 1980s.

Implications for Foreign Policy Making

The rise of Deng Xiaoping and his associates ushered in a new era in China. The thrust of Deng's leadership was a shift in the nation's priority from political mobilization (i.e., the "ideological struggle in command" model) to economic modernization (i.e., the "modernization in command" model). For the reformers, economic growth and the improvement of the material standard of living of the Chinese people became the linchpin of their success or failure as leaders to rebuild the confidence of the Chinese people and to consolidate the party's legitimacy. The emphasis on economic modernization as China's top priority not only fundamentally changed Chinese domestic affairs, but also had a far-reaching influence on China's foreign behavior.

Three new elements were introduced into China's foreign policy making. To begin with, Beijing came to wish for a peaceful and cooperative international environment. Such a setting was crucial to protect China's modernization drive from being disrupted by unwanted external disturbances; to lessen pressure on China to expand its defense spending so that more resources could be used to assist domestic reform; and to justify domestically the overwhelming concentration on economic affairs. Meanwhile, to make Deng's reform effort a success, China became unprecedentedly eager to expand economic interaction with the rest of the world and increased sharply its participation in normal international economic interactions which would provide the country with growing opportunities in trade, inflow of foreign investment, access to advanced technology, and managerial expertise. Thus, seeking international stability in support of domestic economic development and conducive to China's engagement in foreign economic exchange became the central theme of China's foreign activities. In contrast, continuing to confront Moscow and invest huge resources for this purpose became increasingly insupportable within the Chinese leadership.

Second, the demand for establishing a more stable environment and expanding foreign relations reinforced China's awareness that its interests required the use of more effective diplomacy. Previously, China's diplomacy had been rather reactive toward outside pressure. Along with the consolidation of Deng's power, the Chinese leadership took a more activist approach to foreign affairs. In view of the priority placed on economic development, Beijing started to change its assessment of the international balance of power in Asia. The direct result of this reassessment was what Deng Xiaoping called the two major shifts (*zhuan bian*) in China's foreign policy perception: Beijing abandoned the view that another world war was inevitable in favor of the position that such a war could be postponed, if not avoided, for a long period of time. Beijing also realized that the practice of drawing policy lines based solely upon a country's connection with the Soviet Union was somewhat counterproductive.[23] In order to support a modernization drive in China, Beijing boldly adopted a new strategy of "opening to the outside world" to expand economic and cultural exchanges with other countries.

The third new element found in China's foreign behavior was pragmatism. Deng Xiaoping had long enjoyed a reputation as a pragmatist leader who placed much emphasis on facts rather than on dogmas. "It hardly matters whether the cat is black or white. As long as it catches mice, it is a good cat."[24] This oft-quoted statement of Deng summarized an underlying realism and flexibility in his philosophy. To be sure, China's foreign policy was dictated largely by its considerations of national security, prestige and influence. But what was new under Deng was the stress laid on the economic results in foreign policy. There was no shortage of examples of how the abandonment of rigid ideological considerations in favor of pragmatism eased China's diplomatic path. The arms trade was one of the most obvious examples. China sold billions of dollars worth of weapons to both Tehran and Baghdad during the Iran-Iraq war in the 1980s.[25] Typical in this regard also was the new importance given to international trade in China's relations with all kinds of countries no matter whether or not they had diplomatic relations with Beijing and regardless of their political or social systems. As one writer points out, Beijing under Deng "had pursued one of the most 'economic' foreign policy in the world" in the 1980s.[26] It is true that under Deng's leadership China entered a time of relative "de-ideologization" in its foreign policy, focusing on reconciliation and on economic interactions with the rest of the world.

In conclusion, the rise of reformers within the Chinese leadership fundamentally changed China's foreign behavior. The single-minded foreign policy centered on anti-Soviet threat increasingly became irrelevant and counterproductive to serve the needs of Deng Xiaoping's modernization program and started to give way to a new foreign policy.

International Pressures for Change

Domestic changes were fundamental in influencing China's foreign behavior. But they represented only a part of pressures on China for foreign policy restructuring in the early 1980s. New developments in the strategic relations between China and the United States and the Soviet Union constituted another aspect of pressure for change in Beijing's foreign policy.

Difficulties in Sino-American Relations

Realization of full diplomatic ties in 1979 and burgeoning economic, cultural and governmental contacts between China and the United States created high expectations and even euphoria about prospects for Sino-American relations. Remarkable breakthroughs further consolidated security ties between the two countries. The U.S. Defense Secretary and his Chinese counterpart exchanged visits in the first half of 1980, helping lay the basis for transfer of U.S. advanced defense technology to Beijing and for a limited strategic cooperation on matters of common concern against the Soviet Union. The most prominent example was a joint China-United States military intelligence operation in the Xinjiang Uygar Autonomous Region in northwestern China monitoring Soviet nuclear and missile tests.[27] However, the expectations proved premature and soon the "honeymoon" between Beijing and Washington ended with the emergence of serious strains in the Sino-American relations.

The immediate cause of the problem was the reemergence of the Taiwan issue to complicate the relationship between Washington and Beijing. For a long time, the Taiwan issue had been the major obstacle in Sino-American relations. The Chinese government had long held the position that Beijing was the sole legal government of China, Taiwan was a part of China and the unification of Taiwan with the mainland was China's internal affair. In the Shanghai Communiqué of 1972, the United States agreed that it "*acknowledges* that all Chinese on either side of the Taiwan strait maintain there is but one China and that Taiwan is a part of China. The U.S. government does not challenge that position."[28] In the 1978 joint communiqué on the establishment of diplomatic relations between Beijing and Washington, the United States "*recognizes* the government of the People's Republic of China as the sole legal government of China. Within this context, the people of the United States will maintain cultural, commercial and other unofficial relations with the people of Taiwan."[29] At the same time, the United States fully accepted the three conditions regarding Taiwan which Beijing had demanded for normalization since 1974. These were: (1) the withdrawal of all American military forces from Taiwan, (2) the severance of American-Taiwan diplomatic relations, and (3) the abrogation of the U.S.-Taiwan mutual defense treaty of 1954.[30] However, the question of U.S. arms sales to Taiwan was not settled in the course of negotiations on establishing diplomatic relations between the two countries.[31] The United States insisted upon supplying Taiwan with limited and carefully selected defensive weapons for defensive purposes after normalization. On this matter the Chinese disagreed with Washington, but agreed to proceed with the normalization first and raise the issue again following the normalization. After the normalization, U.S. Congress passed the Taiwan Relations Act (TRA) in April 1979. This event was in reaction to Carter's unilateral declaration abrogating the 1954 Mutual Defense Treaty with Taiwan and for the purpose of calming fears in Taiwan as well as stabilizing relations between Washington and Taipei. As American law, the TRA defined the future U.S. commitments to Taiwan's defense and clearly stated that it was proper for the United States to "provide Taiwan with arms of a defensive character."[32]

In spite of the passage of TRA, the Taiwan issue was relatively dormant during 1979 and 1980. The United States sold no military equipment to Taiwan in 1979. In 1980 a total of $292 million in such equipment was sold to Taiwan.[33] Beijing's response to this was mild. But when Ronald Reagan entered the White House, the confrontation over arms for Taiwan suddenly began to intensify. China feared that the new administration might reverse the course taken by Washington toward China since 1972 and return to the "two Chinas" policy. These fears were confirmed in the statements and actions of the Reagan administration.

Even early in the 1980 U.S. presidential elections, Reagan blasted Carter's callous treatment of Taiwan, "an old friend and ally," and promised to upgrade relations with Taiwan to the official level, if elected. He pledged that a Reagan administration would keep American commitments "to its friends, large and small." Taiwan was, of course, the "small friend" being referred to. In response, Carter pointed to Reagan's attitudes toward Taiwan as an indication that a Reagan administration would endanger the newly burgeoning Sino-American strategic partnership.[34]

In 1981 it was apparent from press reports that the new administration was considering moves to upgrade U.S. relations with Taiwan, including the sale of advanced fighter aircraft, FXs or F-5Gs. In June, on his visit to China, Secretary of State Alexander Haig said that the United States would remove some restrictions on the purchase of sophisticated arms by Beijing, but he also indicated to the Chinese that the United States planned to continue arms sales to Taiwan as provided by the Taiwan Relations Act.[35] Later in that year, the Reagan administration decided to offer a "package deal" by providing both China and Taiwan the arms they wanted. For Taiwan, the arms sales involved contracts for F-5Es (equipped with Sidewinder missiles) and the production of spare parts under joint production in Taiwan by Northrop for the island's fleet of F-100s.[36]

The Chinese reaction was swift and unequivocal. Beijing argued on legal grounds that since the United States recognized Taiwan as a part of China and Beijing was the sole legal government of China, the arms sales authorized by the Taiwan Relations Act was an interference in China's internal affairs, constituted an encroachment on China's sovereignty and obstructed China's peaceful reunification process.[37] China hinted strongly a possible downgrading of diplomatic relations with the United States by saying that "If the United States insists on a 'long-term policy' of selling weapons to Taiwan, Sino-U.S. relations will retrogress."[38]

The Reagan administration was confronted with a dilemma: to continue arms sales to Taiwan as authorized by the TRA, or to face a downgrading of relations with Beijing. Related to this dilemma was the question of how important the Sino-American strategic cooperation was and how far the United States should go in that cooperation in offering Beijing modern sophisticated weapons as China was not a formal ally. As a way of resolving the dilemma, a series of consultations between the two countries on the issue of arms sales to Taiwan was initiated in late 1981. The Chinese demanded that the United States set a firm timetable for terminating U.S. arms sales to Taiwan. Under the pressure, Washington announced in early 1982 that it would not sell Taiwan any more advanced aircraft (e.g., FXs or 5-Gs) than it had already provided.[39] On August 17, 1982, after almost ten months of negotiation, the two sides published a joint communiqué providing for at least a partial resolution of the problem. The Chinese made a strong statement that its fundamental policy toward Taiwan was for peaceful reunification with mainland China while Washington appreciated such a Chinese policy and stated that:

> [The United States Government] does not seek to carry out a long-term policy of arms sales to Taiwan, that its arms sales to Taiwan will not exceed, either in qualitative or in quantitative terms, the level of those supplied in recent years since the establishment of diplomatic relations between the United States and China, and that it intends to reduce gradually its sales of arms to Taiwan, leading over a period of time to a final resolution.[40]

The interesting part of the joint communiqué was that the United States did not set a specific timetable for the gradual reduction of arms sales to Taiwan or the termination date for ending such sales. It gave the Chinese only a vague assurance. Although the communiqué forestalled further deterioration for the time being, Beijing and Washington differed in their interpretations of it.[41] The Taiwan issue continued to be a "dark cloud" (to use the Chinese phrase) affecting Sino-American relations to varying degrees in the following years.[42]

In addition to the question of Taiwan, other aspects of U.S.-China relations also produced controversy at the time. Difficulties over commercial relations included Chinese displeasure with American trade quotas and tariffs on Chinese textiles to the U.S. market and a degree of disappointment and frustration within the American business community over the difficulties of doing business in China.[43] Because of the delays in the approval of licenses for the export of U.S. technology to China, the Chinese complained about the level of technology allowed and the slow pace of transfers.[44] The Chinese got very angry also when the United States granted political asylum to a Chinese tennis star, Hu Na, who defected to the United States. On April 1983 Beijing even announced that nineteen planned cultural exchanges with the United States were to be suspended for the remainder of the year.[45] Other irritants included a court judgment that the Chinese government would have to pay principal and interest to American holders of Huguang railroad bonds issued in the waning months of the Qing Dynasty and the decision by Pan American World Airways to resume flights to Taiwan which had been suspended when it began service to the mainland.[46]

None of these incidents was, in itself, a major issue. But together they reflected deeper problems in the Sino-American relationship. Each side was becoming increasingly conscious of the limits and differences in its deepening relationship with the other. Apart from the fundamental differences between the two social-political and economic systems, the difficulties in Sino-American relations also came from the different approaches Beijing and the Reagan administration held in their newly-found coalition partnership based on the strategic cooperation against the Soviet Union. China's policy was based on the united front strategy as a device to preserve Chinese security in a time of relative weakness. A credible anti-Soviet coalition would restrain provocative Soviet actions against China and in other parts of Asia. In Beijing's view, Chinese contributions to countering Soviet power in East Asia were vital to the global goals of the United States since Washington no longer had the capability to compete singlehandedly against the Soviet Union and thus sought supplementary forces to augment its own power. The United States would therefore be extremely forthcoming in its aid to China, economically and militarily, for its four modernization goals (i.e., agriculture, industry, defense, and science and technology).

The election of the Reagan administration and its adoption of a staunchly anti-Soviet orientation appeared to share Beijing's concern about Soviet political and military assertiveness. Yet the Reagan administration emphasized more upon "self-strengthening" than upon the "united front" in resisting the Soviet threat. In Washington's view, a Soviet military buildup and expansion had continued unabated and unanswered for a decade and a half. The most urgent need was to undertake a comparable effort to augment America's own military capabilities in a manner that could challenge the perceived Soviet threat in peacetime and defeat the Soviet Union in wartime. For this purpose, the United States needed "Reaganomics" to restore its economy and on this basis develop an overall anti-Soviet military strategy such as the Strategic Defense Initiatives (SDI). China's role, while not marginal, was only a part of the U.S. global strategy vis-à-vis the Soviet Union. In line with this policy, Washington regarded China only as a local power in East Asia. The Reagan administration even took Beijing for granted, believing that China needed America more than America needed China in countering the Soviet expansion. For this reason, even if some U.S. policies did not give proper considerations to or offended Chinese sensibilities and interests (notably, the Taiwan issue), Beijing would not go too far to take issue with Washington on these policies.

Besides, Beijing and Washington remained quite different in the perception of their respective national interests on many other international issues in the early 1980s. They had different opinions on third world affairs, on the Polish crisis, and on the conflict on the Korean peninsula.[47] All these differences eventually replaced the euphoria in the Sino-U.S. relationship at the time of their diplomatic normalization with a sense of mutual disenchantment. Both sides come back to reality: the two countries had different interests in their strategic cooperation.

New Developments in Relations with Moscow

For a decade, the Soviet Union had maintained large, sophisticated and well-equipped military forces along the Sino-Soviet border and in Outer Mongolia, including ground and air forces, naval power, as well as strategic nuclear weaponry. In late 1978, the Soviet Union established an independent theater command in its Far East.[48] The Soviet political and military presence to the north of China (i.e., in Mongolia and along the Sino-Soviet border), to the east (i.e., the Soviet Pacific Fleet), to the south (i.e., in Vietnam), and to the west (i.e., in Afghanistan) reflected a broad, underlying Soviet commitment to the containment of China and Beijing's alignment with the United States and Japan. In Beijing's eyes, the Soviet Union continued to be the major threat to China's security.

However, after the Soviets invaded Afghanistan in 1979, the Chinese started to notice that Moscow's ability to use military power to extend its influence was sapped by growing economic, political, and military problems the Soviet leaders faced both at home and abroad. Beijing seemed to perceive that the Soviet threat had become long term rather than immediate.[49] In the Chinese analysis, the momentum that the Soviet Union had established since the mid-1970s was now fading. The Soviet Union had too many problems to take care of at the same time. For example, Moscow had met difficulties in Afghanistan and in Poland. It had too many aid commitments to its allies (Eastern Europe, Cuba and Vietnam). At home, the Soviets had a continued decline in economic growth and its military expenditures exceeded 10 percent of Gross National Product (GNP).[50] Besides, the aged and ossified leadership structure and ethnic tensions haunted the Soviet domestic agenda. What was worse, the Soviet Union had to face a more severe confrontation with the United States in the wake of the resurgence of

American military power and tougher responses to the Soviet expansionist activities under the Reagan administration. Meanwhile, Moscow also faced a broad anti-Soviet coalition including the United States, Japan, Western Europe, China, and other countries. All these meant that Moscow's capabilities could not match its presumed hegemonic ambitions and that the Soviet Union would inevitably face an agonizing reappraisal of its external commitments and goals.

This analysis of Soviet power was supported by the Soviet gestures signalling to reduce tensions with China. At the Twenty-Sixth Soviet Party Congress in February 1981, Brezhnev inserted into his report to this Congress the sentence "Sino-Soviet relations remain in a frozen state." At first sight, describing Sino-Soviet relations as a "frozen state" was not astonishing under the circumstances of the Sino-Soviet rift. But at that time, such wording had a special meaning. In fact, Brezhnev would have been able to describe Sino-Soviet relations as a "frozen state" even earlier if he had wanted to. During the Maoist era, he did not do so. Now the signal meaning of it was that a "frozen state" could "thaw."[51]

The "thaw" did start in the Sino-Soviet relationship after this speech. Beginning in 1981, Moscow showed distinctly greater interest in reaching out to China than it had previously. Soviet Foreign Ministry China expert Mikhail Kapitsa visited Beijing twice in early 1981 as "a guest of the Soviet Embassy."[52] On March 7, 1981, Moscow suggested that the two countries discuss the implementation of "confidence-building measures" along the border. But China prudently responded to it and suggested "indefinite postponement" of border talks in protest against the Soviet-Afghan treaty signed on June 1981 which involved Pamir borders. Even so, for the first time since 1963 Beijing signed a transport protocol with the Soviets. In November, the first increase in bilateral exchanges in decades was noted when Chinese gymnasts performing in the Soviet Union were feted by the Sino-Soviet Friendship Society, the first such festivities in over a decade. In December, both sides agreed in principle to resume scientific and technological exchanges. In February 1982, the Soviets proposed a resumption of the Sino-Soviet border talks which were suspended after the Soviet invasion of Afghanistan. The Soviets also proposed exchanges of language students and teachers. In April, the Sino-soviet Trade Payment Agreement was signed in Beijing.[53]

The most conciliatory gesture to China was made by Leonid Brezhnev himself on March 24, 1982, when he gave a speech in the central Asian city of Tashkent. He declared four points towards China in his speech:

> First, despite the fact that we have openly criticized and continue to criticize many aspects of the Chinese leadership's policy..., we have never tried to interfere in the internal life of [China]. We have not denied and do not now deny the existence of a socialist social system in China although Beijing's fusion with the imperialists' policy in the world arena is, of course, at variance with the interests of socialism. Second, we have never supported and do not now support, in any form, the so-called "two Chinas concept".... Third, there has been no threat to the Chinese People's Republic from the Soviet Union.... We are prepared at any time to continue talks on outstanding border questions with a view to reaching mutually acceptable decisions.... Fourth, we well remember the time when the Soviet Union and people's China were united by bonds of friendship and comradely cooperation. We have never considered the state of hostility and alienation between our countries to be a normal phenomenon.[54]

In a September 26 speech at Baku and an October 27 speech to a group of high-ranking military officers, Brezhnev again stated his desire for Sino-Soviet conciliation.[55]

China reacted cautiously, publicly acknowledging Brezhnev's statements and hinting at its awareness of possible Soviet attempts to exploit the difficulties in Sino-American relations over the Taiwan issue.[56] Beijing noted that "it was not the first time for a Soviet leader to make such 'improvement' remarks. But so far, people have not seen any substantive actions taken by the Soviet authorities in this respect." The Chinese pointed out the contradictions between Brezhnev's denial that the Soviet Union posed a threat to China and the deployment of "massive Soviet troops" along the Sino-Soviet border. Beijing stressed the importance of "actual deeds" as against "words" if Moscow wanted to improve its relations with China.[57] In this regard, China continued to stick to the three preconditions for normalizing Sino-Soviet relations: a reduction of Soviet forces along the Chinese border (including the withdrawal of Soviet forces from Mongolia), the withdrawal of Soviet troops from Afghanistan, and the ending of Soviet aid to Vietnam.

Although still remaining unspecific on the more concrete measures, Moscow seemed to judge that its interest would be well served by reducing tensions with Beijing, especially at the time when Sino-American relations were strained. The Soviet Union saw itself at a disadvantage in the American-Soviet-Chinese triangle. As Sino-American strategic cooperation appeared to grow after the normalization of their relations in 1979, Moscow became more concerned about a possible close Sino-U.S. military arrangement. The Soviets presumably judged that a Sino-Soviet thaw would not only lessen China's incentive to move closer to the United States and insert an element of distrust in the anti-Soviet coalition, but that it would also improve Soviet leverage in dealings with the United States. The emerging Sino-U.S. differences over Taiwan and other issues provided an opening for accelerated Soviet efforts to promote improvement, at least on the margins, in Sino-Soviet relations. For China's part, the new situation in the triangular relations presented the pragmatic leaders in Beijing with both constraints and opportunities. In the face of both domestic and international pressures, the Chinese leadership finally felt the limitations of the anti-Soviet united front strategy in securing China's broader interests.

Limitations in Anti-Soviet Policy

In the face of the changed domestic and international environments, Beijing's anti-Soviet united front strategy began to show its fundamental limitations. The most obvious weakness of the strategy was its overreliance on close relations between China and the United States and their parallel interests or actions. The illusion of an implicit Sino-American alliance, on the one hand, largely raised Soviet fear about such a military alignment and thus stimulated further Soviet military buildup in East Asia.[58] On the other hand, it also severely reduced Beijing's leverage in its bilateral relationship with Washington. The Reagan administration seemed to have regarded China as a junior partner in the U.S. global strategy and taken a more pro-Taiwanese stance than its predecessors. Obviously, China's relative importance in American global strategy had unquestionably diminished since the United States intended to confront the Soviet Union on a worldwide scale irrespective of China's involvement or urging.[59] Besides, the Chinese ability to exploit U.S. interests in strategic relations with Beijing in order to compel the United States to meet Chinese demands on Taiwan and on other questions, such as trade relations, technological transfers, and military cooperation, had been sharply reduced.

Under such circumstances, Beijing began to suspect that the United

States, as the far more powerful partner, would inevitably seek to take advantage of China's weakness and vulnerability, and thus could not be expected to support a genuine commitment to "a strong and secure China."[60] Since many of the benefits of the earlier strategy of united front were exhausted, such as the normalization of diplomatic relations with the United States, to continue such a policy would surely increase costs without adequate returns. Beijing also questioned its alignment with a superpower in the security arrangement under the new conditions. Its experience in the 1950s had left China perpetually suspicious of excessive dependence on a major external power.

There were other more deeply rooted weaknesses in the policy. For example, after being put into practice for a number of years, the united front strategy often proved to be too simplistic. To base its policy largely on one factor--whether or not the Soviet interest was hurt--China had once again underestimated the need for some nations to develop close ties with the Soviet Union primarily for their own interests, economic or geo-political. As a matter of fact, to draw a line between those who were pro- and those who were anti-Moscow had prevented China from expanding relations with countries which had certain relations with Moscow. To insist on the anti-Soviet criterion had alienated from China a large number of third world states. The striking parallel between the Chinese and U.S. positions on many third world issues, especially those associated with regional conflicts, aroused suspicion or even resentment in some developing countries which openly or privately viewed it as evidence of China's increasing deviation from its claimed third world position. In the example of China's obsessive anti-Soviet (and anti-Cuban) posture on the issue of Angolan membership in the United Nations, Angolan Foreign Minister attacked both the United States and China for their opposition. He charged that there was an "unnatural alliance" between China, imperialism, and South Africa. He particularly added that mercenaries recruited by South Africa were paid in U.S. dollars and killed Angolans with weapons "made by the Chinese proletariat."[61] Clearly, China was increasing its international reputation in leftist African states as a country aligned with the capitalist, imperialist, and right-wing powers.

In this regard, closer ties with the United States, to some extent, undoubtedly had negative impact on China's third world policy. For a long time, that policy had been an important component of its overall foreign strategy. China had tried to identify itself with the Third World on the basis of its economic status and a common past in the form of a strong collective memory of historical grievance and exploitation. It had also sought a leading role in the Third World as Beijing saw itself as the only permanent representative of the Third World in the United Nations Security Council. In doing so, China had gained support from the Third World and thus consolidated its proper place in world politics. However, by the end of the 1970s, references to the New International Economic Order (NIEO) had virtually vanished from Chinese pronouncements on third world affairs. Instead, Beijing seemed more concerned with preserving the existing international strategic balance of power against the Soviet threat. The Chinese press repeatedly argued that the main focus of third world foreign policy should be resistance to Soviet expansionism, rather than creation of a New International Economic Order.[62] Chinese leverage in the Third World was reduced further by the sharp decline in Chinese economic and military aid commitments, beginning in 1976. Faced with serious economic problems at home, reduced ideological commitment to the Third World in the post-Mao period, and mixed results from past large-scale aid efforts, Chinese aid commitments dropped from $366 million in 1975 to under $200 million for each of the next three years.[63] Relying mainly on diplomacy and propaganda, China condemned perceived signs of Soviet-backed expansion while encouraging the formation of the broadest international front against the Soviet Union. China's image in the Third World, to a large extent, had been tarnished because of its single-minded anti-Soviet efforts. As a consequence, Beijing began to lose wide support in the Third World.

With rapid changes on the Chinese domestic scene and new developments in the international strategic balance of power, China had increasingly become uneasy about the limitations in its single-minded and rigid anti-Soviet foreign policy. Its unproductive results had constantly imposed pressures on the pragmatic leaders in Beijing. In the end, Deng Xiaoping and his associates had to make a decision to move away from the united front strategy and develop a new one in China's relations with the outside world.

Chapter 6

Developing an Independent Stance

The strongly anti-Soviet and pro-West posture in China's foreign policy was directly challenged by both domestic and international pressures triggering leadership debate in Beijing in the early 1980s.

Strong Anti-Soviet and Pro-West Posture in Doubt

Initial Criticisms

Throughout the 1970s China's foreign policy was based on the conviction that the Soviet Union was the major threat to China's security and Moscow was unrelentingly expanding its influence worldwide, while the United States was defending its former spheres of influence with difficulty. As the United States no longer constituted a direct threat to China, Beijing could use Washington as a counterweight to resist the Soviet threat and thus adopted a united front policy. This foreign policy peaked between 1978 and 1980 as the Chinese leadership became alarmed by the Cambodian and Afghanistan incidents. China not only established closer ties with the West in the security arrangement, but also hoped that large-scale economic cooperation with the West would speed up China's modernization process. In a sense, close strategic and economic cooperation with the United States and its allies appeared necessary, possible and mutually reinforcing.

However, some Chinese leaders were not convinced of the logic behind this approach. In the spring of 1979, in the wake of Sino-American normalization and China's attack on Vietnam, a series of historical articles appeared which used allegories from ancient Chinese history and from early Soviet history to question the current policy. Like the past, allegories were again used for political debate over sensitive issues. Some of the articles suggested that China could afford neither to "import" modernization from the West nor to pursue a confrontational foreign policy against the Soviet Union. Rather, they advocated that China should adopt the approach of Lenin during the days of the New Economic Policy in the 1920s. Beijing should relax restrictions on capitalistic practices at home and make amends with enemies abroad.[1] Leadership support for some change in foreign policy was also seen in the rehabilitation of officials who had been criticized for favoring a "pro-peace" foreign policy involving improvement of relations with both the Soviet Union and the United States, and relaxation of tensions with China's neighbors.[2]

Those oblique criticisms came at the time when China faced a variety of difficulties, such as a strained international environment following China's punitive attack on Vietnam, the outbreak of social unrest and political dissidence in several cities at home, and serious imbalances in the economy. In order to consolidate its newly-established power position, the reform leadership had to temporarily engage in economic retrenchment and tighter social controls. In foreign relations, some tactical adjustments in its strongly anti-Soviet stance were also made. The Chinese became somewhat less forceful in pushing opposition to Soviet hegemonic activities and in criticizing Soviet "proxies" in the Third World. Beijing seemed to see its unsophisticated anti-Soviet, pro-Western approach as "excessive, potentially dangerous, and possibly counterproductive" to its basic concern of creating a stable international environment for domestic economic development.[3]

On April 3, 1979, Beijing made a formal decision at the National People's Congress that China would not renew the thirty-year old Sino-Soviet Treaty of Friendship, Alliance, and Mutual Assistance when it expired in 1980. While making the point that "the treaty has long ceased to exist except in name, owing to violations for which the Chinese side is not responsible," the Chinese government proposed normalization talks on the basis of the five principles of peaceful coexistence "to settle the outstanding issues between the two countries and improve bilateral relations."[4] This offer might have caught the Soviets by surprise, for it was the first time since the 1969 border clash that the Chinese made such a gesture. On April 17, 1979, Soviet Foreign Minister Andrei A. Gromyko, in a note handed to the Chinese Ambassador to Moscow, accepted the offer.[5] Between September 27 and November 30 of that year, the talks were held in Moscow at the vice-ministerial level. During these sessions, the Chinese side formally raised the three demands: (1) reduction of Soviet armed forces in the

Sino-Soviet border areas; (2) withdrawal of Soviet troops from Mongolia; and (3) discontinuation of Soviet support for Vietnam's invasion of Cambodia. The Soviet delegation resubmitted its 1978 proposal for a draft declaration on the principles of mutual relations. Both Beijing and Moscow also proposed an expansion of economic, cultural, scientific, technological, and other exchanges between the two countries.[6] At the end of the talks, both sides agreed to resume further discussions in early 1980.

However, Sino-Soviet negotiations did not resume in 1980 because of the Soviet invasion of Afghanistan at the end of December 1979, China suspended the talks and joined the world outcry of condemnation, including the boycott of the 1980 Moscow Olympic Games. International developments seemed to continue to support the anti-Soviet united front strategy. In January 1980, U.S. Defense Secretary Harold Brown came to Beijing. Both sides agreed to take parallel strategic actions vis-à-vis the new Soviet military threat and engage in some military cooperation. China's relations with the West, especially the United States, were thus further developed to an unprecedented level. Later that year, the Chinese Premier visited Japan and one Chinese Vice-Premier and Defense Minister traveled to the United States.[7] The criticisms of strongly anti-Soviet and pro-American foreign policy were stilled in the Chinese news media.

Even under such circumstances, there continued to be evidence of doubt about potential long-term Sino-American strategic cooperation. The notable example was the unusual "mistake" made by China's official news agency *Xinhua* in reporting a toast by Deng Xiaoping at the welcoming banquet for U.S. Defense Secretary Brown in January 1980. *Xinhua* reported that Deng called for an "alliance" with the United States on January 8. But later *Xinhua* formally "corrected" this to read "to unite."[8]

The Suspicion of Reagan's China Policy

The wisdom of the strong pro-American and anti-Soviet posture in China's foreign policy was being brought into question because of increasing tensions in Sino-American relations after Ronald Reagan was elected as the new American president. At first, Beijing appeared optimistic about the prospects for Reagan's foreign policy insofar as the media focused on the new administration's avowed determination to contain Soviet expansionism in an all-around way.[9] Yet Reagan's long-standing sympathies with Taiwan and his campaign pledges to upgrade U.S. ties with the island made leaders in Beijing uncertain about Reagan's China policy. Although many of the new administration's officials were well-known to Beijing[10] and President Reagan personally reassured Beijing that his administration would continue its predecessors' efforts to cooperate with China, the Chinese were perplexed by Reagan's conflicting signals to China.[11] On the one hand, the Reagan administration appreciated China's anti-Soviet stance considering a modernizing and friendly China to be in America's best interest. But on the other hand, the new administration was less convinced of the ideological value of aligning closely with a major Communist state. Moreover, China was treated by the Reagan administration "first and foremost as a part of Asia and only secondly as a counterweight to the Soviet Union." Even if China had "a decidedly global approach to economic and security problems," it remained a modernizing, regional power.[12]

Problems soon emerged in Sino-U.S. strategic collaboration. Within days of Reagan's inauguration, officials in Taipei renewed their long-standing calls for more modern combat aircraft.[13] How to handle the request immediately constituted a challenge to the new administration's broader China policy. For Beijing, American policy toward Taiwan assumed importance well beyond the island's relationship to the mainland. It represented a critical test of whether the United States took China seriously.[14] In order to fulfill his campaign promise toward Taiwan and to continue to keep good ties with Beijing, the Reagan administration made a balanced proposal: the United States would supply new arms to Taiwan and at the same time permit China to purchase some sophisticated American weapons.[15] Leaders in Beijing bluntly responded that arms sales to both Beijing and Taipei were unacceptable and Chinese sovereignty over Taiwan could not be compromised. In an interview with *the Washington Post*, Chinese Vice Foreign Minister Zhang Wenjin said that China wanted to cooperate with President Reagan on a global scale. But he said:

> China has no intention of concealing its poverty and technical
> backwardness. But, it is not an insignificant country. It is determined
> to never barter away its sovereignty and principles. It is an illusion to
> think that China will ever accept "two Chinas."[16]

Obviously, Chinese leaders' concern for their nation's sovereignty and memory of China's historical experiences with foreigners colored Beijing's evaluation and heightened their suspicions about American intentions toward China. Although Beijing continued its strong efforts to shore up American and other international support for checking Soviet power, strains in the bilateral relations between China and the United States made the Chinese doubt that the logic of Sino-American cooperation in the immediate post-Afghanistan period could be extended into the indefinite future.[17]

Both the Reagan administration and China attempted to ease differences as they prepared for Secretary of State Alexander Haig's visit to China in June 1981, the first high-level contact between China and the newly-installed American administration. Before Haig's departure, authoritative reports from Washington clearly indicated that the Secretary of State would propose a further loosening of restraints on sales of sensitive defense technologies to Beijing.[18] However, China remained wary of U.S. intentions, fearing that the United States was trying to buy China's acquiescence in arms sales to Taiwan. A Chinese Foreign Ministry spokesman stated that "we have time and again made it clear that we would rather receive no U.S. arms than accepting continued U.S. interference in our internal affairs by selling arms to Taiwan, to which we can never agree."[19]

At the welcoming banquet for the Secretary, Haig deemed China "a close and valued friend...[whose] strength, security, and well-being [are] fundamental to the global balance." He sought to reassure Beijing that the Reagan administration would abide by the terms specified at the time of normalization and that the two countries would continue to concentrate on the "fundamental strategic imperatives" that drew them together.[20] But Chinese Foreign Minister Huang Hua omitted the assessment of progress in Sino-American relations which was customarily a feature of toasts welcoming high-level U.S. officials. Alluding unmistakably to the Taiwan issue, Huang pointedly stressed the principles of sovereignty and noninterference that were due "mutual respect." In a remark unprecedented on such occasions since the 1970s, he made explicit references to "quite a few differences" in policy and views between the two countries, and went on to allude to specific areas of disagreement, such as the Middle East, South Africa, and the demand of developing nations for a new international economic order.[21]

After several days of talks, Beijing acknowledged that the Haig visit had "helped deepen our national understanding and yielded positive results. "[22] At a press conference, Haig also announced that China would no longer be subject to restrictions on the munitions control list, and that the United States would now consider sales of lethal weaponry to China on a case by case basis. Chinese media approvingly cited Haig's appraisal of the visit as "unusually productive, unusually significant, unusually successful." Huang Hua, in his closing toast, reemphasized a convergence of Chinese and American strategic interests, and credited Haig's visit with having yielded satisfactory results.[23]

However, when Haig was about to leave Beijing, President Reagan reiterated his firm support for U.S. arms sales to Taiwan at a press conference in Washington. He said that "I have not changed my feelings about Taiwan" and "I intend to live up to the Taiwan Relations Act."[24] The Chinese immediately protested in a *Xinhua* commentary that the provision in the Act for sales of arms to Taiwan was "tantamount to a de facto revitalization" of the "'Mutual Defense Treaty'...which places...Taiwan under the military protection of the United States," thus "severely infringing upon China's sovereignty" and demonstrating that some "Americans in the U.S. Government...are bent on giving Taiwan international status as an independent political entity." After criticizing Washington's "superpower mentality," the commentary warned that anyone who thought China would have to "swallow the 'bitter pill'" because it needed "American support on the question of combatting Soviet hegemonism" should remember how China dealt with foreign pressures in the 1950s. Evoking an analogy between the state of Sino-Soviet relations on the eve of the break and the current state of Sino-American relations, the commentary recalled that in the 1950s, China "waged a resolute struggle against...bullying...in order to defend the principles of independence, sovereignty, and equality, not hesitating to bear the consequences of a break," thus showing "the daring spirit of the Chinese people." In the end, the commentary said that the results of Secretary Haig's visit "indicate that the two countries have identical or similar views" on global strategy, and that "some progress has been achieved in their bilateral relations." China hoped that "this identity of views and the progress made in Beijing will stand the test of future actions. But in view of the incessant out-of-tune voices from [some] Americans in the U.S. Government..., we cannot but make the necessary reply."[25]

This kind of tough language, unprecedented since the opening to Washington began in the 1970s, showed the frustration of the Chinese leaders over the mixed signals from the Reagan administration with regard to China policy. Deng Xiaoping made the strongest statement about this when commenting on Sino-U.S. relations:

> The United States thinks that China is seeking its favor. In fact, China is not seeking any country's favor.... China hopes that Sino-American relations will further develop rather than retrogress. However, this should not be onesided.... It is nothing serious even if the United States causes a retrogression in Sino-American relations. If worst comes to worst and the relations retrogress to those prior to 1972, China will not collapse.... The Chinese people...will never bow and scrape for help.... When U.S. Secretary of State Alexander Haig came to China, I told him the same thing.... China and the United States should cooperate on an equal footing. If the United States does not play fair but forces China to act according to the will of the United States, China will not agree.[26]

Clearly, the Chinese nationalist sentiment dominated Beijing's view of the Reagan Administration. As is often the case in China, any dealings with foreigners that are perceived as showing weakness, are likely to cause domestic repercussions threatening the position of incumbent leaders. For this reason, in order to consolidate their newly-established position within the Chinese leadership, reform-minded officials had to show their firmness in upholding China's nationalist position. Just several days after he had replaced Hua Guofeng as the Party's new chief in the middle of 1981, Hu Yaobang found it necessary to project a strong nationalist position. Speaking at a rally on the Party's sixtieth anniversary, Hu assured the assembly that his leadership would not tolerate "any servility in thought or deed" in the face of "hegemonist threats of force" and in relations with "all stronger and richer countries." He juxtaposed with this pledge a vow to reunify Taiwan with the mainland, making the reference quite pointed.[27] To increase pressures on American policy-makers, the Chinese insisted on saying that the Taiwan issue was the "major" obstacle to improved Sino-U.S. relations.

In the face of the unusually strident Chinese position, the Reagan administration had to reassess its China policy and take several steps to meet Chinese complaints. The United States decided as soon January 1982 that it would not sell Taiwan FX aircraft, but would continue selling the type it had been providing in the past. In May 1982, Vice-President Bush visited China with letters from President Reagan to the Chinese leaders which formally disavowed U.S. interest in a "one China, one Taiwan" policy. On August 17, 1982, the United States and China signed a joint communiqué which placed qualitative and quantitative limits on U.S. arms sales to Taiwan and promised that the United States would eventually stop such sales.

Although the communiqué stopped further deterioration in Sino-American relations, Beijing continued to complain about the slow pace of American technology transfer to China and the difficulty of getting Chinese products into the United States. Chinese Foreign Minister Huang Hua said in New York in October 1982 that "the U.S. authorities had made many nice remarks about developing our bilateral relations. Yet what has happened can be described by a Chinese saying, 'loud thunder, but little rain.' "[28]

Chinese concerns seemed to be far more complex than a mere a reflection of national sensibilities. Beijing was becoming aware of problems in its overall foreign policy strategy: its overemphasis on the anti-Soviet threat and too close a security arrangement with the United States had cast China into a disadvantaged position. Reform-minded leaders in Beijing were very unhappy about playing "junior partner" in the alignment with the United States in opposing the Soviet threat. Because of this, the United States had taken China for granted believing that Beijing had no other alternative but to put up with American policies toward Taiwan. Close alignment with the United States had not only reduced Beijing's leverage in Sino-U.S. bilateral relations, but also severely limited Beijing's flexibility and options in its general foreign behavior. Standing too close to the United States risked causing greater hostility from Moscow, which was contrary to China's interest for a stable external environment favorable to its domestic economic development. It also reduced China's ability to press the United States for more concessions on a number of issues that Beijing deemed of greatest importance.

Soon the "never again" mentality of the Chinese leaders prevailed. Their experience in the 1950s had left them suspicious of excessive dependence on a major external power.[29] In the winter and spring of 1981, allegorical articles in the Chinese press warned of the dangers of excessive Westernization and reliance on external powers for technological, economic, and security assistance. The lessons of history, deriving mainly from China's reform movement of the late nineteenth century, appeared relevant to the present as well: China could not depend on other countries and expect to retain initiative and independence in its relations with the outside world.[30]

In 1981 an internal debate over the close alignment with the United States and unyielding anti-Soviet course occurred within the Chinese government. In order to consolidate their newly-installed power position and institute major reform programs, the Chinese reform-mined officials led by Deng Xiaoping and his younger associates, Hu Yaobang and Zhao Ziyang, lost no time in addressing the difficulties in China's foreign policy. The reformers clearly understood that their efforts to institutionalize major domestic policy initiatives and retain momentum in political and economic reform could both be compromised if they proved vulnerable to attacks on their foreign policy. It became clear that thoughtful decisions rather than pressure tactics were needed in China's foreign policy. These would involve a broad range of interrelated changes and affect most of China's important external relationships. Difficulties in the Sino-U.S. relations thus served as a catalyst for a grand reorientation.[31]

Reassessing the International Environment

A strong desire for policy flexibility was reinforced by the debate within the Chinese leadership over the international balance of power affecting China's national interest. Substantial changes in the international environment had not only made the underlying assumptions of the strongly anti-Soviet and pro-American foreign policy less attractive, but also provided China with a chance for freedom of maneuver in pursuing its national interest. Beijing could thus adopt a new foreign policy on the basis of new international developments as well as domestic demand for economic reform.

The Soviet Military Threat to China Not Immediate

Although the Soviet Union still physically constituted a threat to China's security because of its massive military buildup along China's periphery, by mid-1981 the Chinese leaders seemed to be convinced that Moscow had become mired in a host of domestic and international problems which caused the momentum of Soviet expansion developed in the previous few years to be substantially reduced. Beijing thus concluded that the Soviet threat to China was less immediate than before. So it was possible for China to obtain a relatively long period of time to focus on economic development, rather than on defense and on intensifying a strategy of countering Moscow.[32] It was also possible for China to have more foreign policy flexibility. These conclusions were based on three observations.

First, the Chinese noted that the Soviet Union had met serious problems at home and abroad, such as the low economic growth rates, the imbalanced development between defense and civil sectors, and the shortage of foreign exchange. A *Renmin Ribao* commentary accused the Soviets of replacing the meat on the common people's dining tables with "inedible and mass-produced lethal weapons.... If such a state of affairs goes on, the people's discontent is bound to intensify and culminate in a political problem."[33] The Chinese found that low levels of agricultural and industrial output in the Soviet Union necessitated greater imports, which in turn caused shortages of foreign exchange. They closely observed Soviet activities on the international money market. The sale of large quantities of Soviet gold during a period of declining international gold prices was seen as indicative of "the great trouble the Soviet Union is now confronted with."[34]

Second, Chinese observers also noted that the financial and political burdens of supporting Soviet allies and client states like Eastern Europe, Cuba and Vietnam had limited Soviet expansion. One *Renmin Ribao* commentary pointed out that the "Soviet Union's support to Cuba, Vietnam and its 'ever increasing' expenditure in Afghanistan" along with the crisis in Poland was creating "a long-term unfavorable trend" for Moscow.[35] Another article said that Cambodia was a "double burden" because the Soviet aid to Phnom Penh consisted chiefly of grain and petroleum which were both in short supply in the Soviet Union.[36]

Third, the Soviet-U.S. relationship had deteriorated since the Soviet invasion of Afghanistan. Under the Reagan administration, the United States adopted a tougher policy towards Moscow. Washington was determined to restore superpower power balance and even regain superiority over the Soviet Union. In the eyes of the Chinese leaders, Soviet expansion was checked at least for the time being. Thus, Beijing began to revise its view of the international balance of power prevalent since the 1970s, when it had portrayed Moscow as the "rising" and "expanding" superpower, and the Washington as the "declining" and "passive" one. The Chinese had come to the view that there would be a stalemate between the two superpowers. One Chinese foreign policy specialist pointed out:

> The stalemate could last for some time. Marginal gains can be made,
> but parity will continue. The Soviet Union is superior in some areas,
> and the U.S. in some areas. On the whole, there is parity. The source
> of scientific and technological breakthroughs is the United States,
> however. In the long term, the United States could regain
> superiority.[37]

On the basis of these observations, Beijing judged that under the
current difficult circumstances, the Soviet Union might choose strategic
flexibility. It might seize an opportunity to reduce tensions with China
and solve the "China problem" so as to concentrate on its long term
strategy vis-à-vis the United States.[38] The conciliatory gestures made by
Moscow at a time when U.S.-Chinese relations were in trouble seemed
to support this judgement. To Beijing's pragmatic leaders, it was in
China's interest to seek a détente with the Soviet Union depending upon
the extent to which Moscow was willing to compromise on China's
demands (i.e., the withdrawal of Soviet troops from the Sino-Soviet
border, Mongolia and Afghanistan, and the termination of Soviet
support for the Vietnamese invasion of Cambodia). On the one hand,
China hoped to reduce tensions with the Soviet Union and press
Moscow to make more compromises. On the other hand, it could also
advance a bargaining gambit to exact greater payoffs from the United
States for it was in neither superpower's interest to drive China to the
other side. To be sure, Beijing was realistic enough to understand that
a limited reconciliation fell short of a sweeping rapprochement.[39] The
Chinese were quite cautious to manage their relations with both
superpowers and wanted to get compromises from both of them. The
Chinese leaders clearly understood that the Soviet Union still posed a
long-term threat. They did not want to change their basic desire for
good relations with the West out of both security and development
concerns. Rather, they were backing away from their single-minded
efforts of the late 1970s in order to increase their flexibility and
options.

Interpreting Washington's Global Strategy

While Beijing perceived the decreasing Soviet threat as Moscow
became bogged down in a host of domestic and international

difficulties, the Chinese leaders also saw that the Reagan administration instituted a policy of "all around confrontation with the Soviet Union" as a means of reversing American strategic setbacks of the past decade.[40] In contrast to its view of previous U.S. administrations, China claimed to see no advocates of "appeasement" in the Reagan administration. Rather, Beijing highlighted a rapid buildup of U.S. strength seen in such events as the unusually smooth passage--unprecedented since the 1960s--of U.S. defense budget increases larger than any before in peacetime. What Beijing saw was the Reagan administration's firm commitment to counter Soviet power and to build up American military capabilities. Reagan's Strategic Defense Initiatives (SDI) speech in March 1983 was interpreted by Beijing as a show of U.S. determination to use technological and military means to compete with the Soviet Union.[41]

Besides, Beijing saw a unilateralist trend in American global strategy to confront the Soviet Union under the Reagan administration which often ignored the interests of American allies and friends, including China.[42] In the Chinese perception, the United States was determined to engage in large-scale rivalry with the Soviet Union and seemed to be reemerging as an offensive power pursuing hegemonic policies. The Reagan administration's new posture which publicly downgraded China's strategic importance and neglected China's interest in the issue of Taiwan and in other questions further supported this view. The previous tilt toward the United States, which was based upon a combination of "strategic cooperation" against the Soviets and a desire to tap the technological and economic reservoirs of the "developed world" for its own domestic four modernizations, accentuated Beijing's inability to pursue an independent policy.[43] China's enduring suspicions about the motivations of a far more powerful benefactor were fueled by a perception of the United States as a resurgent hegemonic power acted in disregard of the sensibilities and concerns of its allies and friends.

Although both Washington and Beijing subsequently sought to repair the strains in their relations and avoid what threatened to become a serious rupture in their dealings, substantial suspicions and uncertainties had been generated on both sides. From China's perspective, good relations with the United States still remained very important, especially if China were to benefit more fully in the areas of economic collaboration and technology transfer. But it was not in China's interest to join the United States in a new round in the arms race with the Soviet Union as the threat from the latter had gradually reduced.[44] On the contrary, China needed a stable environment and wished to devote more attention and resources to its domestic economic reform. Beijing felt uneasy about intensified superpower contention in the arms race and in the Third World, including the Asia-Pacific region. Chinese leaders concluded that China's security interests would be better served by standing somewhat apart from the superpower rivalry than by being closely aligned with either of them. China should not allow itself to be used as a pawn in the U.S.-Soviet strategic competition. It started to show a strong desire for an independent posture as demonstrated in one article in *Guangming Ribao* (*Intellectual's Daily*) asserting that "maintaining independence and keeping the initiative in our own hands is the fundamental principle" of Chinese foreign policy. "It means that both politically and militarily, we must [not]...be dependent on the pleasure of others, or be controlled by others."[45]

The desire for an independent stance was further reinforced by the view developed in the early 1980s that there would be a certain military parity between the two superpowers, which provided China with greater flexibility in terms of policy options. Although the Chinese saw that the Soviet-U.S. competition, both globally and regionally, would continue or perhaps intensify, they seemed to perceive that neither state was likely to enjoy the strength to overwhelm the other and that superpower confrontation would remain essentially stalemated.[46] According to Huan Xiang, a Chinese senior international affairs specialist:

> Near the end of the Carter administration term and at the beginning of the term of Reagan administration, the Americans determinedly and energetically put up a front against the Soviet Union politically and militarily.... This stopped the Soviet Union.... It seems that the Russians still do not feel strong enough to react to the U.S. offensive. In our view, a certain balance between the two has emerged, especially in the military field.[47]

To the Chinese, the U.S. defense buildup largely eased previous Chinese anxieties of the Soviet threat and restored the balance of power. The Chinese were pleased with this because "the world situation will be more peaceful if there is parity between the United States and the Soviet Union."[48] The balance also meant that Beijing had less need to unite with one superpower against the other. Rather, China could take advantage of the new situation to pursue an independent posture and concentrate on economic development. Beijing clearly believed that both superpowers had their weaknesses and needed to garner additional political support for their increasingly costly and complicated global rivalry sooner or later. Because of this, China would become the object more of superpower solicitation than of criticism, coercion, or isolation even if Beijing adopted an independent stance.[49] Besides, an independent stance would silence domestic critics who continued to be anxious about the negative consequences of the closer relationship with the United States.

War or Peace: from Inevitability to Avoidability

The shift of top priority to economic development at home considerably transformed China's world outlook. Beijing's pragmatic leadership under Deng Xiaoping had a strong desire for a peaceful international environment which would enable China to concentrate its energy on realizing the four modernizations. Beijing started to cultivate good relations with countries which had been less friendly or hostile to China. In the eyes of Chinese reform-minded leaders, developmental-economic priorities had become as important, if not more important than strictly strategic military-security ones.

Internationally, this emphasis was supported by the ongoing assessment of the international balance of power. Although authoritative pronouncements criticized both superpowers for their hegemonic rivalry, Beijing concluded that neither Moscow nor Washington had sufficient power to challenge the other through a test of arms:

> Both the Soviet Union and the United States worry about the serious consequences of a world war in the nuclear era. Both sides have limited their struggle to the brink of war.... Nuclear deterrence has discouraged both superpowers from venturing into launching a major war or a nuclear war.... The U.S.-Soviet balance of military power unfavorable to the United States in the 1970s will possibly be changed in the eighties, but the present balance of comprehensive strength between the superpowers will not be changed to a marked degree and neither will be able to overpower the opposing side.... The strategic balance in the present nuclear era will effectively prevent the outbreak of a major war.[50]

China had changed its previous view that superpower contention was "bound to lead to a world war," and this was said to be "independent of man's will."[51] Although still considering the confrontation between Washington and Moscow as the major source of conflict which would directly affect the peace and security of the world, Beijing seemed to be convinced that the forces opposing superpower hegemonic activities were also growing. To a large extent, it was possible to check the scramble for hegemony between the superpowers by the cooperation of all "peace-loving" and "justice-holding" forces in the world.[52] Therefore, there would be a relatively long period of general peace in international relations.

This view was further developed by the observation of changes in the international structure. Since late 1981, China's world view had shifted from the emphasis on bipolarity in international politics characterized by the confrontation between the West and East, to one of multipolarity.[53] "In overall terms," one Chinese commentary observed in January 1983, "both the Soviet Union and the United States have their weaknesses, but in general there seems to be a balance." However, in relative terms, the influence and position of both powers would "weaken and decline" during the remainder of the decade.[54] As noted by one Chinese official, "our times can be characterized as...multipolarization in politics and economics, competition and coexistence."[55] He argued:

> Manipulation of the world's political situation by the superpowers has been a major phenomenon in international politics since World War II.... The most fundamental aspect of a superpower's character is that it not only has unprecedentedly tremendous economic and military powers, but also exerts these for its own interests and imposes its own will on other countries. The superpowers, if necessary, will go so far as to directly invade and enslave other countries. In this sense, the politics of superpowers is tantamount to the "politics of hegemonism".... China is strongly opposed to power politics and hegemonism...and has firmly supported all peoples oppressed by the superpowers and has opposed every form of hegemonism.[56]

He continued:

> It should be noted that the presence of superpowers is a temporary phenomenon in history. On the one hand, as each superpower has extremely selfish aims and an ever-sharpening conflict of interests and

fierce rivalry inevitably exist between them, it is impossible for them to unite to dominate the world. On the other hand, they are meeting increasing resistance from other countries, including their "allies;" it is impossible for them to fulfil their desire to pull the strength of their "allies" and that of many other countries together for the attainment of their hegemonic aims. The strength of the superpowers has been contained and worn down in the course of their confrontation and rivalry, amidst the conflicts inside their own blocs and by the regional wars outside their blocs. As a result, an odd phenomenon has occurred in international relations that the war capabilities of the superpowers have been augmented to an extent never seen before, while their freedom to use such capabilities to manipulate world affairs and control their own spheres of influence has been unprecedentedly restricted. We must have a profound understanding of the superpowers' dual character of being at once powerful and feeble.[57]

Clearly, the Chinese saw that bipolarism of the superpowers was being challenged by the rise of Western Europe, Japan, China and the Third World in international political and economic affairs. They found that there were centrifugal forces within the two alliance systems. The "guns and butter contradiction" fed the peace movement and caused public disagreements between the United States and its Western European allies as well as amongst the Soviet Union and its allies.[58] Beijing also saw that the emergence of the Third World constituted an important force in the international arena and highly appreciated the efforts of the Third World in world affairs.[59] China saw with satisfaction that the Third World had changed the United Nations from a mere voting machine manipulated by big powers into a forum to condemn imperialism, hegemonism and expansionism.

All in all, Beijing came to the conclusion that multipolarization in the world was a healthy trend against superpower politics.

[There are] two possibilities as to whether a new world war can be averted--either the war will break out or it will be prevented. Which will become reality will be determined by the struggle of the peace-loving countries and peoples throughout the world. A new world war can be prevented if the people all over the world heighten their vigilance, strengthen unity and launch resolute struggle against all manifestations of hegemonism and expansionism.[60]

This view was further developed by Deng Xiaoping later. He said:

The danger of world war still exists. Because of the two superpowers' ongoing arms race, the factors of war will continue to grow. However...the growth of the forces for peace in the world will outpace the growth of the forces for war.... It is possible that large-scale world war will not break out for a relatively long time.... There are hopes for safeguarding world peace.[61]

According to this view, Beijing perceived that in the context that the Soviet threat was declining and the world was becoming more multipolar, it was not in China's interest to attach itself to any big powers. Instead, China should look for more policy flexibility in the form of greater "independence." China's foreign policy goals should not be dominated solely by strategic/military factors as they had been in the 1970s. Based on these perceptions, the pragmatic leaders in Beijing immediately grasped the opportunity to restructure China's foreign policy.

Toward an "Independent Foreign Policy"

Objectives

After a lengthy period of critical evaluation and debate within the Chinese government over the international environment, plus dramatic domestic changes, China's foreign policy restructuring became inevitable in 1982. As the reform-minded leaders consolidated their political power in Beijing, they also reformed China's foreign policy and set forth three basic objectives.

First, the Chinese leaders realized that their national interest would be better served by domestic prosperity and stability based upon sustained economic development. This required an active but balanced foreign policy emphasizing the maintenance of national independence and the promotion of a stable international environment. Since China's security environment would remain reasonably favorable for a period of time because of the declining Soviet threat and the relative balance of power between the superpowers, Deng and his associates hoped that China would devote greater attention to economic modernization and eventually catch up with the rapidly industrializing states of East Asia. For this purpose, China became more cooperative and was willing to adopt a conciliatory stance to reduce tensions with its neighbors and make compromise where possible with her opponents to minimize conflicts.[62]

Second, due to the strategic parity between the superpowers, the objective ground on which China united with the less dangerous one against the other had disappeared. China could pursue a more independent foreign policy in international affairs.[63] Beijing's goal of following an independent foreign policy was to increase its leverage in dealing with the United States and the Soviet Union and get more concessions on China's terms from them. Meanwhile, an independent policy could also improve China's image in the Third World and increase China's foreign policy options and flexibility in international affairs. Besides, a policy of national independence had a direct appeal to Chinese nationalistic sensibilities at home, an essential for reform-minded officials who needed an effective foreign policy in support of their positions of power within the leadership.

Third, in order to promote economic modernization, China had a strong desire for expanding economic ties with foreign countries and obtaining economic assistance and technology from a diversity of suppliers. Beijing not only wanted to continue its good economic and commercial relations with the United States, Western Europe and Japan, but also intended to expand such ties with other countries including the Soviet Union, Eastern Europe, Taiwan, South Korea, and the Middle East. It was generally believed that China urgently needed to upgrade its industrial infrastructure built in the 1950s with Soviet aid and to attract foreign capital from a variety of sources.[64] Deng argued that it was not in China's interest to continue to follow Mao's "self-reliance" strategy in economic development but to adopt a policy of "opening to the outside world." He claimed that China could benefit from effective participation in the international economic system and could attract foreign participation in its economic development. Through increased international involvement China could rapidly attain wealth and power.[65]

As compared with Beijing's foreign behavior in the 1970s, China's new foreign policy which emphasized independence, peace and economic development was more practical and sophisticated. In projecting greater independence from the United States, showing its willingness to deal reasonably with Moscow, and favoring a close association with the Third World, Beijing wanted to pursue steady, independent and pragmatic policies toward the major countries and areas of concern to China. In essence, a foreign policy of independence did not mean that China intended to change its basic desire for good ties with the West for purposes of both security and development. Rather, it was backing away from its single-minded anti-Soviet foreign efforts of the late 1970s and developing omni-directional foreign relations. The Chinese pragmatic leaders hoped thereby to increase their policy flexibility and options. In the meantime, Washington could also be reminded that China had other resources for solving its problems, and thus could not be taken for granted.[66]

New Platforms

Formal enunciation of China's new foreign policy orientation came during the Twelfth Congress of the Chinese Communist Party, held in Beijing on September 1-11, 1982. As an important event, the Congress enhanced the powerful position of the reformers headed by Deng Xiaoping, Hu Yaobang and Zhao Ziyang within the Chinese leadership. The main themes of the Congress were set forth by General Secretary Hu Yaobang in his 34,000-word political report to the Congress. In general, Hu strove to legitimize the more pragmatic reform programs followed by the Party since he and other reformers led by Deng Xiaoping had managed to gain the upper hand in the leadership councils following the Third Plenum of the Eleventh Congress in December 1978. Meanwhile, he continued to discredit the policies associated with Maoist loyalists like former Party chief Hua Guofeng. More importantly, Hu elaborated Dengist pragmatic themes in the country's economic, political, and foreign policies over the next five years. He explicitly declared in his report that China's top priority for the foreseeable future was economic modernization and all other works must focus on this goal.[67]

In the discussion of China's foreign affairs, Hu Yaobang officially announced that China would pursue an "independent foreign policy of peace:"

> Being patriots, we do not tolerate any encroachment on China's national dignity or interests. Being internationalists, we are deeply aware that China's national interest cannot be fully realized in separation from the overall interests of mankind. Our adherence to an independent foreign policy accords with the discharging of our lofty international duty to safeguard world peace and promote human progress.... [W]e have shown the world by deeds that China never

attaches itself to any big power or group of powers, and never yields to pressure from any big power.... China's foreign policy...proceeds from the fundamental interests of the people of China and the rest of the world. It follows an overall long-term strategy, and is definitely not swayed by expediency or by anybody's instigation or provocation.[68]

These words distinctly demonstrated China's resolution to maintain an independent posture in its foreign policy.

Mr. Hu continued to emphasize that China was willing to develop relations with all countries on the basis of "the five principles of mutual respect for sovereignty and territorial integrity, mutual non-aggression, non-interference in each others' international affairs, equality and mutual benefit, and peaceful coexistence." "It is our firm strategic principle," he said, "to carry out the policy of opening to the outside world and expand economic and technological exchanges with foreign countries in accordance with the principles of equality and mutual benefit." He reiterated interest in carefully planned import of foreign technology, in the use of foreign funds, and in the growth of foreign trade.[69]

When talking about Sino-American relations, Hu Yaobang harshly criticized the United States' Taiwan policy as a hegemonic action and described it as "a cloud [that] has all along hung over the relations between the two countries." He concluded that "Sino-US relations can continue to develop soundly only if the principles of mutual respect for sovereignty and territorial integrity and non-interference in each other's internal affairs are truly adhered to." Hu Yaobang's reference to the Soviet Union likewise contained serious complaints about the Soviet hegemonist policy which constituted "grave threats to the peace of Asia and to China." In response to Brezhnev's overture at Tashkent in March in 1982, he said, "deeds, rather than words," were more important to the Chinese. "If the Soviet authorities really have a sincere desire to improve relations with China," they should "take practical steps to lift their threat to the security of our country."[70]

In his report, however, Hu Yaobang did not repeat the vivid portrayal of Soviet expansion as the main danger to world peace that had been presented in the keynote address at the Eleventh Congress in 1977. He only made a more general reference to "imperialism, hegemonism and colonialism" as the "main forces" jeopardizing peace, and said that the rivalry of the two superpowers was the "main source of instability and turmoil in the world." Mr. Hu argued that "the most important task for the people of the world today" was "to oppose hegemonism and safeguard world peace." "Experience shows," he continued, "that the people of the world, by persevering in struggle, can upset the strategic plans of the superpowers." "World peace can be safeguarded, provided the people truly unite and fight resolutely against all expressions of hegemonism and expansionism." He pledged that China opposed world tension "being fomented by the superpowers" and opposed "all the local war of aggression which they instigate or back."[71]

Hu Yaobang devoted many paragraphs in his report to a discussion of the relations between China and the Third World, which had been somewhat neglected over the past several years in Beijing's foreign policy as China followed an overly anti-Soviet and pro-West posture. First, he pointed out that "socialist China belongs to the Third World." He said that China had "experienced the same sufferings as most other third world countries" and faced similar problems and tasks. Second, he listed several examples of the political and economic roles that the Third World had played in international relations. He argued that the emergence of the Third World in the international arena was "a primary event of our time" which had "converged into a mighty current of forces upholding justice in our time and greatly changed the situation in which the superpowers could wilfully manipulate the fate of the world." Third, Mr. Hu promised that China would strongly support the Third World on the issues such as the New International Economic Order (NIEO), South-South cooperation, and political independence and sovereignty of third world countries. Finally, he announced that China would like to develop relations with all developing countries on the basis of the Five Principles of Peaceful Coexistence, irrespective of the differences in their political, social and economic systems, and regardless of their stances towards the two superpowers.[72]

The evolution of China's independent foreign policy was further summarized in Premier Zhao Ziyang's detailed survey of China's foreign relations at the Sixth National People's Congress on June 6, 1983. In laying out the guiding principles of Beijing's independent foreign policy of peace, Zhao reaffirmed the basic elements that had been cited by Hu Yaobang previously:

> Our socialist modernization requires a peaceful international environment. The preservation of peace is the common desire of the

people of China and the rest of the world. The superpower contention for world hegemony is the main source of turmoil in the world today. It is imperative to oppose hegemonism in order to safeguard world peace. The Chinese Government takes opposing hegemonism and safeguarding world peace as *the basic point of departure* of its foreign policy and seeks to develop relations with [*all*] *other countries* on the basis of the Five Principles of Peaceful Coexistence and to promote the progress of mankind.[73]

He continued:

The Third World constitutes a powerful force against imperialism, colonialism and hegemonism. China is part of the Third World. Our *basic stand* in foreign affairs is to strengthen solidarity and co-operation with other third world countries. It is our sacred duty to support other third world countries and people in their struggles to win and uphold their national rights.[74]

When discussing policies with regard to specific countries, Zhao expressed Beijing's continuing wariness of relations with the United States and said that China would "never tolerate any infringement on China's sovereignty or any interference in its internal affairs." He urged the Soviet Union to remove its threat to China's security in order to open the way to improved Sino-Soviet relations. In particular, Zhao emphasized the importance of maintaining and expanding friendly relations with China's neighboring countries including Japan, India and Vietnam. Finally in his report, Zhao adopted an unusually conciliatory approach to the Soviet bloc countries in Eastern Europe and explicitly expressed China's willingness to improve relations with them.[75]

During the course of developing an independent foreign policy, Hu Yaobang and Zhao Ziyang, two of Deng's followers at the time, became more personally associated with the construction of the new framework. As the Party's new General Secretary, Hu Yaobang started to gain influence in foreign affairs. The restructuring of the central organs resulted in considerable turnover among the key actors who were involved in making foreign policy. Officials who had worked with Hu Yaobang in youth organizations in the 1950s and 1960s were placed in key posts. Wu Xueqian, who had worked under Hu in international liaison affairs for both the Party and its youth organization, replaced Huang Hua as new Foreign Minister in late 1982. Besides, Premier Zhao Ziyang also left deep marks on China's pragmatic foreign policy.

He placed great emphasis upon pragmatic development of good relations with all countries for the sake of gaining more practical benefits and diversifying economic ties. With their down-to-earth reputation, reform-minded leaders in Beijing developed a more pragmatic foreign policy which gave equal stress to China's goals of independence, development, and security.

Initiatives under the
New Orientation

Under the new foreign policy orientation, China immediately took a series of specific foreign policy initiatives to restructure its relations with the United States, the Soviet Union and the Third World. Beijing distanced itself from policies of Washington and reopened talks with Moscow. Meanwhile, China again stressed its identification with the Third World. Through these measures, Beijing had laid a good foundation for the overall foreign policy restructuring in the following years.

Keeping a Distance But without Going to Extremes

The declaration that China would "never attach itself to any big power or group of powers"[76] underscored Beijing's positive evaluation of international balance of power vis-à-vis China's interest. This platform allowed China to distance itself from the United States and engage in dialogue with both superpowers without completely aligning with either of them. This independent stance was China's way of saying that it was not interested in being used as "China card" by any powers. Beijing's relations with the superpowers were becoming more and more dependent on the policies that they adopted on issues of interest to the Chinese. Specifically, they included the positions that the United States took on arms sales to Taiwan and the export of advanced technology to China, and the responses that Moscow made to Beijing's preconditions of easing China's security concerns.[77] Premier Zhao Ziyang said clearly in late July 1983 that "there are still obstacles in the development of Sino-Soviet and Sino-U.S. relations, but the obstacles are not on the side of China."[78] He reiterated that China would (1) consistently oppose superpower hegemonism; (2) be willing to pursue normal state-to-state relations with both states on the basis of the Five Principles of Peaceful Coexistence; and (3) continue dialogues with both superpowers.[79]

In an effort to dissociate itself from the Sino-American relationship in anti-Soviet terms, Beijing began to refer to the United States once again as a hegemonic power. This label had been reserved in the recent past for the Soviet Union alone. In talks with Yugoslav journalists on December 15, 1981, Deng told them that he considered both the United States and the Soviet Union to be hegemonists in foreign affairs, the first time he so labeled the United States in many years.[80] Premier Zhao also complained that "the two superpowers in their worldwide rivalry are menacing and encroaching upon the independence and security of many countries."[81]

Beijing was particularly critical of the U.S. attitude toward Taiwan as a hegemonistic action against China's sovereignty. Li Xiannian, one Chinese senior leader, conveyed an indirect but clear message at a leadership meeting in early 1982 that China would not cooperate with the United States at the expense of its claim to sovereignty over Taiwan. After reaffirming Beijing's willingness to develop diplomatic relations and economic and cultural contacts with all countries on the basis of the principles of peaceful coexistence, Li delivered a stern message:

> We will never barter away principle, let alone depend on alms. It is absolutely intolerable that anyone should try to encroach upon China's national sovereignty, interfere in our internal affairs, and obstruct the reunification of our country. We can never tolerate that.[82]

The media were also full of harsh criticism of the United States' policy toward China. A special commentator of *Beijing Review* warned:

> Some people say that because China is backward and faces a Soviet military threat, it needs U.S. assistance. They believe that so long as the United States adopts a hardline towards the Soviet Union, China will swallow the bitter pill on the questions of sovereignty and U.S. arms sales to Taiwan. This is fallacious reasoning based on ignorance of the history of Sino-Soviet relations and the history of Sino-U.S. relations.... The gradual improvement of Sino-U.S. relations...came only after the United States recognized that there is one China.... China did not alter its conditions for the establishment of Sino-U.S. diplomatic relations simply because of the Soviet threat.[83]

Apart from the Taiwan issue, China started to follow a policy less dependent on close strategic bonds with Washington and take issue with Washington's third world policy. First of all, China reiterated its identification with the Third World instead of the United States and other Western countries. To symbolize such an identification, Chinese media began once again to emphasize problems of third world development and to state China's support for a restructuring of the international economic order. Then China began to openly criticize Washington's "superpower complex" and expressed its disapproval of "the erroneous policies of the United States toward certain issues in the Third World."[84] In particular, China criticized Washington's policy in the Middle East, Southern Africa, and Central America. The Chinese said that the American support for Israel and South Africa had pitted the United States "against the Arab and African peoples and the peoples of many other third world countries."[85] Beijing also charged the Reagan administration with making Soviet and Cuban infiltration as the excuse to consolidate and expand U.S. influence in Central America. The criticism of American "hegemonism" in El Salvador and Nicaragua were in particular contrast with earlier Chinese comments in which Beijing positively supported U.S. policy there.[86] In addition, commentaries on the twentieth anniversary of the nonaligned movement attacked both the Soviet Union and the United States as "hegemonists" exploiting smaller states.[87] Beijing publicly mentioned "American hegemonism" in East Asia even though Soviet hegemonism was still regarded as a greater threat there.[88] A lengthy commentary in *Renmin Ribao (People's Daily)* on the superpower rivalry in the Western Pacific criticized American strategies there.[89] It said that China was not satisfied with Washington's encouragement of Japanese pledges to assist U.S. defense policy in Northeast Asia. Japan's readiness to assume increased responsibilities for sea lane defense and commitment to military collaboration with the United States were viewed by China and elsewhere in Asia as portending "a possible revival of Japanese militarism."[90] In the meantime, China strongly protested to Japan over the issue of revisions of school history textbooks by the Japanese Education Ministry which diluted the wording used to describe Japan's aggression against China and other Asian states during the 1930s and 1940s. Chinese accusations were especially harsh:

> This is definitely not a simple dispute over the use of words or over accidental mistakes made by the Japanese authorities concerned. It is

a grave signal that the danger of a revival of Japanese militarism exists in Japan.... The militarist elements have by no means vanished in Japan.... These people are...[bidding] to revive militarism and are vainly thinking of turning Japan from an economic into a great military power.[91]

Beijing also attacked on the Operation Team Spirit, the annual joint American-South Korean military exercises, as a destabilizing factor on the Korean Peninsula.[92]

To demonstrate its independent role, China particularly criticized the hegemonistic behavior of both superpowers. Chinese press accounts implied that China now regarded South Africa and Israel as "regional hegemonists" linked to the United States, just as Beijing had long considered Cuba and Vietnam to be regional hegemonists linked to the Soviet Union.[93] Later Deng Xiaoping told former West German Chancellor Helmut Schmidt that "Washington views Taiwan as an 'unsinkable aircraft carrier,' just as Moscow does Vietnam. The two superpowers are all alike."[94] One Chinese journal summarized China's new policy stating that:

[China would] totally oppose hegemony, no matter who seeks it or where it is sought.... On the Afghan and Cambodian issues, both China and the United States oppose the Soviet Union and Vietnam.... In another case, both China and the Soviet Union oppose the United States in supporting Israeli aggression and the South African apartheid rule. This does not mean that China "allies" with the United States under some circumstances, or becomes a Soviet partner under other circumstances. [Instead], this precisely proves that...China is independent of all the superpowers.[95]

The same journal also pointed out that "China may adopt a similar attitude with this or that superpower on this or that issue, and have a certain 'point of meeting.' " But its point of departure in determining its position was different.[96]

Officially China rejected the concept of "equidistance," as interpreted by the West, in its new relations with the two superpowers. Zhu Qizhen, Chinese Vice-Foreign Minister, explained in an interview that Beijing's independent posture meant that "China determines its policy independently on the merits of each case proceeding as we do from the fundamental interest of the Chinese people and the people of the entire world." This was why on some issues China was close to the

United States, and on others close to the Soviet Union. But he emphasized in the interview that "equidistance is not our policy."[97]

Clearly, even as the Chinese dissociated themselves from an intimate security relationship with Washington and criticized "hegemonist" behavior of the United States, they understood that, in spite of their differences over Taiwan, the United States did not threaten China's security. The Soviet Union remained a major security threat to China even if Beijing asserted that the immediacy of this threat had somewhat diminished in recent years. Furthermore, China was embarking on an economic modernization drive. It needed greater stability in its security environment and substantial assistance from the United States, Japan and West Europe--assistance which Moscow simply could not match even if it wanted to. So if Beijing became "too cocky" in its relations with the West, such assistance from the West could be jeopardized.[98] Thus, even as the Chinese strove for an independent role by opposing "hegemonism" of both superpowers while keeping dialogue open with them, they in fact adopted asymmetrical policies in relations with the two superpowers. China had continuing interest in keeping good relations with the West for economic and technological benefits. But this could be done by pressing the United States to make more compromise on the issue of Taiwan and to permit China greater access to sensitive technologies. In this regard, a more independent stance, instead of playing a role of "junior partner," was more effective. On the part of China, the Sino-Soviet thaw not only helped reduce tensions with the Soviet Union, but could also well serve as a reminder to Washington of China's importance. At least it could raise the fear in the West of possible shift in China's strategic alignment.

With these calculations in mind, the Chinese leadership was careful to separate political issues from economic interests in its foreign policy. While pursuing an independent stance in strategic relations with the United States, Beijing continued to keep or even expand its economic relations with the West. Politically, Chinese nationalism and ideological imperatives made Beijing become increasingly concerned about such issues as Taiwan and the so-called "bourgeois" influences as well as the "spiritual pollution" from the West. But economically, Beijing was very realistic and still eager to reap the benefits of China's new "open door." While pursuing an independent stance in its foreign policy, China significantly expanded the range of economic and commercial transactions with the West. Even later it increased trade relations with the Soviet Union and Eastern Europe, China purposely developed its relations with the West one step ahead of its relations with the Soviets. The asymmetry in relations with the two superpowers became clearer later on when Beijing saw little signs of immediate Soviet willingness to compromise on basic political and security issues during Sino-Soviet talks in October 1982. And the Soviet military buildup in Asia, including the deployment of highly accurate SS-20 intermediate-range missiles, continued.[99] In this case, China was very careful not to risk losing the United States. It was not in China's interest to do so for both security and economic reasons. On security matters, bad relations with Washington would obviously increase China's insecurity when the Soviet threat had not been eliminated. Economically, deteriorating Sino-American relations would not only upset China's ability to gain greater access to American markets, but also affected China's relations with other important capitalist countries for getting more financial and technical assistance. In fact, during the spring and summer of 1982, the Japanese began to express growing concern to Beijing about the deterioration of Sino-American relations.[100] So an uncontrolled overall confrontational posture toward Washington would ill serve China's broader political, technological, and economic goals. Even if Beijing judged the United States a born again hegemonist, the Chinese understood that its independent policy was not to ruin Sino-American relations and upset the balance of power in the Asian-Pacific area but to get more leverage in its dealings with the United States.

Therefore, China had to carefully carry out its "independent foreign policy". On the one hand, Beijing did not want to be overly dependent upon the West and be taken for granted by the United States. An independent position was needed to push Washington on the Taiwan issue as well as on other questions. But on the other hand, China did not want to have an excessively confrontational atmosphere at the risk of ruining relations with the West. It meant that China should keep an appropriate distance from the United States and exert proper pressure without going to extremes. Although Beijing no longer considered a united front metaphor appropriate, it understood that there still existed overlapping security concerns with Washington and Tokyo in such issues as Afghanistan, Indochina, and the Soviet conventional and nuclear buildup in East Asia.[101] On the issues not directly bearing on Chinese security concerns, China might pursue a more independent posture so as to maneuver more freely to seek its advantage. But on the security issues having a direct bearing on China's environment in Asia, Beijing knew that it was irrelevant to equate the two superpowers.[102] Throughout the spring of 1983, Moscow reiterated that it was free to redeploy any missiles dismantled in the European portion of the Soviet Union to positions east of the Urals, which was not addressed by the Geneva talks. In March 1983, it was estimated that there were 230 operational SS-20 launchers west of the Urals, and 95 east of the Urals. By December, European deployment of the SS-20 stood at 243, with Asian deployments at 126. In early January 1984, it was confirmed that the total number of SS-20 in Soviet Asia was 135. In response, Beijing showed great concern and called on Moscow to "cut back drastically" the SS-20s already deployed in Asia and to destroy the launch sites. China also included the SS-20 deployments among the "obstacles" to an improvement of Sino-Soviet relations.[103] In this regard, China was obviously interested in keeping steady Sino-American and Sino-Japanese relations.

For its part, the United States also had an interest in stabilizing its relations with China and did not want to lose China at the risk of upsetting the balance of power in East Asia. The Reagan administration pointed out later that China was a regional power but with global importance. Washington then reemphasized that a strong and healthy Sino-American relationship was a key component of stability in the Asia-Pacific region. It was in the interest of the United States to continue to cooperate with China.[104] Soon Washington began to fix the relationship by accommodating some Chinese concerns through the avoidance of strong rhetorical support for Taiwan that had so inflamed U.S.-China tensions, and by moving ahead on military and technology transfers to China. In May 1983, President Reagan approved the decision to place China in Category "V" along with the Western European nations, India, most of Africa, some Arab countries, Australia, New Zealand, and Japan.[105] The visit of U.S. Defense Secretary Caspar Weinberger to China in September 1983 demonstrated the continuing security interest of the United States in cooperating with Beijing even though China had adopted a more independent role. Weinberger provided a detailed presentation of the long-awaited American policy guidelines on technology transfer. According to the new guidelines, as a "friendly, non-allied nation," China could now purchase a much wider variety of sophisticated dual use technologies.[106]

Beijing was pleased with these developments and saw them as positive steps undertaken by the Reagan administration to improve bilateral ties. During the remainder of 1983 and early 1984, the Chinese responded very positively to Washington and also sought to cultivate bilateral relations by reconciling some of the ambiguities and contradictions in their dealings with the United States. In January 1984, Premier Zhao Ziyang made his long-delayed visit to the United States. Before his visit, he had issued a statement. He said that, in spite of the "twists and turns" in Sino-American ties, on the whole great progress had been made in bilateral relations. China, he continued, would not demand an immediate or complete cessation of American arms sales to Taiwan, but it did expect adherence to various Sino-American agreements on the matter. Zhao stated that China's pursuit of Sino-Soviet normalization was genuine but it did not mean that China was practicing "equal distance diplomacy or equating different countries." The only "major obstacle" to Sino-American relations, according to Zhao, remained Taiwan. But China "attach[ed] importance to relations with the United States," and therefore remained "rather restrained" in its reactions to U.S. arms sales to Taiwan, even though "the Chinese people are most unhappy about this."[107] In a way of showing China's independent stance, Zhao was frank, during his visit, to mention the differences between the two countries on many issues and criticize the Reagan administration's Central American, Middle East, European, and Taiwan policies.

In April 1984, President Reagan made a reciprocal visit to China where he received a warm welcome. While in China, Reagan signed four agreements and protocols and initialed one more agreement on nuclear energy cooperation. In Reagan's own words, the trip raised Sino-American relations to "a new level of understanding."[108] Reagan admitted that his past view on "Red China" as an implacable foe of the United States was wrong. Dramatically shifting his language, he asserted that the United States could get along "with this so-called Communist China" since it was not an expansionist power and since it wanted American investment.[109] The Chinese were also gratified as the New China News Agency proclaimed that "President Reagan's trip to China and his reiteration of his commitment to abide by the Chinese-U.S. communiqués represented a significant step forward."[110]

In spite of Reagan's long list of accommodations, however, China's course of following an independent stance was unswerving. During Reagan's visit, the Chinese reiterated China's desire to normalize Sino-Soviet relations and to develop economic, technological and cultural exchanges with the Soviet Union. Instead of endorsing his anti-Soviet crusade, as Reagan had hoped, the Chinese leaders publicly urged that the United States likewise end its deadlock with Moscow for the sake of world peace. On the other occasion, the anti-Soviet portions of President Reagan's speech were censored by the Chinese in their domestic news coverage. All these episodes served as a reminder to the United States of China's independent stance.[111]

On the whole, the reconsolidation of Sino-U.S. relations did not presage a revitalization of China's united front strategy of the 1970s. Although Beijing indicated that relations with the West, especially with the United States, were essential to China's broad foreign policy goals, and Washington also regarded its relations with China as important, both sides knew clearly that U.S.-Chinese differences on many questions made it impossible to establish a comprehensive and formal strategic alignment. Even so, both sides, for various reasons, still had interest in accommodating each other. Now they were more realistic about their relationship than ever before and seeking to establish "maturing" ties between the two countries.

Bargaining for Sino-Soviet Reconciliation

After adopting an independent posture in its foreign policy, Beijing sought to test Soviet intentions by agreeing to resume bilateral talks on the normalization of Sino-Soviet relations. The Chinese looked for any political opportunities that might result from the impending succession to Leonid Brezhnev. They also tried to demonstrate to Washington that China had options for reducing the Soviet threat other than a close Sino-U.S. collaboration. In the words of one Chinese official,

> China...wants to relax its relations...with its neighbor, the Soviet Union, for the sake of the four modernizations. What it wants is normalization, that is, to conduct dialogue, build balanced state relations, and carry out normal trade and cultural exchanges. To that end we are asking the Soviet authorities to take steps to dispel our suspicions.[112]

In October 1982, China and the Soviet Union resumed bilateral talks at vice-foreign ministerial level. Labeled only as "consultation," the talks, which had been suspended by the Chinese after the Soviet invasion of Afghanistan, met semi-annually, alternating between Beijing and Moscow. The chief Chinese negotiator was Vice-Foreign Minister

Qian Qichen; his Soviet counterpart was Vice Foreign Minister Leonid Ilichev, a veteran of the Sino-Soviet border talks.

However, the talks were unable to bridge a major gap between the positions of the two sides on basic security and political issues immediately. China stuck to its preconditions for improved Sino-Soviet relations involving withdrawal of Soviet forces from along the Sino-Soviet border and from Mongolia (later China added specific reference to Soviet SS-20 missiles targeted against China); an end to Soviet support for Vietnam's occupation of Cambodia; and withdrawal of Soviet forces from Afghanistan. Moscow remained unwilling to compromise, stating that the Soviet Union would not discuss matters affecting third countries. After the talks ended without success, Premier Zhao Ziyang was reported to have said that talks would continue and that China's opposition to Soviet hegemonism and Beijing-Moscow dialogue were not contradictory to one another.[113]

Brezhnev's death in November 1982 offered an opportunity for Sino-Soviet contacts at the highest level. Beijing dispatched its Foreign Minister Huang Hua to the funeral in Moscow where he held talks with his counterpart, Andrei Gromyko. Border trade between the two countries was restored in April 1983 along the Amur and Ussuri rivers and near Mongolia after a fifteen-year suspension.[114] In August 1983, in an interview Soviet President Andropov called for greater Sino-Soviet cooperation, but insisted that improvement in relations between Moscow and Beijing must not harm third countries.[115] In response, Chinese leader Hu Yaobang told an Italian newspaper *L'Unità* that Soviet actions in Afghanistan and support for Vietnam's occupation of Cambodia were a threat to China and therefore should be included in the Sino-Soviet consultations. "What is at stake and is threatened [by the Soviet presence in Afghanistan and Moscow's backing of Vietnam's takeover of Cambodia]," Hu argued, "is our security." He asked rhetorically, "Against whom are the five Soviet divisions in Mongolia lined up? Obviously against China."[116]

One month later, the second forum of "consultations" began during the visit of Soviet Vice-Foreign Minister Mikhail Kapitsa to China. He talked with his Chinese counterpart Qian Qichen, and met with Chinese new Foreign Minister Wu Xueqian. The discussions covered each side's views of recent developments in the Middle East, Central America, the Indian Ocean, Afghanistan, and Indochina; and concerns over arms control including the deployment of the SS-20 missiles in Asia. But no agreement was reached on the security and political issues in this round of talks.[117] During the talks, China reacted cautiously to the Soviet shooting down of Korean Airlines Flight 007, allowing itself only to express regret but not to join in any international sanctions against Moscow.[118] Even so Chinese officials were not optimistic that any substantive results would be soon achieved in the Sino-Soviet talks. They stated explicitly that until Moscow responded to Beijing's demands to eliminate or reduce its threats to China's security, the development of relations would be limited to secondary areas of trade, technology transfer, and educational and cultural exchanges. The Chinese were suspicious that the Soviets wanted better relations with China but did not want to make any concessions on security matters.[119]

In February 1984, China sent its ranking vice-premier as well as a Politburo member, Wan Li, as its representative to the funeral of Andropov. It was the signal of China's positive assessment of the deceased Soviet leader as well as hopes for better relations in the future. But Wan received a cool welcome in Moscow. Beijing found that the rigid and uncompromising Chernenko government was resorting to stronger military means in both Europe and Asia in order to assert Soviet power and determination at a time of leadership transition in the Kremlin. Although the Soviets were on the defensive on a whole range of international issues and failed to halt the deployment of American Pershing and cruise missiles in Western Europe, Moscow was now engaged in new demonstrations of its military power. The Soviet Union deployed two of its three aircraft carriers in the Western Pacific in February and March 1984; one of them passed near China on its way to Vladivostok. In March 1984, the Soviets and Vietnamese conducted their first joint amphibious exercises fairly close to China and near the Vietnamese port city of Haiphong. Shortly before the exercise, there were reports about the stationing of Soviet medium bombers at Cam Ranh Bay, Vietnam. Moreover, the Soviets appeared to go out of their way to publicize strong support for Mongolia and Vietnam against China, again indicating their unwillingness to make compromises with China at the expense of third countries. Meanwhile, Chernenko had canceled a scheduled visit to China by Soviet First Deputy Prime Minister Ivan Arkhipov in May 1984.[120]

In response, China hardened its line and highlighted public complaints against Soviet pressure and intimidation. As the time of President Reagan's visit to China in April 1984, China and Vietnam were engaged in the most serious border armed clashes in years. The incidents underlined an area of important strategic common ground between Beijing and the strongly anti-Soviet Reagan administration. At the same time, China escalated charges regarding the Soviet threat to Chinese security, especially via Vietnam, and attempted to consolidate an identity of interests with both Japanese Prime Minister Nakasone, during a visit to China in March, and President Reagan in April, on the basis of opposition to the Soviet threat in Asia.[121]

The result was the postponement of bilateral "consultations" by the Soviets, who warned China that it could not take Moscow's conciliatory gestures for granted to strengthen China's relationship with Washington and its anti-Vietnam policy. Both sides revived polemical exchanges. Sino-Vietnamese confrontation along their common border continued into the summer of 1984, well beyond the usual period of fighting coincident with the annual Vietnamese dry season campaign against the Chinese-supported resistance forces in Cambodia. This escalation of fighting prompted Chernenko to publicly condemn China by name, the first such occurrence since Brezhnev's Tashkent speech in 1982. The Sino-Soviet relations remained chilled through the summer and fall of 1984.[122]

Although both sides did little to ease their differences on major political and security issues, they were still extremely interested in stabilizing their relations and resuming a forward movement in the less sensitive economic and technical areas. Beijing agreed to undertake a delimitation of the frontier with the Soviet satellite Mongolia, and agreed to set up joint commissions to discuss economic exchanges with Moscow's close East European allies. The Chinese leaders also indicated that they would like to do the same in China's relations with the Soviet Union. In December 1984, two weeks prior to Soviet Foreign Minister Gromyko's meeting in Geneva with U.S. Secretary of State Schultz on U.S.-Soviet arms control, Moscow reinstated the canceled trip to Beijing by its First Deputy Prime Minister Ivan Arkhipov, the highest-level Soviet official to visit China since 1969. Arkhipov himself had been a senior Soviet economic adviser in China in the 1950s. He was warmly received as "an old friend of China" by high level Chinese leaders such as Zhao Ziyang and Chen Yun. This visit saw the signing of three agreements and set up a Joint Commission for Economic, Trade, Scientific, and Technical Cooperation. Both sides agreed to conclude a five-year trade agreement and decided that the trade levels in 1985 would be 60 percent greater than the value of their trade in 1984.[123]

Initiatives in the Third World

By taking an independent stance, Beijing was in a better position to revise its third world policy. In the past, China had not treated individual events occurring in the Third World in their own right. Very often, the lines between friends and enemies were drawn depending on whether they followed anti-Soviet policies. Now in an effort to improve its image and regain support in the Third World, China publicly announced that "China is a developing socialist country belonging to the Third World."[124] Departing from its past alignment with one superpower against the other, China claimed its opposition to hegemony no matter who sought it and where, and China would determine its policy independently on the merits of each case. Such a differentiated opposition to both superpowers brought China's global posture more or less into line with that of the Third World. At the Cancùn summit meeting of October 1981, Premier Zhao stressed China's strong support for developing countries' demands for establishment of a new international economic order (NIEO), opposed by the United States and some other developed countries. China also criticized the U.S. position on other global issues, including the United Nations Law of the Sea Convention, the United Nations Educational Scientific and Cultural Organization (UNESCO), and the International Monetary Funds (IMF). Besides, Beijing continued to oppose Soviet hegemonic behavior in Indochina and Afghanistan. In 1983, it condemned external interference in Chad and considered the conflict in Chad as purely an internal matter of no concern to the United States, France, or the Soviet Union.[125]

In late 1981 Beijing worked hard to identify with the Third World when it actively supported a third world candidate from Africa for the United Nations Secretary-General. In a closed session for the election of the Secretary-General, China cast 16 vetoes to block the reelection of Kurt Waldheim supported by the West. In the end, a compromise third world candidate, Javier Pàrez de Cuàllar from Peru, was chosen.[126] China's voting behavior in the United Nations also reflected its growing independence of the two superpowers. In 1983, for example, China voted for the anti-American draft resolution condemning the invasion of Grenada and abstained on the U.S.-sponsored anti-Soviet draft resolution on the Korean Air Lines incident. In the meantime, through propaganda coverage, international exchanges, leadership meetings, and action in international organizations, Beijing placed much emphasis on North-South and South-South issues. As a result of these and other steps, China had gradually consolidated its ties with developing nations and recovered some of its lost political ground in the Third World.[127]

Chinese leaders also made extensive trips to third world countries. The most notable of these was that of Premier Zhao to eleven African countries between December, 1982 and January, 1983.[128] Throughout these visits, China was trying hard to underline a strong reassertion of its third world credentials and its more independent posture toward both superpowers. During the trip, Zhao held low-key discussions with African leaders of varying political views. In an effort to eliminate African and other third world countries' tendencies to associate Chinese policy with the United States, Zhao singled out unpopular American policy in the Third World for criticism. At the same time, he avoided caustic references to either Washington or Moscow in public, presumably out of deference to his hosts' sensibilities. In order to maximize political gains and minimize the risk of alienating important regional actors, Zhao carefully tailored his statements over issues that divided the region, including the civil war in Chad, the West Sahara dispute among Morocco, Algeria, and Libya, the Iran-Iraq war, and the disagreement between Ethiopia and Somalia over their border. During the trip, Zhao refused to commit China to many new aid programs, at most stops he offered to conclude economic cooperation agreements, emphasizing joint investment in small projects that would have a fairly rapid and relatively high political impact with low cost. For this end, Zhao put forward four principles of China's economic and technical cooperation with developing countries: "equality and mutual benefit, stress on practical results, diversity in form, and common progress."[129]

On the whole, China's third world policy had become more realistic. Politically, Beijing intended to win the Third World's support by showing more sensitivity to problems of the developing nations. In the eyes of Beijing, identifying with the Third World and voicing concerns over the issues with regard to the Third World would raise China's political reputation among developing countries and increase its influence in international affairs. Besides, Beijing was careful not to make any political and/or economic commitments to the Third World beyond its ability because such overcommitments might in turn affect China's dealings with the West. Beijing adopted a practical policy in which it insisted on China's flexibility and independence in backing the

Third World and tended to give moral support to the Third World on many issues. However, China did not physically join the two leading third world caucuses--the Group of 77 in global developmental politics and the Non-Aligned Movement in global geo-politics. The Chinese believed this as another demonstration of their "independent foreign policy." Finally, China no longer indiscriminately attributed third world difficulties to the damaging consequences of ex-colonial rule or the vicious effects of the world capitalist system. It began to equally stress the role of mismanagement on the part of third world governments themselves and their inappropriate use of foreign models. When discussing specific measures to speed up economic development in the Third World, China tended to give much emphasis on the need to utilize and not simply reject the existing international system. To China, dialogue and cooperation, especially among developing nations, were more relevant in their modernization efforts.[130]

China's realistic attitudes towards the Third World were also reflected in its economic relations with the developing countries. Beijing dropped its past policy to throw a substantial amount of money into a handful of countries in order to fulfill its political commitment to the so-called third world causes. Instead, most economic exchanges between China and developing nations in the 1980s were conducted on strict business terms. In fact, China was more a recipient, rather than a supplier, of foreign aid during this period.[131] Moreover, the Chinese were interested in seeking economic benefits through improved relations with the Third World. In the Middle East, for example, Chinese trade grew as new markets were opened. It remained highly favorable for China, resulting in a surplus of over $1 billion in 1982 alone. China also used good political ties to send tens of thousands of contract workers, especially to Iraq and other Middle Eastern countries.[132] Perhaps the most lucrative source of foreign earnings China gained from its good relations with the Middle East was arms sales. In the early 1980s, China provided Egypt with a large quantity of arms, including warships, aircraft, missiles, spare parts, ammunition and maintenance services. When asked whether China would meet its third world commitment and increase its military aid to Egypt during Egyptian President Mubarak's visit to China in 1983, Egyptian Foreign Minister Kamal Hasan Ali replied candidly: "It is not aid, it is sales, and I think China is one of the countries that deal with Egypt with very reasonable prices and steady supply."[133] As openly viewed by Beijing, selling arms abroad was an ordinary practice in international relations.

During the Iran-Iraq war, China engaged in arms sales on a larger scale. China sold tanks, aircraft, field artillery, missiles, and large amounts of ammunition, and spare parts to Iraq. According to American reports, a quarter of Iraq's military purchases were said to have come from China and half of Chinese military sales were to Baghdad. It was assumed that Iraq was spending about $12 billion a year on foreign supplies for the war effort; hence the Chinese share would have been about $3 billion.[134] Iran was also receiving Chinese weapons through North Korea.[135] In 1983 alone China sold about $5 billion in arms to the Middle East. In addition to the arms aid to China's long-standing allies, North Korea and Pakistan, these sales represented the largest arms transfer ever undertaken by Beijing.[136] The foreign policy implications were obvious: China's arms sales to the Middle East added a new element to Beijing's relations with the two superpowers, especially the United States.

Chapter 7

Seeking Peace and Economic Development (I)

As adaptive behavior, foreign policy restructuring is reflected not only in the change of a country's foreign policy orientation, but also in the application of that new orientation to the country's specific foreign policy activities. Starting in the mid-1980s, the reformers in Beijing's leadership made great efforts to translate the new orientation of "independent foreign policy of peace" into all the aspects of China's foreign relations and activities. Departing from a single-dimensional foreign policy centered on the strategic-military factor against a principal enemy, China adopted an omni-directional foreign policy pursuing the goal of "peace and development" which placed economic modernization as the overriding priority of foreign relations.[1] At a meeting of Chinese ambassadors in 1985, the Party chief Hu Yaobang and Premier Zhao Ziyang emphasized the concept of "economic diplomacy," which they defined as the use of foreign relations to serve modernization. As a pro-Beijing newspaper in Hong Kong commented on the meeting, since foreign policy was "the extension of a country's domestic policy," Chinese foreign policy should therefore be placed in the service of China's "greatest national interest," which was now economic development.[2]

The economic emphasis had several implications for China's foreign policy. First, in the strategic/military aspect of China's foreign policy, Beijing had a strong desire for a tranquil and stable international environment so that China could concentrate on the task of modernization and reform. Second, in the economic/developmental aspect, China would accept (rather than reform) the current international system and play a cooperative role in it. China started to downplay the role of ideology and took pragmatic steps to expand economic ties with all potential trading partners. China eagerly sought to use foreign capital, technology, and expertise to speed up its modernization program and integrate itself into the world economy. Third, in the diplomatic/political aspect, China sought to reduce tensions and establish friendly relations with all countries, especially China's neighbors. Finally, by placing more stress on the reunification of Hong Kong, Macao, Taiwan with the mainland, on China's growing wealth and power, and on its independent role in international politics, China's foreign policy strongly emphasized nationalist feelings. In 1985, Hu Yaobang elaborated the details of China's new foreign policy as:

(1) Establishing and developing friendly ties with other countries on the basis of the Five Principles of Peaceful Coexistence; (2) Following an independent foreign policy in which China will never attach itself to, or foster strategic relations or an alliance with, any big power or bloc of powers; (3) Working with other nations in opposing hegemonism and protecting world peace; (4) Upholding the open policy. On the basis of equality and mutual benefit, China will boost economic and technological exchanges and co-operation with all countries--socialist, developing and developed alike; (5) Standing by other third world nations in sympathy and support; (6) Never seeking hegemony or succumbing to the pressure of hegemonism; (7) Emphasizing principles and acting in good faith in foreign affairs. Accordingly, China will never fraternize with, or turn its back on, any country for temporary gains or losses or because of different opinions. Nor will it play "cards" at the expense of its principles; and (8) Treasuring all friendly ties with foreign countries, although this does not mean China will relinquish its stand just for the sake of relationship; and even less will it allow anyone to hurt its national dignity.[3]

Restructuring China's Strategic/Military Posture

Beijing's foreign and defense policies have been largely based upon a careful analysis of the international balance of power affecting China. In the mid-1980s, China was even more confident about the international environment than ever before. The Chinese perceived that a strategic stalemate between the United States and the Soviet Union was likely to persist for some time. They argued that in the world only Washington and Moscow were capable of conducting a major war. But now neither of them could be confident of victory. As a result, the probability of a world war's occurring was very slim and there was no major immediate military threat to China's security. Such a secure situation presented Beijing with greater flexibility to seek an independent foreign policy . This assessment also had substantial influence upon Beijing's security thinking, upon its defense policy and upon the allocation of resources within China's economic modernization programs.

China's Security Confidence

The Chinese evaluations of the superpower relationship since the reelection of President Reagan in the United States and Gorbachev's coming to power in the Soviet Union seemed very optimistic. On the one hand, Beijing continued to believe that the core of the Soviet-American relations remained based upon a "fierce rivalry" and both of them would "struggle" to maintain their military strength.[4] The goal of the Strategic Defense Initiative (SDI) was seen as an attempt to achieve nuclear superiority over the Soviet Union by breaking the "balance of nuclear deterrence."[5] Gorbachev's *perestroika* was interpreted as the Soviet effort to catch up with the Western industrial states and to achieve a "balance of interests with the United States."[6] But on the other hand, the Chinese perceived that the inability of either superpower to break the nuclear stalemate and to attain nuclear superiority might compel each superpower to pursue "certain partial agreement" with the other.[7] Beijing noticed that both the United States and the Soviet Union were facing economic and financial difficulties forcing them to undertake reforms or readjustments. Both of them needed time to implement their long-term strategies. Gorbachev himself announced that he needed a period of peace to strengthen the Soviet economy. At first, the Chinese remained fearful that a success of Gorbachev's reform program and growing weakness in the American economy could result in a shift in the balance in Moscow's favor as early as the 1990s. But by early 1988, this fear was overcome by the developments inside the Soviet Union. They became more sober about the prospects for a Soviet economic resurgence in the short run.[8] As for Washington, Beijing saw that the Reagan Administration undertook a massive military build up and launched an ideological crusade against Moscow in the first half of the 1980s. In this regard, the United Stated succeeded in shifting the balance of power in its favor. But high levels of military spending exacerbated American economic difficulties and could no longer be sustained.[9] In judging the difficulties that the United States and the Soviet Union faced, Beijing concluded that under both internal and external pressures, a new escalation of arms race between the superpowers was unlikely in the second half of the 1980s. On the contrary, both Moscow and Washington were likely to enter a period of détente by avoiding new military confrontation, resuming serious efforts to achieve arms control agreements, and reducing regional conflicts.[10]

The general tenor of Chinese reaction to the 1987 Intermediate-range Nuclear Forces (INF) Treaty was supportive. According to the treaty, Washington and Moscow would eliminate all their intermediate-range and shorter-range missiles. To Beijing, the treaty was strong evidence that both superpowers, especially the Soviet Union, were suffering from arms-race fatigue and sought a way of reducing pressures. Clearly, Gorbachev was impelled toward further arms control negotiations as a means of assisting his reform programs and alleviating domestic economic pressures.[11] Gorbachev's "new thinking" was viewed by Beijing as a foreign policy restructuring ending the Brezhnev Doctrine. In November 1987, Gorbachev stated publicly for the first time that the "arrogance of omniscience," referring to the Brezhnev Doctrine, could no longer be accepted as a norm for Moscow's foreign relations. He pronounced that the principle of peaceful coexistence should be applied to international relations.[12] Détente and disarmament became the two main international goals of the new Soviet leadership. The concepts of global interdependence and a comprehensive world security system were matched, to a greater extent than most people had expected, by paying Soviet arrears in the United Nations, withdrawing Soviet troops from several hot spots, dismantling SS-20 missiles, and reducing Soviet naval activities in the Pacific. These dramatic changes in the Soviet foreign policy led to a notable relaxation of East-West and, more broadly, international tensions.

The Chinese definition of global reality then became even more optimistic. Beijing saw potential future East-West agreements on the elimination of battlefield nuclear weapons and the reduction of conventional forces. It was very confident that the easing of Soviet-American tensions constituted a long-term, strategic readjustment of the superpower relationship.[13] In Beijing's eyes, the new American-Soviet détente would not only benefit the two but would also undergird a broader global détente.[14] As noted by one Chinese article, "fundamental changes in the contents and forms of the competition and contention between the United States and the Soviet Union" would "probably become the starting point for a new and more stable postwar worldwide détente. "[15] China soon noticed that the impact of the new American-Soviet détente was spreading beyond the easing of East-West tensions and providing a stimulus to the resolution of third world conflicts. Regional hot spots would begin to cool down one after another.

This situation was, no doubt, beneficial to China's interest as the Asian-Pacific region would become stable and no longer pose any imminent threat to China. Confident about China's security and perceiving no need to align itself with one superpower against the other, Beijing reaffirmed its position that it would no longer enter into alliance or establish strategic relations with either Washington or Moscow. Instead, it would independently decide its policies on international issues.[16] Beijing stated that an nonalignment position meant that China would not do anything to "break the basic equilibrium of strength between [the superpowers]." By keeping its thumb off the scale, it aimed to "reduce the danger of war which might arise from a break of such an equilibrium. "[17] One Chinese article justified Beijing's independent foreign policy of peace by saying:

> China has realized that its strength cannot compare with that of the two superpowers, but it has a position of great importance in the world and can play a significant role in international affairs. So it should not depend on either of the superpowers. On the contrary, it should maintain its independence and keep the initiative in its own hands at all times, dealing with all international affairs according to their own relative conditions.[18]

New Security Thinking

While the Chinese perceived that their security environment would remain relatively stable for quite a while, they also contended that the global standing of both the United States and the Soviet Union was declining relative to other major powers, including Japan, China, and Western Europe. A number of articles were published in China on the ongoing changes from bipolarity to multipolarity in international relations. The Chinese argued that the bipolar structure had been eroded and the dispersion of economic, political, and military strength among new power centers would be the continuing trend toward a multipolar international system. As a result, more complex configurations of power would appear. Some articles even put forward that a quadrangle structure of power involving China, the United States, the Soviet Union and Japan had emerged in East Asia. They pointed out that the strategic triangle concept was exhausted and no longer captured the new complexities that China confronted. Responding to the new strategic setting, China should adapt to it in time and its foreign policy of the mid-1980s should become multifaceted accordingly.[19]

In the eyes of the Chinese leadership, one reason for the development of multipolarization in international relations was the increasing importance of scientific and technological developments in determining a nation's power. The Chinese argued that, in a new period of rapid technological change, all nations had to undertake reform and readjustment in the economic, political, military, social, and cultural life of their societies. In the course of this intense global competition, some countries would rise in importance, while others would fall. One Chinese said that "countries in the world are all aware that only by developing advanced science and technology and by introducing them into production as quickly as possible can they achieve superiority in aggregate strength and that this superiority will determine their places in the world in the next century."[20] The Chinese seemed to realize that the primary determinant of national power was not military might alone as had been the case in the 1970s. The concept of power should be broadened including a multitude of factors, such as economic, military, political, scientific, technological, and even cultural strength. This trend had already forced every country in the world to adapt to the direction of "overall national strength."[21] In this situation, China concluded that world peace would be a clear and continuing possibility in the foreseeable future because countries, one after another, were turning their attention to their own economic development.[22]

Under such circumstances, Beijing began to emphasize security in a broader sense, including domestic economic prosperity and thus sociopolitical stability as well as the survivability of the state in terms of external threats. The reform-minded leaders in Beijing argued that China's national interest would be well served when sustaining and taking advantage of the general relaxation of tensions in international relations and concentrating on domestic reform and development. Otherwise the economic and technological gap between China and advanced countries would be larger and that would be the real danger to China. Thus, "the acceleration of scientific and technological progress in China is a task which brooks no delay."[23]

Soon China's new security thinking emerged which stressed the notion that security was to be found in economic growth and general modernization as well as in military strength. Economic development was then considered the most reliable source of national strength. In Deng Xiaoping's words, economic modernization was "the basis for the solution to China's external and internal problems."[24] Beijing seemed to have understood that military power, unlike money power, was neither easily usable nor readily fungible. The traditional concept of military power as the main indicator of a nation's strength was now said to be diminishing and the traditional concept of national security obsolete.[25] Emphasis was placed more on overall national strength than on military power alone. In supporting this view, some Chinese argued that military overspending had stifled the political economy of the Soviet Union and actually diminished its power and prestige in world affairs.[26] Finally, Hu Yaobang said in mid-1986 that "we have come to the conclusion that the right thing for us to do is to concentrate on economic development and gradually improve the people's livelihood, and on that basis, to strengthen our defense capabilities step by step."[27]

Defense Reduction

The new security thinking and the optimistic interpretation of China's security environment led Beijing to believe that China was not faced with a major military threat. Beijing forecast that the country was unlikely to become embroiled in a major conflict by the end of this century, which would allow China to concentrate on domestic economic reform.[28] This projection permitted Beijing to restructure the military component of its security policy and focus on political strategies consonant with its view of the enduring trends of multipolarization and emphasis on economic and technological development.[29]

As a result, Deng Xiaoping and his associates decided to engage in major military cutbacks. Placing it as a crucial step in their reform programs, they argued that China's future military strategy and the size of the People's Liberation Army (PLA) should be proportional to the military threat and to the country's priorities. The reformers clearly understood that there was a close linkage between the economic development and the military. The role of the military was important in determining the extent, speed, and likelihood of success of the economic reform program because the military establishment in China had long occupied a central position in the country's economic set-up, both in its large share in the allocation of state resources--financial, industrial, technological, and human--and its massive economic organization with major assets and responsibilities. So a military reduction could substantially contribute to China's overall economy. For instance, the PLA had a relatively advanced technological base. Its organizational and command network could reach isolated and remote regions. Its infrastructural resources could also ease bottlenecks in the transportation sector. In short, the reduction could provide resources and assistance in areas of China's economy that were fundamental but inadequately developed.[30]

After two years of debate (1983-1985) within the Chinese leadership, the major reduction measures were finally decided upon at an enlarged session of the Party's Central Military Commission (CMC), chaired by Deng Xiaoping, in mid-1985.[31] At the meeting, the CMC's Secretary-General Yang Shangkun, Deng's associate in the PLA, announced that the military situation China faced in the 1980s was different from that in earlier decades. Based on a "scientific analysis of the current situation at home and abroad, and on a realistic assessment of our armed forces,"[32] the military should make a positive contribution to the country's economic development. For this purpose, the PLA needed extensive reorganization, a reduction of its size, and a conversion of large portions of the military-industrial complex into the civilian sector. Yang argued that the cuts were vital to the success of the nation's economic development program and promised that the cutback would strengthen national security in the long term. Expanding and improving the country's economic base in turn could support additional military spending and maintain a more sophisticated military posture. Military modernization could only be carried out following the attainment of a certain level of economic development, and a major reduction of the PLA would eventually speed arrival at this threshold. In this way, economic development was seen as integral and more fundamental to national defense than the military component.

Five specific reduction measures were taken. First, the principal emphasis was the reduction of the military's spending in the national economy (Table 1). During the 1980s, there was a steady and progressive decline in the defense budget. From 16.9 percent of the national budget in 1980, the army's share declined to 8.3 percent in 1989, representing an average seven percent annual drop in monetary terms. These figures, however, did not include appropriations for defense-related spending such as research and development (R&D), but they did indicate spending on weapons and administrative and maintenance costs. Considering the rapid growth rate of inflation during the same period, the retrenchment of military spending, was much bigger than the actual statistics. Defense modernization was now placed as the last priority in Deng's proclaimed "Four Modernizations," meaning that the military would suffer major contractions in the amount of resources allocated to it. This actually happened at the same time that the Chinese economy was experiencing significant rates of growth.

Table 1 Chinese Military Spending, 1980-1989
(In billions of U.S. dollars)

Year	Expenditure	Percent of GNP
1980	5.207	16.9
1981	4.518	15.5
1982	4.739	15.8
1983	4.758	14.5
1984	4.855	13.1
1985	5.145	11.9
1986	5.334	10.5
1987	5.492	8.30
1988	5.856	8.17
1989	6.758	8.34

Source: *White Paper on National Defense*, Ministry of
Defense (Taiwan).[33]

Second, in order to reduce military outlays, PLA Chief of Staff Yang Dezhi, a Deng appointee, said that it was necessary to "reform" and "further streamline" the armed forces and "reduce noncombatant personnel." One million soldiers out of the four-million-member PLA were demobilized. It represented a 25 percent cut in the number of the PLA.[34] Many units considered superfluous for the redefined operational functions of the PLA were cut. In one organization reform, several hundred thousand PLA security troops were reassigned to a civilian paramilitary force known as the People's Armed Militia. In a related move, the PLA Railway Corps was placed under civilian jurisdiction. The regional command structure of the PLA was also consolidated from eleven military regions into seven.[35] Indeed, large-scale reductions allowed widespread structural reforms in the dated and inefficient command system and paved the way for the much-needed technological modernization of the Chinese army. It not only reduced the bureaucracy and improved the military's professionalism, but also made more room for weapon modernization, which in turn strengthened the PLA's combat capabilities.

Third, significant portions of the defense industries were transferred to civilian-oriented functions. Premier Zhao Ziyang said in January 1986 that "China's defense industry is at a juncture at which it should and can make greater contributions to the country's four modernizations."[36] The conversion of defense output to serve civilian needs was far-reaching. Forty percent of the defense establishment's production was for the civilian market in 1985, and in some priority sectors, the ratios were even higher. The aircraft industry's production was 80 percent nonmilitary by 1990 and the civilian share of the nuclear industry's output was between 60 and 70 percent.[37] The output value of weapons produced by factories under the Ministry of Ordnance in 1986 dropped to 60 percent of 1985 values. Thousands of factories engaged in defense production were turned over to the manufacture of nonmilitary consumer goods such as motorcycles and electronic appliances.[38] The impact of the switchover was considerable as resources were reallocated to civilian priority sectors. The effort of transferring large portions of the military-industrial complex into the civilian or dual uses included large slices of the defense industries and major military infrastructural installations, such as military bases, airfields, railroads, and naval ports. All these transfers had consolidated the country's civilian communications, transportation and production of energy, machinery, and consumer goods.[39] In addition, in order to earn hard currency, a lot of defense industries were also turned into production for exporting arms.

Fourth, the most significant military reform was the substantial replacement of aging, conservative PLA veteran officers by younger and better-educated professionals. The Chinese military had long been the fortress of Maoist thinking. Many conservatives continued to believe in the Chinese military strategy as it had evolved during the 1930s and 1940s. Dissatisfied with the deviation from Mao's doctrine, many aging veterans who now staffed the upper reaches of the military hierarchy, were unmoved by the logic of reform. They complained about or even resisted the military cutbacks.[40]

In the face of their opposition, Deng bluntly criticized the PLA's senior officer corps as "undisciplined, arrogant, extravagant and lazy" and took the offensive. In December 1984, forty senior officers of the PLA general staff retired, representing the largest top-level "voluntary" group retirement in the army's history. Deng made it clear that he "hoped to see more open-minded people in the army."[41] He pushed on and restored insignias of rank which had been abolished at Mao's behest in 1965 on the eve of the Cultural Revolution. In 1985, it was announced that 47,000 officers, approximately 10 percent of the entire officer corps, would retire by the end of 1986. By 1990, 20,000-30,000 more officers would leave the PLA. Most demobilized officers were men who had joined the PLA during the anti-Japanese and civil wars of the 1930s and 1940s, and many of them had attained high rank in the PLA.[42] In consolidating the eleven military regions into seven, Deng pensioned off several superannuated regional commanders, including the hitherto "untouchable" generals. The *Xinhua* News Agency dispatch which announced the shakeup pointedly noted that "younger, better educated, and professionally more competent" officers were selected to succeed the retiring commanders.[43] The "readjustment" resulted in a full 50 percent reduction in the number of senior officers in the seven newly consolidated regional commands, and a 24 percent cut in the number of ranking officers at the PLA general staff headquarters and its political and logistics departments. At the Thirteenth Party Congress in November 1987, the military received the weakest representation on the Politburo (two out of eighteen) since the establishment of the PLA in 1927. In order to promote younger, more technically and professionally oriented officers, one month after the Congress, new commanders of the General Staff, Logistics, and Political Departments were appointed, who were on average, about twenty years younger than their predecessors.[44]

Finally, Chinese defense strategy was gradually shifting away from relying on sheer weight of numbers to emphasizing the need for more technological, mobile, three-dimensional, and machine-oriented posture.

This shift reflected China's changed threat perceptions. Strategic parity between the United States and the Soviet Union had created a situation in which increasing attention would be devoted to the probability of localized low-intensity conflicts, especially around the periphery of China.[45] Beijing was worried that these conflicts would flare up because individual countries would be more capable of determining their own courses of action without reference to the superpowers. So China's security interest would be served in defending sea-lanes, offshore resources, and contested islands and borders.[46] One article, reviewing major "local" wars over the past ten years (e.g., the Iran-Iraq War, and the Falklands War), concluded that the principal cause of these wars was territorial disputes. A proposal was made that the Chinese army should change its strategy "from fighting an overall war into that of mainly dealing with incidents which happen because of territorial issues, and fighting local wars."[47] Obviously, the new situation demanded the military forces to be significantly different from what the PLA currently possessed. The 1979 Sino-Vietnamese conflict vividly demonstrated the PLA's inability to conduct a limited war beyond its borders. In order to meet the new demand, the PLA began to focus on specific military readiness for limited wars. With limited resources allocated to the military, the PLA intended to become a more technologically advanced and mobile force, capable of responding quickly to localized challenges.[48]

One thing that China did not restructure much, however, was the qualitative improvement of its nuclear arsenal and the continuous development of its nuclear program. In 1986, Beijing pledged to cease above-ground nuclear tests, suggesting that China might have passed from the stage of atmospheric nuclear testing to a more advanced weapons testing and development stage. By the end of the 1980s, China had established a relatively complete nuclear weapon system including full-range intercontinental ballistic missiles (ICBM), sea-launched ballistic missile (SLBM), and strategic bombers.[49] In order to allay the fears generated in its neighbors by these developments, China adopted a minimum-deterrent posture, saying that such a minimum-deterrent strategy was characterized as "a strategy of limited self-defensive counterattack," a strategy designed to oppose and check, not to launch or win, any nuclear war. China promised its "no-first-use" policy while continuing its nuclear programs.[50]

Active Participation in International Peace Efforts

The primary purpose of Chinese foreign policy restructuring in the 1980s was to seek a stable international environment conducive both to China's domestic economic reform and its engagement in foreign economic exchange. Realizing that there was now only one interdependent and fragile world and China was an integral part of it, Beijing concluded that a full and constructive participation in world peace and development was a functional necessity, moral duty, and in its national interest.[51] Within this general pattern of policy, China began to play a more active role in international affairs in search of peace. On the one hand, Beijing stopped advocating armed struggle and people's war as the strategy for national liberation movements and revolutionary organizations in other countries. It publicly announced that revolution was not exportable.[52] On the other hand, China began to make active efforts fostering international peace and stability. The evolution of China's attitudes toward international organizations and toward arms control and disarmament issues in the 1980s boldly underlined the restructuring of China's policy in the military/strategic domain.

The most outstanding change was China's attitudes towards the United Nations in settling international conflicts. In the past, China only regarded the organization as a propaganda platform against the two superpowers. But in September 1985, Beijing made an overall reassessment of the United Nations. Praising the United Nations in unprecedented terms, Zhao Ziyang, the first Chinese Premier ever to address the United Nations General Assembly, said, "In world history it is rare for a political international organization to have such enduring vitality like that of the United Nations, whose universality and importance grow with the passage of time." "Despite twists and turns and its present weakness," he continued, "the United Nations is irreplaceable in the international mission it shoulders and the impact it exerts on the world."[53] Chinese Foreign Minister Wu Xueqian further elaborated, "We should affirm [the United Nations] active efforts to maintain peace, prevent and ease conflicts, accelerate decolonization, and promote international cooperation."[54] This rhetoric indicated a growing Chinese interest in the United Nations. As a permanent member of the Security Council and the spokesmen of the Third World, China wanted to play a more active role in the organization and pledged to take its responsibilities and obligations to contribute to maintaining world peace and promoting international cooperation.[55] In this context, Beijing started to introduce its "concrete contributions to world peace."[56] In the Security Council, China unexpectedly changed its stand on U.N. peace-keeping activities. In their first decade of the People's Republic representative with the United Nations, (1971-1981), the Chinese, on numerous occasions, had acted as outside observers, rather than full and responsible members. On the matter of U.N. peace-keeping, the Chinese had opposed the deployment of U.N. peace-keeping forces to conflict-ridden areas. They suspected the U.N. role and rejected their involvement in any U.N. peace-keeping. Beijing also did not participate in the votes on almost all the resolutions concerning peace-keeping operations.[57] This pattern was very consistent. For example, of the 21 votes on the periodic extension of the mandate of the United Nations Force in Cyprus (UNFICYP), China did not participate in 16, and abstained on five. China did not participate in the vote on the establishment of United Nations Emergency Force (UNEF II) to disengage the Israeli and Egyptian troops in the Sinai Peninsula on October 25, 1973, nor in any of the subsequent seven votes on the renewal of its mandate nor on the financing of UNEF II. The last instance of nonparticipation occurred on November 1981 on the extension of the mandate of the United Nations Disengagement Observer Force (UNDOF) to maintain and supervise the cease-fire agreement between Israeli and Syrian troops on the Golan Heights.[58]

The pattern changed dramatically on December 14, 1981. For the first time, China voted for the extension of UNFICYP. Beijing began to support the extension of the mandate of the United Nations Interim Force in Lebanon (UNIFIL) and the United Nations Disengagement Observer Force (UNDOF) and has done so ever since. In the General Assembly, the Chinese voted for 258 of the 262 resolutions related to the Middle East up to the end of 1989. By late 1985, the Chinese not only encouraged the United Nations to play an active role in settling international conflicts, but also stipulated that China could and should contribute its due share, actively, in these efforts. Consequently, Beijing started to pay its share of expenses for U.N. peace-keeping operations.[59] On October 15, 1984, Lian Yufan, China's deputy permanent representative, acknowledged, "In this most turbulent and volatile world, there is a universal demand for strengthening the peace-keeping capability of the United Nations. The United Nations Organization should not fail to meet such expectations."[60] The Chinese began to explore in late 1985 the possibility of sending a group to join U.N. peace-keeping forces in the Middle East. In June 1986, U.N. officials in New York confirmed that a Chinese delegation, which included two senior PLA officers and the deputy director of the Department of International Organizations in the Chinese Foreign Ministry, had made an inspection tour of the United Nations Truce Supervision Organization (UNTSO). It was later reported that Beijing would contribute 20 officers to the UNTSO observer force in Beirut known as Observation Group Lebanon (OGL). In September 1988, Ambassador Li Luye officially applied for China's membership in the United Nations Special Committee on Peace-Keeping Operations (also know as the Committee of 33). China, the only permanent member of the Security Council outside the committee, now called for making a greater contribution "to further enhance the efficiency of the United Nations peace-keeping operations."[61] China was immediately admitted as a full member to the United Nations Special Committee on Peace-Keeping Operations in that year, which laid the groundwork for a more active Chinese participation in these operations.[62]

On October 31, 1989, China's ambassador to the United Nations, Yu Mengjia, told the Special Political Committee of the General Assembly that China was "ready to join the international community in contributing to the greater success of the United Nations peace-keeping operations." He subsequently confirmed that 20 Chinese would go to Namibia to take part in peace-keeping operations under the United Nations Transitional Assistance Group (UNTAG) for the first time. China offered a contribution of five military observers to serve in UNTSO on November 15, 1989 and the offer was accepted. In 1988 and 1989 China voted for the formation of three U.N. groups: the United Nations Iran-Iraq Military Observer Group (UNIIMOG), the United Nations Good Offices Mission to Afghanistan and Pakistan (UNGOMAP), and the U.N Observer Group in Central America (UNOGICA).[63] In 1990, China joined the other four permanent members of the Security Council in sponsoring the U.N. framework to settle the Cambodian issue, the largest peace-keeping effort ever undertaken by the United Nations.[64] In April 1992, Beijing sent 47 military observers and 400 military engineers to join the U.N. transitional forces charged with keeping peace in Cambodia.[65]

In addition to its active participation in peace-keeping activities sponsored by the United Nations, China's position on arms control and disarmament issues was also restructured. It had progressively shifted over the years from initial nonparticipation to reluctant participation and then to active participation in global forums, especially in the Conference on Disarmament in Geneva. In the 1970s, China had criticized all the disarmament talks between the two superpowers and other talks such as the Conference on European Security and Co-operation. It refused to participate in various peace movements because China thought that they would have little effect on both the United States and the Soviet Union.[66] Not only that, the Chinese criticized the East-West arms control and disarmament efforts as Western appeasement at the expense of China's interest.

In the 1980s, however, China's attitude on arms control and disarmament issues underwent a positive change. It actively participated in the activities of the United Nations Disarmament Commission (UNDC). In the period of 1982-1987, China attended seven out of the eleven Conferences of the Committee on Disarmament in Geneva.[67] In order to seek peace and development, Beijing highlighted the dangers of the buildup of nuclear forces by the superpowers to international stability and called for renewed negotiations on banning weapons of mass destruction. It publicly expressed that superpower "dialogues are better than confrontations."[68] At the United Nations Conference on Disarmament in 1982 and the General Assembly the following year, Beijing claimed that the United States and the Soviet Union possessed the biggest nuclear arsenals in the world and they had the special responsibility to cut their nuclear weapons significantly first. China announced that if the superpowers cut their nuclear weapons by 50 percent, China would consider participation in international nuclear disarmament.[69] China obviously had little expectation that this proposal would be accepted, but its call served to focus critical attention exclusively on the superpowers in a way that would please the broad ranks of the international peace movement. This line of reasoning was almost certainly behind Premier Zhao Ziyang's support for the European peace movement during his trip to Europe in mid-1984.

Partly for propaganda purposes, Beijing publicized its own peace efforts. It pointed out that China had not set up military bases or stationed troops abroad. Moreover, it had cut military expenditure and demobilized one million servicemen. Many defense industries and installations had been converted into civilian-oriented functions. It repeated China's undertaking not to be the first to use nuclear weapons "under any circumstances," or to conduct atmospheric nuclear tests in the future. In addition, Beijing had been active in helping push through a convention based on the 1925 Geneva Protocol to comprehensively ban the development, production, stockpiling, acquisition, transfer, and use of chemical warfare agents, and stipulate the destruction of existing production facilities including dual-purpose plants.[70]

Beijing's public posture on the control and ultimate elimination of nuclear arms during the 1980s presented China as a constructive contributor to arms control and disarmament. Beijing was pleased by the 1987 Intermediate-Range Nuclear Forces (INF) Treaty and the Soviet pledge in 1982 to respect the principle of no-first-use in nuclear weapons. However, China was very careful about its own nuclear capabilities and attempted to balance between normative and geo-political concerns. For decades, Chinese leaders had given high priority to nuclear weapons development in order to help deter outside aggression and intimidation, to secure a strategic retaliatory capability, and to demonstrate China's international importance. Beijing had been refusing to sign the Nuclear Nonproliferation Treaty and regarded the treaty as discriminatory.[71] This position later was softened in 1991 as the French government announced its participation in the treaty that year. On December 29, 1991, China publicly pledged to join the treaty and on March 9, 1992, Chinese Foreign Minister handed over Beijing's Instrument of Accession to Treaty on the Non-Proliferation of Nuclear Weapons.[72] Besides, Beijing stressed that the two superpowers should take the lead in reducing nuclear weapons.[73] So before any of the "medium nuclear powers" (i.e., France, Britain, and China) enter negotiations for the elimination of nuclear weapons, the superpowers must drastically reduce armaments and agree to terminate testing and manufacturing nuclear arms. Along with the dramatic progress in nuclear arms reduction between the superpowers in the second half of the 1980s, China further raised the pledge for the superpowers to reduce their nuclear stockpiles. Chinese Foreign Minister made it clear in June 1988 that an agreement by the United States and the Soviet Union to reduce their strategic weapons by 50 percent did not fully meet Beijing's measure for a drastic reduction which should include all kinds of nuclear weapons, not just strategic forces.[74] Without further significant and verifiable reductions in the superpowers' nuclear arsenals, Beijing would continue its own strategic program.

On the issue of international terrorism, China changed its previous ambiguous attitude and explicitly condemned terrorist activities. The Chinese began to favor "the settlement of international disputes by peaceful means and on a fair and reasonable basis" and started to see that international terrorism preyed on innocent lives and was "cruel, inhuman, and extremely unpopular." "It not only terrorizes people in their daily life, damages normal international exchange but also brings in a destabilizing factor affecting international peace and security."[75] Zhao Ziyang unequivocally announced that "we oppose all forms of terrorism and the practice of using terrorism as a means in political struggle."[76]

Finally, Beijing participated in a wide range of international organizations and groupings during the 1980s. As a part of the efforts to pursue economic modernization, China entered a number of the specialized agencies of the United Nations system. Specifically, it joined the International Monetary Fund (1980) and World Bank (1980), the Multi-Fibre Arrangement (MFA, 1984), Asian Development Bank (1986), and applied to rejoin the General Agreement on Tariffs and Trade (GATT, 1986). In order to acquire credentials to pursue its development goals, Beijing was accepted as a full-fledged member by over 250 international science and technology organizations.[77] The acceptance not only gave the Chinese access to scientific and technical resources, but also provided recognition of Beijing as the sole government of China, a high-priority goal in Chinese leadership since 1949. For the purpose of obtaining advanced technology, Beijing joined the International Atomic Energy Agency in 1983. In addition, China became active in its participation in such international organizations as the United Nations Conference on Trade and Development, (UNCTAD), the United Nations International Children's Emergency Fund (UNICEF), the United Nations Educational, Scientific and Cultural Organization (UNESCO), and the World Health Organization (WHO) in the 1980s.

In the wake of China's participation in a multitude of functional multilateral conventions and regimes, Beijing started to place much emphasis on international law in its interaction with the rest of the world. In late 1986 China acceded to two U.N. conventions: the Convention on the Recognition and Enforcement of Foreign Arbitral Awards, and the Convention on Contracts for the International Sale of Goods. Following this, the Beijing government officially declared that the two treaties would now take precedence over its own economic contracts law and that Chinese courts would enforce foreign arbitral awards. Thus, a floodgate opened for international commercial arbitration cases in Chinese courts.[78]

Chinese Arms Sales

In the 1980s, Beijing's plunge into international arms trade was a contradictory and hidden side of China's peace posturing. Over 97 percent of China's exports went to the Third World, including North Korea, Pakistan, Thailand, Iran, Iraq, Egypt, Saudi Arabia, Algeria, Bangladesh, Sudan, Tanzania, Somalia, Zimbabwe, Sri Lanka, Libya, Syria, Nicaragua, Afghan guerrillas, and the anti-Vietnamese forces in Cambodia.[79] Evidence of Chinese arms could be seen in every region of the world. Having an "across-the-board" manufacturing capacity, China offered a variety of items in different degrees of sophistication to its clients. They included artillery, battle tanks, aircraft, naval ships, armored personnel carriers, various types of missiles, and an assortment of guns and ammunition.[80] On the whole, Chinese-made weapons had the advantage of being sturdy, relatively cheap, and easy to operate and maintain, making them a more attractive buy for many third world countries.[81] In the period between 1980 and 1987, China ranked fifth in the value of arms delivered to the Third World, behind only the Soviet Union, the United States, France, and the United Kingdom. Actually its deliveries ranked fourth in the period 1984 to 1987, overtaking the United Kingdom, and the percentage increase of its sales from 1980-1983 to 1984-1987 far exceeded that of the other frontrunners.[82] Between 1985 and 1989, the top ten buyers of Chinese made weapons included Iran, Pakistan, Saudi Arabia, Iraq, Egypt, Thailand, North Korea, Zimbabwe, Bangladesh and Sri Lanka.[83]

Chinese arms transfer agreements with the Third World between 1980 and 1987 amounted to nearly 11.1 billion U.S. dollars. Nearly $8.2 billion (i.e., 74 percent) was with Iraq and Iran. Among foreign providers, China's share of arms agreements with Iraq and Iran amounted to 13 percent, compared with the Soviets' 29 percent and Western Europe's 31 percent.[84] Iraq was Beijing's initial Persian Gulf customer in the first half of the 1980s. In the latter half of the decade, China shifted its arms sales emphasis to Iran. In 1988, China sold CSS-2 intermediate-range ballistic missiles (IRBMs) to Saudi Arabia, earning $3 billion for Beijing.[85]

The principal motive of China's arms sales to the Third World was to earn foreign exchange. With its last-place priority in China's four modernizations, Beijing's defense spending was shrinking steadily in the central budget during the 1980s (Table 1). The PLA faced cutbacks in procurements as well as in research and development (R&D). In order to offset budget limitations and continue to support defense modernization, the PLA not only demobilized one million servicemen and converted excess capacity to production of civilian goods which were then sold on domestic and foreign markets, but also sold arms overseas to earn hard currency. The arms sales were important because foreign exchange could allow China to purchase foreign military technology and equipment and to engage in research and development as well as production for its own defense. According to one source, 25 percent of the profit from arms sales abroad was used for PLA's own procurement of foreign advanced military equipment.[86] Evidently, selling arms abroad became an acceptable, relatively easy, and lucrative way to help finance China's defense modernization.

There was an open endorsement from Chinese leaders for international arms sales. Zhao Ziyang said in public at a weapons show that China would increase its arms sales.[87] Deng Xiaoping also allowed this other avenue for the PLA to help fund its modernization. A decree reportedly issued by Deng supported the idea that the military could buy Western advanced equipment as long as it gained foreign exchange to pay for it.[88] There was solid domestic support for selling arms abroad and little dispute in China as to the correctness of this policy. As a result, China speeded up its arms sales abroad and its defense industry turned a huge profit. The products were made by China's defense industries and were aggressively marketed and sold by trading corporations associated with them.[89] Following 1983 China hosted several ordnance exhibitions and participated in a number of international arms exhibition and air show overseas.

Through arms deals abroad, China not only earned much foreign exchange, but also purchased advanced foreign defense technology and obtained know-how abroad. For example, through the deal with Pakistan it is believed that Beijing obtained French Mirage jet fighters, American Sidewinder air-to-air missiles and TOW anti-tank missiles and American artillery technologies. American F-16 jets in Pakistan were reportedly examined by Chinese personnel. Both Egypt and Iraq permitted China to acquire relatively new versions of Soviet and Western equipment, such as Soviet-made MiG-23s and French-produced Exocet ship-to-ship and Magic air-to-air missiles with manuals of operation and maintenance included.[90] China also obtained assistance from Israel. Between 1976 and 1988 Israel was believed to have supplied China with an estimated $4 billion in arms and equipment.[91] All these efforts helped China's defense industry produce weapons of greater technological sophistication as a result of indigenous research and Western know-how. The lure of hard currency and know-how needed for China's defense modernization drew China deeper and deeper into the international arms market.

The second motive for China to engage in international arms sales was Beijing's political considerations, if any. Supporting North Korea, Pakistan, Thailand, Afghan guerrillas, and Cambodian resistance forces was aimed at consolidating Beijing's geo-strategic security concerns and countering threats along China's periphery. It could also enhance China's political influence in the region. To some extent, selling arms was the Chinese way to maintain its own initiative in foreign policy without relying heavily on any foreign country. Arms sales to the Middle East not only extended China's range of influence, but also raised China's prestige and "big power" status in that region. The CSS-2 sale to Riyadh also served as a catalyst to help establish diplomatic relations between the two countries in 1989 even when China faced international crisis after the Tiananmen Square events.

Chinese arms sales became an international issue in July 1987 when the U.S. navy began Persian Gulf escort operations for reflagged Kuwaiti oil tankers. The Americans found themselves threatened by the Silkworm antiship missiles China had sold to Iran.[92] Besides, in 1988 Washington worried that China's sale of the CSS-2 intermediate range ballistic missiles to Saudi Arabia would affect the military balance in the region. The CSS-2 missiles with a range of 1,700 to 2,200 miles, were "among the longest-range missiles ever exported from one nation to another."[93] Seeing that the Chinese arms sales policy was in conflict with U.S. interests, Washington severely criticized both the Silkworm and the IRBM sales as irresponsible and endangering the region's stability.[94]

Initially, Beijing denied that any such sales to Iran had ever taken place and criticized American escort operations in the Persian Gulf as "destabilizing."[95] When China ignored Washington's request to stop supplying Silkworm missiles to Iran, the United States decided to curb the export of some high-technology products to China and the Reagan administration showed Chinese officials photographs of Chinese weapons being loaded in China and unloaded in Iran.[96] It was not until September 1988 that China formally proclaimed its "three principles of arms sales:

China is a responsible country. We always assume a serious, prudent, and responsible attitude toward the military products export question. In this regard, we strictly adhere to three principles: First, our military products export should help strengthen the legitimate self-defense capability of the countries concerned; second, it should help safeguard and promote peace, security, and stability in the regions concerned; and third, we do not use the military sale to interfere in the internal affairs of other nations.[97]

In short, the preaching of pragmatism as the highest priority in China's modernization process had already made its mark on the Chinese arms sales policy. The Chinese sold arms to almost any customer with money on hand, and even adopted a double-dealing strategy vis-à-vis belligerent parties to a conflict to ensure arms sales as a way of earning foreign exchange and channels of input of military technology from abroad. Indeed, China became an arms salesman whose arms-sales patterns followed the logic of market demand forces. As commented on by one writer, "Dengist unprincipled pragmatism is rampant--it doesn't matter whether the cat is black or white (or whether the PLA is red or white), as long as it catches greenbacks."[98]

Restructuring China's Foreign Economic Relations

The reform of China's foreign economic relations was the most amazing part of China's foreign policy restructuring in the 1980s. China's pragmatic leadership led by Deng Xiaoping sharply altered national development strategy from self-reliance and autarky to emphasis on economic interdependence. Accordingly, China greatly expanded its participation in the world economy through increased international trade and financial activities. Beijing became more willing than ever to accept economic aid and direct foreign investments. With the dramatic increase of foreign trade, foreign investments and loans, and tourism, as well as the introduction of science and technology, and management methods from abroad, China made remarkable economic progress in the 1980s.

Opening to the Outside World

As a major part of the reform program, the policy of "opening to the outside world" (*duiwai kaifang*) represented a fundamental change of China's former suspicious rejection of the outside world and its decades of largely self-imposed autarky and ideological rigidity. Actually, it was "a wholesale rejection of the Maoist economic ideology."[99] The purpose of opening up was stated initially in the communiqué of the Third Session of the Eleventh Central Committee in December 1978:

> We are now...adopting a number of major new economic measures, on conscientiously transforming the system and methods on terms of equality and mutual benefit with other countries on the basis of self-reliance, striving to adopt the world's advanced technologies and equipment and greatly strengthening scientific and educational work to meet the needs of modernization.[100]

Since the 1960s, China had stuck to Mao's principle of "self-reliance" and refused to accept foreign investment, foreign aid, or foreign loans, except for short-term suppliers' credits, to finance their imports. After the Chinese reform-minded leaders had effectively taken control of the state in the early 1980s, the restructuring of China's economic strategy as well as its foreign economic policy began in earnest. Zhao Ziyang argued that "by linking our country with the world market, expanding foreign trade, importing advanced technology, utilizing capital, and entering into different forms of international economic and technological cooperation, we can enhance our capacity for self-reliant action."[101] Evidently, self-reliance was effectively reinterpreted to permit the use of foreign contribution to serve China's needs in meeting the ultimate goal of modernization. Accepting foreign assistance and the principle of self-reliance were then regarded as complementary rather than contradictory. Cloaked in the legitimizing rhetorical goals of "socialism with Chinese characteristics" and long-term self-reliance, the Chinese reform-minded leaders more and more accepted such concepts as supply, demand, savings, loans, investment, incentives, rewards, profits, efficiency, competition, productivity, the international division of labor, and comparative advantage.

Throughout the 1980s China, step by step, integrated itself into the world economy. Beijing largely restructured its foreign trade, banking, and financial systems to facilitate the open door policy. As a result, it not only substantially expanded its foreign trade and got access to more foreign markets, but also accepted all common practices of international economic transactions. For example, China began to welcome direct foreign investment and accepted aid, loans and credits from foreign governments, international organizations, and private banks. In order to attract foreign capital, to absorb advanced technology and managerial experience, and to expand Chinese exports to foreign markets, the Chinese government established four Special Economic Zones (SEZs) in 1980 in Southeast China where the local administration could enjoy special autonomous powers, foreign investors obtained preferential treatment, and more importantly, capitalism was allowed to be practiced.[102] These zones were supposed to attract foreign firms to bring in capital, technologies, management methods and even raw materials. Foreign investors could employ cheap local labor, and then sell goods produced in these zones overseas without having to pay the usual import and export duties and fees. Some other preferential treatment for foreign investors included tax-free privileges or lower rates for a certain period of time, land-use rights (e.g., the sale, transfer, lease, mortgage of real estate, etc.), no control of the flow of foreign exchanges, simplified visa procedures, and right to open financial institutions.[103] In this way, China hoped to encourage more foreign direct investment, absorb more modern technologies and management methods, and earn more foreign exchange.

In April 1984, following the initial success of SEZs, China designated fourteen more "open coastal cities" to foreign investment.[104] Another three "development zones" were set up in that year.[105] On April 13, 1988, Hainan Island, China's second largest island next to Taiwan, was changed into a new Special Economic Zone province.[106]

Initially the major type of foreign investment was primarily in the form of joint ventures. In this arrangement both foreign and domestic investment were involved. The ratio of investment was deliberately fixed at 49:51 to symbolize that control of the venture was in China's hands. But it seemed unrealistic to introduce more foreign technology, especially foreign management in practice. As time went by, the ratio became flexible, depending on specific projects. Later, in order to attract more foreign investors, the government encouraged the establishment of wholly foreign-funded or owned enterprises in China.

Foreign banks were also allowed to open their branch offices in China. On February 6, 1988, China officially adopted Zhao Ziyang's Coastal Development Strategy which attempted to link the coastal areas with the global market place and to promote export-oriented economic development by developing labor-intensive industries. This strategy focused on importing more raw materials and export more products on the world market. In doing so, China could attract more foreign investment, increase foreign trade, earn more foreign exchange, and reduce domestic investment pressure for raw materials.[107] The introduction of this innovative strategy was described as vital to China's economic reform. Zhao himself claimed that this strategy would enable China to achieve rapid economic development.[108]

Policy Basis

The policy of "opening to the outside world" was based on the assumption that China would not be able to modernize rapidly and effectively unless it expanded economic relations with the outside world. The Chinese reformist leaders began to see that "the present world is an open world, in which economies of all countries are more and more closely interrelated and interdependent."[109] They realized that an autarkic development strategy could only prevent China from absorbing the advanced experience and modern technology of other countries, and that an isolated China would remain relatively poor and weak. In this regard, they acknowledged that China's relative autarky in the 1960s, when most of the other East Asian countries were enjoying rapid economic growth, caused Beijing to lag further behind its neighbors. As pointed out by Deng Xiaoping, "Isolation landed China in poverty, backwardness, and ignorance. No country can now develop by closing its door."[110] In October 1984 he argued that the "open policy" was essential if China was to overcome 300 years of "impoverishment, backwardness and ignorance" caused by its self-imposed isolation from the outside world.[111] In an article entitled "Why China Has Opened its Door," Deng emphasized that China was at a turning point in its history and had to learn to use the "favorable international climate" to accelerate the advance toward the Four Modernizations. He declared that "China has now adopted a policy of opening its doors to the world in a spirit of international cooperation.... To accelerate China's modernization we must not only make use of other countries' experience. We must also avail ourselves of foreign funding."[112] Following this line of reasoning, Beijing placed increased emphasis on the benefits to be derived from active participation in the international economy, such as lower costs of production, greater economic efficiency, and technological advances.

However, Deng's open door policy was not without its opponents. Old fears and humiliations died hard. Some Chinese felt that the special economic zones and the granting of "preferential treatment" to foreign investors were too reminiscent of the special privileges that foreign powers had forced China to grant them in the nineteenth century. They insisted that their country should not become unduly penetrated by foreign interests. Others nervously viewed numerous effects of Western influence in China on business, education, science, culture, entertainment, dress and so on. They vigorously argued that an infusion of Western ideas, such as individualism, consumerism, political pluralism and human rights, would endanger China's political stability, social order, and cultural integrity. During the 1980s, there were at least four political campaigns aimed at reducing or eliminating the "spiritual pollution" and "bourgeois liberalization" generated by foreign life-styles and political and moral concepts. Still others feared that if the Chinese economy were fully opened to the outside world, domestic firms would be unable to compete effectively with foreign imports, Chinese consumers would demand expensive foreign products, and China's economy would become dependent upon foreign countries. Using this rhetoric, they called for continued restrictions on the import of foreign products. Since the reform of China's foreign economic policy began in 1978, disputes often occurred within the Chinese leadership when Beijing faced the balance of payments deficit, the excessive import of foreign consumer goods, the sharp fall of Chinese foreign exchange reserves, and other related difficulties.[113]

In the face of a mounting criticism over the experiments of special economic zones and open coastal cities, Deng Xiaoping made a strong public defense of "open policy" and reassured nervous foreign investors: "To open to the world is a fundamental policy for China." He asserted that "[if] there is to be any change in the policy, it will be that China's doors will be opened even wider."[114] As a compromise, the reform-minded leaders promised to use the power of the state to regulate their country's cultural and economic relations with the rest of the world. They claimed that, as a large country with a strong national government, China, while avoiding the costs, had the ability to secure the gains of international involvement. They argued that the situation was completely different from that during the Qing Dynasty which had been forced to open its door to foreigners a century before. China could now use its own power to avoid dependence on any single supplier, to press to gain access to new markets, to keep its national market from foreign goods that would harm domestic industries, to control the level of national indebtedness, and to insist that all foreign investment projects carry advanced technology or some other obvious benefit for China. Similarly, Beijing could protect China from cultural contamination by maintaining substantial control over who could go abroad, who might come to China, and what forms cultural and educational exchange should take. In their own words, China could place a screen across the passageway to admit the technology it wanted and the capital that it needed while excluding the ideas and influences it feared.[115] It seemed to the reform-minded leaders that the details of "open policy" could vary, but the policy itself was not negotiable.

In this regard, Chinese leaders have long been facing a dilemma in the country's development. On the one hand, China could not be modernized and become strong without openness to the outside world. China desperately needed Western technology, scientific knowledge, capital, and markets. On the other hand, Chinese leaders were terrified by Western cultural influences and political ideas such as individual liberty and democracy. Thus, they attempted to avoid Western ideological influence while importing Western science and technology. In reality, it was not possible to fully prevent foreign influence, especially in terms of unorthodox ideas, from penetrating the Chinese society. In fact, lots of foreign advanced technologies themselves were based on Western thinking. In the 1980s, along with rapid economic progress, plenty of foreign things did arrive in China with tremendous impact on the minds of the Chinese people, especially the youth. This was an unavoidable consequence of the open door policy which Deng did not like to see. Eventually, this development contributed to challenging the Communist rule, as shown in Tiananmen Square in June 1989. In a general sense, the balance between foreign factors in China's economic modernization and the challenges they have posed for the Communist rule would continue to be an unsettled question not only for the current Chinese leaders but also for the next generation of the Beijing leadership.

Economic Progress through Opening Up

In the 1980s, China, under Deng's open door policy, achieved remarkable progress in economic development and surprised the world. One American scholar commented on this by saying:

> K-Mart, Sears, and most other U.S. department stores sell Chinese clothing, by now finely cut at a cheap price; Nike and Voit make athletic equipment in China for export; Honeywell and Hewlett-Packard have helped with small computers for China's textile industries; new world-class hotels, with foreign restaurants served by Chinese women in sleek slit skirts, seem to sprout like mushrooms after a rain. American Motors produces Jeeps in a joint venture; R.J. Reynolds produces cigarettes; and U.S. buyers of screws and nuts are trooping to China.[116]

This picture represented only a tip of the iceberg. Apart from American firms, China attracted a large number of foreign investments from Hong Kong, Japan, Taiwan, South Korea, and Western European countries as well. Consequently, the average annual growth rate of China's Gross National Product (GNP) between 1979 and 1988 was 9.6 and the average growth rate of national income was 9.2. In 1989, China ranked number eight in the world in GNP.[117]

One of the most impressive achievements of the open door policy was the expansion of China's foreign trade. Before 1978, foreign trade and foreign exchange were monopolized by the state. Self-reliance was the guiding principle. Too much international trade was seen as a form of economic reliance resulting in a loss of political independence.[118] In carrying out the open door policy, China realized that there were mutual gains from trade. In the 1980s, Beijing liberalized some restrictions and decentralized the foreign trade system.[119] With these reforms, China's foreign trade in total rose dramatically after the adoption of the open door policy. Total foreign trade increased 5.4 times from $20.64 billion in 1978 to $111.6 billion in 1989, with an average annual increase of 16.6 percent.[120] In 1978, foreign trade accounted for less than 10 percent of China's GNP. But in 1989 it rose to over one-quarter of GNP, indicating much greater openness of the Chinese economy to the international economy.[121] In fact, by the end of the 1980s, China became the fifteenth-largest trading country in the world. Even after the June 4 events, China's foreign trade continued to expand. Its total foreign trade reached $115.41 billion in 1990 and $ 135.7 billion in 1991.[122] The high rate of expansion in foreign economic relations had a big effect on China's overall economy and on the pattern and direction of Chinese trade. The composition of exports changed in the direction of manufactured goods, especially light industry. Manufactured goods accounted for 46.4 percent and raw materials for 53.6 percent of the total value of exports in 1979. By 1988, manufactured goods accounted for 68.7 percent and raw materials for 31.3 percent of the value of Chinese exports. China vigorously developed labor-intensive industries and increased production of labor-intensive products. The rapid improvement in the structure of Chinese exports reflected both the progress made by the Chinese economy and the success of economic cooperation with foreign investors. In 1988, exports of textiles and clothing earned 27.4 percent of China's total foreign exchange earnings, or $13 billion.[123] Exports of toys in 1988 accounted for about four percent of the annual world market.[124] Imports, to a considerable extent, were from the industrialized countries and concentrated on machinery and equipment; and semi-finished goods. In summary, China's major two-way trade partners in the 1980s were Japan, the United States, countries in the European Community, the Soviet Union, ASEAN countries and Taiwan. To a great extent, Hong Kong served as a transfer point in the trade between China and the rest of the world.[125]

There were, however, problems in China's balance of trade. For example, the most dramatic deterioration in the balance was in the period between 1982 and 1985 when China's trade surplus of $3 billion in 1982 became a deficit of $15 billion in 1985.[126] Trade surplus was regained only after 1990 when China expanded its exports.[127]

Opening China up to foreign direct investment in the 1980s was another restructuring of Beijing's foreign economic relations under Deng's open door policy. The scale of utilization of foreign capital expanded rapidly during this period. By the end of 1988, some 16,325 contracts (370 loan agreements and 15,955 contracts), involving total foreign capital of $79.17 billion, were signed. Of this total, $47.34 billion, or 59.8 percent were actually invested (Table 2).

The total number of ventures undertaken was a little over 10,000 at the end of 1987, with 2,200 of them finalized in that year alone. In 1988 there was a sharp increase of 5,890 ventures for a total of 15,955. Of these, 8,532 were Sino-foreign joint ventures, 6,778 cooperative enterprises and 594 exclusively foreign-funded business. Nearly 6,000 of them started operation, with 85 percent of these generating sound economic returns. Most foreign-funded enterprises performed strongly. In 1988 some 2,600 foreign-funded enterprises exported goods worth $1.7 billion. In general, most of them were small or medium-sized, with an average investment of about $1.6 million. Besides, co-operative development contracts included the joint exploration and exploitation of China's offshore oilfields. By 1988, 51 such contracts had been approved with a total value of $2.93 billion in investment.[128] On the whole, Hong Kong and Macao were by far the largest investors, followed by Japan, the United States, and about forty other countries.[129] In addition, Taiwan significantly increased its direct investment on the mainland starting in late 1989. To a certain extent, the rise of investment from Taiwan offset China's loss of the Western investment caused by the Tiananmen Square Incident in June 1989.[130]

Table 2   Composition of Foreign Investment in China, 1979-1988 (In billions of U.S. dollars)

	Amount Contracted	Amount Utilized	Percent Spent
Foreign Loans (370 Agreements)	46.99	33.12	70.5
Direct Foreign Investment (15,955 Contracts)	28.20	11.56	41.0
-Equity Joint Ventures (8,532 Contracts)	9.89	4.81	48.6
-Contract Joint Ventures (6.778 Contracts)	13.86	3.97	28.6
-Wholly Foreign-owned (594 Contracts)	1.52	0.29	19.1
-Co-operative Development (51 Contracts)	2.93	2.49	84.9
Compensatory Trade and Assembling Operations	3.98	2.69	67.6
Total	79.17	47.34	59.8

Source: The State Statistics Bureau (China).[131]

In restructuring China's investment policy, the Chinese not only invited foreigners to invest in China, but they themselves also ventured forth. According to one study in 1990, China had invested over $2 billion abroad. About half the investment was in Hong Kong, making China one of the largest, if not the largest, investors in the territory. The remaining investments were scattered over 100 countries, including the United States, Britain, and Australia.[132] The Chinese invested in banking, real estate, ore mines, manufacturing and other projects. The China International Trust and Investment Corporation, the leading Chinese investor abroad, invested its capital in forest land and computer firms in the United States and in an aluminum smelter in Australia. In the period of 1979-1988, 553 non-trade enterprises invested in by the Chinese were set up abroad.[133] Profit and experience were two objectives of these projects. One Chinese official said that "we've been using foreign money to earn foreign money."[134] In addition, China sent contract workers to foreign countries. From its modest beginning in the Arabian Peninsula, China's overseas construction business expanded to such countries as Jordan, Kuwait, Egypt, and Iraq. In Iraq alone, China won 84 construction contracts between 1981 and 1984.[135] China collaborated in third country projects with France, Brazil and South Korea. From 1979 to 1988, China signed 6,750 contracts worth $10.1 billion for projects and labor services overseas. Some 300,000 Chinese workers were sent abroad, mainly in the Middle East, Africa and Asia, earning $5.7 billion in foreign exchange. In 1988, China also sent workers to Guam, the Soviet Union and Eastern Europe.[136]

Another amazing aspect of the restructuring of Beijing's foreign economic policy was that China started to accept a large amount of foreign financial help. It was a natural consequence as China increasingly integrated itself into the world economy. In fact, external funds became more important in the process of capital formation for China. China's foreign debt increased from $4.5 billion in 1980 to $41.1 billion in 1989, a nine-fold increase in just nine years.[137] In 1980 total foreign debt accounted for 1.6 percent and in 1988 for approximately 10.5 percent of GNP. Until 1982 all debt had been medium and long term. Then short-term borrowing (i.e., debt repayment under one year) took off. In 1984 the amount more than doubled, reaching $5.6 billion, nearly 50 percent of China's total debt. Since then the share of short-term debt had been reduced to about a quarter of the total debt outstanding. In 1980 some 90 percent of China's medium- and long-term loans came from private creditors (nearly 75 percent of the total from financial markets), while only 10 percent came from foreign governments. By 1988 medium- and long-term debt had been growing at an average annual rate of 27 percent, and amounted to $23.7 billion. About 60 percent came from private creditors (of which nearly 90 percent from financial markets) and 40 percent from official creditors (e.g., international organizations and governments).[138] To a certain extent, this reflected the progress of China's relations with international economic organizations.

As a part of the restructuring of China's foreign economic relations, Beijing participated in major international economic organizations. It joined the International Monetary Fund (IMF) in April 1980 and the World Bank and its affiliated agencies in May 1980. In March 1986, China was admitted to the Asian Development Bank. After it was granted observer status to the General Agreement on Tariffs and Trade (GATT) in 1983, Beijing officially applied for full GATT membership in July 1986. By joining these international economic institutions, China obtained many benefits. First, it could get access to a huge pool of lending capital on which to draw to cope with temporary adverse monetary and trade imbalances and to finance a large array of essential but costly and initially unprofitable infrastructure projects. Second, memberships in these organizations enabled China to draw upon valuable foreign professional economic expertise to analyze in depth the strengths and weaknesses of the Chinese economy, jointly draft a long-range development blue print, and provide broad and diversified training for Chinese technocratic personnel. Third, these organizations provided a valuable economic negotiating framework within which China could communicate and bargain to its best advantage with other countries. Finally, Beijing's participation and commitment conferred legitimacy on China's modernization program and economic reform. It would greatly help raise international business, banker, and investor confidence and expand foreign investment and trade arrangements for China's economic development.[139]

In opening up, China's tourist industry also developed rapidly in the 1980s. In 1988 alone, China received 31.69 million tourists from 168 countries and regions, earning $2.22 billion foreign exchange. The number of visits was 5.6 times as many as that in 1980. The tourist industry was greatly hurt by the 1989 Tiananmen Square events. But starting in 1990, there was a big recovery with 27.46 million foreign tourist visiting China. In 1991, China earned $2.84 billion from the tourist industry.[140]

Last but not least in China's open door policy, Beijing dispatched unprecedented numbers of Chinese students and scholars for training and research abroad. It was an important channel for China to acquire advanced science and technology. According to official figures in the period between 1978 and 1989, China sent some 60,000 students to study abroad, plus another 10,000 management and technical personnel.[141] In June 1989, about 40,000 Chinese students and scholars were studying in the United States alone. In the first half of the decade, most of the Chinese students were sponsored by the Chinese government. Only a small number of Chinese students took up their studies with private support from relatives overseas or from foreign universities. In addition, many students originally funded by the Chinese government subsequently obtained fellowships from foreign sources after their first year abroad. In the second half of the 1980s, most Chinese students were self-sponsored.[142]

All in all, China had become much integrated into the world economy in the 1980s as it adopted the open door policy. Each year China engaged in international trade worth billions of dollars, attracted a huge amount of foreign investment, and received both official and private financial assistance. The foreign presence in China was found in many quarters, such as new international hotels, advertisements on Chinese television, foreign tourists, offices and shop floors of the new joint ventures, wholly foreign-owned enterprises, and foreign teachers and experts in Chinese schools and research institutions. Besides, many Chinese went abroad to study or work. They were either officers in international organizations, or students and scholars in foreign universities, or workers on foreign construction projects. Through their contacts, the Chinese gained not only access to the most advanced knowledge and technology, but also experience in negotiating with major banks and corporations. All these activities were hardly seen in China in the 1970s. Through opening up, China did make amazing economic progress in the 1980s in contrast with economic disasters in other Communist countries during the same period. Even after the Tiananmen Square events in June 1989, China continued to accelerate its economic opening up and dramatically expanded its exports to the world market. It is true that the Chinese economy cannot grow and even China's Communist rule can hardly survive unless China is tied to the global economy. This perception has been shared by the majority of the Chinese leaders and the reform policy has a broad public support. As China continued to benefit from the open door policy and further developed its economy, it would be highly unlikely for the Beijing government to turn back the clock on reform and close its door.

Chapter 8

Seeking Peace and Economic Development (II)

Restructuring Relations with Key Countries

Its application of the "independent foreign policy of peace" to China's major foreign relations was an indispensable part of Beijing's foreign policy restructuring during the 1980s. In order to adapt to changed conditions at home and abroad, Beijing used all diplomatic means available to soften international tensions for the purpose of creating an international environment favorable to China's domestic economic reform. Chinese Premier Zhao Ziyang pointed out in 1985 that, to China, striving for lasting peace, developing international cooperation and promoting joint prosperity were the sole reasonable choices in our age.[1] The Chinese government took pragmatic steps to improve relations with all countries, regardless of their different political, social, and economic systems. In the 1980s, Beijing successfully improved relations with all its major external contacts.

Toward Mature and Multi-dimensional Relations with the U.S.

The underlying theme of Sino-American relations since the mid-1980s was how to consolidate a new basis for stable, long-term ties to replace the eroding strategic rationale (i.e., the shared need to contain the Soviet Union) which was central to their relationship from 1972 to 1982. In this process, both Beijing and Washington were working hard to seek a much sounder basis on which to continue to construct their bilateral relations. Both China and the United States began to devote more attention to such bilateral issues as economic relations, technology transfers, Taiwan, and to regional questions in East Asia. After years of efforts by both sides, progress was made in almost every sphere of the Sino-American relationship despite the occurrence of disagreements and disputes between the two countries. Both of them recognized that a workable relationship between them was in their respective national interests and carefully managed their relations to the extent that friction in any one area of their bilateral relations was less likely to jeopardize the entire relationship. Besides, the two countries had learned to absorb disagreements and conflicts in one way or another by working together. Although such experience did not completely eliminate misunderstandings or clashes of interest, it did provide institutionalized channels for resolving differences through communication and compromise.[2]

Generally speaking, Sino-American relations involved four basic areas: international security policy, economic relations, cultural ties, and social and political values. In the area of security policy, China made it clear in the second half of the 1980s that it would never "attach itself to either superpower or enter into alliance or strategic relations with either."[3] While claiming an independent stance, the Chinese, in reality, continued to follow an asymmetric policy toward the superpowers, favoring the United States. The Soviet threat was seen as declining because the Soviets were preoccupied with their internal problems. Strategic cooperation with the United States against the Soviets thus receded in importance. But in Beijing's eyes, relations with the United States still played the most important part in China's foreign policy. Not only did the U.S. presence in the Asian-Pacific region directly affect the international balance of power there, but also the two countries still shared many common interests in maintaining stability and promoting prosperity in the region. Besides, the advantages that China's modernization program received from the United States exceeded what China had received from other countries. To a certain degree, positive U.S. support for China's economic reform influenced the attitudes of other Western nations. So at a Politburo meeting in late 1988, Beijing decided to keep relations with the United States "one step ahead" of its ties with Moscow.[4] Despite the persistence of several problems in Sino-U.S. relations (e.g., Taiwan, difficulties regarding access to the American market, limits on technology transfers, congressional complaints about human rights violation in China, Chinese criticisms of U.S. policies elsewhere in the world, and U.S. concern over the possible destabilizing consequences of Chinese arms sales in the Middle East) in the second half of 1980s, the Chinese quietly valued the important relations with the United States and said that "Sino-U.S. relations are gaining more pull in the international arena as the Asian-Pacific area is beginning to have more importance in the world affairs."[5]

At the same time, Washington also reiterated the importance of its relations with Beijing following the decline of the Soviet military threat. As U.S. Undersecretary of State for Political Affairs Michael Armacost said, "the geopolitical dimensions of our relations with China--though more muted and nuanced than in the past--remain important."[6] To the United States, China, as a big country, would continue to wield its long-term influence over Asia. Washington could not disregard China's position and influence on issues affecting U.S. interests such as arms sales, proliferation of nuclear technology and cooperation in the settlement of regional conflicts. In February 1990, U.S. Deputy Secretary of State Lawrence S. Eagleburger in testimony before Congress said that a modernizing China at peace with itself and its neighbors was "critical to stability in Asia."[7]

As the two countries were refocusing their relationship under the new circumstances, they continued official consultation on such security matters as the Korean peninsula, Indochina, Afghanistan and the Soviet Union. There were frequent exchange visits of top-level officials to discuss both bilateral, regional and global issues. Through these contacts, they effectively improved mutual understanding and coordinated the two countries' policies in dealing with the international issues in which they shared common interests.[8] Moreover, the exchange visits also underscored the relative normalcy of the Sino-U.S. relationship. President Bush's visit to Beijing in February 1989 was such an example indicating endorsement of the continued importance of the Beijing-Washington connection. It was particularly true in view of the fact that his visit was made on the eve of Gorbachev's historic visit to Beijing.

In this sense, even though China claimed not to align with any big power, it did not mean that China would not have common interests with Washington. Even under an independent foreign policy, limited forms of military cooperation continued between the United States and China. The working relations between the Chinese and U.S. military establishments progressed considerably since the early 1980s. There was a well-known "three pillars" approach taken by both sides in pursuit of an enduring military relationship: high-level visits, functional-level exchanges, and military technology cooperation. Defense Secretary Caspar Weinberger visited Beijing for the second time in three years in the fall of 1986. His successor Frank Carlucci made the same trip in September 1988. Yang Shangkun, Permanent General Secretary of the Chinese Central Military Commission (CMC), visited the United States in May 1987. Working-level functional groups in several areas of military technology continued to exchange information. The monitoring installation erected by the United States in western China in 1980 for the purpose of intelligence gathering with reference to Soviet nuclear tests remained in operation for years.[9] Small numbers of PLA personnel received training at American military facilities, while U.S. military and civilian defense specialists were given access to Chinese military bases and defense production facilities. In November 1986, American Navy ships paid a port call at Qingdao in China, the first such visit since 1949.[10] The U.S. Air Force (USAF) Thunderbirds demonstration team visited Beijing in 1987. The first port call by a Chinese warship to Pearl Harbor was also made in April 1989. The highlight of Sino-American military relations was American arms sales to China. Since 1986, Washington licensed munitions technology and avionics equipment for sale to China, including $22 million large-caliber artillery plant modernization program, the $8 million MK 46 Mod 2 torpedo sale, the $62 million AN/TPQ-37 artillery-locating radar sale, and the $500 million F-8 interceptor avionics modernization program (in order to give it all-weather and night-fighting capabilities).[11]

In this connection, U.S. export controls, designed to curb the flow of sensitive technology to Communist countries, became a point of contention in U.S.-Chinese relations. In response to Chinese complaints, Washington gradually liberalized certain restrictions on transfer of technology to China and treated Beijing differently from other Communist countries. Consequently China imported a substantial amount of technology (some of which had military implications), industrial equipment, and selected weapon systems from the United States. By the late 1980s only a small number of product categories on the cutting edge of technology remained restricted or required individual approval for export licenses.[12]

Of course, significant Sino-U.S. discord arose out of Chinese arms sales to the Middle East. As the dominant external power in the Middle East, the United States was dismayed at China's Silkworm missile sales to Iran. In October 1987 the State Department announced the decision to suspend additional liberalization of high technology transfers to China because of Chinese arms sales to Iran. In managing their relations, Washington and Beijing held a series of consultations through diplomatic channels. Finally, the State Department lifted the freeze on liberalization of high technology exports to China in March 1988 and

Reagan administration officials said China had given clear assurances that it would take steps to stop delivery of Silkworms to Iran.[13]

While Beijing was circumspect about strategic cooperation with Washington, it was fully enthusiastic about economic relations. The Chinese viewed the United States as a key outside factor in its economic modernization because of its potential role as a major trading partner and as a source of high technology, investment capital, and managerial skills for China. In restructuring its relations with Washington, Beijing attempted to make economic cooperation a new cornerstone of Sino-American relations.

As early as 1980, U.S. Congress ratified an extension of most-favored-nation (MFN) trade status to China. Since then trade turnover between the two countries expanded rapidly. Two-way trade was $2.3 billion in 1979 and $4.8 billion in 1980. In 1985, the figure rose to $7.7 billion. By 1988 the United States became China's fourth largest trade partner, after Hong Kong, Japan and the European Community.[14] According to U.S. statistics, the volume of Sino-American trade exceeded $10 billion for the first time in 1987, a 25 percent increase over the previous year. In 1989, China became America's tenth-largest trading partner. The volume of Sino-U.S. trade reached the $20 billion mark in 1990 and $25.3 billion in 1991.[15]

Through joint ventures and investment, U.S. companies were transcending the limits of purely trading relations and becoming more deeply immersed in the Chinese economy. By 1988, U.S. corporate giants such as IBM, Chrysler, Boeing, and Occidental Petroleum, along with literally hundreds of smaller firms, had made investment commitments in China totaling some $3.1 billion in nearly 400 joint ventures. The largest joint venture between the United States and China was the $650 million Antaibao opencast coal mine which went into operation in September 1987.[16] Besides, the world's largest Kentucky Fried Chicken outlet was established as a joint-venture in Beijing in November 1987. From chewing gum to automobiles, baby food to airplane parts, American investors discerned significant opportunities in China. In 1988, the United States ranked number two (after Hong Kong but before Japan) on the list of foreign investors in China.[17]

Certainly, there were many problems in Sino-U.S. commercial relations. Chinese exports to the United States ballooned since 1987. This created a trade imbalance in China's favor (i.e., $3.4 billion in 1987, $3.5 billion in 1988, $6.2 billion in 1989, $10.4 in 1990, and $12.7 billion in 1991).[18] The American side complained about China's unfair trade practices, such as dumping, prisoner-made products, and protectionist measures against importing durable consumer goods from the United States. On the one hand, Americans urged China to open its door wider; on the other hand, they made efforts to limit Chinese imports; this elicited firm complaints from Beijing. In addition to complaining about U.S. export restrictions on high technology goods, Chinese officials in the second half of the 1980s, frequently voiced alarm about increasing U.S. protectionist sentiment expressed in congressional attempts to curb imports from China. Textile negotiations remained hard and protracted between the two countries. Even so, commercial relations between China and the United States expanded to an unprecedented scale in the 1980s, and especially in the late 1980s.

Cultural ties between the two countries also developed rapidly in the 1980s. Under numerous official and quasi-official protocols and agreements, thousands of institutional and individual exchanges were conducted. Cooperative research and training in scientific and technological fields flourished under the umbrella of more than thirty governmental scientific and technological protocols. The influx of Chinese students onto hundreds of American college and university campuses was perhaps the most dramatic development in Sino-American exchanges in the 1980s. According to statistics released for the protection of Chinese students studying in the United States in the wake of the Tiananmen Square Incident in June 1989, there were over 40,000 such persons.[19] Meanwhile, American culture was also appreciated by the Chinese. Mickey Mouse and Donald Duck were shown on Chinese television. The American Peace Corps also went to China. Cultural exchanges, whether initiated privately or under official auspices, were intended to bridge the gap between China and the United States and promote greater understanding.[20]

To be sure, U.S.-Chinese relations often encountered constraints with respect to differing social and political values. Tensions frequently occurred resulting from U.S. criticisms of Chinese internal policies on such issues as Tibet, population control, and political dissidents (i.e., human rights violation). In most cases, Chinese officials angrily condemned American criticism as meddling in China's internal affairs. In February 1985, a wrinkle appeared in Sino-American relations when Washington decided to withhold $23 million from the United Nations Fund for Population Activities because of concern by the Reagan administration that American funds might be used to support coerced abortions in China.[21] The Chinese government expressed "deep regret"

over the American decision and blamed the administration's action on
"distorted reports and rumors in the American press. "[22] In September
1987 riots in Tibet caused Congress to issue statements concerning
China's human rights violations. The Chinese considered this
interference in their domestic affairs. For a long time, Washington had
followed a double standard of making much fuss about human rights
violations in the Soviet Union and Eastern Europe while overlooking
them in China. But following the changes in the Soviet Union, more
voices regarding human rights questions in China were heard in the
U.S. Congress. After the Tiananmen Square Incident in June 1989, the
human rights question emerged as one of the most important issues
between the two countries.

In response, Beijing, in early 1988, addressed six problems in
Sino-U.S. relations (i.e., the Taiwan issue, U.S. Congress objection to
China's family-planing policies, human rights in Tibet, Chinese arms
sales to the Middle East, difficulty in technology transfers, and
American efforts to spread American ideas of freedom of speech and
publication in China). An article published in *Beijing Review* argued
that "the six problems amount to nothing short of interference in
China's internal affairs and political blackmail. "[23] However, strong in
its rhetoric criticizing Washington, Beijing still carefully managed to
avoid letting these tensions get out of hand. In the same article, the
Chinese put forward four principles for managing Sino-U.S. relations:
learn to respect each other; increase mutual understanding; prevent
differences in ideology from becoming an obstacle to development of
bilateral relations; and treasure improvements already made in their
relations.[24]

In general, Beijing's relations with Washington since the mid-1980s
had become more mature than before. Indeed, the two countries shared
many common interests while having differences in their ideologies and
social values. Both sides were making strong efforts to separate, to the
degree possible, those issues over which they differed with each other
from those in which they shared common interests. To do this, both
countries tried ways to understand the other's national interest, political
practices, social policies, and values. Compared with the early 1980s,
Beijing had become much better informed about various issues. China
had acquired a much greater knowledge of how the U.S. government
operated, including the role of Congress. Aware of the institutional gap
between the two countries and the complex nature of domestic politics
in each, the Chinese approach to the United States became much more

"rational, reasonable, and thus effective."[25] Beijing clearly understood that its relations with the United States occupied a most important position in China's overall foreign policy. The new type of relationship between Beijing and Washington included not only security interests shared in the Asian-Pacific area, but also economic, cultural, and political interests.[27] Of course, differences existed between the two countries. This situation required both political will and political wisdom from the two countries to shape their multi-dimensional relationship.

The political test of the new relationship was the Tiananmen Square Incident and its after-effects in 1989. The United States responded vehemently to Beijing's brutal suppression of the pro-democracy movement in Tiananmen Square, including bitter condemnations, economic sanctions, and suspensions of high-level exchange visits and military cooperation. U.S.-Chinese ties reached the lowest point since 1972. Nonetheless, while condemning Beijing's brutality and its human rights violation, the Bush Administration's China policy was to maintain contact with China and avoid isolating the latter from the rest of the world. The White House argued that it was not in America's interest to see an isolated China returning to a destabilizing role in Asia.[27] President Bush tried to convince the American public that cutting ties with China or hurting its economy by suspending China's most-favored-nation trade status would isolate China. A positive participation by Beijing in international affairs was needed especially in establishing a new international order and in maintaining regional stability in the Asian-Pacific area. The United States needed to talk with China on such issues as human rights, bilateral trade, arms sales, nuclear proliferation, and even cooperation in settlement of regional conflicts. On the Chinese side, although Beijing's propaganda machine bitterly charged the United States with attempting to subvert China's socialist system and warned its people against Western ideology and the "peaceful evolution" plot of the West, efforts were being made to repair China's relations with the United States. One such example was Beijing's compromise to allow Fang Lizhi, a well-known Chinese dissident, to leave for the United States from his shelter in the U.S. Embassy in Beijing. Besides, Beijing cooperated with the United States in 1990 by not vetoing U.N. Resolution 678 which authorized the United Nations to use force against the Iraqi invasion of Kuwait. Clearly, China was very realistic about its national interest and adopted a flexible policy toward the United States. Truly enough, Beijing's policy toward the United States was and will continue to be a central part of overall Chinese foreign policy. It has a strong influence not only on China's security strategy, but also on China's relations with other parts of the world. To some extent, it even plays an important role in shaping China's domestic policy.[28] In short, cultivating a stable Sino-U.S. relationship is really in the interests of both China and the United States.

Normalizing Relations with Moscow

Accommodation in Sino-Soviet relations was cautious but steady since 1982. Sino-Soviet cultural, educational, scientific, and technological ties were resumed and trade was expanded. Despite this warming trend, further improvement in the political climate of Sino-Soviet relations was impeded by the "three obstacles," namely, withdrawal of Soviet troops from Afghanistan, termination of Soviet support for the Vietnamese occupation of Cambodia, and substantial reduction of the military buildup in Mongolia and the Soviet Far East. These three obstacles were advanced by China in 1980 when the Chinese felt threatened by Soviet encirclement in the aftermath of the Soviet occupation of Afghanistan. The Chinese insisted that the three obstacles hurt their national interest and inhibited normalization of Sino-Soviet relations. Beijing made it firm and clear that normalization was "out of the question" unless Moscow acted to remove these obstacles.[29] Nevertheless, progress was slow in this regard and deep-seated suspicion persisted on both sides.

In March 1985, China sent a delegation headed by Vice-Premier Li Peng to attend the funeral of Konstantin Chernenko in Moscow. Meeting with the new Soviet leader Mikhail Gorbachev, Li expressed hope that "major improvement would be made in Sino-Soviet relations." Gorbachev replied that Moscow would like a serious improvement in relations with China.[30] But Gorbachev's accession to power in Moscow brought no immediate restructuring in Sino-Soviet relations because he was busy consolidating his power in preparation for the 1986 Twenty-Seventh Soviet Communist Party Congress and Soviet-U.S. relations topped his foreign policy agenda. At the same time, Beijing continued to insist that "normalization" of relations depended on the resolution of the "three obstacles." In April 1986, at the conclusion of the eighth round of the semi-annual Sino-Soviet consultations, China again rejected Soviet Foreign Minister Shevardnadze's proposal to "upgrade the level of political dialogue and hold meetings between the leaders of the two countries."[31]

A significant break in the deadlocked negotiations between the two countries came on July 28, 1986 when Mikhail Gorbachev made a landmark speech on Moscow's new Asian policy in the Soviet Far East city of Vladivostok. In this speech, Gorbachev made three specific concessions to Beijing. First, he promised to withdraw six regiments from Afghanistan by the end of 1986. This was not a large scale pullout, involving only about six percent or 6,000 of a total of more than 100,000 Soviet troops in Afghanistan. In the meantime, Gorbachev also laid down, as a condition, that the pullout was to be matched by a reduction of Western aid to the *mujahedin*, the Afghan guerilla fighters. The second concession to China was his willingness to discuss reduction of force levels along the Sino-Soviet border. Gorbachev said that "the Soviet Union is prepared--any time, at any level--to discuss with China questions of additional measures for creating an atmosphere of good-neighborliness. We hope that the border dividing...us will soon become a line of peace and friendship." Gorbachev's third proposal was that some Soviet troops would be withdrawn from Mongolia. He promised to initiate talks with Mongolia about reduction of Soviet troops stationed there.[32] In January 1987, Gorbachev announced that an agreement had been reached and a motorized rifle division and several smaller units would withdraw from the Sino-Mongolian border beginning in April 1987. This was only a small reduction as the Soviets still stationed four divisions in Mongolia.[33]

In addition to his conciliatory initiative to meet at least partially two of three obstacles that the Chinese demanded, Gorbachev further proposed to Beijing a joint development of the Amur River, saying that "we do not want the Amur River border to be 'a water obstacle'."[34] This proposal was followed by another visit in August 1986 from Ivan Arkhipov.[35] He brought to Beijing a unilateral concession of considerable importance: Moscow was willing to negotiate a border settlement on the Amur River and the Ussuri River based on the Chinese claim that the border line should be the middle navigable channel of the two rivers, not the river bank on the Chinese side.[36]

The Chinese were rather cautious in their reaction to Gorbachev's initiatives. On the one hand, they did not reject his offer to reduce tensions and expand contacts. Beijing accepted Arkhipov's proposal by agreeing to resume border negotiations with Moscow, which had been broken off in 1978. In February 1987, both sides reached a procedural agreement to review the entire length of the Sino-Soviet border, beginning with the eastern sector divided by the disputed Amur and Ussuri rivers, the site of border clashes in 1969.[37] On the other hand, the Chinese noted that the 8,000 soldiers the Russians had withdrawn from Afghanistan in October 1986 were "insignificant" given the total number of Soviet troops in Afghanistan. Beijing pointed out that this did not meet the Chinese demand of a complete Soviet withdrawal, there even being no complete withdrawal timetable.[38] As for reduction of military forces in Mongolia, the Chinese retorted, the size of the troops involved was rather small.[39] On the matter of Vietnamese occupation of Cambodia, Deng Xiaoping himself was quick to note that the Soviet leader in his speech had on purpose excluded Indochina from the areas in which the Soviets were prepared to accommodate Chinese interests. In a television interview with Mike Wallace on "60 Minutes," Deng charged that Gorbachev "evaded" the Cambodian issue in his Vladivostok speech. He argued that without Moscow's backing, armed conflict by the Vietnamese in Cambodia would end. Deng reemphasized in his interview that "the Vietnamese invasion of Cambodia constituted the main obstacle in Sino-Soviet relations." Deng added a personal note by saying that he had decided not to take any more trips abroad because of his advanced age. But he would make an exception to meet with Gorbachev anywhere in the Soviet Union if Moscow would "take a solid step toward the removal of these major obstacles in their relations, particularly urging Vietnam to end its aggression in Cambodia and withdraw its troops from there."[40]

In an attempt to break the political impasse, Moscow finally agreed to include the Cambodian issue in Sino-Soviet consultations. In October 1986, for the first time, bilateral talks between the Soviet Union and China included the issue of Cambodia. Until that time Moscow had steadfastly insisted that the issue had nothing to do with their bilateral relationship and should not be included in bilateral consultations. The problem should be decided directly between Beijing and Hanoi.[41] This time the Chinese expressed satisfaction while the topic dominated the week-long discussions.

The Cambodian concession was paralleled by Soviet foreign policy restructuring initiated by Gorbachev under his "new thinking." Moscow decisively adopted a brand new foreign policy pursuing peace and reducing tensions with the United States. Between 1985 and 1989, the Soviet-U.S. détente developed very rapidly. The two sides held six summit meetings during this period. The key December 1987 summit resulted in the signing of the Intermediate-Range Nuclear Forces Treaty (INF) which demonstrated the seriousness of the Soviet Union on détente.[42]

Gorbachev was also determined to restructure Soviet-Chinese relations and moved closer toward elimination of the "three obstacles." Progress toward a reduction of the Soviet military presence on China's borders came when Moscow agreed to destroy intermediate and short-range nuclear missiles (including SS-20s) in the Soviet Far East as part of the December 1987 INF agreement. In December 1988 at the United Nations, Gorbachev announced a 500,000-man reduction in the Soviet army within two years; 40 percent of this cut was to be in the Soviet Far Eastern region. During his visit to Beijing in February 1989, Soviet Foreign Minister Shevardnadze elaborated on the offer, stating that the Soviet Union would reduce the numerical strength of its troops in Asia by 200,000 men and that it would withdraw three-fourths of its troops from Mongolia. He indicated that reductions would be completed in two years and called the plan a "component part of the process of normalizing relations with China."[43] In March 1989 the Soviet and Mongolian governments announced that two Soviet air force and three ground divisions, including two armored divisions would be withdrawn from Mongolia during 1989 and 1990.[44] In April 1988, the Soviet Union formally agreed in Geneva to remove its forces from Afghanistan by February 15, 1989, following a U.N.-sponsored agreement.[45] Moscow also, for the first time, denied any linkage between a Soviet troops withdrawal and the nature of the regime in Kabul.[46]

These developments in themselves suggested the reduction of threats to China. Beijing welcomed Moscow's new initiatives. Deng repeated his personal interest in meeting with Gorbachev if further progress could be made to end Hanoi's occupation of Cambodia.[47] To Beijing, Soviet support for Vietnamese occupation of Cambodia was now the most serious "obstacle" to "normal" Sino-Soviet relations. Chinese firmness paid off. As Gorbachev maneuvered towards better relations with China he began to push Hanoi and Phnom Penh toward a policy of national reconciliation and withdrawal of Vietnamese troops from Cambodia. The Vietnamese-Indonesia Joint Communiqué of July 1987 opened the process of constructing a solution to the Cambodia question through political means. Talks among the various parties to the dispute soon started. In May 1988 Hanoi reiterated the plan to withdraw its forces from Cambodia by the end of 1990.[48] Gorbachev expressed "confidence" that Vietnam would keep its promise.[49] In August 1988, Soviet Vice Foreign Minister broke with the previous practice and told his Chinese counterpart for the first time that withdrawal of Vietnamese troops from Cambodia was the key to solving the Cambodian problem. Meanwhile, Soviet assistance to Vietnam was substantially cut.[50] In his speech at Krasnoyarsk in September 1988, Gorbachev indicated that he hoped to settle the Cambodian conflict as soon as possible.[51] In December 1988, new Chinese Foreign Minister Qian Qichen visited Moscow to confer on this issue. Substantial agreement on Cambodia was reached during his visit, whereupon the two sides agreed that a summit should be held in the first half of 1989 ushering in a "new type" of Sino-Soviet relations.[52]

On January 6, 1989, Hanoi announced that it would speed up withdrawal of all its forces from Cambodia by the end of September 1989. Hanoi's announcement represented Vietnam's acceptance of a Chinese proposal to Soviet Deputy Foreign Minister Igor Rogachev in September 1988 to the effect that Vietnam withdraw from Cambodia over a nine-month period.[53] In sharp contrast to China's reaction to earlier Vietnamese withdrawal schemes, of which there had been seven by Chinese count, Beijing welcomed Hanoi's January 1989 plan. According to a *Renmin Ribao* commentator, it was "a step forward" and advanced an "acceptable schedule."[54]

In February 1989, Soviet Foreign Minister Shevardnadze paid a reciprocal visit to Beijing. His visit mainly concerned the Cambodian issue. After a series of talks, the participants reached a nine-point agreement.[55] Moscow showed confidence that Hanoi would keep its promise of withdrawing Vietnamese troops from Cambodia. In return, the Chinese promised to gradually cease military aid to "any of the parties in Cambodia" along with other countries once the Vietnamese withdrew their troops. For the first time, the Soviets did not echo the Vietnamese demand of linking their troop withdrawal to the dismantling of the Khmer Rouge.[56] Besides, both China and the Soviet Union favored a fair and reasonable political settlement of the Cambodian issue and supported the role of the United Nations in the Cambodian settlement. With an international guarantee, the two sides endorsed establishment of a provisional government under Prince Sihanouk with quadripartite representation (including Sihanouk's faction, the Hanoi-backed group, the Khmer Rouge and the West-supported group).

In the end, Beijing and Moscow promised to discontinue the policies and practices of the recent past in Cambodia and expressed hope that settlement of the Cambodian issue would contribute to removal of that source of tension in Southeast Asia.[57]

With progress on settlement of the Cambodian issue, the focus of Sino-Soviet diplomacy soon shifted to the summit meeting between Deng and Gorbachev. As early as October 1985, Deng asked Rumanian President Nicolai Ceausescu, who was visiting China, to pass on a message to Gorbachev proposing that the summit could be arranged once the "three obstacles" were removed.[58] In November 1987, while meeting with a Japanese delegation, Deng repeated that he would be 85 and too old to make a journey to Moscow. So he hoped withdrawal of Vietnamese forces from Cambodia should take place within two years.[59] Judging from Gorbachev's words and deeds since he took office, the Chinese gradually came to the conclusion that the new Soviet leader was serious about domestic reform, about the need for an international "breathing space," and about rapprochement with China. Thus, China's attitude toward the Soviet Union became much more relaxed than before. During Shevardnadze's visit to Beijing in February 1989, the timing of the planned summit was finalized.[60]

The symbolic and substantive highlight of Sino-Soviet rapprochement was Gorbachev's historic visit to China May 15-18, 1989. It was the first Sino-Soviet summit since Nikita Khrushchev's visit to China in 1959. The Deng-Gorbachev summit meeting officially ended the Sino-Soviet dispute after almost thirty years of hostility and rancor. It marked the beginning of "normal" and "good-neighborly" relations between the two countries.[61] Deng summed up the summit in eight words: "End the past and open up the future."[62] As chief of the Soviet Communist Party, Gorbachev also met his Chinese counterpart Zhao Ziyang[63] and formally restored party relations between the two countries. In the joint communiqué issued at the end of the visit, both sides agreed that normalization of relations between the two countries was in conformity with the interests and aspirations of the Chinese and Soviet peoples and contributed to maintenance of world peace and stability. They particularly pointed out that normalization of Sino-Soviet relations was "not directed at any third country," nor did "it harm its interests." On the contrary, they stated that the new Sino-Soviet relationship would develop on the basis of the Five Principles of Peaceful-Coexistence. Besides, the two sides, in the communiqué, expressed readiness to "resolve all the disputes between the two countries through peaceful negotiations, and neither side would use or threaten to use arms against the other by any means, including the use of the territorial land, water or air space of a third country bordering on the other side. " For this purpose, both sides agreed to take measures to cut down military forces in areas along the Sino-Soviet boundary to a minimum level commensurate with normal, good-neighborly relations between the countries and to work for increased trust and continuous tranquility in border areas. Meanwhile, they favored a fair and reasonable settlement of the Sino-Soviet boundary question left over from history on the basis of treaties concerning the present Sino-Soviet boundary and of the generally recognized principles of international law, and in a spirit of consultation on an equal footing and of mutual understanding and accommodation. Interestingly enough, both Beijing and Moscow stated in the communiqué that neither side would seek hegemony of any form in the Asian-Pacific region or other parts of the world. With this promise, Moscow and Beijing supported international efforts in disarmament and settlement of global problems and regional conflicts. As far as the Cambodian issue was concerned, the two countries in the communiqué sustained their positions on the matter expressed in their nine-point statement reached in February 1989. Finally, they also agreed to further expand their economic, trade, scientific, technological, cultural and other relations.[64]

The normalization of Sino-Soviet relations greatly accelerated commercial, cultural, scientific-technological exchanges between the two countries. Since 1982 when Beijing decided to include the Soviet Union and Eastern Europe in its open door diplomacy, Sino-Soviet economic relations developed rapidly. In 1982, two-way trade between China and the Soviet Union was $362 million. Starting in 1983, the volume of bilateral trade increased significantly. It was over $1 billion in 1983, $1.2 billion in 1984, $1.9 billion in 1985, $2.5 billion in 1986, $2.9 billion in 1987, and over $3.5 billion in 1988. In 1985, a five-year trade agreement was concluded, which would raise bilateral trade arrangements to $3.5 billion by 1990. In fact, Sino-Soviet trade was $3.9 billion in 1989. By 1988, the Soviet Union had become China's fifth largest trading partner, after Hong Kong, Japan, the European Community and the United States.[65] The Soviet Union exported steel, plate glass, transportation equipment, chemical products and machinery while China exported mineral products, meat, cotton, silk, textiles, tea, and other consumer goods to the Soviet Union.[66] Border trade also expanded rapidly between the two countries. At the

Third Session of the Sino-Soviet Commission for Economic, Trade, and Science and Technological Cooperation in 1988, an agreement was reached to increase the number of ministries and subministerial departments, provinces, autonomous regions, republics, cities, enterprises, and associations authorized to engage in Sino-Soviet commercial relations. Throughout 1989, a large number of such subcentral delegations flowed both ways across the border. Senior officials from both countries visited each other frequently, exchanging views and experiences regarding their economic reform programs.[67] From 1986 to 1988, teams of Soviet experts surveyed the 1950s industrial enterprises built by the Soviets. A small number of Chinese laborers were sent to work in Siberia.[68] Sino-Soviet cultural and sports exchange programs were resumed. The two sides also sent students to be enrolled in each other's universities.[69]

The normalization of relations between Beijing and Moscow greatly influenced China's ties with Soviet bloc countries. While continuing to keep good relations with Yugoslavia and Romania, China actively improved relations with other East European countries. In 1984 it signed a ten-year agreement on economic, trade, scientific, and technological cooperation with Poland and the two governments set up a committee to implement the agreement. They also set up general consulates respectively in Shanghai and Gdansk. One after another, Poland's Wojciech Jaruzelski in September 1986, East Germany's Erich Honecker in October 1986, Czechoslovakia's Premier Strougal in April 1987, Bulgaria's General Secretary Zhivkov in May 1987 and Hungary's General Secretary Kador in October 1987 visited Beijing. In June 1987, Zhao Ziyang, both as Acting General Secretary of the Chinese Communist Party and as Premier, made a much-publicized trip to Poland, East Germany, Czechoslovakia, Hungary, and Bulgaria. By 1987 the Chinese Communist Party had resumed party-to-party relations with all East European countries except Albania. Even Sino-Cuban relations were improved. In 1987 Cuba sent its highest level delegation to China in at least 20 years.[70]

In sum, both China and the Soviet Union had excellent reasons to restructure their bilateral relations from hostility to good neighborliness. Both of them had serious domestic problems and initiated substantial reforms. Motivated by the same idea that international détente was an external precondition for success of their reform programs, Moscow and Beijing sought to reduce tensions between the two countries and lower their military spendings.

Meanwhile, they had strong desires to expand bilateral economic ties through improved relations. Even though dramatic changes took place in both countries after the Tiananmen Square events in June 1989, Beijing and Moscow were very cautious not to criticize each other's domestic politics publicly. Although each might not like the other's internal political development, they avoided a return to the old hostility. By putting aside political differences, Beijing and Moscow continued to carefully cultivate their newly-improved relations and concentrate on practical cooperative initiatives for their mutual benefits.

Sino-Japanese Relations

Japan is a very important country to China. Indeed, except for the two superpowers, China's most important bilateral relationship is with Japan. Due to historical ties, cultural affinity, geo-graphical proximity, and economic attraction, these two major powers in East Asia have come to realize the importance of maintaining a good relationship. As a leading trade partner and major supplier of technology and loans for China's modernization, Japan's active participation in China's economic development is one of the essential elements of Deng's open door policy. For this reason, Hu Yaobang put the Sino-Japanese relationship as the first item discussed in his report to the 1982 Party Congress.[71]

Maintaining and developing stable relations with China is a major pillar of Japan's diplomacy. To this end, Japan has adopted a comprehensive China policy in which economic and political objectives complement one another. The assistance that the Japanese afforded China's modernization program is intended not only to promote the interest of Japanese commerce and industry but, more importantly, to draw China into the Western-dominated international economy, with a view to deradicalizing Chinese politics, encouraging political stability and thus ultimately serving Japan's politico-strategic interest. It is no wonder that in the wake of the Tiananmen Square Incident, Japan only had restrained responses to the events and soon a large number of Japanese businessmen were in a hurry to return to China to capitalize on the huge market there.[72]

The importance of Sino-Japanese ties was realized by leaders of both countries and regularly reinforced by top-level visits between the two nations. Virtually all senior Japanese political leaders visited China. Since 1972, all prime ministers travelled to China while in office. On the Chinese side, all top leaders, including Deng Xiaoping, Hu Yaobang and Zhao Ziyang visited Japan.[73] During his visit to Japan in June 1982, Zhao proposed a set of principles to promote bilateral ties: continued peaceful and friendly relations, equality and mutual benefit, and a lasting and stable friendship "from generation to generation, impervious to international storms."[74]

The complementary economies and proximity of the two countries have made their relations attractive to each other. China has natural resources Japan needs, while Japan has technology and money to assist China in a number of ways. Beyond resources, technology, and money, each side has a market which hold a great potential for each other, and their proximity significantly keeps down transportation costs. To be sure, the complementary relationship between China and Japan is due to the different levels of economic development of the two countries.[75] Chinese economic development is beneficial to both countries and will not cause competition between them in the foreseeable future. Thus, economic cooperation and interaction between the two countries proves beneficial to both nations.

By the end of the 1980s, Japan was China's second-largest trading partner after Hong Kong, while China was Japan's fifth-largest trading partner.[76] Two-way trade in 1989 was $19.7 billion, with Chinese exports exceeding $10 billion for the first time.[77] A degree of interdependence had developed between the two countries in the 1980s. But China needed Japan's credit, technology and industrial goods more than Japan needed Chinese energy and mineral resources. The Chinese market was a big lure, but overall Japanese economic health depended far more on the United States and Western Europe than it did on China. Conversely, Japanese purchases of Chinese oil and coal were essential to China's foreign exchange earnings. Nearly half of China's crude oil went to Japan, but comprised only 6.5 percent of total oil imports. With the drop of oil prices in the international market, China developed a massive trade imbalance with Japan which rose to record levels in the mid-1980s.[78] Like many other nations in the 1980s, China had difficulty penetrating the Japanese market. Yet, as a state-controlled economy, China had the capability and could lower trade volumes if it saw fit. It did exactly that in 1987 after the deficit with Japan had reached alarming levels over the previous two years. This paid off in the short run at least because in 1987 China's exports to Japan rose and imports fell, thus resulting in a sharp deficit reduction.[79] The long standing Chinese complaint about their trade imbalance was addressed even further by imposing tighter controls over imports, which in turn led to a drop in Japan's share of China's total trade from the high point of 30 percent in 1985 to less than 20 percent after 1987.[80] There was a perception among Chinese leaders that they should make conscious efforts to diversify trade relationship in order to avoid possible dependence on Japan.

Beyond trade matters, other economic links were further testimony to Japan's importance to China. Beginning in 1982, China for the first time became the top recipient of Japan's official development assistance (ODA). Following the 1981 extension of $1.3 billion of credit to China so as to enable it to complete the first phase of the Baoshan Steel Complex, Japan made another loan of $2.1 billion in March 1984 to help China finance construction of key projects including railroads, ports, hydroelectric power plants, mineral mines, and aluminum plants. The loan carried a low 3.5 percent interest rate and was payable in thirty years.[81] Altogether the Japanese government committed $3.5 billion in low-interest loans between 1979 and 1988 which became the most important international financial source for China.[82] In August 1988, Prime Minister Noboru Takeshita approved a new round of loans to China, amounting to $6.25 billion. Immediately after the Tiananmen Square Incident in June 1989, the loan was frozen temporarily. But Japan was quick to lift the ban during the Group of Seven Summit in Houston in July 1990.[83] In fact, Japan was the first industrial country which was pragmatic enough to lift economic restrictions against China in the wake of the Tiananmen Square events.

While the Japanese provided loans for China and sold products there, they were very cautious about getting involved in direct investments in China. Beijing was very disappointed with Japan's reluctance in this regard in the 1980s. The Chinese complained about it, contrasting the large trade surplus with the relatively small number of production ventures. As compared with American investors, Japanese firms were usually invested in small and short-term projects rather than in long-tern and big ones. For this reason, Japan ranked as the third-largest source of foreign investment behind Hong Kong and the United States in China in 1989.[84] Despite improvements in investment climate, Japanese investors remained cautious. In this sense, Japan was more interested in making money from China through selling manufactured products than in seeing the rise of an economic giant as its neighbor. To change the situation, the two countries signed the Sino-Japanese investment protection protocol in April 1989.[85] Japan's investments in China rose gradually since then.

China saw technology transfer as an integral part of its foreign investment strategy to upgrade the nation's economic level. But this was the field in which Japan remained most reluctant to cooperate. The Chinese complained in particular that Japanese technology transfer was inadequate, evidenced by the fact that whereas 48 percent of hardware imports came from Japan as against 13 percent from the United States, only 13 percent of production know-how came from Japan as against 26 percent from the United States.[86] Only one indicator of technology transfer showed that the Japanese led the way: of 10,000 foreign experts working in China in 1986, around 40 percent (or roughly 4,000) were Japanese.[87] Some relief to this problem came in 1986 when restrictions of the North Atlantic Alliance Coordinating Committee for Export to Communist Countries (COCOM) were considerably loosened for China, following a major relaxation of American export licensing procedures.[88] On balance, China's positive economic relations with Japan far outweighed the negatives.

In addition to economic relations, other aspects of Sino-Japanese relations also received great attention in the two nations. Some events were essentially bilateral in nature, while others were part of the larger scene of East Asian geo-politics. Chinese Premier Zhao Ziyang once warned that if those problems were "not handled correctly," they would "do greater harm to Sino-Japanese relations than economic problems."[89] A few well-publicized cases illustrated the point. In 1982, some changes were made by Japanese Education Ministry in school textbooks which in fact whitewashed Japan's invasion and predatory occupation of China during the 1930s and 1940s. This incident brought forth Beijing's wrath. The Chinese government officially protested and severely criticized the changes. Beijing made it clear that relations would be gravely damaged if Tokyo did not make amends. Together with China, South Korea and some Southeast Asian countries also protested against Japan. Under such pressure, the Japanese finally rectified the situation.

It is true that resentment of Japan persisted among a populace which still recalled the brutality of the 1931-45 invasion and occupation. Chinese leaders gave voice to these memories, as when they vigorously protested against Prime Minister Yasuhiro Nakasone's August 1985 official visit to the Yasukuni Shrine honoring Japan's war dead. China saw this as a visit to the graveyard of war criminals.[90] Next year, Japan's Education Minister Fujio Masayuki made some public remarks which minimized Japan's wartime actions in China. China protested and Fujio later was fired.[91] In any case, China seemingly had no reluctance to remind Japan of its past war crimes from time to time.

But on the other hand, reformers in Beijing for economic reasons tried hard to cultivate favorable popular sentiment toward Japan. In this regard, Hu Yaobang was very active. During his trip to Japan, Hu invited three thousand Japanese young people to visit China in October 1984 as guests of the Chinese government.[92] But the Chinese public resisted becoming heavily dependent upon Japan. It is necessary to distinguish between officially inspired and genuinely spontaneous popular reactions in China. Having seen Japan's continued trade surplus and the flooding of Japanese goods into Chinese markets, students in Beijing went on to the streets against Japan's alleged "economic aggression" in 1985. Wall posters bearing anti-Japanese slogans such as "Down with Nakasone," "Second Japanese Invasion," and "Boycott Japanese Goods" were on display on several university campuses.[93] The drastic move taken by the Chinese government to reduce Japanese imports was then maintained due to this domestic pressure. This move might also have been motivated by China's declining foreign exchange reserve and mounting criticism raised by orthodox hardliners against an excessive tilt toward Japan.[94] Under such circumstances, the reformers had to act tough toward Japan. Deng deliberately stated that the unfavorable balance of trade must be reversed and that Japan must buy more from China.[95]

Tension also mounted briefly in Sino-Japanese relations in 1987 in a lawsuit involving the ownership of the Kokario student dormitory. This incident came from the different political systems of the two countries. Japan has an independent judiciary, whereas China does not. The dormitory had housed Chinese students since the days of the Chinese Kuomintang's rule. A Kyoto court awarded the property to Taiwan. But Beijing viewed the case, the civil lawsuit and the ruling by the Kyoto court, as a political case and complained that some people in Japan wanted to foster a "two Chinas" policy. The Chinese insisted that Beijing was the recognized government and therefore the Japanese court had violated the Sino-Japanese Peace and Friendship Treaty. The Chinese government called on the Japanese government to reverse the decision by taking "the question seriously and earnestly" and handling it properly so as to avoid affecting the friendly relations between the two countries."[96] Deng told the visiting Japanese Foreign Minister

Kuranari in June 1987 that Japan was solely to blame for chilly Sino-Japanese relations and that Tokyo must solve it without delay. To Japan, however, it was just a legal matter for the courts. The Chinese were furious when a Japanese Deputy Foreign Minister responded by saying that Deng Xiaoping was a man above the clouds.[97] Although the Japanese official resigned afterwards and the government later expressed regret for "discourteous remarks," Sino-Japanese relations were greatly hurt by those incidents.[98]

Other Sino-Japanese problems arose because of changing geo-political circumstances in East Asia. Chinese analysis and forecasting of Japan's Pacific role was a subject of major strategic as well as political sensitivity. As the Chinese adopted a nonalignment policy toward the superpowers, Beijing's policies toward Japan also changed. By the late 1970s and early 1980s, the Sino-Japanese relationship was subsumed under strategic considerations. At that time, alignment with Washington and opposition to Moscow dictated Chinese policy toward Japan. In early 1979, Deng Xiaoping declared that China, Japan, and the United States should unite to further develop their relationship and contain Russian expansion.[99] One Chinese Deputy Chief of Staff, Wu Xiuquan, said, "I am all for Japan's increasing its self-defense capabilities.... Generally speaking, Japan is one of the economic powers and it is entitled to become a big power militarily, too."[100] Beijing also encouraged American-Japanese security cooperation.

In 1982, however, the political mood changed. East Asia was now perceived by the Chinese as a new but delicate power balance based on four power centers: Beijing, Moscow, Tokyo, and Washington. On the one hand, China welcomed the declining contention between the superpowers in the region. On the other hand, it publicly expressed concern over Japan's future role in the region. Beijing was worried that Japan, with its economic power and military potential, would fill the vacuum and extend its political influence in the region. At a time when China was engaged in reducing its own military forces, Beijing altered its tone on Japan's. Chinese spokesmen frequently stated that Japan's military spending should not exceed self-defense requirements. They also warned that its military capabilities "should be moderate and of a defensive nature, and should not cause concern to its neighboring countries."[101] Beijing was alert to any signs of the rise of "militarism" or "chauvinism" in Japan or significant increases in Japan's military spending. In 1987 Tokyo's lifting of the one percent of GNP ceiling on

Japanese defense expenditures elicited critical comment in China. Chinese Foreign Minister voiced concern that China did not like to see Japan become a major military power.[102] Deng Xiaoping called Japan "a chauvinist country" and warned about the threat of Japan's growing militarism in East Asia. A memorial hall was dedicated in Beijing on July 7, 1987 to commemorate the fiftieth anniversary of the war against Japan. This deliberate affront to the Japanese was a clear indication of potential tensions that existed between the two.[103]

The memory of the Second World War was still fresh. From time to time China issued finger-pointing warnings to Japan calling upon it to avoid the road to militarism, typically laced with acid commentary describing how China had suffered under the boots of Japan's military. The Chinese also made some sharp cautionary remarks about Japanese military potential. They complained that at a time when Americans, Russians and the Chinese were reducing their military expenditures, Japanese military spending was continually rising.[104] Beijing carefully pointed out that Japan had already built up an impressive military machinery. China was worried that Japan's high technology could be rapidly transformed into military capabilities and warned that China and other Asian countries were very sensitive about the issue.[105] China and other Asian countries severely criticized Japan's decision to send military personnel abroad for the first time since the end of World War II to participate in the U.N. peacekeeping operation in Cambodia.[106] In essence, balance between economic benefits and geo-political concerns is crucial for China in managing relations with her neighboring economic superpower.

Good Relations with Neighboring Countries

China's search for a peaceful international environment, and its efforts to expand foreign economic relations led Beijing to improve ties with all its neighbors in the 1980s. Chinese Foreign Minister Qian Qichen wrote at the end of 1990 that China attached special importance to developing closer relations with its neighbors. This statement articulated the dominant thrust of Chinese foreign policy in recent times: good-neighborly relations.[107] Indeed, China's major military and political interests focus primarily on the Asian-Pacific region. Because of its importance (i.e., its size and population, its political and socio-cultural influence, its status as the only Asian permanent member of the

United Nations Security Council, its possession of the largest military power in the area, and its influence on regional tensions from the Korean peninsula to Indochina and South Asia), China's policies, domestic stability, economic prospects, and military strength are of deep concern to and are watched closely by all its Asian neighbors.

Therefore, China's did all it could in the 1980s to convince its neighbors of Beijing's benign attitude toward peace and economic development, and to gain long-term acceptance as a cooperative and nonthreatening neighbor. Over time, Beijing's efforts at détente with its Asian neighbors paid off. Politically, while keeping good relations with Japan, North Korea, Pakistan, and most Southeast Asian countries, China reestablished or eased relations with virtually all other neighbors, including Indonesia, Singapore, South Korea, India, and even Vietnam. China relieved Malaysian, Indonesian, Burmese, and Philippine security concerns by suspending or halting support for insurgencies and Communist parties in the region, including ending "liberation radio" broadcasts from Chinese territory.[108] Beijing publicly stated that there was no such thing as world revolution in state relations, which should be guided only by the Five Principles of Peaceful Coexistence.[109] In addition, China's dramatic reduction in military spending also had a positive impact on its neighbors. On regional issues, Beijing supported relaxation of tensions on the Korean peninsula and cooperated closely with the Association of Southeast Asian Nations (ASEAN), both regionally and in the United Nations to press Vietnam to withdraw its troops from Cambodia. Meanwhile, Beijing also cooperated with other major powers in encouraging a political settlement in Cambodia. Economically, China actively joined the economic dynamics in the Asian-Pacific region. Chinese trade with Asia, as a whole, tripled in the 1980s, rising from $21 billion to $65 billion between 1983 and 1989. Asia's share of total Chinese world trade grew from 49 percent to 60 percent. China's trade was heavily concentrated in Hong Kong and Japan, representing over 80 percent of its total trade with Asia during the 1980s. Trade with other Asian countries also grew from $2.8 billion in 1983 to $10.3 billion in 1989.[110]

Korea   The success of China's policy of détente was exemplified by Beijing's policy toward the Korean peninsula. On the one hand, China still remained a strategic-military ally of North Korea, proclaiming their relations as sealed in blood and ideological bonds. Because of the downturn in Soviet-North Korean economic and political relations, China actually further consolidated its ties with Pyongyang.

Besides, normalization between Beijing and Moscow limited Kim Il Sung's ability to continue to exploit Sino-Soviet differences to his advantage as he had done before.[111] As a result, North Korea had to tilt toward Beijing.

On the other hand, in order to obtain economic benefits, the Chinese leadership followed a policy which combined Beijing's pragmatic open-door economic policy with efforts to separate politics and economics in its foreign activities. Thus, China adopted a two-track policy toward both North and South Korea. It advanced relations with South Korea while maintaining standard friendly relations with North Korea. There was a rapid growth in trade between China and South Korea. The total value of this indirect trade was estimated to be about $20 million in 1979, and it increased, in spite of the North Koreans' discontent, to $1.5 billion in 1987 and $3 billion in 1988, while China's trade with North Korea was only $519.4 million in 1987.[112] China became one of South Korea's major trading partners. Besides, South Korean industrial giant Daewoo signed a joint-venture agreement with China and opened an assembly plant to build television sets and refrigerators in Fuzhou in China. Samsung also established joint ventures in China with a refrigerator plant in Beijing producing half a million units per year and a color television operation in Shenzhen, and a videorecorder (VCR) plant in Zhuhai.[113] Before China and South Korea formally establish diplomatic relations in August 1992, trade offices with consular privileges were opened in the capitals of the two countries. Cultural ties, from sports to intellectual exchanges to tourism, also developed rapidly between Beijing and Seoul. Chinese athletes participated in the Tenth Asian Games held in Seoul in 1986 whereas the North boycotted the games.[114] In 1988 the Chinese also went to the Twenty-Fourth Olympic Games in Seoul.

Given the crucial role that the Korean peninsula played in Chinese national security considerations and long-standing personal and ideological ties to North Korea, Beijing was very careful not to offend or isolate North Korea and carefully controlled the speed and scope of China's rapprochement with South Korea. To be sure, Pyongyang was not pleased about China's contacts with Seoul. In order to retain good relations with the North, China was sensitive to Pyongyang's displeasure. In order to keep political support for the North, the Chinese leadership consulted frequently with their North Korean comrades though exchanges of high-level visits. One example was North Korean leader Kim Il Sung's visit to China in 1987 which was meant to show that, despite China's increasingly visible relationship with South Korea, the two Asian Communist nations were still as close "as lips and teeth."[115] China promised its continued support for North Korea's call for a withdrawal of U.S. troops from the peninsula and the ending of joint American-South Korean military exercises. Beijing also advised and encouraged North Korea to open its door to the outside world as well. Later on North Korea agreed to join China and Russia in establishing a special economic zone at the Tumen River Delta area between North Korea, China and Russia.[116] After Beijing and Seoul officially established diplomatic relations in 1992, China continued its promise of no changes in its existing treaties or agreements with Pyongyang.[117]

China had long regarded inter-Korean contact as a major means of increasing regional stability and solving the Korean problem. For this, China welcomed talks between the North and the South and for the first time began to support simultaneous admission of both Koreas to the United Nations.[118] In working with other major powers, such as the United States and Russia, China contributed much to stability on the Korean peninsula by easing its relations with South Korea, refusing to increase its military assistance to North Korea or help on its nuclear programs, and pressuring North Korea to moderate its domestic economic policies.[119] In general, China's Korean policy gave Beijing much leverage and flexibility and helped ease tensions on the Peninsula.

　　Indochina　　Sino-Vietnamese relations deteriorated rapidly as Vietnam invaded Cambodia in December 1978. Tensions between China and Vietnam included territorial disputes, the treatment and deportation of ethnic Chinese living in Vietnam, and the cutback of Chinese economic assistance. From a geo-political viewpoint, Beijing perceived that Vietnamese collaboration with Moscow constituted a direct threat to China's southern flank. In order to oppose Vietnamese domination in Indochina, Beijing waged a border war against Hanoi in 1979. Since then both sides remained deadly enemies and deployed a large number of troops on both sides of their common frontiers. Throughout the 1980s, military clashes occurred from time to time on their borders (including those at the disputed islands in the South China Sea). In addition, China joined the rest of the world, especially the United States and the countries of the Association of Southeast Asian Nations (ASEAN), in their efforts to isolate Vietnam and press Hanoi to withdraw its troops from Cambodia. Meanwhile, Beijing actively backed Cambodian resistance groups including the Khmer Rouge, and provided them with weapons. In response to its diplomatic isolation, Hanoi became even more dependent upon Russia, politically and economically.[120]

But things changed after Gorbachev decided to exercise more pressure on Vietnam so as to improve Soviet relations with China. Moscow dramatically cut back its aid to Hanoi.[121] Meanwhile, military operations in Cambodia and direct confrontation at the border area with China placed much pressure on Vietnam's crumbling economy.[122] In the face of both domestic and international pressure, Vietnam had to change its domestic and foreign policies. In December 1986, under the new Vietnamese leader Ngyen Van Linh, Hanoi announced at the Party Congress that Vietnam would start an economic innovation (*doi moi*), introducing market factors into its economy. Vietnam declared that it would withdraw troops from Cambodia by 1990 and cut military spending.[123] At the same time, Hanoi attempted to improve relations with both the United States and China so as to end its international isolation.

Vietnam then appeared to be eager about normalizing relations with China. In early 1989, both countries exchanged ambassadors and soon talks on their border issues were resumed.[124] Hanoi also pulled back its antiaircraft batteries from the Sino-Vietnamese border and began using ethnic Chinese to rebuild the economy.[125] Radio Hanoi made a commentary on "gratifying changes" by saying that gunshots had basically died out along the border and people on both sides started cross-border trade.[126] In 1990, top Vietnamese leaders, including the Party General Secretary and Prime Minister, secretly travelled to China to have a summit meeting with top Chinese leaders.[127]

But Beijing was not in a hurry for rapprochement and showed no great enthusiasm about the Vietnamese offers. The Chinese were careful to point out that improved ties would be mainly dependent on settlement of the Cambodian conflict. China welcomed withdrawal of Vietnamese troops from Cambodia, but it stuck to saying that normalization could only take place after a settlement in Cambodia.[128] Clearly Beijing wanted to press Hanoi for more compromises. Like the United States, China stated explicitly that the Cambodian settlement was the precondition to improve bilateral relations between Beijing and Hanoi.

After long and hard bargaining among the different interests involved, Hanoi and the regime backed by it in Phnom Penh finally accepted the comprehensive settlement designed by the five permanent members of the United Nations Security Council to end the 12-year civil war in Cambodia. China achieved almost everything it had sought from Hanoi. First, the Soviets agreed to leave Indochina. In exchange for upgrading of Sino-Soviet relations, Moscow also promised to pressure Vietnam for concessions. Second, the Vietnamese pulled out of Cambodia and compromised on China's terms that the Khmer Rouge must be included in the Cambodian Supreme National Council under the United Nations framework. China made concessions as well. Beijing agreed to halt arms shipments to the Khmer Rouge as part of its contribution to building regional and international consensus on Cambodia.[129] Beijing also agreed to include the Hanoi-backed regime in the Cambodian settlement. After the Peace Treaty on a Comprehensive Political Settlement of the Cambodian Conflict was signed in Paris on October 23, 1991, China finally agreed to normalize its ties with Vietnam.[130] From November 5 to 10, 1991, the Vietnamese Communist Party Chief and Vietnamese Prime Minister paid an official visit to China, formally ending hostilities between the two countries.[131]

Reconciliation between Beijing and Hanoi also promoted accommodation between China and Laos. There had been a renewed warmth between Beijing and Vientiane since 1989 as China ventured into closer commercial, diplomatic, and party links with Laos. Between 1988 and 1990, more than half of all foreign investments in Laos came from China.[132] In December 1990, Chinese Premier Li Peng officially visited Laos.

ASEAN In the 1980s, China was very successful in developing friendly relations with the countries of the Association of Southeast Asian Nations (ASEAN). When Vietnam turned to Russia for support and became its ally, especially after Hanoi invaded Cambodia, the ASEAN nations quickly improved their relations with China and more or less sided with China on the issue. China also strengthened its security and political relationships particularly with Thailand, through which Beijing provided arms to resistance groups in Cambodia. Initially, Beijing called for formation of a united front against the expansionism of Vietnam and of the Soviet Union in the region. Later, China and the ASEAN cooperated with one another to work on a political settlement of Cambodian issues. On the whole, the ASEAN countries viewed China as a balancing power in the region to contain Hanoi and Moscow. But it was mainly a short-range rather than a long-term goal because of differences between China and the ASEAN in ideology, geo-political considerations and ethnic problems. Unlike

Thailand, Indonesia, Malaysia and the Philippines were much concerned about China's future role in Asia, especially China's potential military capability as a dominant power in the region.[133] They closely watched China's increasing activities in the South China Sea.

Beijing seemed to have realized the problem. Chinese Premier Li Peng in 1988 set forth "Four Principles for Sino-ASEAN" relations during his tour to Southeast Asia. The four principles included: (1) peaceful coexistence despite differences in social and political systems; (2) anti-hegemonism (i.e., China would not seek to be a hegemonist power and it would not interfere in the domestic affairs of the ASEAN countries); (3) further development of economic relations; and (4) continuing support for regional cooperation and initiatives from the ASEAN.[134] One problem which was deliberately removed in Beijing's relations with the ASEAN countries was that China terminated its support for the Communist guerrilla movement in Southeast Asia and paid more attention to state-to-state relations. As a result, In 1990, Indonesia reestablished diplomatic relations with China, thus ending the formal rupture caused by the 1965 attempted coup by Communists supported by China. China also established diplomatic relations with Singapore in the same year. Its stable relations with the Philippines, Malaysia and Thailand remained on track.

Beijing was very careful to follow a low-key policy toward overseas Chinese living in Southeast Asia. There are some 30 million ethnic Chinese living outside of China. Most of them live in Southeast Asia. In Malaysia, Chinese made up 35 percent of the population (5.2 million), the next largest ethnic group to the Malays (50 percent). In Singapore, Chinese comprise 77 percent of the population. In Thailand, there are 5.8 million Chinese while in Indonesia, 7.2 million.[135] Although Chinese constitute a minority ethnic group in Southeast Asia, they are generally successful in running business and play an important role in the local economy. From time to time, ethnic Chinese are the target of racial and religious conflict in countries where they live. In search of peace and development, Beijing, on the one hand, actively invited those overseas Chinese to bring back money to invest in their homeland. On the other hand, China advised them to cooperate, politically and economically, with local authorities where they lived. It particularly encouraged overseas Chinese living in Southeast Asia to give up dual citizenships and choose to become local citizens.

Trade relations between China and ASEAN members developed rapidly in the 1980s and two-way trade between them reached $6.6

billion in 1989. The ASEAN was becoming a major trading partner of China and the trend was toward as much economic activity and commerce as the traffic would bear. Improvement in relations with both Singapore and Indonesia further helped stimulate the Sino-ASEAN trade. Singapore became one of the important investors in China with contracts valued at $698 million at the end of 1989. Thailand had $157 million of investment in China. Sino-Thai trade was $800 million in 1988. Direct trade between China and Indonesia was resumed after some twenty years, and the value of annual trade was around $100 million.[136]

India Since the armed clashes on the Sino-Indian borders in 1962, relations between China and India had remained tense. In order to improve relations with India, China made several efforts. It repeatedly stated its recognition of India's importance in both regional and global politics and its interest in seeing a political settlement of Indo-Pakistan disputes. Beijing appealed to South Asian nations to settle their conflicts by peaceful means and refrained from statements in support of Pakistan, Beijing's long-standing ally, on Indo-Pakistani tensions over the Kashmir issue.[137]

Most importantly, both China and India agreed on further measures to lessen the possibility of armed conflict on their disputed borders. This long-standing issue was the principal source of friction between the two countries. During his Delhi visit in 1981, Chinese Foreign Minister Huang Hua and Indian leaders agreed to hold a series of talks on border and other territorial issues. Eight rounds of talks were held in the decade. But China's proposal, known as the "complex deal" which retained the status quo (i.e., India's formal recognition of the cession to China of the Aksai in the Western part of their common borders and China's recognition of the MacMahon Line as an international border in the east) was not accepted by New Delhi. No actual results were achieved. However, both sides were sincerely seeking to settle the problem and wanted to alleviate tensions in bilateral relations and find a way out of an impasse in the solution of the territorial issue.[138] Both of them restrained their behavior in the face of incidents which occurred on their common borders and did not interrupt their border talks. For example, the Chinese protested in 1986 against the Indian Parliament's decision to upgrade Arunachal Pradesh, a disputed area in the eastern sector between India and China, from a federal territory to a state of India. The Chinese even made incursions in an area known as Sumdrong Chu in Arunachal Pradesh. In April

1987, three times in less than a month, China charged India with provocative troop movements and air incursions. In 1986 India criticized Chinese involvement in Pakistan's nuclear program. But the approach of both sides to the conflict was relatively low-key, and the subject was discussed in a nonprovocative manner at the eighth Sino-Indian talks in New Delhi in November 1987.[139]

While continuing to work on settlement of border disputes, other aspects of bilateral relations between China and India developed in the 1980s. One major advance was Rajiv Gandhi's visit to Beijing in December 1988, the first such visit by an Indian prime minister since 1954. Both sides agreed to set up a joint working group mandated to seek a solution to the long-standing border dispute. The two nations also agreed to broaden cultural, educational, and scientific contacts and agreed in a diplomatic communiqué to maintain "peace and tranquility" along the border. The biggest gain for Beijing was the announcement by Prime Minister Gandhi that Tibet was an internal affair of China.[140] In December 1991, Chinese Premier Li Peng paid a reciprocal visit to New Delhi. This was the first visit to India by a Chinese head of government in 31 years. Besides, bilateral trade between the two countries amounted to $270 million in 1989.[141]

Mongolia China and Mongolia embarked on a new course in the late 1980s. Along with dramatic changes inside Mongolia, a younger generation of leaders sought to introduce political pluralism and a market economy there. They also sought to lessen dependence on the Soviet Union and remove Soviet military forces from their territory. Therefore, Mongolia broadened its contacts with the world and aimed at improved ties with China.[142] But both Beijing and Ulan Bator were cautious. In Mongolia, there was uncertainty as to whether the Chinese might again try to incorporate their country into a Greater China. On the Chinese side, there was uneasiness about new Mongolian nationalism which might appeal to nearly three million Mongols living in China's Inner Mongolia. Even so, cultural and economic relations between the two countries expanded. In August 1986, China and Mongolia signed their first consular treaty since diplomatic relations had been established in 1949.[143] More importantly, both sides singed a new border agreement in 1987.[144]

To sum up, in search of peace and development, Beijing must carefully deal with its Asian neighbors on such issues as territorial disputes, ethnic Chinese and China's defense development. Indeed, China has border disputes with most of the nations with which it shares a land frontier: North Korea, Russia, Vietnam and India. It also has territorial disputes over offshore marine zones and islands with Japan, South Korea, Vietnam, Indonesia, Malaysia, and the Philippines. Besides, China has to pay particular attention to the ethnic dimension in its relations with Southeast Asia because of the large number of overseas Chinese living in the region who are often the target of racial and religious conflict with local people. More importantly, Asian countries have long been very concerned about China's military strength and its potential dominant role in the region. In the 1980s, China's military reduction was well received among its Asian neighbors. But after 1989, they again got very worried about the increase in China's military spending, China's purchase of advanced weapon systems from abroad, and China's new push through the South China Sea.

Clearly, China must be very careful to balance different policy objectives. On the one hand, Beijing, with its rapid economic growth and rising nationalist mood, is determined to become a powerful country in the Asian-Pacific region. But on the other hand, China's primary interest is to create a stable international environment favorable to its domestic development. Therefore, China must cautiously balance different policy objectives. Otherwise, other countries will be perplexed by China's ambiguous behavior. In the 1980s China seemed to place more emphasis on improving relations with all of its neighbors than on pursuing either military or ideological expansionism in Asia. Indeed, if China wants to strengthen economic relationships with its Asian neighbors and to be accepted as a full partner in regional developments and consultative activities, it has to follow a stated policy of peace and development while carefully promoting its modernization program in national defense.

China and Western Europe

Although in the 1980s China paid more attention to its relations with the United States, the Soviet Union, Japan, and its Asian neighbors, Sino-Western European ties were important in Beijing's overall foreign policy because such relations were useful in improving China's position with the superpowers and Japan. China found it easier to deal with Europeans as simply distant but rich states. In fact, Europeans had always been more pragmatic than the United States (but not Japan) in their dealings with China. In the early days of the People's Republic, Britain, Switzerland, and the Scandinavian states recognized the Beijing regime just after the Communists came to power. In the 1960s, more Western European companies started to trade with Mainland China and in 1964, taking advantage of the Sino-Soviet conflict and a more relaxed international environment, France was the first major western power to normalize relations with Beijing. But because of their closer links with the United States, and then the Cultural Revolution in China, other European countries established diplomatic relations with Beijing only following the Sino-U.S. rapprochement in the early 1970s. In the 1980s, all Western European states, plus the European Community (EC) but not the Vatican, established diplomatic relations with China. Sino-Western European links were regularly buttressed in the 1980s by all kinds of exchange visits between the two sides. In contrast to Mao's period, all Western European heads of state or prime ministers had been to China during the 1980s and most Chinese leaders of the post-Mao period, including Deng Xiaoping, Hu Yaobang, Zhao Ziyang, Li Peng, and Jiang Zemin, visited Western Europe.[145] During twenty-six years in office as premier (October 1949-January 1976), Zhou Enlai hardly ever visited Western Europe (except for participation in the 1954 Geneva Conference) even though he made a score of trips abroad.

To be sure, strengthening of ties between China and Western Europe in the 1980s was far more in the economic area than in political and strategic terms.[146] The situation was different from China's policy toward Western Europe in the 1970s. At that time, China had placed more emphasis upon strategic factors vis-à-vis the Soviet threat, and both China and Western Europe adopted convergent positions on many international issues. But after China adopted an independent foreign policy in 1982, the "pro-NATO" stance became muted as part of Beijing's efforts to improve its ties with Moscow.[147] Thus, the strategic position of Western Europe was of less concern in Beijing's policy. In Hu Yaobang's report to the 1982 Party Congress, the United States, the Soviet Union, Japan and the Third World deserved attention, but Europe was not even mentioned.[148] Western Europe was seen more and more as an economic partner. In April 1989, Li Peng listed China's foreign relations in the following order of importance: the United States, the Soviet Union, China's Asian neighbors (Japan,, Korea, Pakistan, India, the ASEAN countries and Vietnam), and Europe (both Western and Eastern). Western Europe was listed just before Canada,

Australia and New Zealand, the Middle East, Africa, and South America.[149]

This shift resulted from China's perception of the international strategic balance of power. Beijing began to favor cooperation between countries regardless of their political, ideological and strategic differences. It welcomed greater international détente and saw it as the international condition for success of domestic economic reform.[150] Because of this, China adopted a new policy which encouraged Western Europe to engage in disarmament negotiations with the Soviet Union, supported the European peace movement, and enhanced cooperation between Western and Eastern Europe to contribute greater détente.[151]

As a consequence, relations between China and Western Europe in the 1980s, concentrated more on economic links. Western European technology, talent and money were given great attention by the Chinese. In Beijing's eyes, Western Europe was almost a perfect alternative to Japan or the United States, putting Beijing in a fine position to get good trading terms or long-term loans. In fact, Western Europe was an extremely fertile area for top-level technology transfer. China could shop around for the best goods and the best prices among a number of competing investors and traders in Western Europe. As a Chinese scholar bluntly put it, "of particular interest to China is the fact that Western European countries have been more liberal than other Western countries in sales of technology."[152]

The Chinese were quick to learn how to play on competition among European countries and on the complexity and contradictions of their two-level (national and European) export regulations.[153] In 1978, France signed an agreement on scientific and technological co-operation, the first of this kind between China and a Western country. In 1983-1985, West Germany, France, Italy and the Netherlands signed nuclear co-operation agreements with China. Moreover, Western European capitals were praised by Beijing for their contribution to relaxation of the North Atlantic Alliance Coordinating Committee for Export to Communist Countries (COCOM) approval procedures for exports to China. In 1988, the European Community's technology and equipment exports to China accounted for about 50 percent of China's total technology imports.[154] In this sense, China had "priority relations" with the European Community for it might provide Beijing with technology and equipment which the United States and Japan were reluctant to offer. In addition, one-fifth of China's total foreign loans came from the four major members of the European Community, France, West

Germany, Britain, and Italy. In the period 1979-1987, Western Europe invested $1.75 billion in China, just behind Hong Kong, the United States and Japan.[155] One of the most successful cooperative projects between China and Western Europe was the joint-venture of the Shanghai-Volkswagen Automobile Corporation (between China and Germany), manufacturing thousands upon thousands of "Santana" vehicles each year. This cooperation greatly upgraded China's automobile industry.[156]

In the 1980s, the European Community was the third largest trading partner of China (after Hong Kong and Japan).[157] But to some extent, the European share in China's foreign trade slowly deteriorated in relative terms. Totalling 20 percent of China's trade in the 1970s, the European Community did not take full advantage of the Chinese open door policy. Its share was 15.7 percent in 1986 and 12.5 percent two years later. Among EC members, West Germany was the largest trade partner with China. China traded three times more with Bonn (38 percent of European Community total trade with China) than with Paris (12 percent). Although in 1979, the European Community had signed a textile agreement and in 1980 decided to grant China general preferential treatment, the country still belonged to the fifth category of trade partners (i.e., state-controlled countries). Thus, China's exports were subject to more restrictions than those of many other countries. This obstacle also slowed down China's request to join the GATT. Quotas (especially for textiles), anti-dumping measures and duties kept China's trade deficit with the European Community high. In 1987 it was $3.5 billion. From the point of view of the European Community, China remained a minor trade partner accounting for only one percent of European Community's total foreign trade.[158]

Sino-Western European ties were hurt by the Tiananmen Square Incident in June 1989. The European Community and most Western European governments took a very tough stance condemning Chinese authorities for their brutality against unarmed citizens. They imposed economic sanctions, including prohibition of arms sales and government-funded or guaranteed loans. The European Community countries suspended all bilateral and high-level official contacts. However, they did not want to totally cease their relations with China. Britain and France did not interrupt their civil nuclear project in China which had been under construction for many years. West Germany froze its government-funded loan for the building of the Shanghai underground network, but since it had invested so much time and effort in winning this huge contract over other foreign competitors, it reconsidered the issue as the pressure of public opinion decreased.[159] For obvious economic and political reasons, Western European countries were interested in keeping China open and maintaining stable relations with it. And indeed, in just two years, most private firms and many individual Western European governments resumed business with China. In October 1990, the European Community decided to resume ministerial visits, aid, and loans to China.[160] In the fall of 1991, British Prime Minister John Major and Italian Prime Minister Giulio Andreotti travelled to China, indicating full restoration of high-level contacts between China and Western Europe. China's trade with Western Europe amounted to $17.32 billion in 1991, a 11.38 percent increase over the previous year.[161] To China, relations with Western Europe remained important as the latter was its major trading partner, technology supplier and money lender. For this reason, Beijing took a series of damage control measures after the Tiananmen events. It softened its stand and agreed to talk with the West about human rights issue and even cooperated with the West on some major regional and international issues. Despite the growing concern in the West about human rights violations in China and clashes within China between the desire for economic prosperity and domestic ideological concerns, Sino-Western European cooperation would continue to develop as long as China was on the track of economic modernization.

National Reunification Efforts

The reunification of Hong Kong, Macao and Taiwan with the mainland is an extension of Chinese domestic politics and reflects on the basic legitimacy of Beijing's rule. In fact, national integration has long been seen as proof of effective and successful leadership in China. In early 1980 Deng Xiaoping made national reunification one of three principal goals of his leadership for that decade (the other two: economic   modernization,   and   preserving   peace   and anti-hegemonism).[162] To reformist leaders, the way of handling the national reunification issue had a substantial impact on China's national interest. Any mismanagement of the Hong Kong or Taiwan question would destabilize the situation there and cast shadows on China's foreign relations. In return, it would block China's efforts to construct a peaceful external environment and its domestic economic development. Thus, consistent with China's foreign policy goals of peace and development, Deng Xiaoping and his associates took pragmatic steps in managing both the Hong Kong and Taiwan issues. On the one hand, Beijing firmly adhered to the principle of Chinese sovereignty over these areas. On the other hand, China agreed to maintain Hong Kong and Taiwan's current social, economic and political systems unchanged at least for fifty years. This is the so-called "one country, two systems" model initiated by Deng Xiaoping:

> The reunification of China is a national desire.... This goal, in my opinion, can only be reached by using the "one country, two systems" concept.... There are two ways to settle the issues [of Hong Kong and Taiwan]: peacefully and non-peacefully. The non-peaceful way, or the way to settle the issues by force, was deemed inappropriate. How could these issues be settled peacefully? It requires taking into full consideration the history and present conditions of Hong Kong and Taiwan.... All work should be based on reality. So, it is indispensable for us to respect the history and reality of Hong Kong and Taiwan when we consider the question.... After the reunification is realized, Taiwan [and Hong Kong] can still practice capitalism while the mainland maintains socialism, or "one country, two systems." ... If the capitalist system in Hong Kong and Taiwan is not guaranteed, stability and prosperity there cannot be maintained and peaceful settlement will become impossible.... So, on the Hong Kong question, China must first of all guarantee that the present capitalist system and lifestyle will remain unchanged for 50 years after 1997. The social system and lifestyle, and its position as an international financial center and free port will be kept.[163]

The "one country, two systems" model was the centerpiece of Beijing's policy toward Hong Kong, Macao and Taiwan in the 1980s. Under this model, Beijing succeeded in signing agreements with Britain (1984) and with Portugal (1987) respectively to settle the Hong Kong and Macao issues. Although the Taiwan question did not involve regaining sovereignty from a foreign government, the essential appeal in Beijing's drive for reunification with Taiwan also rested on this model. With dramatic changes on both sides of the Taiwan Strait in the 1980s, substantial political adaptation took place in the policies of Beijing and Taipei.

The Settlement of Hong Kong and Macao

Chinese policy toward Hong Kong reflected Beijing's political as well economic interests. Politically, Chinese leaders were pushed by anti-imperialist ideological imperatives, stemming from the deep and bitter experience of China over the past century, to reassert strongly their sovereignty over the colony. Moreover, reformist leaders in Beijing were aware that they could use a successful recovery of such "lost" territory as a way to build nationalist support for their leading positions and other programs at home. A firm stand regarding sovereignty over Hong Kong also made clear to foreign leaders with an interest in other territories claimed by China (such as Taiwan, the Spratly Islands in the South China Sea, and some border areas with China's neighbors) that China was determined to reassert its right to rule lands it regarded as Chinese.[164] At the same time, China wanted to keep social and economic stability in Hong Kong so as to demonstrate the feasibility of the "one country, two systems" model to Taiwan. Through settlement of Hong Kong, Beijing wanted also to enhance its credibility and confidence in relations with the United States, Japan, Britain, and other Western countries.

Economically, Hong Kong is of vital economic importance to China. As one of the world's major financial and communication centers, Hong Kong's share in China's total trade rose from 11 percent in 1978 to 25 percent in 1987. In 1987 two-way trade between China and Hong Kong amounted to $20.6 billion, making the territory for the first time China's largest trading partner, followed by Japan with $15.6 billion. Since then Hong Kong steadily remained this position.[165] In fact, China increasingly used the territory as an entrepôt between itself and its trading partners. Sixty percent of Hong Kong's imports from the mainland were now reexported. Between 1978 and 1987, around two-thirds of foreign direct investment in China came from Hong Kong.[166] China received over 35 percent of its annual foreign earnings from exports to and through Hong Kong, and from investments there. In 1986 China's investments in Hong Kong topped $5 billion, ranking first in the area. Since then China remained the largest foreign investor there.[167] Besides, most of China's technology purchases and managerial advice came through Hong Kong. Hong Kong also enjoyed many favorable advantages in American-Chinese entrepôt trade, including roles in training Chinese managers and analyzing policy changes in

China, technology transfer, availability of China experts, banking service support, connections to Chinese trading companies, geographic location, housing facilities, information collection, international communications, and recreation facilities.[168]

During the 1980s, Hong Kong served as the "third party's place" for China to contact Taiwan and the countries which had no diplomatic relations with China. These countries included South Korea, Indonesia and Israel. Via the Hong Kong market, there was substantial indirect trade between China and those countries. In July 1987, Taipei authorities lifted the ban on direct trips to Hong Kong from Taiwan in order to facilitate a "detour" to the mainland for "unofficial business."[169]

With these considerations in mind, Deng's policy toward the future of Hong Kong was to resume sovereignty over the territory without destroying stability and prosperity there. The issue of the future of Hong Kong was raised by the British government because the impending end of the lease (1997) governing the New Territories began to affect individual property leases, mortgages (often made for at least 15 years), and other financial and real estate arrangements in Hong Kong. It prompted British authorities to raise the issue in discussions with Chinese leaders at the time of British Prime Minister Thatcher's visit to China in September 1982. The visit produced an agreement between China and Britain to "enter into talks through diplomatic channels with the common aim of maintaining stability and prosperity of Hong Kong."[170] The visit was marked by pointed differences over the legal status of the territory at a press conference in Hong Kong, following her China stay. Mrs. Thatcher emphasized that nineteenth-century treaties governing the status of the colony remained the basis of Britain's position, although she added that London would talk with Beijing in the hope that the treaties could be amended by mutual agreement. Mrs. Thatcher insisted that British rights drawn from the three nineteenth-century treaties concerning Hong Kong be ensured and that the issue of the colony be settled "legally."[171]

This position appeared to have enraged Beijing which saw the treaties as unequal and humiliating. To China, Hong Kong must be returned to Beijing's control in 1997 when Britain's lease on most of the colony's territory expires according to the Second Beijing Convention between China and Britain (1898).[172] The Chinese Foreign Ministry's spokesman replied that Beijing's "consistent position" was that "China is not bound by the unequal treaties and that the whole

Hong Kong area will be recovered when conditions are ripe."[173] Clearly, sovereignty over Hong Kong appeared to be the most important principle for the Chinese leadership. To counter the British position, Beijing insisted that London's recognition of China's sovereignty over Hong Kong be the basis on which to negotiate the issue. Beijing also rejected London's stance that the "British presence" politically in Hong Kong after 1997 was a condition for stability and prosperity of the region as a "de facto renewal of the unequal treaties."[174] During the whole process of negotiation, Beijing made its position clear that the principle of sovereignty was not negotiable.

After months of secret diplomatic communications, the two sides issued a joint statement on July 1, 1983 announcing the start of formal negotiations on Hong Kong's future. Talks continued into 1984 and were supplemented in June 1984 by discussions of a working group of Chinese and British diplomats who were trying to come up with a draft agreement by Beijing's September 1984 deadline. This deadline had been set by Deng when he told Mrs. Thatcher in September 1982 that a Sino-British agreement on Hong Kong had to be reached in two years. Beijing subsequently announced that if agreement were not reached by that time, China would announce its plans for Hong Kong unilaterally.[175]

London had little leverage over China as Great Britain had only a small economic interest in Hong Kong, it trailed far behind the United States, China, and Japan as Hong Kong's leading trading partners and accounted for only a modest share of foreign investment in the territory.[176] According to the Second Convention of Beijing (1898), the New Territories must revert to China in 1997. Without that land (i.e., 90 percent of the territory of Hong Kong), the colony was not viable as a British possession. Britain hoped to renew the lease on the New Territories or continue the status quo after 1997. But Beijing was determined to recover complete sovereignty over all of Hong Kong by 1997. Under this pressure, London gave in and accepted China's sovereignty and control of Hong Kong after 1997. In April 1984 it also accepted Beijing's two year deadline. Finally, the accord on the future of Hong Kong was initialed in September 1984 and officially signed by the Chinese and British governments in December of that year.[177]

The agreement illustrates China's flexibility in separating principle from practice. In the negotiations, Beijing refused to budge on the principle of sovereignty, thus forcing the British to give up their goal of retaining a role in the territory's government beyond 1997. But once

Britain had conceded this point, China's nationalistic and pragmatic leaders were able to make a bilateral, binding agreement that spelt out in detail a remarkable degree of autonomy for the "Special Administrative Region" of Hong Kong according to the design of "one country and two systems."[178] To Beijing, it was in China's interest to maintain Hong Kong's dynamic economy. After decades of development, Hong Kong's economy had become one of the miracles of Asia. Therefore, prosperity in Hong Kong must be preserved. For this purpose, Beijing made determined efforts to keep capital and trained people from flowing out of the territory. Realizing the substantial social, economic, and political differences between China and Hong Kong, Beijing's basic position as written in both the Sino-British Joint Declaration and the Basic Law for Hong Kong was as follows. In order to maintain Hong Kong's social and political stability, Beijing agreed that current economic, social, judicial systems, and life-style would remain unchanged, but stripped of the British presence. It promised that socialism would not be introduced before 2047. Economic and individual rights in Hong Kong would remain in place. Residents would have their own travel documents and travel freely. Hong Kong would be allowed to issue its own currency, maintain a free port, and conclude a wide range of economic and cultural agreements with other countries. Besides, Hong Kong's chief executive officers were to be chosen from among local residents, appointed by Beijing after "election or consultation." Beijing promised not to send its own officials. Beijing, however, would control Hong Kong's foreign affairs and defense.[179] Through all these measures, Beijing wanted to reduce panic in Hong Kong. Even after the Tiananmen Square events, Chinese President Yang Shangkun reconfirmed in April 1990 that "the socialist system and policies will not be practiced in Hong Kong."[180]

The settlement of Hong Kong soon led to resolving the issue of Macao, a colony controlled by Portugal. Three years after the Sino-British Joint Declaration, the Macao issue was settled to Beijing's great satisfaction. Four rounds of negotiation between China and Portugal in less than a year, from June 1986 to March 1987, were held smoothly and in a friendly and cooperative atmosphere. Being well aware of China's strong position on the issue of sovereignty, Lisbon did not even bother attempting to bargain with Beijing in this regard. On March 26, 1987, both sides signed a Joint Declaration regarding the future of Macao. By the terms of the agreement, Beijing will resume sovereignty over Macao in 1999. Almost all Beijing's promises toward Hong Kong after 1997 were repeated in the agreement regarding the future of Macao.[181]

The successful resolution of the Hong Kong and Macao issues had a far-reaching impact. Reform-minded leaders in Beijing could then claim added legitimacy for their rule. They could also claim a substantial achievement in their open door policy and proceed to open the door even wider. Further reform plans were adopted to develop Special Economic Zones along China's coast in order to blur the lines between the former colonies and the mainland. Success in this venture would eventually mean that the larger prize of Taiwan might also be won.

Relations between the Mainland and Taiwan

Although in 1980 Deng Xiaoping made reunification of Taiwan with the mainland one of three goals for that decade, he later suggested that that might take longer and expressed hope that it should be realized in his lifetime. For this, Beijing made broad proposals to Taiwan for negotiations under the formula of "one country, two systems" and conducted "unification diplomacy" vis-à-vis Taipei's "pragmatic diplomacy" in which Taipei tried hard to win international recognition. The Chinese President made it clear in his interview with a Taipei-based newspaper that, under the notion of "one China," Taiwan would have more autonomy than any other part of China, permitting it to maintain its own economic and political system, and even allowing it to retain its own military forces. Moreover, China pledged that it would not send any officials to Taiwan to take part in civil or military affairs, although Taiwan could send representatives to the mainland to participate in the central government. In order to avoid a deviation from "one China" position, he called for negotiations between the Kuomintang (KMT) and the Communist Party instead of between "two governments."[182]

Meanwhile, political developments on Taiwan took a dramatic turn. Under both internal and external pressures, President Chiang Ching-kuo, son of Chiang Kai-shek, loosened the long-established authoritarian rule on the island in his last days in office. In 1986 he allowed formation of opposition parties to challenge the virtual monopoly of the ruling Kuomintang. In September that year, the

Democratic Progressive Party (DPP) was established. This marked a potentially epochal step in Taiwan's democratization. The next move of Chiang was to abolish martial law (i.e., "the Decree of the State Emergency") which had been imposed on the island to repress any political opposition in the name of preventing Communist penetration since the late 1940s. As a result, public demonstrations could now take place in Taiwan. Control of news media was also loosened and the press became increasingly free of censorship and self-imposed restrictions. Finally, on July 28, 1987, authorities changed their rigid attitudes toward the mainland and allowed people from Taiwan to visit their relatives on the mainland. When Chiang Ching-kuo died in 1988, his power was smoothly transferred to his hand-picked successor, Lee Teng-hui, a native-born Taiwanese. This was a remarkable event in the mainlander-dominated regime. All these events of democratization in Taiwan had a far-reaching impact on relations between the mainland and Taiwan.

The initial contact occurred in May 1986 in Hong Kong as Taipei negotiated with Beijing representatives for return of a Taiwan-owned civilian transport plane that had been hijacked to the mainland by one dissident pilot. This was the first direct talk between the mainland and Taiwan since 1949. As a result of the negotiation, the plane and the other two pilots were returned to Taiwan while the dissident pilot remained in the mainland.[183] In 1987 small but significant steps opened up contacts across the Taiwan Strait. Mainland books on nonpolitical subjects could be published on the island, provided that the simplified characters were replaced by traditional script. Permission was granted for unlimited travel to Hong Kong, opening the gate for unofficial crossing into the mainland. This was followed by authorized visits to the mainland for family reunions, triggering more than 100,000 requests in the first month. Taiwan-mainland trade reportedly surpassed $1 billion in 1987, mainly through Hong Kong.[184]

Beijing reacted ambivalently to these changes. On the one hand, it welcomed visits as one of its long-standing proposals, the others including direct mail, transport, and trade. On the other hand, it was worried that political liberalization might tempt Taiwanese independence advocates to pursue the goal of separating the island from the mainland permanently. Beijing warned that development of an independent Taiwan would prompt the mainland to use force even though Beijing hoped to reunify the island peacefully.

Taipei further loosened its control over contacts between the two sides of the strait following the Thirteenth Congress of Kuomintang. On July 12, 1988, the Taiwan Olympic Committee announced its willingness to send a delegation to participate in the Asian Games to be held in Beijing in 1990. (Taiwan athletes in the name of "Chinese Taipei" went to the Eleventh Asian Games in Beijing in September 22-October 7, 1990.[185] Meanwhile, commercial, cultural and sports institutions were allowed to send members to the mainland to take part in different meetings and activities. Such decisions indicated that Taiwan was beginning to redefine its "three nos" policy (i.e., no compromise, no negotiation, and no contact) toward Beijing.[186]

Reform in the mainland provided greater economic attraction for Taiwan than at any previous time. It offered the promise of profitable investment opportunities and expanding markets in exchange for badly needed natural and human resources that were readily accessible and priced competitively. In 1988 many of the barriers to Taiwanese direct trade, investment, cultural exchanges and visits to the mainland were further lowered. Between November 2, 1987 and August 31, 1988 nearly 230,000 people formally applied to visit the mainland. Trade via Hong Kong reached $2 billion in 1988. Beijing called these developments a "turning-point."[187]

The growth of economic and cultural ties between the two societies was explosive. The cross-Taiwan strait trade rose from nothing in 1978 to $4 billion in 1990 and to $5.79 billion in 1991, and Taiwanese investment on the mainland increased to $2.5 billion in 1991.[188] According to some reports, Taiwan had accumulated a $10 billion surplus with China over previous years.[189] By the end of 1990, an amazing total of 600,000 to 700,000 individuals from Taiwan had made a total of 1.6 million visits to the mainland, and 6,000 to 7,000 mainland residents had visited the island.[190] Quasi-formal arrangements were made for direct mail, telephone calls, and repatriation of persons "wanted" for crimes or involved in incidents at sea. Not only were military tensions between Taiwan and the mainland sharply reduced, but Beijing and Taipei also even supported each other over the disputed Diaoyutai Islands with Japan and the disputed islands in the South China Sea with other claimants. Further liaison at a semi-official level was set up to handle various matters.[191] Both sides seemed to seek to strengthen ties with each other to reduce the risks of misunderstanding and potential miscalculation. In November 1990, Taiwan established the Foundation for Exchanges Across the Taiwan Strait to function as a nongovernmental intermediary between China and Taiwan.[192] In response, Beijing also established a similar semi-official organization (i.e., the Association for Relations Across the Taiwan Strait) in 1991 to promote contacts across the Taiwan Strait.[193] Yet, when investment flow toward China risked getting out of hand, Taiwan tried to cool the "mainland fever" by discouraging major petrochemical and other investments.[194]

But Beijing was strongly hoping for still closer economic integration with Taiwan that would restart social and cultural interdependence between the two societies. Indeed, such integration had significant political overtones. Economic and cultural reinteractions were regarded as tangible results of reunification efforts. However, like previous decades, political issues continued to dominate relations between the mainland and Taiwan. Their incompatible political systems continued to block further integration between the mainland and Taiwan. Beijing was very upset by the tendency toward Taiwan's independence of the mainland which had gained more strength as Taiwanization developed within the Kuomintang and as the Democratic Progressive Party which publicly promoted Taiwanese independence grew. Taiwan's economic prosperity and political democratization also gave the island more bargaining chips with the mainland. Beijing found that people on the mainland had become impressed by Taiwan's economic progress and closely watched political developments on the island. Internationally, Taipei, with its economic strength, was very active to pursue "flexible diplomacy" as a way to upgrade Taiwan's international status. Taiwan successfully changed the status of its economic representation in some key countries to semi-diplomatic status. By using economic aid as means to attract some developing countries, Taiwan even restored diplomatic relations with them.[195]

Although relations between the mainland and Taiwan had moved from no-contact to substantial contacts in various fields, reunification still remained a distant goal for both sides. Beijing refused to promise that it would not use force to solve the Taiwan issue. Beijing clearly understood that it was in the best interests of both Beijing and Taipei to solve the reunification issue peacefully. A military attack on or blockade of Taiwan would undermine the very core of foreign policy restructuring pursued by China since 1982. But in order to deter the tendency toward Taiwanese independence, China persistently maintained its right to use military force if Taiwan declared independence or if a foreign power directly interfered in the Taiwan issue. Although the portion of Taiwan's electorate favoring formal independence was small and no major foreign countries publicly supported it,[196] Beijing was still worried that more international recognition of Taiwan and continuous foreign military sales to Taipei could prompt authorities on the island to distance themselves from the mainland. Besides, democratization and the weakening of political leaders who favored a reunification policy in Taiwan could eventually erode the island's commitment to "one China." So Beijing would make double efforts to call for negotiations with Taipei under the "one China" concept, the very foundation of China's policy toward Taiwan. Meanwhile, Beijing would offer favorable terms to attract more Taiwanese investment on the mainland and increase trade and cultural ties with Taiwan. Politically, Beijing would continue to block Taiwan's moves to gain international recognition, making the Taiwan issue one of the most sensitive aspects in Beijing's relations with other countries.

Chapter 9

Conclusion

Policy Effectiveness

China's "independent foreign policy of peace" in the 1980s included four specific aspects: (1) pursuing a nonalignment strategy and maintaining peace to foster a stable external environment; (2) developing friendly relations with all countries, especially China's neighbors, on the basis of the principle of peaceful coexistence; (3) expanding foreign economic ties; and (4) making efforts to reunify the country. In a decade of unremitting efforts, Beijing achieved remarkable successes in all these aspects.

By claiming not to align itself with either the United States or the Soviet Union, Beijing became more able to handle its relations with both superpowers. It not only increased the ability to bargain with the United States, but also succeeded in ending the adversarial relations with the Soviet Union. With this success and the emergence of a new international détente, China had achieved the most stable security environment at any point since the founding of the People's Republic in 1949.[1] For the first time, China no longer faced an overwhelming strategic threat to its national security from a superpower. Under the new relaxed climate of international relations, the local and regional conflicts around China's periphery were also in the process of being diffused. Ties with all of China's traditional rival neighbors, such as Russia, India, Vietnam and Indonesia, were greatly improved and a new type of good neighborly relations emerged. China was glad to see no real danger of a major war in Asia. This was the situation to which the Chinese leadership had long aspired, allowing China to wholeheartedly pursue its long-awaited goal of economic modernization.

China's confidence in its own security could be seen in Beijing's big military cutbacks in the 1980s. Because of its dedication to the task of economic reform under the leadership of Deng Xiaoping, China needed a peaceful and stable international environment conducive to its modernization drive. The search for reduced tensions in international relations thus became a constant and consistent aim of China's foreign policy during this period.[2] By promoting international détente, Beijing began actively participating in international peace efforts, ranging from U.N. peace-keeping operations to arms control and disarmament negotiations. Unlike their previous critical attitudes, the Chinese began to favor the arms talks between the superpowers. On the regional conflict in Asia, Beijing supported a political settlement of the Cambodian and Afghan issues. It also welcomed further relaxation of tensions on the Korean peninsula.

By abandoning Mao's "three worlds" theory, China no longer followed an anti-Soviet line to establish a "united front." Instead, it actively developed relations with all countries in the world in accordance with the principle of peaceful coexistence, irrespective of the differences in their political, economic, and social systems. By the end of 1980s, China had established diplomatic relations with over 133 countries in the world.[3] China was no longer an anti-Soviet or an anti-American country, but rather, it sought stable relations with both of them on the basis of what its leaders perceived to be in China's best interest.

The most striking progress was seen in Beijing's foreign economic relations. Through opening up, China dramatically expanded its foreign economic relations with all possible partners in the world. In its quest for advanced technology, capital investment and managerial know-how, China, by the end of 1980s, had established a widening network of trade, scientific, technological and cultural ties with the outside world.. Also China joined almost all the major international organizations. Through all these activities, China deepened its involvement in the global system. Amazing successes were achieved in greatly broadening China's range of trading partners and increasing its foreign trade volume to an unprecedented level. Billions of dollars of investment and loans from abroad went to China annually. Cultural, educational, scientific, and tourist exchanges between China and the rest of the world expanded drastically in the 1980s.

The success of Beijing's diplomacy in the 1980s was also seen in its pragmatic handling of the Hong Kong and Macao questions in negotiations with Great Britain and Portugal. On the Taiwan issue, the Chinese succeeded in pushing Washington to promise to end U.S. arms sales to the island eventually. Substantial progress was also made in the bilateral relationship between the mainland and Taiwan.

In short, Beijing's multi-dimensional foreign policy of the 1980s was a blend of strategic independence, peaceful coexistence, economic opening and policy flexibility. Of course, it was also combined with nationalistic sentiments over the issues regarding Hong Kong, Macao and Taiwan, and with several campaigns of anti-Western ideological influence in China's foreign activities. On the whole, the policy produced tangible economic benefits for the Chinese populace at large, brought technological gains for the country's economic infrastructure, and created unprecedented peace and security for China. The success of the external component of Deng Xiaoping's reform program not only greatly reinforced his domestic reform programs, but also had a tremendous impact of the Chinese society.

Driving Forces behind China's Foreign Policy Restructuring

In retrospect, the fundamental reasons for China's foreign policy restructuring in the 1980s were the shifts that had taken place in China's external strategic environment, the domestic demand for reform and economic modernization, and the change in the composition of the Chinese leadership. Other reasons, such as Dengist pragmatism, China's nationalistic feelings, and an increased foreign policy agenda, also played important parts in shaping China's foreign policy in the 1980s.

International Strategic Factors

The way Deng Xiaoping and his close supporters perceived China's external environment was an important aspect of restructuring Beijing's foreign policy in the 1980s. The international balance of power remained central to China's definition of global reality with attendant constraints and opportunities. Given the dramatic changes in the international environment in the 1980s, China's post-Mao leaders questioned the wisdom of alignment with one or the other superpower as a way of protecting the country's interest.

In the 1970s, China's foreign policy had mainly focused on opposing the perceived Soviet military threat and Beijing had to advocate the need to form a "united front" with the United States, Western Europe, Japan and the Third World to fight against Soviet military expansion. This policy of China stemmed from its estimation of the international situation at the time and arose out of Mao's "three worlds" theory. Beijing maintained that Moscow was the main threat both to China's security and to world peace since the Soviet Union was on the offensive while the United States was on the defensive in the world strategic pattern.

But in the 1980s, great changes took place in the international situation which challenged the basic assumptions of China's "united front" foreign policy. First, after Ronald Reagan came to power, the United States began seeking military superiority over the Soviet Union in deploying nuclear weapons in Europe and in developing new strategic defensive weapon systems. Washington was firm on rolling back the Soviet influence in the Third World. A most vivid example of its determination was the United States invasion of Grenada in October 1983. Meanwhile, the Soviet Union was struggling with a sagging domestic economy, the mire of Afghanistan and overcommitment to its allies and clients. Beijing concluded that the superpower balance of power had shifted from the Soviet offensive policy to a certain strategic parity and that such a parity was likely to persist for a long period of time. As a result, the objective ground for China to unite with one against the other had disappeared and Mao's "three worlds" theory was no longer applicable. Thus, China could follow a more independent and flexible policy. The relaxed international situation also provided a good opportunity for China to concentrate on domestic economic reform.[4]

Second, China met difficulties in its bilateral relations with the United States over such issues as U.S. arms sales to Taiwan and technology transfers. On these issues, the Chinese sensed that the United States took China for granted since Beijing had to look to Washington for help in security and economic cooperation. Also the United States could act as it pleased on sensitive questions concerning China while Beijing had no option but to accept all the outcomes. Under such circumstances, China started to take advantage of the flexibility presented by the change in the global balance of power and distance itself from the United States in strategic cooperation. It announced that Beijing would not be subordinate to or ally itself with either superpower. Instead, it would keep a working relationship with Washington and tried to develop broad-based ties not just on the single basis of strategic cooperation. In dealing with the Soviets, Beijing insisted that the obstacles be removed before normalization between the two countries. It seemed to Chinese leaders that a policy of nonalignment was the best choice because China could take advantage of the basic equilibrium of strength between the superpowers and keep initiatives in their own hands while dealing with international affairs according to their own interest. Starting in the mid-1980s, China's assessment of the strategic balance became even more optimistic. It perceived that the forces of peace were growing due to the declining influence of the superpowers and the development of multipolarity in international relations. The Chinese were finally convinced that superpower détente was real and that the Soviet Union under Gorbachev was changing. The "new thinking" in Soviet foreign policy led to Moscow's own version of the open door, détente with the United States and a winding down of many regional conflicts. The 1987 INF Treaty and the subsequent agreements between the superpowers to negotiate seriously on arms reductions and on cutting back involvement in regional conflicts further enhanced China's confidence in world peace and international cooperation. Beijing concluded that the world was entering into a relatively long period of relaxation. This long-term confidence made the Chinese engage in major military cutbacks and concentrate on economic development. In short, strategic changes during the 1980s shifted the Chinese assessment of the world situation, their approach to the question of peace and war, and their attitude towards the superpowers.

Modernization Drive

Another fundamental driving force behind China's foreign policy restructuring in the 1980s was internal economic reform under Deng Xiaoping. Indeed, China had faced combined economic, political and social problems at the time when Mao died in 1976. Economically, it experienced little or no growth during that time because of the failure of Mao's policies and natural disasters. China's economy was almost on the verge of collapse. Politically, Beijing was confronted with widespread disillusion and cynicism because of the devastating consequences of the Cultural Revolution. Ideologically, the Chinese people were at best confused. In theory, Communism appeared to be able to offer a more consistent and attractive alternative to China than other social theories. In practice, however, what had happened in China was not convincing. This was particularly shocking in comparison to other Asian countries such as Japan, South Korea, Taiwan, Hong Kong and Singapore, where economic miracles were taking place during the time when China was in a political turmoil. An awareness of China's backwardness was increasingly felt by the Chinese elite and the masses alike.

After several years of power struggle within the Chinese leadership, the reformers led by Deng Xiaoping came to power in Beijing. In order to consolidate the tottering rule of the Communist Party and strengthen China's national power, the reformers argued that the only way out of difficulties was to deliver good economic results and improve the people's living standards. For this purpose, an economic reform program was introduced. Deng Xiaoping clearly understood that economic development was the linchpin determining the success or failure of his reform leadership. Unlike Mao, who could base his leadership claim on the success of the Chinese Communist revolution, Deng and his reform-minded colleagues had to base their legitimacy on economic development.[5] For this reason, they redefined China's top priority from Mao's revolutionary struggles to a modernization drive. In reforming Mao's policies and promoting economic development, the reformers followed an unprecedentedly pragmatic, often trial-and-error approach to their reform programs.

The emphasis placed on economic modernization led to major restructuring in China's foreign policy in two aspects. The most fundamental one was Beijing's desire for a peaceful and stable international environment to serve China's long-term development needs. As Deng Xiaoping put it in 1984, "China needs at least twenty years of peace to concentrate on our domestic development."[6] In keeping with this principle, China adopted what could well be described as a policy of omni-directional peaceful coexistence. Beijing improved ties with its traditional adversaries. Moreover, modernization sharply reduced the possibility for China to become again a destabilizing force in Asia. No longer was China a revolutionary force that supported insurgencies against neighboring governments or sought to reform the international system, as was true during parts of the Maoist period.[7] Instead, China became much more cooperative in its foreign activities.

The second outcome of the emphasis on economic modernization was the expansion of China's foreign economic contacts. Opening to the outside world represented one of the most dramatic aspects of Beijing's foreign policy restructuring in the 1980s. The Chinese leaders realized that they could never make the modernization drive a success by closing their country to international contacts. Modernization of China depended in the long term on continued and deepening integration with the world economy because it was the international economy that set criteria for modernity and efficiency.[8] Therefore, China must open itself and participate in the international economic system. Clearly, openness itself not only meant a major change in China's foreign policy, but also meant that China had accepted the current international economic structure.

It is not difficult to see that China's foreign policy in the 1980s was no longer driven solely by security considerations as it had been in the 1970s. The modernization factor dramatically increased its influence on China's foreign policy making. This result came from inside China and was reinforced by the message from the outside world. Because of this, opening up was no longer motivated only by strategic need, but also by the necessity for domestic economic development. Thus, China's diplomacy in the 1980s increasingly reflected the stress of economic considerations as shown in the efforts to preserve peace, improve ties with other nations, and expand business contacts. In conclusion, the all-directional peace policy of Beijing in the 1980s could be largely explained by the fact that China needed an external environment favorable to its economic development.

Political Leadership

The most decisive factor which led to the restructuring of China's foreign policy was the dominance of Beijing's reform-minded leadership headed by Deng Xiaoping and his principal associates, Zhao Ziyang and Hu Yaobang. This leadership emerged as China faced the adverse political and economic crises of the immediate post-Mao era. Defeating their opponents in the leadership power struggle, the reformers finally gained political control in Beijing. Their main rivals were prominent individuals identified with Mao's policies with their extreme emphasis on revolutionary values as the basis for the country's development. This approach was discredited because of its severely negative consequences, especially during the Cultural Revolution.[9] With a strong commitment to modernization as the logical alternative to the Maoist approach to the country's development, Deng Xiaoping and his supporters swiftly steered China onto a course of decidedly un-Maoist reforms.

It was this political change in the composition of the top Chinese leadership that had a direct impact on Beijing's foreign policy in the 1980s. In fact, China's "independent foreign policy of peace" stemmed from the careful calculations by the reformers concerning Beijing's adaptation to the changes in the international environment and to the domestic demand for economic development. They found that the past foreign policy was no longer productive in serving China's national interest and needed restructuring. Under the new circumstances, China's foreign policy was no longer to forge an anti-Soviet "united front" but to foster a stable and peaceful international environment in support of the country's modernization. They hoped to adopt an effective foreign policy better serving China's national interest and reinforcing their leadership status at home as well. Luckily enough, the positive changes in the international strategic balance of power presented opportunities rather than constraints for Beijing to pursue a more flexible stance in its foreign behavior. The leadership quickly recognized that the U.S.-Soviet strategic parity and international multipolarity made it possible for China to enjoy a tranquil environment in Asia long enough for the country to concentrate on domestic reform. Before long China dropped the "united front" policy and adopted a new one centered on independence, peace and economic development.

Adoption of the "independent foreign policy of peace" typifies the fact that China's foreign policy is determined by its national interest as understood by its ruling circles. As before, individuals play decisive roles in the formulation and implementation of China's foreign policy restructuring. It is Deng Xiaoping's leadership and vision that have led China to domestic reform and foreign policy restructuring. To Deng, economic development is the basic solution for the domestic and international problems faced by China. Not only the positive changes in the international situation assured Beijing that peace was possible, but also economic dynamics elsewhere in East Asia convinced the Chinese reform leadership that China could also prosper once it opened up. China's foreign policy restructuring in the 1980s took place as the Chinese reform-minded leaders perceived the objective conditions at home and abroad and acted upon them. Much emphasis, thus, must be placed on the role of decision-makers and their perceptions in foreign policy restructuring. This point is especially important in a country such as China where personal relationships among the leaders are of vital importance and policy agenda is shaped primarily by the dynamics of intra-elite interactions.

It is worth pointing out that the reform leadership under Deng Xiaoping was not immune to political opposition throughout the process of China's foreign policy restructuring. Like Deng's other reform programs, the open door policy was criticized for making too many compromises on Chinese sovereignty to lure foreign investment. It was also blamed for corrupting Chinese values and civilization.[10] Setting up special economic zones was considered as ideological surrender to capitalism. The military establishment strongly opposed defense cutbacks and was not ready for the reconciliation with Vietnam that took place, they believed, too soon. In keeping manageable relations with Washington, Deng Xiaoping also had to carefully deal with overreaction in the name of national sovereignty from the conservatives on issues related to Taiwan. Besides, in reopening relations with Moscow, Deng deliberately developed relations with the West one step ahead of that with Moscow and restrained the sentiment of the party's pro-Soviet group to speed up Sino-Soviet reconciliation.

Although Deng Xiaoping met many problems in his domestic programs, he dominated China's foreign policy making in the 1980s. His strategy of consolidating power within the Chinese leadership was characterized by supremely adept coalition formation and manipulation.[11] Compared with Mao, Deng did not have the absolute authority and power of his predecessor to silence or eliminate different opinions from other senior leaders, such as Chen Yun who for a long time prior to the Cultural Revolution had ranked higher than Deng within the party hierarchy. Deng and Chen shared many similar ideas on a broad range of domestic and foreign policy issues. There were, however, differences between the two. Domestically, Chen was known to favor a more centrally planned economy than Deng did. Internationally, Deng supported a foreign policy that would draw China closer to the West. By contrast, Chen was virtually the only top Chinese leader who had not made a single public statement criticizing the Soviet Union during the Sino-Soviet confrontation. Long before the formal normalization of relations between China and the Soviet Union in 1989, Chen had advocated a more conciliatory policy toward Moscow.[12]

There was consensus among Chinese leaders on the need for dismantling the irrational features of the Maoist era in the 1980s. But they differed on the question of how far and how fast they should go. Openly voiced differences at the top level required more time for consultation, coordination, and compromise. Deng had to tolerate different opinions at the top level. However, through masterful political dealings, Deng managed to control the political agenda and insure that the core of his reform program was not interrupted. He adopted a "middle course" to deal with leadership differences.[13] On the one hand, Deng spared no pains to put forward opening up and his other economic reform programs. But on the other hand, he advocated no political liberalization and believed that political liberalization in China would inevitably lead to chaos making economic reforms impossible. This is Deng's reform strategy labeled as "one center and two basic points." One center (*zhongxin*) meant that economic work was the central task of the government and all other work must be subordinated to and serve it. Two basic points referred to the two policies to support the central task. The first policy was that rapid economic development could only be made through the bold restructuring of the planned economy and through the opening up to the outside world. Deng strongly criticized the conservatives and their "leftist" and "ossified" thinking. He believed that the introduction of the market mechanism was the only way to lead China's economic reform to a success. The second basic point was to oppose any political liberalization and adhere to the political rule of the Communist Party. Deng argued that this policy was to prevent China from any social instability or chaos in the process of economic reform. For this purpose, he specified four cardinal principles of upholding socialism, the people's democratic dictatorship, the leadership of the Communist Party, and Marxism-Leninism and Mao Zedong Thought. Obviously, Deng's reforms were economic, not political, and he still insisted that China was Communist.[14]

This strategy produced an oscillating political cycle over the decade of the 1980s. On the one hand, continuing economic reform tended to generate pressures for political liberalization. As a result, a relaxation of political restrictions and criticism of the Cultural Revolution and Mao culminated in a crackdown on "democracy wall" advocates as Deng enunciated the "four cardinal principles" in 1979-1980. Another round of relaxation and reform culminated in Deng's call for the campaign against Western "spiritual pollution" in the fall of 1983. In early 1987 after about three years of reform, Deng was angered by the student demonstrations and sided with the conservatives to wage a campaign against "bourgeois liberalization." Because of his unorthodox political views and his resistance to the campaign, Hu Yaobang, Deng's principal protégé, was removed from his post as General Secretary of the Party. In June 1989, Deng again sided with the conservatives by cracking down the student demonstration in the Tiananmen Square and ousted another protégé of his, Zhao Ziyang, from power because of his sympathy with the pro-democracy movement.

To Deng Xiaoping, the primary purpose of tightening up was to maintain "stability and unity" which he had valued so highly. He felt that pluralism was not compatible with China's tradition and that political liberalization in China could only lead the country into chaos and weaken China's power. He saw stability and order as indispensable for his modernization program. Learning lessons from the Cultural Revolution, Deng firmly believed that without social stability, China could achieve nothing in economic development. Personally, Deng was an authoritarian and always believed in decisive power as the means to suppress political liberalization. The fall of Hu and Zhao were big blows to Deng's credibility, but it did not mean the end of reform in China. Each time Deng managed to consolidate his power through new coalition-building and keep his economic reform program on track. Even though he had retired from all his public posts, Deng was still behind the scenes and having the last say in politics. Because of this, the basic direction of China's reform as well as Beijing's "independent foreign policy" remained unchanged during the 1980s and even in the early 1990s.

Pragmatism

The far-reaching socio-economic reform under the leadership of Deng Xiaoping in the 1980s initiated a general process of "deideologizing" Chinese society,[15] as a result of which, the role of ideology was drastically downplayed in China's foreign policy making. Rationality, flexibility and pragmatism started to guide China's foreign relations. In this regard, the Chinese quietly abandoned the ideological framework that had once provided consistency and rigidity to Beijing's conduct of foreign affairs. China's analyses of international affairs became more realistic and factual, and were not constructed around the same ideological categories as in the past. Since the adoption of the independent foreign policy in 1982, Beijing abandoned the Maoist policy of depicting the world as shaped by a single principal contradiction between the superpowers to which all other contradictions or differences should be subordinated. Nuclear war between the United States and the Soviet Union was no longer regarded as inevitable but could be prevented. A growing world stability was seen in the progressing multipolarization in international affairs. Neither the United

States nor the Soviet Union was as a rule described as an imperialist power, although many of their policies were still called examples of "hegemonism." By following an independent line, China, on some issues, shared common interests with the United States or the Soviet Union, while on others, Beijing was critical of Moscow or Washington.[16] In normalizing relations with the Soviet Union, ideological disputes between Beijing and Moscow were deemphasized.

In essence, the dominance of pragmatism meant that national interest rather than revolutionary values were used to guide Beijing's foreign policy making. Zhao Ziyang made it clear in 1986 that Beijing determined its position on international issues "on the merits of each case" according to the interest of the Chinese people. He claimed that China would not base "closeness with or estrangement from other countries on the basis of their social systems and ideologies."[17] In line with pragmatism, China's foreign policy goals started to reflect Chinese national interest as interpreted by its reform-minded leadership and focus on nonalignment, peace and development rather than on strategic alliances or revolutionary struggles between socialism and imperialism. In search of the goal of peace and development, Beijing followed a lower-cost and lower-risk foreign policy and paid more attention to economic results in conducting its foreign relations.[18]

This new pragmatism enabled Beijing to be more flexible and rational in dealing with sensitive issues than it had been in the past. In establishing good-neighborly relations, Beijing recognized that exporting revolution was nonproductive, and started cultivating good state-to-state relations. In opening up to the outside world, China was no longer confined by ideological taboos. Not only did it accept a wide range of economic practices which previously had been considered as capitalism, but also established capitalist-like "special economic zones" to attract foreign investment and capital. Interdependence rather than total "self-reliance" was favored. In taking realistic, differentiated, and reciprocal attitudes, the Chinese separated economic interests from political differences and developed commercial relations with all countries no matter whether or not they had diplomatic relations with China and regardless of their political or social systems. One of the outstanding examples of China's pragmatism in conducting diplomacy was Chinese arms sales to any buyers in the world who had money on hand. Similarly, on issues related to national sovereignty, Beijing was firm on the principle but flexible on specific measures. According to the pragmatic model of "one country, two systems," Beijing successfully settled the problems of Hong Kong and Macao. Even on the matter of U.S. arms sales to Taiwan, China was pragmatic enough to express its sovereignty concerns while still keeping Sino-U.S. relations on track. In the 1980s, China's foreign policy was characterized by the abandonment of rigid ideological considerations in favor of pragmatism.

Nationalist Elements

The determination to advance national interest through modernization reflected the Chinese reform leadership's strong commitment to the ultimate goal of making China prosperous and powerful. In a sense, China's new foreign policy was strongly influenced by Chinese nationalism. The nationalist elements in Chinese independent foreign policy were manifested in several ways. Strategically, there was a strong desire for China to become an influential as well as an independent force in international politics. For this purpose, China seriously developed its national capabilities. In return, the steady growth of China's national capabilities further upgraded China's power status in the world. On territorial issues, China stressed sovereignty over Hong Kong and Macao, reunification with Taiwan, and resolution of all border issues and disputed islands offshore on terms favorable to China.

A growing national pride in China's foreign policy had both official and popular components. The impact of nationalist elements on Chinese foreign policy was an integral part of the party's increasing invocation of nationalist appeals to bolster the legitimacy of a regime whose ideology provided a less powerful source of enthusiasm and support. Thus the Chinese reformist leaders emphasized the need for reunifying the country under a single national government, stressed China's growing wealth and power, and promised that, under their leadership, China would once again play a major role in the politics and economics of the Asian-Pacific region. This appeal struck a responsive cord among the Chinese people, even independent of official sponsorship and, frequently, outside central control. Spontaneous demonstrations frequently took place after international sporting events, bearing a patriotic flavor when the Chinese team won. A nationalist mood was readily evident among younger Chinese when a wave of student protests occurred in several Chinese cities at the end of 1985, protesting, among other things, against the alleged revival of militarism in Japan and the growing Japanese economic presence in China.

In fact, the reform leadership was no less nationalist than Mao and his supporters, but the nature of its nationalistic attitudes was different. In the past, Mao had pursued a limited and cautious Chinese involvement in world affairs as a way of seeking to reduce the country's vulnerabilities. Mao's foreign policy was full of ideological fervor, acerbic rhetoric and even militant assertiveness. But Deng presented a kind of "confident nationalism"[19] as China played an independent role between superpowers and as the policy of economic reform and opening to the outside world greatly enhanced China's economic and technological development. In the 1980s, China's foreign behavior had become more confident and assertive under the leadership of Deng Xiaoping.

One way to show China's confidence toward the outside world is Deng Xiaoping's open-door policy. Deng Xiaoping ascribed Chinese weakness to its underdeveloped economy and thus urged his countrymen to open up to the outside world. Importing foreign capital and advanced technology was considered the most efficient way to remedy China's economic deficiencies. This long-term strategy of modernization was aimed at the eventual enhancement of China's power and influence without eroding the commitment to preserve Chinese identity or generating dependence and causing the country to be flooded by foreign ideologies and institutions that could undermine the very Chinese identity which modernization was designed to protect.[20] As shown in the campaigns of "anti-spiritual pollution" and "anti-bourgeois liberalization," there was also a strong desire to maintain a distinctively Chinese culture, uncontaminated by Western ideas and values.[21] Deng and his associates constantly revealed their pride in China's national heritage and their dedication to making China a major actor in the world affairs. In this sense, opening to the outside world was a calculated decision which was "flexible in tactics, subtle in strategy, but deeply committed to the preservation of national independence...and the attainment of national wealth and power."[22] In fact, the adoption of Western technologies and the influx of foreign capital reflected the confidence of the reform leadership in pursuing its modernization goals. The success of the Chinese in increasing their exports in the 1980s further strengthened this confidence.

Increased Foreign Policy Agenda

The scope of China's foreign relations considerably expanded in the 1980s as the country's foreign policy concerns were no longer dominated by strategic issues. As a result, China's foreign relations became more varied and complex in their functional orientation. The direct result of the increased policy agenda was enhanced participation of various interests in foreign policy making. Although the charting of broad foreign policy guidelines, especially major strategic or political decisions, remained the prerogative of a few people at the top (principally Deng Xiaoping), refining and implementing foreign policy became much more bureaucratic and diffused.[23] In several ways, China's foreign policy making process was not an exclusive preserve of a small number of people as had been previously the case.

First, as China opened to the outside world, foreign policy decisions became much more diversified and complicated than before, especially in the areas of foreign economic and cultural exchanges. Since these issues involved more participants in the policy making process, more players representing a greater variety of interests emerged. In the field of foreign economic relations, a number of government institutions, such as the Ministry of Foreign Economic Relations and Trade, the National Planning Commission, the Ministry of Finance, the People's Bank, and even the China International Trust and Investment Corporation, entered into policy making. The open door policy also broadened powers of those organizations which engaged in international cultural and educational exchanges, such as the Academy of Sciences, the Academy of Social Sciences, the National Commission of Education, and the National Commission of Sciences and Technology. To some extent, the Ministry of Foreign Affairs lost its previous predominance in the conduct of Chinese foreign relations.[24] One remarkable development in this regard was Chinese arms sales in the international market. To some extent, this issue seemed to be outside of the foreign ministry's control. The People's Liberation Army (PLA) became a major arms supplier to the world. The Ministry of Foreign Affairs pledged openly the three principles of Chinese arms sales while the PLA continued to sell weapons to possible buyers without any limitations. In a way, conflicting interests emerged in foreign policy making and there was a need to coordinate foreign policy and international activities among key institutions.[25]

Second, the expansion of China's functional relations with foreign countries caused the development of a large new policy community in which professional expertise acquired new importance in policy making.[26] With the multiplication of external contacts and decreasing reliance on ideology in the assessment of international issues, bureaucracy became increasingly more sophisticated. In the 1980s, administrative reforms also brought a generation of technocrats into the ranks of the government bureaucracy. These technocratic bureaucrats were relatively young, well educated, and had expertise in their respective fields of specialization. Besides, because of decentralization and the establishment of special economic zones and open areas, local governments obtained a higher degree of authority in terms of local economic activities and external economic relations. They began enjoyed unprecedented autonomy in conducting external economic activities.

Third, think tanks assumed an increasingly important role in foreign policy making in the 1980s.[27] They not only prepared background information on international affairs, but also prepared proposals and analyses on foreign policy issues. The Chinese foreign policy establishment became much better informed than ever before. The cumulative effect of foreign travel, the steady stream of foreign leaders and strategic thinkers to Beijing, and the outpouring of translated materials provided a more realistic picture of world affairs. To a considerable extent, the sophistication and pragmatism of Chinese external conduct stemmed from a greater awareness of international trends and domestic politics of other countries. The reduced ideological rigidity at home also enabled Chinese diplomats and scholars to provide more honest reporting. In the Mao era, China's American specialists had portrayed the United States in rather crude Marxist categories: American politics involved a struggle among a few competing financial cliques, and the government was an instrument of the capitalist class to oppress the workers. By the mid-1980s, the leading America watchers had accepted a pluralistic interpretation. They considered the clash among interest groups and bureaucratic politics to be at the heart of the American system.[28] Think tanks played a more or less advisory and consulting role in the foreign policy making process. From 1978 to 1985, there were long-lasting debates about Soviet socialism among these think tanks and intellectuals as well as among government bureaucrats.[29] These debates had prepared the ground necessary for Beijing's normalization of its relations with Moscow by the end of the

1980s.

The impact of the think tanks upon foreign policy making cannot be overexaggerated, however. They may have had a fairly high degree of freedom to conduct internal discussions on a variety of issues, but it was difficult, if not impossible, for them to openly voice their viewpoints when they departed from the official line. In China there is still no open forum for international affairs experts to discuss foreign policy issues. If a scholar is allowed to discuss these issues in public, he is expected to reflect the official line, thereby justifying the policy.[30] Indeed, sensitive and strategically important issues such as China's relations with major powers and the Taiwan issue in China's foreign policy making are still handled by a small group of top leaders. But leadership outlooks are evidently shaped to a considerable extent by timely information flows and by assessments of professionals.[31] The greater involvement of experts and the broadening of consultation are another important development which helps explain the complexities and sophistication of Chinese diplomacy in the 1980s.

Theoretical Implications of the Chinese Case

James N. Rosenau says that any study of a single country's foreign policy synthesizes both "idiographic and nomothetic knowledge, that is, the most salient aspects of a country's uniqueness as well as the dynamics it shares with other countries."[32] Indeed, China's foreign policy in the 1980s is only a single case of foreign policy restructuring. But the preceding analysis provides not merely an insight into change in China's foreign policy, but also suggests a number of useful implications for the study of foreign policy restructuring as a special type of foreign policy behavior.

First, a country's foreign policy restructuring is largely driven by the unproductive results of the current policy in major issue areas to which the country's vital interests are closely related. These major issue areas usually involve national security, economic development, major foreign contacts, and domestic political control. They represent the basic components of a country's foreign policy. The test of the effectiveness of a country's foreign policy is to see whether the policy can meet the country's basic needs. During the 1980s, Mao's "united front" foreign policy no longer corresponded to the global reality concerning China's security. The grounds for a strategic alliance with the West had eroded as the Soviet threat declined. Difficulties were encountered in the Sino-U.S. relationship. Overly close ties with the United States reduced China's foreign policy flexibility and also damaged China's image in the Third World. Strained relations existed between China and some of its neighbors. Domestically, Mao's policies also led to devastating economic, social and political crises inside China. His "self-reliance" policy allowed only limited economic contacts with the outside world which failed to promote China's economic progress. As a result, China was left behind by other Asian nations. The unproductive consequences of Mao's policies resulted in large-scale discontent and triggered major debates and power struggles within the Chinese hierarchy. It was the failure of Mao's policies that made the reformers come to power in Beijing who eventually restructured China's foreign policy. Judging from the Chinese case, *if a country's existing foreign policy becomes increasingly unproductive in the core issue areas and no longer serves the basic needs of the country, that country is likely to embark upon foreign policy restructuring in terms of redefining its major foreign partnerships and engaging in different types of foreign activities.*

Second, *major external events affecting a country's basic interest areas (i.e., national security, economic situation, foreign contacts, and domestic political control) often exercise pressures on the country's existing foreign policy and may trigger foreign policy restructuring.* Normally, most international events do not affect a country's basic interests and are treated routinely because their scope is modest and their immediate impact is limited. Unless they are repeatedly reinforced by other events, most of them do not have an immediate impact on the country's current foreign policy pattern. By contrast, major international events, especially external shocks, are not only visible but also have an immediate impact on the recipients' vital interests. They cannot be ignored and treated routinely but must be taken seriously. As major international events may either pose threats to or provide opportunities for the recipient countries, those countries must respond to the events sooner or later for the purpose of better serving their vital interests. In the 1980s, the declining Soviet threat and a new superpower strategic parity greatly improved China's security environment. In response to the changed strategic surroundings and to the difficulties which occurred in Sino-U.S. relations, Beijing distanced itself from close strategic cooperation with the United States and adopted an independent foreign policy. Encouraged by the new international détente, China shifted its attention to economic development. To this end, it became increasingly cooperative in international relations and was active in creating an external environment favorable to China's domestic economic reform. Meanwhile, attracted by the economic dynamics of the Asian-Pacific region, China adopted an open door policy and pragmatically developed economic relations with all possible foreign partners.

Third, *the domestic dynamics of a country, such as its economic performance and internal political stability, may also have an impact upon the country's foreign policy making and sometimes lead to foreign policy restructuring.* A regime needs domestic endorsement of its policies for its continuance and legitimacy. In the Chinese case, the economic and political crises caused by the failure of Mao's Cultural Revolution in the late 1970s, resulted in the de-Maoification movement inside the Chinese society and the shift of domestic priorities to the modernization drive. Indeed, the open door policy was a direct response to this change. In essence, the essential motivation for Beijing's foreign policy restructuring in the 1980s came from inside China and was reinforced by favorable developments in the international environment. China's new security thinking and defense policy were closely related both to its domestic economic reform and its positive reassessment of the international balance of power.

Fourth, a country's foreign policy restructuring originates in the determined efforts of authoritative policy-makers. Usually it is made by the head of government, who imposes his own vision of a redirection of foreign policy. Such a leader must have the conviction, power, and energy to compel the government to change course.[33] In the post-Mao China, it was Deng Xiaoping's effective leadership and his personality that made China's foreign policy restructuring possible. It was his vision and conceptualization of China's objectives within the changing international system as well as the country's domestic dynamics that contributed to China's foreign policy reform. In a way, foreign policy restructuring is more directly related to interpretation of objective conditions by decision-makers rather than external and/or internal circumstances themselves. Therefore, *without an effective leadership that recognizes the objective pressures and the inadequacy of its existing foreign policy (Of course, these pressures may be interpreted either as major threats to or as new opportunities for the country), and that defines the need for a change under the new circumstances, there will not be any foreign policy restructuring.* To be sure, the shift in the key decision-makers' perceptions and preferences and/or the change in the composition of the government elite assume critical importance in a country's foreign policy restructuring.

Obviously, foreign policy restructuring may be conceptualized as the interaction among domestic politics, external environment, and political leadership. The interplay of these three factors linked by the self-preservation need of a country produces foreign policy restructuring. They may work in tandem. Or one (e.g., external event) may activate another (e.g., a leader-driven initiative) which in turn stimulates a redirection of foreign policy. None of the three operates by and for itself, in isolation from others. However, the relative weights of these factors in shaping foreign policy may vary from country to country or from situation to situation due to the differential impact of the external environment on each country, the unique character of each domestic system, and the quality of certain political leadership. In the final analysis, a country's foreign policy restructuring is influenced not only by the country's need for self-preservation, but also by the inevitable disparity between objective conditions (i.e., international and domestic politics) and the subjective manner in which they are perceived by the country's decision-makers. It is the political leadership that consciously affects policy direction on behalf of its own state. But how it decides the policy direction is largely determined by the values it seeks to maximize or the vision it pursues, by the will and courage it musters, and by its intelligence and skill.[34]

Fifth, *a country's foreign policy restructuring is measured by the changes in its basic attitudes towards its major foreign partnerships and in the way it manages its major foreign policy sectors (i.e., military, economic, political and cultural contacts) over a period of time.* China's foreign policy restructuring in the 1980s started first in the strategic/military aspect as China abandoned its decade-old "united front" policy and adopted a position of nonalignment with respect to the superpowers. Soon it followed a policy in search of peace and development. On the one hand, it actively participated in international peace efforts and engaged in major military cutbacks. On the other hand, Beijing vigorously improved relations with its neighbors and expanded ties with all possible countries. In the economic domain, Beijing no longer followed the policy of "self-reliance" but opened its door to the outside world.

Finally, foreign policy restructuring involves adapting behavior to changing circumstances. Adaptation means "a class of activities through which a system adjusts to changes in its internal and external environment so that it can continue to function as a system."[35] For a country, the very function of foreign policy restructuring is to better serve its national interest in the face of unproductive results of the country's current foreign policy under external and/or internal pressures. By the same token, *the effectiveness of foreign policy restructuring is judged by whether the new policy can remedy the problems of the previous policy and enhance the country's basic interests under the new circumstances.* Not surprisingly, given the shifts that had taken place in both global and domestic politics in the 1980s, China's foreign policy underwent substantive changes as Beijing's reform leadership adapted to the external environment and accommodated domestic modernization needs. The triumph of Dengist pragmatism in search of independence, peace and development in China's foreign behavior represented Beijing's "genuinely self-serving" purpose and brought about positive results both in China's security environment and its economic growth.[36]

China's Foreign Policy
After the Tiananmen Events

The huge success of China's diplomacy in the 1980s was suddenly damaged by the military crackdown on the student pro-democracy movement in Tiananmen Square in Beijing in June 1989. The tragedy was the inevitable consequence of Deng's ambivalence in China's reform program. On economic issues, he was in favor of market mechanisms and recognized that China had no alternative but to open up and to liberalize its economic system. On the political front, however, Deng insisted that the authoritarian rule of the Communist Party was the only effective way to keep China stable and in order. Having experienced the chaos of the Cultural Revolution, he argued that without political stability economic modernization would be impossible. Deng firmly believed that political liberalization and pluralism could only loosen the party's rule and destroy the social order which would eventually lead the country into turmoil and even a civil war.

But a decade of economic reform had created pressures for political liberalization. Some 80,000 Chinese students and scholars had gone to study in Western countries. Western values came to China along with the introduction of foreign advanced technology and management methods. Thousands of Westerners taught in Chinese institutions. China was also widely open to foreign tourism. Access to Western television, radio, literature and culture had never been greater in China's history. All these developments occurred at a time when the prestige of Communism and the control of the party were eroding rapidly. This disaffection was exacerbated by corruption, official profiteering and social divisions that resulted from disparities of income, deemed to be unfair and the product of Deng's reforms.[37] Signs of popular discontent and democratic demands led to the pro-democracy movement in the Tiananmen Square in the spring of 1989 which directly challenged the dictatorship of the party. Chaos, as Deng had feared, did happen in many cities across the country. In fighting for party predominance and control and in the name of order and political stability, Deng sided with the conservatives of the party and used the army ruthlessly to suppress the pro-democracy movement. In this process, Deng's economic reform program was severely challenged by the conservatives within the party. "Bourgeois liberal" influence from the West was pointedly criticized together with Deng's open door policy. Western influence was labeled as a plot of "peaceful evolution" to overthrow the Communist Party in China.

The impact of the Tiananmen Square Incident upon China's foreign relations was damaging and created huge difficulties. The international community was outraged by the brutality of Beijing's government and widely condemned it. To varying degrees, most western governments imposed sanctions against China which involved postponement of high-level contacts, withholding of military sales, suspension of major loans and credits, and cancellation of cultural exchanges. China experienced a sharp decline in tourism, economic aid, commerce, and investment from the outside world after the events of June 1989.

The repression of the democratic movement also widened the ideological gap between China and the West. Political relations with the West reached their lowest point since 1972. This deterioration was manifested not only in an adverse reaction in the West towards Beijing's brutality, but also in the conservative stance of Beijing. The basis on which the Communist regime was seeking to assert its legitimacy was "anti-bourgeois liberalism" leading China into a confrontationist attitude toward the West. This was compounded by the fact that some western governments, such as the United States, France and Great Britain, gave refuge to Chinese dissidents sought by the Beijing authorities. These foreign governments were under attack for their alleged involvement in the Tiananmen events by the Chinese propaganda apparatus controlled by party conservatives. The human rights problem which had long been silenced in Sino-Western relations suddenly emerged as an outstanding issue in the relations between China and the West in the post-Tiananmen era.

The human rights issue also raised questions about the future of Hong Kong after 1997. The suppression of the students in Beijing was a big blow to the political confidence of the people of Hong Kong. They were suspicious of the Chinese promise of "one country, two systems" and their loss of confidence accelerated the exodus of professionals and the flow of large amounts of capital out of the territory. Those in Hong Kong who placed confidence in China called for greater democracy and the right to use British passports to live in Britain as an "insurance policy" for the future.[38]

Motivated in part by moral scruples and in part by prudence, the sanctions against China varied in their scope and intensity. Britain was opposed to economic sanctions lest they rebound upon Hong Kong. President Bush sought to limit sanctions because of the geo-political significance of China and tried to resist pressures from Congress for a tough stand on the human rights issue. The Japanese government made it clear that it did not wish to go beyond formal condemnation. Moreover, for political and economic reasons, some of China's neighbors, such as South Korea, Taiwan, Indonesia, Singapore, and Russia, just expressed regret on what had happened in Tiananmen and continued to expand economic relations with China. Less than three years after Tiananmen, Beijing established diplomatic relations with Indonesia, Singapore, Saudi Arabia and Israel. Thus, the picture was not wholly gloomy for China.

To be sure, after June 1989 China did face acute problems in its foreign relations. Politically, Beijing could not bypass the question of human rights in its relations with the West any longer. Economically, it had to regain the confidence of the international business community by speeding up economic reform and opening the country wider. On the diplomatic front, China, in order to reverse the downward trend, initiated a series of damage control campaigns, including recurrent reaffirmation of the open-door policy, assurance of Beijing's promise of "one country, two systems" toward Hong Kong and Taiwan, release of some dissidents, agreement to discussing human rights issues with the West, and tacit cooperation with the West in the United Nations on the resolution regarding the Iraqi invasion of Kuwait. Meanwhile, Beijing particularly strengthened relations with its neighbors and the Third World.

Most foreign investors returned to China within two years. Following Japan's lead, many western governments lifted economic sanctions. The World Bank again provided loans to China. High-level visits between China and the outside world were restored and the United States still maintained most-favored-nation trade status for China. In fact, Chinese foreign trade, especially its exports, expanded to an unprecedented level after the Tiananmen Square Incident. Whereas in 1989, China's products had accounted for 37.3 percent of the American toy market, in 1991 the share reached 51.1 percent. In 1991, China started to enjoy a trade surplus with the United States second only to Japan's. By April 1992, China's foreign exchange reserves amounted to over \$40 billion.[39]

Initial pessimism after the Tiananmen event gradually declined. The outside world soon recognized that the possibility of another major shift in China's domestic and foreign policies suggested by Tiananmen was unlikely. The outside world also recognized that there was little they could do to pressure China. While relations between China and the West had deteriorated to some extent and China would have preferred this not to happen, Beijing seemed prepared to pay such a price, at least in the short term. After Tiananmen, a widespread prior misconception about China in the West that reforms had changed the nature of China was replaced by a more mature attitude towards Chinese Communism. The essentials of the Chinese regime were recognized more clearly for what they always had been. In the past, Beijing had used force many times to repress dissent and the outside world knew little about it. Because of the open door policy and the wide coverage by the world news media (especially by the foreign news corps which came to China originally to report Gorbachev's historic visit to Beijing in May 1989), the outside world for the first time witnessed Beijing's brutality. In this sense, what really changed was the view on China held by the West rather than in the nature of Beijing's government.[40]

On the whole, the agenda of Chinese foreign policy did not change much as a result of the Tiananmen Square Incident. There were several reasons for this continuity. First, despite the presence within the post-Tiananmen Square Chinese leadership of some conservative elements who would evidently like to turn back the clock on the reform and open-door policies, this did not happen. To be sure, some of reformist policies were challenged, but they still remained on the policy agenda. As a matter of fact, reform policies continued to enjoy the support of a broad spectrum of the Chinese people. After ten years of reform, they had already tasted their fruits. Not only had the country quintupled its foreign trade and achieved a high economic growth rate, but also people's living standards had improved. Each year, China had received billions of dollars of foreign investment and aid. Under such circumstances, changes brought by reform were irreversible. Moreover, as more Chinese had come into contact with the outside world, they found that their prosperity depended upon making a success of their foreign contacts. The Chinese economy could not grow unless China was further integrated into the global economy. A return to pre-1978 isolation could only be a severe blow to China's scientific and technological--hence industrial and military--progress. This perception was shared by most of the Chinese leaders and the people at large. Even conservative ideologues within the party could not ignore this fact, finding it difficult to re-emphasize their orthodox values.[41]

More importantly, Deng slowly recovered from his unfavorable position after the Tiananmen Square Incident. In the spring of 1992, he suddenly ended three years of silence and resumed control of China's political agenda. At the age of 87, he made an unexpected inspection tour to the Shenzhen Special Economic Zone, next to Hong Kong, to re-boost his reform and opening-up programs nationwide.[42] The most important message he delivered on the tour was to open China wider to the outside world and boldly use capitalist methods to speed up economic progress. Deng pointed out that failure to develop the economy and to improve people's livelihood could only lead socialist China to a dead end which reminded people of the collapse of Communism in Eastern Europe and in the former Soviet Union. To avoid this, the country should be bolder in reform and opening up. In fact, the Beijing government realized the achievements of China's reform in the 1980s explained why the Chinese pro-democracy movement in 1989 was one step short of becoming the "popular movement" that led to the collapse of the Communist system in Eastern Europe and the Soviet Union. The experience in Eastern Europe and the Soviet Union convinced Beijing that, to stay in power and make the system work, the Chinese Communist Party had no choice but to continue and deepen the reform started in 1978.[43] On his tour, Deng Xiaoping criticized some people's failure to take a step forward in reform and to dare make breakthroughs because of the fear of introducing capitalist ways. The crux of the matter was whether a move was dubbed "capitalist" or "socialist." In Deng's opinion, the criterion was not an ideological one but whether the move facilitated the development of productive forces, whether it helped increase China's overall national strength, and whether it brought about better living standards. Soon after Deng's tour, the Politburo totally accepted Deng's reform message at a meeting on March 9-10, 1992 and decided that the party's basic line was "one central task and two basic points" which should persist one hundred years and brook no vacillation.[44]

The second reason for the continuity of China's "independent foreign policy of peace" is also related to factors inside China. Since Deng's economic reform started in the early 1980s, the eastern and southern coastal regions of China had benefitted from stronger economic relations with Pacific Basin countries. They enjoyed preferential policy treatment by Beijing, their level of economic and social development became higher than in other regions in China and they were in the vanguard of national economic reform and modernity, representing an important constituency and pressure group for the policies of the open door.[45] Because of this, they had a large stake in developing and maintaining extensive economic ties with the outside world, especially the United States, Japan, Western Europe, and the four "small tigers" (South Korea, Taiwan, Hong Kong and Singapore) in East Asia. In this regard, Guangdong Province took the lead. Because the Shenzhen and two other special economic zones are located in the province and Hong Kong is its next door neighbor, Guangdong's economy took off and began to play a locomotive role in China's economic reform. In 1991, the economic growth of Guangdong was faster than nearly any other in the world, reaching 27.2 percent. Guangdong's exports accounted for a third of China's total exports in 1990.[46] The 1989 Tiananmen Square crackdown hardly slowed the boom. *Newsweek* magazine even called Guangdong the "fifth tiger" of Asia.[47] With its growing economic strength, on many occasions, Guangdong opposed the recentralization measures taken by Li Peng's cabinet in Beijing after June 1989.

The third reason for policy continuity is that, the major powers, including the United States, Japan and some western European countries, concluded that it was not in their interests to isolate China.

Only one month after the Tiananmen Square Incident, at the Group of Seven Summit Meeting held in Paris Japan strongly advocated not driving China into isolation. The Bush Administration also held the position that it was harmful to see an isolated China return to an irresponsible role in Asia, and that the United States needed China's participation in maintaining international stability in the "new world order" whatever that meant. In accordance with this view, President Bush maintained China's most-favored-nation trade status by vetoing Congressional bills which imposed conditions on the renewal of such a status. After China had abstained from rather than vetoed the United Nations Security Council Resolution 678 permitting the use of force against Iraq, the Chinese foreign minister was invited to Washington, signalling the restoration of high-level contacts between the two countries.[48]

As a matter of fact, a substantial number of American foreign-policy elites believe that "because the underlying forces supporting reform and development in China are strong, the present period of political repression will be temporary and transitional" and that "more moderate policies are likely to reemerge in time, primarily in response to domestic pressures, possibly even under the present leadership, [or] probably under their successors."[49] According to this view, some American foreign policy experts suggested that the United States avoid external actions that could lead both to downturns in China's domestic politics and to a prolonged deterioration of bilateral ties. Otherwise, restoration of close cooperation would be difficult when trends toward reform and moderation reappeared in China. This view was shared by Japan which concluded that China remained a major pillar of Japan's diplomacy and that the existence of such a relationship was important not only for Japan and for the United States but also for the peace and stability of Asia. As a result, although China still encountered political obstacles (e.g., the human rights issue) in its relations with the West, the actual economic and cultural exchanges between them were restored.

Fourth, the partial return of conservative ideologues within the Chinese leadership in the wake of Tiananmen could not effectively respond to the fundamental changes in the post-Cold War international relations. On the contrary, Deng's pragmatic diplomacy still dominated the scene at the time when the world was experiencing the end of the Cold War era. The collapse of Communism in Eastern Europe and the disintegration of the Soviet Union were indeed big blows to the Chinese

Communists. The Chinese conservative leaders had long been dissatisfied with Gorbachev's "new thinking" and regarded it as a surrender to western imperialism. Gorbachev himself had been described as a traitor of proletariat.[50] In the face of the defeat of Communism in Eastern Europe, especially the failure of the military coup in Moscow in 1991, Beijing's conservatives attempted to revitalize ideological campaigns both in China's domestic and foreign policies. But Deng's instruction was not to publicly criticize what had happened in the former Soviet Union and Eastern Europe. Instead, he decided that Beijing should carefully watch unfolding developments in overall international relations. With this low-profile attitude, Beijing's position was that China respected the choice made by the people of Eastern Europe and the former Soviet Union.[51] Clearly, Beijing did not want to add more problems in its external relations already strained after Tiananmen. A low-key and pragmatic attitude was conducive to reforging an external environment favorable to China's domestic economic construction. Deng repeatedly stressed that strengthening economic development was more important and that was the basis for the solution of internal and external problems. Any public ideological disputes were only a waste of time. Therefore, conducting a pragmatic diplomacy instead of ideological crusade was more in China's interest. While Beijing was pragmatically restoring economic ties with the West and making attempts at dealing with the question of human rights violations, it was also rapidly developing normal state-to-state relations with the Eastern European countries and with successor states of the former Soviet Union.

Other than that, the end of the Cold War also meant a new situation in the international balance of power, which certainly had a substantial impact upon China. Like other powers, Beijing had to reassess its security environment and the future policies of the United States, Russia and Japan. The end of the Cold War inevitably concluded the so-called strategic triangle, the concept which had been the strongest determinant of China's foreign policy throughout the Cold War era. China now faced a new situation in Asia characterized by the interaction among four major powers involving the United States, Japan, Russia and China, the resurface of many regional problems (e.g., human rights violations, economic frictions, territorial disputes, ethnic and religious disharmony, Japanese military potential, etc.) which used to be concealed under the superpower contention, and the economic dynamics in the Asian-Pacific region.

New developments both inside China and in international relations have posed challenges as well as opportunities for Beijing. On the whole, China continues to perceive its external environment as favorable. Japan is still anchored to the United States in the strategic arrangement in East Asia, Russia has turned inward concentrating on its domestic problems and economic development, the United States continues to play a substantial strategic role in maintaining a balance of power in the Asian-Pacific region. Besides, all the countries in the region share a common interest in easing tensions, maintaining regional stability, and further promoting the area's economic prosperity. At least in the 1990s, China does not face any direct military threats to its security such as it had experienced in the previous several decades. On the contrary, after opening to the outside world for more than a decade, China has tasted the fruits of rapid economic progress which has surprised the rest of the world. In the early 1990s, the country registered double-digit economic growth and from 1980 to 1995, China's GNP level has doubled twice. The People's Republic has rapidly emerged as a major economic power house. Meanwhile, Beijing has reversed its downward trend in the country's military spending by reincreasing defense expenditures since 1989. As a matter of fact, China is making a surprisingly huge impact everywhere, from the Taiwan Strait to shop floors in America. Along with this development, China's national pride among both Chinese leaders and the general public has been greatly enhanced. Increasingly, China's deeds and words carry growing weight in influencing courses of action of other countries.

While China is feeling proud of its newly obtained status which it has been seeking for almost a century, Beijing faces challenges in its foreign policy as this century draws to a close. The core of these challenges is the tension between the country's quest for wealth and power and its international responsibilities as a big power to conform to established international norms and standards.

On the one hand, mounting economic strength and renascent national pride have made the Chinese see their country once again as a great power. But on the other hand, the traditional realist and state-centered approach to world affairs still dominate the minds of the Chinese leadership. As China's power continues to grow, China's foreign behavior seems to become more confident and Beijing has toughened its line on a range of issues. Increasingly, China's political and military agenda is at odds with that of its neighbors and the West.

China's assertive move in the South China Sea in recent years, for instance, has made its neighbors worry that a powerful China will handle international affairs only on its own terms. China's recent military buildup, the flow of advanced Russian weapons to China at record speed, and China's military exercises in the Taiwan Strait have given a bigger role to the People's Liberation Army in China's foreign policy-making. All these developments are accompanied by the rise of Chinese nationalism. In fact, Chinese nationalism now couched in terms of safeguarding Chinese sovereignty in rebuffing western charges of human rights abuses, unfair trade practices, and irresponsible Chinese arms sales, has replaced the communist ideology as the unifying force in China. At time of the post-Deng leadership struggle, contenders for the next head of China cannot look soft on matters related to national sovereignty or appear weak by kowtowing to the West.

Indeed, international tensions are not in China's best interest to sustain a favorable international situation in the Asian-Pacific region in support of China's continuous efforts toward modernization. Beijing has to make efforts to ease tensions and manage to balance its diplomacy between competing policy objectives. This balancing act requires good foreign policy coordination among departments with differing agendas and interests within the Chinese government to carry out an integrated and explicit foreign policy. Otherwise, antithetical objectives in Beijing's foreign policy can only send ambiguous signals to other countries. Besides, as China expands its role as a major international power, Beijing is facing more international responsibilities than ever before. But China seems not to be well prepared for this because it lacks professionals who are familiar with modern international practices.

Nevertheless, China, in the 1990s, will learn to adapt to the new environment and modernize its diplomacy as long as the country continues to be driven by its desire to develop its economy. In this process, the international community should respond to China's foreign acts properly. Proper response means that the rest of the world should encourage positive moves made by China while disencouraging any of its irresponsible acts. Integrating China into the world community will help Beijing accept established international rules and make the country a responsible world power. To this end, the international community needs to understand China and China also needs to understand the rest of the world. Otherwise, improper interactions between China and the rest of the world will only lead to misunderstanding and confrontation.

NOTES

Chapter 1

1. Zhao Ziyang, "Report on the Work of the Government at the Fifth Session of the Sixth National People's Congress, March 25, 1987," *Beijing Review*, Vol. 30, No. 16, (April 20, 1987), p. XX.
2. Zhang Jingyi, "Analysis of the Reagan Administration's Military Strategy," *Renmin Ribao. (People's Daily)*, May 5, 1983, in Foreign Broadcast Information Service (*FBIS* hereafter) *Daily Report-China*, May 6, 1983, pp. B1-6.
3. *Pravda*, March 25, 1982, p. 2.
4. "An Independent Foreign Policy of Peace," *Beijing Review*, Vol. 35, No. 13, (March 30, 1992), p. 13.
5. Zhao Ziyang, "Report on the Work of the Government at the Fifth Session of the Sixth National People's Congress, March 25, 1987," *Beijing Review*, Vol. 30, No. 16, (April 20, 1987), p. XX. The Five Principles of Peaceful Coexistence was jointly put forward by Zhou Enlai, premier of China and by Jawaharlal Nehru, prime minister of India at the first Bandung Conference in 1955. The five principles are: mutual respect for sovereignty and territorial integrity, mutual non-aggression, non-interference in each others' internal affairs, equality and mutual benefit, and peaceful coexistence.
6. Edward Friedman, "Maoist and Post-Mao Conceptualizations of World Capitalism: Dangers and/or Opportunities," in Samuel S. Kim, ed., *China and the World: New Directions in Chinese Foreign Relations*, 2nd ed., (Boulder, CO: Westview Press, 1989), p. 74.
7. This model was put forward by Deng Xiaoping in the early 1980s. According to this model, after China regains its sovereignty over Hong Kong and Macao in 1997 and in 1999 respectively, capitalist system and lifestyle in the two territories will remain unchanged for at least 50 years. See "A Significant Concept," *Beijing Review*, Vol. 27, No. 44, October 29, 1984, pp. 16-17.
8. Yufan Hao and Guocang Huan, eds., *The Chinese View of the World*, (New York, NY: Pantheon Books, 1989), p. xi.
9. The bibliography at the end of this research gives a relatively comprehensive survey in this regard. Some influential studies on China's foreign policy in the 1980s, for example, include Harry Harding, ed., *China Foreign Relations in the 1980s*, (New Haven, CT: Yale University Press, 1984); Jonathan D. Pollack, *The Lessons of Coalition Politics*, (Santa Monica, CA: Rand Corp., 1984); Doak Barnett, *The Making of Foreign Policy in China: Structure and Process*, (Boulder, CO: Westview Press, 1985); Robert G. Sutter *Chinese Foreign Policy: Developments after Mao*, (New York, NY: Praeger Publishers, 1986); James C. Hsiung, ed., *Beyond China's Independent Foreign Policy: Challenge for the U.S. and Its Asian Allies*, (New York, NY:

Praeger Publishers, 1985); Samuel S. Kim ed., *China and the World: New Directions in Chinese Foreign Relations*, 2nd ed., (Boulder, CO: Westview Press, 1989); Yufan Hao and Guocang Huan, eds., *The Chinese View of the World*, (New York, NY: Pantheon Books, 1989); Gerald Segal, ed., *Chinese Politics and Foreign Policy Reform*, (London: Kegan Paul International Ltd., 1990); and Frank J. Macchiarola and Robert B. Oxnam, ed. *The China Challenge: American Policies in East Asia*, (New York, NY: the Academy of Political Science, 1991).

10. Michel Oksenberg, "China's Confident Nationalism," *Foreign Affairs*, Vol. 65, No. 3, (1987), p. 508.

11. James N. Rosenau, "Toward Single-Country Theories of Foreign Policy: the Case of the USSR," in Charles F. Hermann, Charles W. Kegley, Jr. and James N. Rosenau, eds., *New Directions in the Study of Foreign Policy*, (Boston: Allen & Unwin, 1987), p. 64.

12 K.J. Holsti, ed., *Why Nations Realign: Foreign Policy Restructuring in the Postwar World*, (London: George Allen & Unwin, 1982), p. ix.

13. Reviews of the literature which underscore this viewpoint are in Charles F. Hermann, Charles W. Kegley, Jr. and James N. Rosenau, eds., *New Directions in the Study of Foreign Policy*, (Boston, MA: Allen & Unwin, 1987).

14. Barry Buzan and R.J. Barry Jones, eds., *Change and the Study of International Relations: The Evaded Dimension*, (Chapel Hill, NC: The University of North Carolina, 1981), p. 1.

15. Holsti, Ole R., Randolph M. Siverson, and Alexander L. George, eds., *Change in the International System*, (Boulder, CO: Westview, 1980).

16. Robert Gilpin, *War and Change in World Politics*, (Cambridge: Cambridge University Press, 1981), p. 10.

17. Gilpin lists five assumptions to guide his study. These five assumptions are: "(1) an international system is stable if no state believes it profitable to attempt to change the system; (2) a state will attempt to change the international system if the expected benefits exceed the expected costs; (3) a state will seek to change the international system through territorial, political, and economic expansion until the marginal costs of further change are equal to or greater than the marginal benefits; (4) once an equilibrium between the costs and benefits of further change and expansion is reached, the tendency is for the economic costs of maintaining the status quo to rise faster than the economic capacity to support the status quo; and (5) if the disequilibrium in the international system is not resolved, then the system will be changed, and a new equilibrium reflecting the redistribution of power will be established." See *Ibid.*, p. 10.

18. *Ibid.*, p. 13.

19. Gavin Boyd and Gerald W. Hopple, eds., *Political Change and Foreign Policies*, (New York, NY: St Martin's Press, 1987).

20. Kjell Goldmann, *Change and Stability in Foreign Policy*, (Princeton, NJ: Princeton University Press, 1988)., p. 16.

21. International stabilizers involve international agreements, international transaction patterns, and power balances. Cognitive stabilizers include the beliefs on which the policy is based. Political stabilizers are identified by domestic support and policy institutionalization factors. Administrative stabilizers refer to bureaucratic and organizational factors. See *Ibid.*, pp. 26-69.

22. K.J. Holsti, ed., *Why Nations Realign: Foreign Policy Restructuring in the Postwar World*, (London: George Allen & Unwin, 1982). pp. ix, 2.

23. Charles F. Hermann, "Changing Course: When Governments Choose to Redirect Foreign Policy," *International Studies Quarterly*, Vol. 34, No. 1, (March 1990), pp. 3-21.

24. James N. Rosenau, *The Study of Political Adaptation*, (New York, NY: Nichols Publishing Company, 1981).

25. On the criticisms of the adaptation model, see Steve M. Smith, "Rosenau's Adaptive Behaviour Approach: A Critique," *Review of International Studies*, Vol. 7, (1981), pp. 107-126 and Ib Faurby, "Premises, Promises, and Problems of Comparative Foreign Policy," *Cooperation and Conflict*, Vol. XI, No. 3, (1976), pp. 139-162.

26. See, for example, Jerone Stephens, "An Appraisal of Some Systems Approaches in the Study of International Systems," *International Studies Quarterly*, Vol. 16, No. 3, (September 1972), pp. 321-349; Patrick J. McGowan, "Problems in the Construction of Positive Foreign Policy Theory," in James N. Rosenau, ed., *Comparing Foreign Policies: Theories, Findings, and Methods*, (New York, NY: Sage Publications, 1974), pp. 25-44; Patrick J. McGowan, "Adaptive Foreign Policy Behavior: An Empirical Approach," *Ibid.*, pp. 45-54; Michael K. O'Leary, "Foreign Policy and Bureaucratic Adaptation," *Ibid.*, pp. 55-70; Stuart J. Thorson, "National Political Adaptation," *Ibid.*, pp. 71-116.; Stuart J. Thorson, "Adaptation and Foreign Policy Theory," in Patrick J. McGowan, ed., *Sage International Yearbook of Foreign Policy Studies*, Vol. II, (Beverly Hills, Sage, 1974), pp. 123-139; Patrick J. McGowan and Klaus-Peter Gottwald, "Small State Foreign Policies: A Comparative Study of Participation, Conflict, and Political and Economic Dependence in Black Africa," *International Studies Quarterly*, Vol. 19, No., (December 1975), pp. 469-500; and Nikolaj Petersen, "Adaptation as a Framework for the Analysis of Foreign Policy Behaviour," *Cooperation and Conflict*, Vol. XII, No. 4, (1977), pp. 221-250.

27. Peter Hansen, "Adaptive Behavior of Small States: The Case of Denmark and the European Community," in Patrick J. McGowan, ed., *Sage International Yearbook of Foreign Policy Studies*, Vol. II, (Beverly Hills, Sage, 1974), pp. 143-174; and James Rosenau and Ole Holsti, "The United States In (and Out of) Vietnam: An Adaptive Transformation?" in James N. Rosenau,

The Study of Political Adaptation, (New York, NY: Nichols Publishing Company, 1981), pp. 169-186.

28. K.J. Holsti, ed., *Why Nations Realign: Foreign Policy Restructuring in the Postwar World*, (London: George Allen & Unwin, 1982), p. 1.

29. James N. Rosenau, "Toward Single-Country Theories of foreign Policy: the Case of the USSR," in Charles F. Hermann, Charles W. Kegley, Jr. and James N. Rosenau, eds., *New Directions in the Study of Foreign Policy*, (Boston, MA: Allen & Unwin, 1987), p. 71; and Michael Haas, *International Conflict*, (Indianapolis, IN: The Bobbs-Merrill Company, Inc., 1974), p. 487.

30. Donald E. Nuechterlein, "The Concept of 'National Interest': A Time for New Approaches," *Orbis*, Vol. 23, (Spring 1979), p. 76; and James N. Rosenau, *The Study of Political Adaptation*, (New York, NY: Nichols Publishing Company, 1981), pp. 88-95.

31. Bruce E. Moon, "Political Economy Approaches to the Comparative Study of Foreign Policy," in Charles F. Hermann, Charles W. Kegley, Jr. and James N. Rosenau, eds., *New Directions in the Study of Foreign Policy*, (Boston, MA: Allen & Unwin, 1987), p. 37.

32. For an excellent discussion of the logic of comparative case studies, see Theda Skocpol, *States and Social Revolution, A Comparative Analysis of France, Russia, and China*, (New York, NY: Cambridge University Press, 1979), pp. 33-43.

Chapter 2

1. James N. Rosenau, "Comparing Foreign Policies: Why, What, How," in James N. Rosenau, ed., *Comparing Foreign Policies*, (New York, NY: John Wiley, 1974), p. 6.

2. Charles F. Hermann, "Changing Course: When Governments Choose to Redirect Foreign Policy," *International Studies Quarterly*, Vol. 34, No. 1, (March 1990), p. 5.

3. James N. Rosenau, "The Study of Foreign Policy," in James N. Rosenau, Kenneth W. Thompson and Gavin Boyd, eds., *World Politics: An Introduction*, (New York, NY: The Free Press, 1976), p. 17.

4. *Ibid.*, p. 16.

5. A state's salient external environment means its immediate international environment which is directly related to its national interest. To most states, their salient external environment are not as encompassing as the entire international system. For example, under normal circumstances Burma is not likely to be a part of the salient environment of Bolivia, whereas Cuba and its other Latin American neighbors are, that is, the flow of men, ideas, and material from Burma into Bolivia is likely to be a bare trickle, if it exists at all, while the inward flow to Bolivia from elsewhere in the Western Hemisphere

is likely to be substantial. But if Burma were a superpower, then it might have become a part of the salient environment of Bolivia. See James N. Rosenau, *The Study of Political Adaptation*, (New York, NY: Nichols Publishing Company, 1981), pp. 41-42.

6. James N. Rosenau, "The Study of Foreign Policy," in James N. Rosenau, Kenneth W. Thompson and Gavin Boyd, eds., *World Politics: An Introduction*, (New York, NY: The Free Press, 1976), p. 16.

7. *Ibid.*

8. K.J. Holsti, "Restructuring Foreign Policy: A Neglected Phenomenon in foreign Policy Theory," in K.J. Holsti, ed., *Why Nations Realign: Foreign Policy Restructuring in the Postwar World*, (London: George Allen & Unwin, 1982), p. 2.

9. Kjell Goldmann, *Change and Stability in Foreign Policy*, (Princeton, NJ: Princeton University Press, 1988), p. 3.

10. Charles F. Hermann, "Changing Course: When Governments Choose to Redirect Foreign Policy," *International Studies Quarterly*, Vol. 34, No. 1, (March 1990), p. 3.

11. K.J. Holsti, *Why Nations Realign: Foreign Policy Restructuring in the Postwar World*, (London: George Allen & Unwin, 1982), pp. iv, 2.

12. *Ibid.*, p. 2.

13. *Ibid.*

14. *Ibid.*, p. 4.

15. Brigid A. Starkey, "Foreign Policy in the Muslim World: Exploring Domestic-International Linkages." A paper presented at the 1991 Annual Meeting of the American Political Science Association, Washington, D.C., (August 29/September 1, 1991), p. 8.

16. According to K.J. Holsti, a state may choose a foreign partnership pattern at one period of time as the base of is foreign policy. It may be either isolation, self-reliance, non-alignment-diversification, dependence, or alliance. A state's foreign engagement activities are closely related to its basic foreign partnership pattern. For the detailed discussion on the types of foreign relationship patterns, see K.J. Holsti, ed., *Why Nations Realign: Foreign Policy Restructuring in the Postwar World*, (London: George Allen & Unwin, 1982), pp. 4-7. Also see K.J. Holsti, *International Politics: A Framework for Analysis*, 5th ed., (Englewood Cliffs, NJ: Prentice Hall, 1988), pp. 97-101.

17. In 1970, James N. Rosenau published his two pioneering works on adaptation. One was "Foreign Policy as Adaptive Behavior: Some Preliminary Notes for a Theoretical Model" in *Comparative Politics*, Vol. 2, No. 3, (April 1970), pp. 365-387. The other was *The Adaptation of National Societies: A Theory of Political System Behavior and Transformation*, (New York, NY: McCaleb-Seiler, 1970).

18. James N. Rosenau, *The Study of Political Adaptation*, (New York: Nichols Publishing Company, 1981), p. 3.

19. James N. Rosenau, *The Adaptation of National Societies: A Theory of Political System Behavior and Transformation*, (New York, NY: McCaleb-Seiler, 1970), p. 21.

20. Stuart J. Thorson, "Adaptation and Foreign Policy Theory," in Patrick J. McGowan, ed., *Sage International Yearbook of Foreign Policy Studies*, Vol. II., (Beverly Hills, CA: Sage, 1974), p. 131.

21. James N. Rosenau, "Foreign Policy as Adaptive Behavior: Some Preliminary Notes for a Theoretical Model," *Comparative Politics*, Vol. 2, No. 3, (April 1970), p. 372.

22. James N. Rosenau, *The Study of Political Adaptation*, (New York, NY: Nichols Publishing Company, 1981), pp. 39-42.

23. Nikolaj Petersen, "Adaptation as a Framework for the Analysis of Foreign Policy Behavior," *Cooperation and Conflict*, Vol. XII, No. 4, (1977), p. 237.

24. James N. Rosenau, *The Study of Political Adaptation*, (New York, NY: Nichols Publishing Company, 1981), p. 15.

25. The four fundamental choices or strategies are: *promotive, preservative, acquiescent,* and *intransigent.* The first strategy, called a *promotive* foreign policy, exist where decision-makers choose to pursue certain goals which are not designed to respond to changes in the international environment and in essential structures. This kind of strategy is usually initiated by charismatic leaders. In the second strategy, the *preservative* foreign policy, decision-makers are responsive to changes in both the environment and essential structures. The third strategy refers to *acquiescent* foreign policy in which decision-makers are responsive only to external factors. And the fourth strategy involves *intransigent* foreign policy in which decision-makers are responsive mainly to changes in essential structures. See James N. Rosenau, *The Study of Political Adaptation*, (New York, NY: Nichols Publishing Company, 1981), pp. 56-87.

26. Rosenau says that only one of the four strategies is pursued at a given time in a society. See *Ibid.*, pp. 59, 80-87.

27. James N. Rosenau, *The Scientific Study of Foreign Policy*, revised and enlarged edition, (New York: Nichols Publishing Company, 1980), p. 504.; and James N. Rosenau, *The Study of Political Adaptation*, (New York, NY: Nichols Publishing Company, 1981), p. 89.

28. Donald E. Nuechterlein, "The Concept of 'National Interest": A Time for New Approaches," *Orbis*, Vol. 23, (Spring 1979), p. 76.

29. See James N. Rosenau, *The Study of Political Adaptation*, (New York, NY: Nichols Publishing Company, 1981), pp. 88-95.

30. K.J. Holsti, *Why Nations Realign: Foreign Policy Restructuring in the Postwar World*, (London: George Allen & Unwin, 1982), p. 3.

31. The concepts of sensitivity and vulnerability were put forward by Robert O. Keohane and Joseph S. Nye in *Power and Interdependence: World*

Politics in Transition, (Boston, MA: Little Brown, 1977), pp. 12-13.

32. Donald E. Nuechterlein, "The Concept of 'National Interest'": A Time for New Approaches," *Orbis*, Vol. 23, (Spring 1979), p. 79.

33. The original Rosenau model fails to define the role of decision-makers with sufficient clarity and does not specify the mechanics of national adaptation. As a result, his model only points out the need of adaptation for national societies and lacks further explanation of how national adaptation proceeds. In developing a framework for the analysis of foreign policy restructuring, this book modifies Rosenau's original model and gives much emphasis on the role of decision-makers in foreign policy restructuring. Also see Nikolaj Petersen, "Adaptation as a Framework for the Analysis of Foreign Policy Behavior," *Cooperation and Conflict*, Vol. XII, No. 4, (1977), p. 237.

34. Power struggle in the decision-making process involves competition, bargaining, and conflict among different groups of people, such as political factions and bureaucrats within a government. They either directly or indirectly get involved in the process and try to influence policy outcomes according to their own respective interests. More on power struggle within the foreign policy decision-making process, see Graham T. Allison, *Essence of Decision: Explaining the Cuban Missile Crisis*, (Boston, MA: Little Brown And Company, 1971.); Graham Allison and Morton H. Halperin, "Bureaucratic Politics: A Paradigm and Some Policy Implications," in Raymond Tanter and Richard H. Ullman, eds., *Theory and Policy in International Relations*, (Princeton, NJ: Princeton University Press, 1972), pp. 40-79; and Morton H. Halperin with assistance of Priscilla Clapp and Arnold Kanter, *Bureaucratic Politics and Foreign Policy*, (Washington, D.C.: The Brookings Institution, 1974).

35. On the role of perception in foreign policy making, see Robert Jervis, *Perception and Misperception in International Politics*, (Princeton, NJ: Princeton University Press, 1976); Alexander George, "The Operational Code: A Neglected Approach to the Study of Political Leaders and Decision-Making," *International Studies Quarterly*, Vol. 13, No. 2, (June 1969), pp. 190-220; and Irving L. Janis, *Victims of Groupthink*, (Boston, MA: Houghton Mifflin, 1972). Also see next note for more information.

36. Different political leaders as well as a number of motivational, attitudinal, and intellectual factors affect decision-makers' interpretation of the reality and policy choices in front of pressures caused by the external and/or internal changes. As a result, the problem of discrepancies between the "operational and psychological environments" occurs. The concepts of operational and psychological environments were put forward by Harold and Margaret Sprout in their article of "Environment Factors in the Study of International Politics," *Journal of Conflict Resolution*, Vol. 1, (December 1957), pp. 309-328. These two concepts were well studied first in Michael Brecher, Blema Steignberg, and Janice Stein, "A Framework for Research on

256   *Foreign Policy Restructuring As Adaptive Behavior*

Foreign Policy Behavior," *Journal of Conflict Resolution*, Vol. 13, No. 1, (March 1969), pp. 75-101. Later Michael Brecher applied the concepts to his case study of Israel foreign policy as in *The Foreign Policy System of Israel: Setting, Images, Process*, (New Haven, CT: Yale University Press, 1972) and *Decisions in Israel's Foreign Policy*, (New Haven, CT: Yale University Press, 1975). The operational environment refers to the circumstances of domestic and international situations as they really are, whereas the psychological environment means the existing circumstances as they are perceived by decision-makers. In fact, decision-makers' subjective world and the objective reality are not always identical. Unrealistic perceptions towards changes taking place at home and abroad may lead to over-estimate and over-reaction or under-estimate and under-reaction in foreign policy making. In this sense, the change of decision-makers' perceptions towards their outside world and the power struggle among competing domestic elites are two important intervening variables affecting the interpretation of pressures and policy choices. To be sure, the incorrect responses can hardly reduce the pressures on a country's vital interests and re-satisfy the country's basic needs. Thus, the country's long-term demand for self-preservation will continue to require a search for new effective courses of action.

37. David Bachman, "Domestic Sources of Chinese Foreign Policy," in Sameul S. Kim, ed., *China and the World: New Directions in Chinese Foreign Relations*, 2nd ed., (Boulder, CO: Westview Press, 1989), p. 31.

38. Michael Ng-Quinn, "International Systemic constraints on Chinese Foreign Policy," in Samuel S. Kim, ed., *China and the World: Chinese Foreign Policy in the Post-Mao Era*, (Boulder, CO: Westview Press, 1984), p. 101.

39. Samuel S. Kim, "New Directions and Old Puzzles in Chinese Foreign Policy," in Samuel S. Kim, ed., *China and the World: New Directions in Chinese Foreign Relations*, (Boulder, CO: Westview Press, 1989), pp. 3-30.

40. Richard C. Snyder, H.W. Bruck, and Burton Sapin, *Decision-Making as an Approach to the Study of International Politics*, (New York, NY: Free Press, 1962), p. 2.

Chapter 3

1. Suzanne Ogden, *China's Unresolved Issues: Politics, Development, and Culture*, (Englewood Cliffs, NJ: Prentice Hall, Inc., 1989), p. 20.

2. For example, China opened almost all important Chinese ports to foreign countries. Foreign powers obtained from the weak Chinese government various privileges, such as extraterritoriality, most-favored-nation status, control over the rate and collection of tariffs, and control over banks, transportation and communications. For more accounts, see John K. Fairbank,

The Great Chinese Revolution: 1800-1985, (New York, NY: Harper & Row, Publishers, 1987).

3. Yufan Hao and Guocang Huan, eds., *The Chinese View of the World*, (New York, NY: Pantheon Books, 1989), p. xvi.

4. Sun Yat-sen, *San Min Chu I: The Three Principles of People*, (Shanghai: The Commercial Press, 1928), p. 35.

5. Mao Zedong, "Opening Speech at the First Plenary Session of the Chinese People's Political Consultative Conference" in *The Selected Works of Mao Tsetung*, (Peking: Foreign Language Press, 1977), pp. 17-18.

6. Jiaju Qian, "China Can be Saved Only through Peaceful Evolution" in *Central Daily News* (International Edition), October 25, 1991, p. 4.

7. Deng Xiaoping "Opening Address to the Twelfth Party Congress," in Harold C. Hinton, ed., *The People's Republic of China 1979-1984: A Documentary Survey*, (Wilmington, DE: Scholarly Resources, Inc., 1986), p. 185.

8. Xinhua News Agency, September 29, 1995.

9. Frank N. Trager and Frank L. Simonie. "An Introduction to the Study of National Security," in Frank. N. Trager and Philip S. Kronenberg, eds., *National Security and American Society*, (Lawrence, Kansas: University Press of Kansas, 1973), p. 36.

10. Harry Harding, "China's Changing Roles in the Contemporary World," in Harry Harding, ed., *China's Foreign Relations in the 1980s*, (New Haven, CT: Yale University Press, 1984), p. 210.

11. Thomas W. Robinson, "Restructuring Chinese Foreign Policy, 1959-76: Three Episodes," in Kalevi J. Holsti, ed., *Why Nations Realign: Foreign Policy Restructuring in the Postwar World*, (London: George Allen & Unwin, 1982), p. 163.

12. Thomas W. Robinson, "Restructuring Chinese Foreign Policy, 1959-76: Three Episodes," in Kalevi J. Holsti, ed., *Why Nations Realign: Foreign Policy Restructuring in the Postwar World*, (London: George Allen & Unwin, 1982), p. 163.

13. For background analyses, see Robert S. Ross, *The Indochina Tangle: China's Vietnam Policy 1975-1979*, (New York, NY: Columbia University Press, 1988).

14. William S. Turley, "Vietnam/Indochina: Hanoi's Challenge to Southeast Asian Regional Order," in Young Whan Kihl and Lawrence E. Grinter, eds., *Asian-Pacific Security: Emerging Challenges and Responses*, (Boulder, CO: Lynne Rienner Publishers, Inc., 1986), pp. 178-179.

15. Donald Shanor and Constance Shanor, *China Today*, (New York, NY: St. Martin's Press, 1995), p. 15

16. Hua Guofeng, "Report on the Work of Government Delivered at the First Session of the Fifth National People's Congress, February 26, 1978," *Renmin Ribao (People's Daily*, February 28, 1978, p. 1.

17. David Shambaugh, "The United States and China: A New Cold War?" *Current History*, Vol. 94, No. 593, September 1995, p. 244.

18. Kenneth Lieberthal "Domestic Politics and Foreign Policy," in Harry Harding, ed., *China's Foreign Relations in the 1980s*, (New Haven, CT: Yale University Press, 1984), pp. 43-70. In addition, Michel Oksenberg and Steven Goldstein identify four clusters: fundamentalist, radical conservativist, eclectic modernizational, and total westernizational. Since 1949, the center of gravity in China's foreign policy has been radical conservatism. At times, it moved close toward fundamentalist position or toward eclectic modernizational position. Seldom has China followed a foreign policy of complete westernization. See Michel Oksenberg and Steven Goldstein, "The Chinese Political Spectrum," *Problems of Communism*, Vol. 23, No. 2, (March/April 1974), pp. 1-13.

19. This slogan was very popular in China's "Self-Strengthening Movement" in the late nineteenth century. It was first put forward by Zhang Zidong (Chang Chih-tung), one of the leading figures in the movement. More on this, see John K. Fairbank, *The Great Chinese Revolution: 1800-1985*, (New York, NY: Harper & Row, Publishers, 1987), pp. 100-121.

20. "Complete Westernization Negates Socialism" in *Beijing Review*, Vol. 30, No. 3, (January 19, 1987), p. 16.

21. Michael Yahuda, *Towards the End of Isolationism: China's Foreign Policy After Mao*, (New York, NY: St. Martin's Press, 1983), p. 131.

22. In 1955, 29 newly independent Asian and African countries held the Bandung Conference in Indonesia. They discussed their common concerns against imperialism and neocolonialism. They also discussed their common interest in developing economy. China participated in this conference.

23. Hu Yaobang, "Create a New Situation in All Fields of Socialist Modernization: Report to the 12th National Congress of the Communist Party of China," *Beijing Review*, Vol. 25, No. 37, September 13, 1982, p. 30.

24. Zhao Ziyang, "Report on the Work of the Government at the First Session of the Sixth National People's Congress, June 6, 1983," *Beijing Review*, Vol. 26, No. 27, (July 4, 1983), (Supplement), p. XXII.

25. *Ibid.*

26. Robert L. Worden, Andrea Matles Savada, and Ronald E. Dolan., *China: a country study*, (Washington D.C.: Headquarters, Department of the Army, 1988), p. 478.

27. Greg O'Leary, *The Shaping of Chinese Foreign Policy*, (New York, NY: St. Martin's Press, 1980), p. 37.

28. Jean-Luc Domenach, "Ideological Reform," in Gerald Segal, ed., *Chinese Politics and Foreign Policy Reform*, (London: Kegan Paul International Ltd., 1990), p. 28.

29. Robert L. Worden, Andrea Matles Savada, and Ronald E. Dolan., eds., *China: a country study*, (Washington D.C.: Headquarters, Department of

the Army, 1988), p. 480.

30. Simon Long, "Political Reform," in Gerald Segal, ed., *Chinese Politics and Foreign Policy Reform*, (London: Kegan Paul International Ltd., 1990), p. 46

31. Seweryn Bialer, "Soviet Foreign Policy: Sources, Perceptions, trends," in Seweryn Bialer, ed., *The Domestic Context of Soviet Foreign Policy*, (Boulder, CO: Westview Press, 1981), pp. 409-441.

32. Jean-Luc Domenach, "Ideological Reform," in Gerald Segal, ed., *Chinese Politics and Foreign Policy Reform*, (London: Kegan Paul International Ltd., 1990), p. 25.

33. Robert G. Sutter, *Chinese Foreign Policy: Developments after Mao*, (New York, NY: Praeger Publishers, 1986), p. 7.

34. Doak Barnett, *The Making of Foreign Policy in China: Structure and Process*, (Boulder, CO: Westview Press, 1985), p. 14. Also see Quansheng Zhao, "Domestic Sources of Chinese Foreign Policy: from Vertical to Horizontal Authoritarianism." A research paper presented at the 1991 Annual Meeting of the American Political Science Association, Washington, D.C., (August 29/September 1, 1991), p. 4.

35. The classic studies on the subject include Lucian W. Pye, *The Dynamics of Chinese Politics*, (Cambridge, MA: Oelgeschlager, Gunn & Hain, 1981); Andrew Nathan, "A Factionalism Model for Chinese Politics," *The China Quarterly*, No. 53, (January/March, 1973), pp. 34-66; and Tang Tsou, "Prolegomenon to the Study of Informal Groups in Chinese Communist Party Politics," *The China Quarterly*, No. 65, (January 1976), pp. 98-114.

36. Gavin Boyd, "The Foreign Policy of China," in James N. Rosenau, Kenneth W. Thompson and Gavin Boyd, eds., *World Politics: An Introduction*, (New York, NY: The Free Press, 1976), p. 115.

37. Lucian W. Pye, *The Dynamics of Chinese Politics*, (Cambridge, MA: Oelgeschlager, Gunn & Hain, 1981), p. 13.

38. *Ibid.*, p. 8.

39. Kenneth Lieberthal, "Domestic Politics and Foreign Policy," in Harry Harding, ed., *China's Foreign Relations in the 1980s*, (New Haven, CT: Yale University Press, 1984), p. 45-46.

40. Michel Oksenberg and Steven Goldstein, "The Chinese Political Spectrum," *Problems of Communism*, Vol. 23, No. 2, (March/April 1974), p. 3.

41. Thomas Fingar, *China's Quest for Independence: Policy Evolution in the 1970s*, (Boulder, CO: Westview Press, 1980), p. 28.

42. *Zhongyang* usually includes the members of the senior leaders, the Standing Committee of the Politburo, the Politburo itself, the Central Committee Secretariat, the State Council, and the Military Affairs Commission of the Central Committee.

43. Robert G. Sutter, "China: Coping with the Evolving Strategic

Environment," in Young Whan Kihl and Lawrence E. Grinter, eds., *Asian-Pacific Security: Emerging Challenges and Responses*, (Boulder, CO: Lynne Rienner Publishers, Inc., 1986), p. 111.
44. Michael B. Yahuda, "Sino-American Relations," in Gerald Segal, ed., *Chinese Politics and Foreign Policy Reform*, (London: Kegan Paul International Ltd., 1990), p. 182.

Chapter 4

1. Robert G. Sutter, *Chinese Foreign Policy: Developments after Mao*, (New York: Praeger Publishers, 1986), p. 13.
2. Steven I. Levine, "The Superpowers in Chinese Global Policy," in James C. Hsiung and Samuel S. Kim, ed., *China in the Global Community*, (New York, NY: Praeger Publishers, 1980), p. 56.
3. Alan J. Day with Peter Jones and Siân Kevill, eds. *China and the Soviet Union 1949-84*, (New York, NY: Facts On File, Inc., 1985), pp. 89-91; Alfred D. Low, *The Sino-Soviet Confrontation Since Mao Zedong*, (New York, NY: Columbia University Press, 1987), p. 77; and Thomas W. Robinson, "The Sino-Soviet Border Dispute: Background, Development, and the March 1969 Clashes," *American Political Science Review*, Vol. 66, (December 1972), p. 1178.
4. Michael Yahuda, *Towards the End of Isolationism: China's Foreign Policy After Mao*, (New York, NY: St. Martin's Press, 1983), p. 118.
5. Robert L. Worden, Andrea Matles Savada, and Ronald E. Dolan, eds., *China: a country study*, (Washington D.C.: Headquarters, Department of the Army, 1988), p. 490.
6. For a detailed account, see Roy Medvedev, *China and the Superpowers*, (New York, NY: Basil Blackwell, Inc., 1986), pp. 45-47.
7. Alan J. Day with Peter Jones and Siân Kevill , eds. *China and the Soviet Union 1949-84*, (New York, NY: Facts On File, Inc., 1985), pp. 87-91.
8. Thomas W. Robinson, "The Sino-Soviet Border Dispute: Background, Development, and the March 1969 Clashes," *American Political Science Review*, Vol. 66, (December 1972), p. 1178; and Alfred D. Low, *The Sino-Soviet Confrontation Since Mao Zedong*, (New York, NY: Columbia University Press, 1987), p. 77
9. Thomas W. Robinson, "The Sino-Soviet Border Dispute: Background, Development, and the March 1969 Clashes," *American Political Science Review*, Vol. 66, (December 1972), p. 1177.
10. Alan J. Day with Peter Jones and Siân Kevill, eds. *China and the Soviet Union 1949-84*, (New York, NY: Facts On File, Inc., 1985), pp. 92-93; Roy Medvedev, *China and the Superpowers*, (New York, NY: Basil Blackwell, Inc., 1986), p. 48; and Michael B. Yahuda, *Towards the End of Isolationism:*

Notes 261

China's Foreign Policy After Mao, (New York, NY: St. Martin's Press, 1983), p. 118.

11. The Chinese side stated that the battle had lasted about eleven hours while the Soviet side said the clash had taken about seven hours. Up to 2,000 men from the Chinese side and nearly 3,000 soldiers from the Soviet side engaged in the battle. For the detailed account, see Thomas W. Robinson, "The Sino-Soviet Border Dispute: Background, Development, and the March 1969 Clashes," *American Political Science Review*, Vol. 66, (December 1972), pp. 1175-1202; and Alan J. Day with Peter Jones and Siân Kevill, eds. *China and the Soviet Union 1949-84*, (New York, NY: Facts On File, Inc., 1985), pp. 92-96.

12. Roy Medvedev, *China and the Superpowers*, (New York, NY: Basil Blackwell, Inc., 1986), p. 49.

13. For the detailed account, see Thomas W. Robinson, "The Sino-Soviet Border Dispute: Background, Development, and the March 1969 Clashes," *American Political Science Review*, Vol. 66, (December, 1972), pp. 1175-1202; and Roy Medvedev, *China and the Superpowers*, (New York, NY: Basil Blackwell, Inc., 1986), pp. 5-65; and Robert G. Sutter, *Chinese Foreign Policy: Developments after Mao*, (New York, NY: Praeger Publishers, 1986), p. 18.

14. Henry Kissinger, *The White House Years*, (London: Weidenfeld and Nicolson and M. Joseph, 1979), pp. 183-186.

15. Michael Yahuda, *Towards the End of Isolationism: China's Foreign Policy After Mao*, (New York, NY: St. Martin's Press, 1983), p. 119.

16. Thomas W. Robinson, "Restructuring Chinese Foreign Policy, 1959-76: Three Episodes," in Kalevi J. Holsti, ed., *Why Nations Realign: Foreign Policy Restructuring in the Postwar World*, (London: George Allen & Unwin, 1982), p. 149.

17. Michel Oksenberg, "A Decade of Sino-American Relations," *Foreign Affairs*, Vol. 61. No. 1, (Fall, 1982), pp. 175-177. Also see Doak Barnett, "Peking and the Asian Power Balance" in *Problems of Communism*, Vol. 21, (July/August 1976), pp. 36-40.

18. Kenneth G. Lieberthal, *Sino-Soviet Conflict in the 1970s: Its Evolution and Implications for the Strategic Triangle*, (Santa Monica, CA: The Rand Corporation, 1978), pp. 49-50.

19. *Renmin Ribao (People's Daily)*, October 7, 1969, p. 1.

20. For more background information, see Thomas M. Gottlieb, *Chinese Foreign Policy Factionalism and the Origins of the Strategic Triangle.*, (Santa Monica, CA: Rand Corporation, 1977); Greg O'Leary, *The Shaping of Chinese Foreign Policy*, (New York, NY: St. Martin's Press, 1980); and Robert G. Sutter, *Chinese Foreign Policy: Developments after Mao*, (New York, NY: Praeger Publishers, 1986).

21. Harry Harding, "China's Changing Roles in the Contemporary

World," in Harry Harding, ed., *China's Foreign Relations in the 1980s*, (New Haven, CT: Yale University Press, 1984), p. 190.

22. James C.F. Wang, *Contemporary Chinese Politics: An Introduction*, 3rd ed., (Englewood Cliffs, NJ: Prentice-Hall, Inc., 1989), p. 309.

23. Robert G. Sutter, *Chinese Foreign Policy: Developments after Mao*, (New York, NY: Praeger Publishers, 1986), p. 17.

24. For a detailed account of the Lin Biao Affairs, see Michael Y.M. Kau, ed., *The Lin Piao Affair: Power Politics and Military Coup*, (White Plains, NY: Institute of Arts and Sciences Press, 1975).

25. In late 1969, Mao asked Marshal Ye Jianyin and several other senior military leaders to review China's strategic position and options. See *Renmin Ribao (People's Daily)*, October 30, 1986, p. 2.

26. Banning Garrett and Bonnie Glaser, *War and Peace: The Views from Moscow and Peking*, (Berkeley, CA: University of California Press, 1984), p. 57.

27. Robert G. Sutter, *Chinese Foreign Policy: Developments after Mao*, (New York, NY: Praeger Publishers, 1986), pp. 15-19; and Thomas W. Robinson, "Restructuring Chinese Foreign Policy, 1959-76: Three Episodes," in Kalevi J. Holsti, ed., *Why Nations Realign: Foreign Policy Restructuring in the Postwar World*, (London: George Allen & Unwin, 1982), p. 148.

28. The Second Foreign Language Institute of Beijing, ed., *Guo Ji Zhi Shi Sou Ce (The Handbook of World Knowledge)*, (Nanning, China: People's Press, 1981), pp. 281-290.

29. Robert G. Sutter, *Chinese Foreign Policy: Developments after Mao*, (New York, NY: Praeger Publishers, 1986), p. 23.

30. *The White House Years*, (London: Weidenfeld and Nicolson and M. Joseph, 1979), p. 192.

31. "Joint Communiqué by China and the United States (February 28, 1972)," in *Beijing Review*, Vol. 15, No. 9, (March 3, 1972), pp. 4-5.

32. Robert G. Sutter, *Chinese Foreign Policy: Developments after Mao*, (New York, NY: Praeger Publishers, 1986), p. 23.

33. Editorial Department of *Renmin Ribao (People's Daily)*, "Chairman Mao's Theory of the Differentiation of the Three Worlds is a Major Contribution to Marxism-Leninism," *Peking Review*, Vol. 20, No. 45, (November 4, 1977), p. 11.

34. Deng Xiaoping (Teng Hsiao-ping), "Speech by the Chairman of Delegation of the People's Republic of China at the Sixth Special Session of the United Nation's General Assembly," *Peking Review*, Vol. 17, No. 16, (April 12, 1974), pp. 6-11.

35. Editorial Department of *Renmin Ribao (People's Daily)*, "Chairman Mao's Theory of the Differentiation of the Three Worlds is a Major Contribution to Marxism-Leninism," *Peking Review*, Vol. 20, No. 45, (November 4, 1977), p. 34.

36. *Ibid.*, pp. 10-43.

37. *Ibid.*, p. 35.

38. *Ibid.*

39. Zhou Enlai (Chou En-lai), "Report to the Tenth National Congress of the Communist Party of China," *Peking Review*, Vol. 16, No. 35/36, (September 7, 1973), pp. 17-25.

40. Editorial Department of *Renmin Ribao* (*People's Daily*), "Chairman Mao's Theory of the Differentiation of the Three Worlds is a Major Contribution to Marxism-Leninism," *Peking Review*, Vol. 20, No. 45, (November 4, 1977), p. 35.

41. *Ibid.*, pp. 10-43.

42. Alfred D. Low, *The Sino-Soviet Confrontation Since Mao Zedong*, (New York, NY: Columbia University Press, 1987), pp. 48-49.

43. Robert G. Sutter, *Chinese Foreign Policy: Developments after Mao*, (New York, NY: Praeger Publishers, 1986), pp. 24, 38, 85.

44. The Second Foreign Language Institute of Beijing, ed., *Guo Ji Zhi Shi Sou Ce* (*The Handbook of World Knowledge*), (Nanning, China: People's Press, 1981), pp. 281-290.

45. Zhimin Lin, "China's Third World Policy," in Yufan Hao and Guocang Huan, eds., *The Chinese View of the World*, (New York, NY: Pantheon Books, 1989), pp. 237-238.

46. Zhou Enlai (Chou En-lai), "Report to the Tenth National Congress of the Communist Party of China," *Peking Review*, Vol. 16, No. 35/36, (September 7, 1973), pp. 17-25.

47. *Ibid.*

48. Robert G. Sutter, *Chinese Foreign Policy: Developments after Mao*, (New York, NY: Praeger Publishers, 1986), pp. 39-41.

49. *Ibid.*, p. 41.

50. Most of these plants were for basic industries, such as steel, electricity, petroleum, and chemical fertilizer. See James C.F. Wang, *Contemporary Chinese Politics: An Introduction*, 3rd ed., (Englewood Cliffs, NJ: Prentice-Hall, Inc., 1989), p. 292.

51. Chi Kuo, "Foreign Trade: Why the 'Gang of Four' Created Confusion?" *Peking Review*, Vol. 20, No. 9, (February 25, 1977), pp. 16-18.

52. On October 6, 1976, only one month after Mao's death, four radical Politburo members, including Mao's widow Jiang Qing, Zhang Chunqiao, Yao Wenyuan, and Wang Hongwen, were arrested by their political opponents. These four people later were labeled as the "Gang of Four."

53. Robert S. Ross, *The Indochina Tangle: China's Vietnam Policy: 1975-1979*, (New York, NY: Columbia University Press, 1988).

54. David Armstrong, "The Soviet Union," in Gerald Segal and William T. Tow, eds., *Chinese Defense Policy*, (Urbana and Chicago: University of Illinois Press, 1984), p. 184.

55. "Asian Situation: Developments and Trends," *Beijing Review*, Vol. 22, No. 32, (August 10, 1979), pp. 26-27; and "Increasing Soviet Menace," *Beijing Review*, Vol. 23, No. 34, (August 25, 1980), p. 11.

56. Qi Ya and Zhou Jirong, "Expansionist Soviet Global Strategy," *Beijing Review*, Vol. 24, No. 25, (June 22, 1981), pp. 22-25.

57. Robert G. Sutter, *Chinese Foreign Policy: Developments after Mao*, (New York, NY: Praeger Publishers, 1986), p. 115.

58. *Renmin Ribao (People's Daily)*, January 30, 1980, p. 1.

59. Robert G. Sutter, *Chinese Foreign Policy: Developments after Mao*, (New York, NY: Praeger Publishers, 1986), pp. 67-68, 116.

60. "Treaty of Peace and Friendship Between the People's Republic of China and Japan," *Peking Review*, Vol. 21, No. 33, (August 18, 1978), pp. 7-8; and "Joint Communiqué on the Establishment of Diplomatic Relations between the People's Republic of China and the United States of America," *Peking Review*, Vol. 21, No. 51, (December 22, 1978), p. 8.

61. Harry Harding, "China's Changing Roles in the Contemporary World," in Harry Harding, ed., *China's Foreign Relations in the 1980s*, (New Haven, CT: Yale University Press, 1984), p. 193.

62. Jonathan D. Pollack, *The Lessons of Coalition Politics*, (Santa Monica, CA: Rand Corp., 1984), pp. 39-72.

63. "An Interview with Teng Hsiao-P'ing," *Time*, Vol. 113, No. 6, (February 5, 1979), p. 34.

64. Harry Harding, "China's Changing Roles in the Contemporary World," in Harry Harding, ed., *China's Foreign Relations in the 1980s*, (New Haven: Yale University Press, 1984), p. 194.

Chapter 5

1. Harry Harding, *China's Second Revolution: Reform after Mao*, (Washington, D.C.: Brookings Institution, 1987), pp. 11-12.

2. *Ibid.*, p. 31.

3. *Ibid.*, p. 32.

4. On Chinese political crisis in the latter years of Mao's life, see Harry Harding, *China's Second Revolution: Reform after Mao*, (Washington, D.C.: Brookings Institution, 1987), pp. 35-38.

5. Qingguo Jia, "China's Foreign Economic Policy," in Yufan Hao and Guocang Huan, eds., *The Chinese View of the World.*, (New York, NY: Pantheon Books, 1989), p. 63.

6. Harry Harding, *China's Second Revolution: Reform after Mao*, (Washington, D.C.: Brookings Institution, 1987), p. 52.

7. Lowell Dittmer, "Bases of Power in Chinese Politics: A Theory and an Analysis of the Fall of the 'Gang of Four,'" *World Politics*, Vol. 31, (October

1978), pp. 26-60.

8. On Hua's struggle to maintain power, see Dorothy G. Fontana, "Background to the Fall of Hua Guofeng," *Asian Survey*, Vol. XXII, No. 3, (March 1982), pp. 237-260; and Jürgen Domes, *The Government and Politics of the PRC: A Time of Transition*, (Boulder, CO: Westview Press, 1985), pp. 140-191.

9. For a detailed account, see Hua Guofeng, "Report to the Eleventh National Congress of the Communist Party of China, August 1977," in *The Eleventh National Congress of the Communist Party of China (Documents)*, (Peking: Foreign Languages Press, 1977), pp. 1-111.

10. People's Republic of China, State Statistical Bureau, *Statistical Yearbook of China, 1984*, (Hong Kong: Economic Information and Agency, 1984), pp. 26, 395.

11. *Ibid.*

12. Li Chengrui and Zhang Zhuoyuan, "An Outline of Economic Development, 1977-1980" in Yu Guangyuan, *China's Socialist Modernization*, (Beijing: foreign Languages Press, 1984), pp. 29-52.

13. *Renmin Ribao (People's Daily)*, February 7, 1977, p. 1.

14. On Deng Xiaoping and his political career in China, see Uli Franz, *Deng Xiaoping*, (Boston, MA: Harcourt Brace Jovanovich, 1988); Harry Harding, *China's Second Revolution: Reform after Mao*, (Washington, D.C.: Brookings Institution, 1987), pp. 40-69; and Jürgen Domes, *The Government and Politics of the PRC: A Time of Transition*, (Boulder, CO: Westview Press, 1985), pp. 145-191.

15. Jürgen Domes, *The Government and Politics of the PRC: A Time of Transition*, (Boulder, CO: Westview Press, 1985), pp. 156-158.

16. Deng Xiaoping, "The 'Two Whatevers' Do Not Accord with Marxism," May 1977, in *Selected Works of Deng Xiaoping, 1975-1982*, (Beijing: Foreign Languages Press, 1984), pp. 51-52.

17. "The Communiqué of the Third Plenary Session of the Eleventh Central Committee of the Chinese Communist Party," *Peking Review*, Vol. 21, No. 52, (December 29, 1978), pp. 6-16.

18. The core of the rural reform program was the introduction of the "household responsibility system" which was, in essence, an incentive system. This system decentralized the power to the household which could determine its own production plans and function as both the basic production and accounting unit. The key elements of the system were the clear linkage between income and output and the contract between the peasant producers and the production team. The team collected the grain or produced contracted for, and the peasants might keep any surplus after they met the quotas. Peasant producers were free to market any surplus in the rural free markets. Households were encouraged to produce whatever crops grew best in their area, a mandate limited, however, by planned quotas imposed on each

production unit and by the forces of market demanded. More on the "household responsibility system," see James C.F. Wang, *Contemporary Chinese Politics: An Introduction*, 3rd ed., (Englewood Cliffs, NJ: Prentice-Hall, Inc., 1989), pp. 253-259.

19. Jürgen Domes, *The Government and Politics of the PRC: A Time of Transition*, (Boulder, CO: Westview Press, 1985), p. 170.

20. *Ibid.*, p. 175.

21. "Resolution on Certain Questions in the History of Our Party since the founding the People's Republic of China" adopted by the Sixth Plenary Session of the 11th Central Committee of the Communist Party of China on June 27, 1981, *Beijing Review*, Vol. 24, No. 27, July 6, 1981, pp. 10-39.

22. On May 16, 1989, Zhao Ziyang told the Soviet President Mikhail Gorbachev, who was on his historic tour to China, that "Comrade Deng Xiaoping has been the leader of our party since the third plenary session of the Eleventh Chinese Communist Party Central Committee (1978). Comrade Deng Xiaoping stepped down from the Central Committee and the Standing Committee of the Politburo of his own accord at the Thirteenth Party Congress (1987). However, all the comrades in our party hold that in the interests of the party we still need Comrade Deng Xiaoping, his wisdom and his experience. This is of vital importance to our party. Therefore, the first plenary session of the Thirteenth Party Congress made the solemn decision that we still need Comrade Deng Xiaoping at the helm when it comes to most important questions. Since the Thirteenth Party Congress, we have always made reports to and asked for opinions from Comrade Deng Xiaoping while dealing with most important issues." *Renmin Ribao (People's Daily)*, May 17, 1989, p. 1.

23. Robert G. Sutter, *Chinese Foreign Policy: Developments after Mao*, (New York, NY: Praeger Publishers, 1986), p. 60.

24. Quoted in James M. Ethridge, *China's Unfinished revolution: Problems and Prospects since Mao*, (San Francisco, CA: China Books & Periodicals, Inc., 1990), p. 71.

25. Simon Long, "Political Reform," in Gerald Segal, ed., *Chinese Politics and Foreign Policy Reform*, (London: Kegan Paul International Ltd., 1990), p. 51.

26. Jean-Luc Domenach, "Ideological Reform," in Gerald Segal, ed., *Chinese Politics and Foreign Policy Reform*, (London: Kegan Paul International Ltd., 1990), p. 27.

27. Strobe Talbott, "The Strategic Dimension of the Sino-American Relationship," in Richard H. Solomon, ed., *The China Factor: Sino-American Relations and the Global Scene*, (Englewood Cliffs, NJ: Prentice-Hall, Inc., 1981), p. 92. See also *The New York Times*, April 4, 1987, pp. A1, A3.

28. The United States used the word "acknowledge" instead of "recognize" in the joint communiqué. See "Joint Communiqué by China and the United States (February 28, 1972)," *Peking Review*, Vol. 15, No. 9, (March 3, 1972),

pp. 4-5. (Emphasis Added)

29. "Joint Communiqué on Establishment of Diplomatic Relations between the People's Republic of China and the United States of America," *Peking Review*, Vol. 21, No. 51, (December 22, 1978), p. 8. (Emphasis Added).

30. Bureau of Public Affairs, The Department of State. "Text of U.S. Statement, December 15, 1978," in *U.S. Policy Toward China: July 15, 1971-January 15, 1979*, Selected Documents No. 9. (Washington, D.C., January 1979), p. 48.

31. "U.S.-China Joint Communiqué, August 17, 1982," *Beijing Review*, Vol. 25, No. 34, (August 23, 1982), pp. 14-15.

32. "Taiwan Relations Act," in *The United States Statutes At Large, 1979*, Vol. 93, (Washington, D.C.: U.S. Government Printing Office, 1981), pp. 14-21.

33. John W. Garver, "Arms Sales, the Taiwan Question, and Sino-US Relations," *Orbis*, Vol. 26, (Winter 1983), p. 1009.

34. *Ibid.*, p. 1013.

35. James C.F. Wang, *Contemporary Chinese Politics: An Introduction*, 3rd ed., (Englewood Cliffs, NJ: Prentice-Hall, Inc., 1989), p. 337-8.

36. Robert G. Sutter, "U.S. Arms Sales to Taiwan: Implications for American Interests," *Journal of Northeast Asian Studies*, Vol. 1, No. 3, (September 1982), p. 29.

37. "Sino-U.S. Relations," *Beijing Review*, Vol. 25, No. 1, (January 4, 1982), p. 3.

38. "Critical Point in Sino-U.S. Relations," *Beijing Review*, Vol. 25, No. 11, (March 15, 1982), pp. 10-11.

39. Harry Harding, "China's Changing Roles in the Contemporary World," in Harry Harding, ed., *China's Foreign Relations in the 1980s*, (New Haven, CT: Yale University Press, 1984), p. 195.

40. "U.S.-China Joint Communiqué, August 17, 1982," *Beijing Review*, Vol. 25, No. 34, (August 23, 1982), pp. 14-15.

41. *The New York Times*, August 17, 1982, pp. A1, A8; and "The U.S. Should Strictly Observe Agreement," *Beijing Review*, Vol. 25, No. 35, (August 30, 1982), pp. 25-26.

42. Allen S. Whiting, "Assertive Nationalism in Chinese Foreign Policy," *Asian Survey*, Vol. XXIII, No. 8, (August 1983), p. 921.

43. Donald Hugh McMillen, "Chinese Perspective on International Security," in Donald Hugh McMillen, ed., *Asian Perspectives on International Security*, (New York, NY: St. Martin's Press, 1984), p. 176; and John F. Copper, "Sino-American Relations: on Track or off Track?" *Asia Pacific Community*, No. 19, (Winter 1983), pp. 17-18.

44. Robert L. Worden, Andrea Matles Savada, and Ronald E. Dolan, eds., *China: a country study*, (Washington D.C.: Headquarters, Department of the Army, 1988), p. 494.

45. Donald Hugh McMillen, "Chinese Perspective on International Security," in Donald Hugh McMillen, ed., *Asian Perspectives on International Security*, (New York, NY: St. Martin's Press, 1984), pp. 176, 192(n22).

46. Harry Harding, "China's Changing Roles in the Contemporary World," in Harry Harding, ed., *China's Foreign Relations in the 1980s*, (New Haven, CT: Yale University Press, 1984), p. 196.

47. During the Polish crisis in 1981, Beijing joined Washington in condemning the Soviet policy. But the Chinese leaders refused to support the Solidarity for the fear of similar labor problems at home and dissent against the Communist Party in China. See John F. Copper, "Sino-American Relations: on Track or off Track?" *Asia Pacific Community*, No. 19, (Winter 1983), p. 21. On the Korean issue, China supported North Korea while the United States backed South Korea. As far as third world issues were concerned, the United States and China held quite different attitudes towards many issues such as the New International Economic Order.

48. Jonathan D. Pollack, "China and the Global Strategic Balance," in Harry Harding, ed., *China's Foreign Relations in the 1980s*, (New Haven: Yale University Press, 1984), pp. 164, 166.

49. Banning Garrett and Bonnie Glaser, *War and Peace: The Views from Moscow and Peking*, (Berkeley, CA: University of California Press, 1984), p. 61.

50. *Ibid.*

51. Yasuhiko Ono, "Sino-Soviet Reconciliation and its Impact on Asia," *Asia Pacific Community*, No. 19, (Winter 1983), p. 3.

52. Chi Su, "China and the Soviet Union: 'Principled, Salutary, and Tempered' Management of Conflict," in Samuel S.Kim, ed., *China and the World: Chinese Foreign Policy in the Post-Mao Era*, (Boulder, CO: Westview Press, 1984), p. 137.

53. Yasuhiko Ono, "Sino-Soviet Reconciliation and its Impact on Asia," *Asia Pacific Community*, No. 19, (Winter 1983), p. 5; and Chi Su, "China and the Soviet Union: 'Principled, Salutary, and Tempered' Management of Conflict," in Samuel S.Kim, ed., *China and the World: Chinese Foreign Policy in the Post-Mao Era*, (Boulder, CO: Westview Press, 1984), pp. 137-138.

54. *Pravda*, March 25, 1982, p. 2.

55. Chi Su, "China and the Soviet Union: 'Principled, Salutary, and Tempered' Management of Conflict," in Samuel S.Kim, ed., *China and the World: Chinese Foreign Policy in the Post-Mao Era*, (Boulder, CO: Westview Press, 1984), p. 137.

56. *Renmin Ribao (People's Daily)*, March 27, 1982, p. 6; also see "Chinese Spokesman on Brezhnev's Remarks," *Beijing Review*, Vol. 25, No. 14, (April 5, 1982), p. 7.

57. Quoted in Banning N. Garrett and Bonnie S. Glaser, *War and Peace: The Views from Moscow and Peking*, (Berkeley, CA: University of California

Press, 1984), p. 74.

58. Ya-chun Chang, "Dilemma in Bush's China Policy under Utopianism," *Central Daily News* (International Edition), January 15, 1992, p. 3.

59. Jonathan D. Pollack, "China and the Global Strategic Balance," in Harry Harding, ed., *China's Foreign Relations in the 1980s*, (New Haven: Yale University Press, 1984), p. 163.

60. The United States first expressed such a commitment to the Chinese during Zbigniew Brzezinski's visit to Beijing in May 1978. See President Carter's instructions to Brzezinski, in Zbigniew Brzezinski, *Power and Principle--Memoirs of the National Security Advisor, 1977-1981*, (New York, NY: Farrar, Straus and Giroux, 1983), pp. 551-55.

61. Ironically, China had long condemned that the Soviet Union interfered with Third World affairs in the name of "natural alliance" with the Third World. See Samuel S. Kim, "China and the Third World: In Search of A Neorealist World Policy," in Samuel S. Kim, ed., *China and the World: Chinese Foreign Policy in the Post-Mao Era*, (Boulder, CO: Westview Press, 1984), p. 190.

62. Harry Harding, "China's Changing Roles in the Contemporary World," in Harry Harding, ed., *China's Foreign Relations in the 1980s*, (New Haven: Yale University Press, 1984), p. 193.

63. Harry Harding, "China and the Third World," in Richard Solomon, ed., *The China Factor*, (Englewood Cliffs, NJ: Prentice-Hall, 1981), p. 274.

Chapter 6

1.Carol L. Hamrin, "Emergence of an 'Independent Chinese Foreign Policy' and Shifts in Sino-U.S. Relations," in James Hsiung, ed., *U.S.-Asian Relations*, (New York, NY: Praeger, 1983), p. 66.

2. An article containing a posthumous rehabilitation of former Party leader Wang Jiaxiang appeared on *Gongren Ribao* (*Worker's Daily*), April 5, 1979. In the early 1960s and again in the early 1970s, Wang had proposed to reduce tensions with all China's neighbors for the sake of economic recovery and social stability.

3. Robert G. Sutter, *Chinese Foreign Policy: Developments after Mao*, (New York, NY: Praeger Publishers, 1986), p. 92.

4. *FBIS-Daily Report-China*, April 3, 1979, p. C1.

5. Peter Berton, "A Turn in Sino-Soviet Relations?" in James C. Hsiung, ed., *Beyond China's Independent Foreign Policy: Challenge for the U.S. and Its Asian Allies*, (New York, NY: Praeger Publishers, 1985), p. 33.

6. Chi Su, "China and the Soviet Union: 'Principled, Salutary, and Tempered' Management of conflict," in Samuel S. Kim, ed., *China and the World: Chinese Foreign Policy in the Post-Mao Era*, (Boulder, CO: Westview

Press, 1984), p. 136.

7. Peter Berton, "A Turn in Sino-Soviet Relations?" in James C. Hsiung, ed., *Beyond China's Independent Foreign Policy: Challenge for the U.S. and Its Asian Allies*, (New York, NY: Praeger Publishers, 1985), p. 35.

8. *FBIS-Daily Report-China*, January 8, 1980, p. B1.

9. Zhang Jingyi, "Analysis of the Reagan Administration's Military Strategy," *Renmin Ribao* (*People's Daily*), May 5, 1983, in *FBIS-Daily Report-China*, May 6, 1983, pp. B1-6.

10. For example, Vice President Bush was the former head of the American Liaison Office in China, and Secretary of State Haig was a member of Henry Kissinger's National Security council Staff.

11. On an early Chinese assessment of Reagan administration foreign policy, see Zhuang Qubing, "Reagan's Diplomatic Strategy," *Shijie Zhishi* (*World Knowledge*), No. 6, (March 16, 1981), in *FBIS-Daily Report-China*, April 15, 1981, pp. B1-6.

12. Richard Nations, "A Tilt Toward Tokyo," *Far Eastern Economic Review*, Vol. 120, No. 16, (April 21, 1983), pp. 36-37.

13. Henry Scott Stokes, "Taiwan's Premier Hopes Reagan Sends New Arms," *The New York Times*, January 25, 1981, p. A6; Richard Halloran, "New Jets for Taiwan: An Issue Surrounded by Nettles," *The New York Times,*, January 27, 1981, p. A2; and Henry Scott Stokes, "Taipei Hopes Reagan Will Act on Campaign Pledges," *The New York Times,*, January 27, 1981, p. A2.

14. Jonathan Pollack, *The Lessons of Coalition Politics*, (Santa Monica, CA: Rand Corp., 1984), p. 75

15. Michael Getler, "Ford Hopeful Taiwan Arms Sales Issue Can Be Solved," *Los Angeles Times*, March 28, 1981., p. 12.

16. Jim Hoagland and Michael Weisskopf, "China Renews Bid to Cooperate But Cautions Reagan on Taiwan," *The Washington Post*, November 23, 1980, pp. A1, A8.

17. Carol L. Hamrin, "Emergence of an 'Independent Chinese Foreign Policy' and Shifts in Sino-U.S. Relations," in James Hsiung, ed., *U.S.-Asian Relations*, (New York, NY: Praeger, 1983), p. 69.

18. Leslie H. Gelb, "Military Aid for China Considered as Haig Prepares to Visit Peking," *The New York Times*, June 5, 1981, pp. A1, A9; Don Oberdorfer, "U.S. Plans to Sell High Technology Material to China," *The Washington Post*, June 6, 1981, pp. A1, A10.

19. *FBIS-Daily Report-China*, June 10, 1981, p. B1.

20. Jonathan Pollack, *The Lessons of Coalition Politics*, (Santa Monica, CA: Rand Corp., 1984), p. 84.

21. Huang Hua cited China's support for the "Arab and Palestinian peoples in their struggle against Israel's policy of aggression," for "the people of Southern Africa in their struggle for national independence," and for the

"reasonable demand" of developing countries for a new international economic order. See *FBIS-Daily Report-China*, June 15, 1981, p. B2-3.

22. *FBIS-Daily Report-China*, June 17, 1981, p. B1.

23. Robert G. Sutter, *Chinese Foreign Policy: Developments after Mao*, (New York, NY: Praeger Publishers, 1986), p. 141.

24. Jonathan Pollack, *The Lessons of Coalition Politics*, (Santa Monica, CA: Rand Corp., 1984), p. 86.

25. *FBIS-Daily Report-China*, June 19, 1981, p. B1-2.

26. Deng Xiaoping Talks to *Ming Bao* Director on July 18," Hong Kong *Ming Bao*, August 25, 1981, in *FBIS-Daily Report-China*, August 25, 1981, p. W6.

27. *FBIS-Daily Report-China*, July 1, 1981, p. K52.

28. *FBIS-Daily Report-China*, October 8, 1982, p. B2.

29. Jonathan D. Pollack, "China and the Global Strategic Balance," in Harry Harding, ed., *China's Foreign Relations in the 1980s*, (New Haven: Yale University Press, 1984), p. 160.

30. For some representative examples, see Yang Dongliang, "A Tentative Analysis of the 'Debate on Coastal Defense Versus Land Border Defense,'" *Guangming Ribao* (*Intellectual's Daily*), February 10, 1981, in *FBIS-Daily Report-China*, March 5, 1981, pp. L3-7; Qiao Huantian, "A Discussion of Li Hongzhang's Westernization Activities," *Renmin Ribao* (*People's Daily*), March 30, 1981, in *FBIS-Daily Report-China*, April, 1981, pp. K8-12; and Qiao Huantian, "The Diplomatic Activities of the Westernization Proponents Should Not Be cut Off From the Westernization Movement," *Renmin Ribao* (*People's Daily*), May 7, 1981, in *FBIS-Daily Report-China*, May 15, 1981, pp. K4-7.

31. Carol L. Hamrin, "Emergence of an 'Independent Chinese Foreign Policy' and Shifts in Sino-U.S. Relations," in James Hsiung, ed., *U.S.-Asian Relations*, (New York: Praeger, 1983), p. 68.

32. Banning Garrett and Bonnie Glaser, *War and Peace: The Views from Moscow and Peking*, (Berkeley, CA: University of California Press, 1984), p. 61.

33. He Li, "No Meat to Eat," *Renmin Ribao* (*People's Daily*), February 17, 1982, in *FBIS-Daily Report-China*, February 24, 1982, p. C2.

34. Zhong He, "Why Does the Soviet Union Want to Sell Large Amounts of Gold?" *Heilongjiang Ribao* (*Heilongjiang Daily*), May 29, 1982, in *FBIS-Daily Report-China*, June 18, 1982, p. C1.

35. "Signs of Crisis as the Soviet Economy Enters a New Year," *Renmin Ribao* (*People's Daily*), January 30, 1982, in *FBIS-Daily Report-China*, February 2, 1982, p. C1.

36. Xiu Qing, "What the Power Failure in Phnom Penh Shows," *Renmin Ribao* (*People's Daily*), February 27, 1982, in *FBIS-Daily Report-China*, March 3, 1982, p. C3.

37. Banning Garrett and Bonnie Glaser, *War and Peace: The Views from Moscow and Peking*, (Berkeley, CA: University of California Press, 1984), p. 70.

38. *Ibid.*, p. 62.

39. Parris H. Chang, "Trends and Prospects for U.S.-China Relations," *Asia Pacific Community*, No. 17, (Summer 1982), p. 126.

40. Zhang Jingyi, "Analysis of the Reagan Administration's Military Strategy," *Renmin Ribao* (*People's Daily*), May 5, 1983, in *FBIS-Daily Report-China*, May 6, 1983, pp. B1-6.

41. Alex Gliksman, "Emerging Technology and Changing Security Requirements: Focus on the People's Republic of China," in Dora Alves, ed., *Pacific Security toward the Year 2000*, (Washington, D.C.: National Defense University Press, 1988), p. 15; and Jonathan D. Pollack, "China's Changing Perceptions of East Asia Security and Development." *Orbis*, Vol. 29, (Winter 1986), p. 773.

42. Banning Garrett and Bonnie Glaser, *War and Peace: The Views from Moscow and Peking*, (Berkeley, CA: University of California Press, 1984), pp. 80, 98.

43. Thomas W. Robinson, "Choice and Consequence in Sino-American Relations," *Orbis*, Vol. 25, (Spring 1981), p. 38.

44. Donald Hugh McMillen, "Chinese Perspective on International Security," in Donald Hugh McMillen, ed., *Asian Perspectives on International Security*, (New York, NY: St. Martin's Press, 1984), p. 175.

45. Lu Ding, "The Principle of Independence Has the Significance of Methodology," *Guangming Ribao* (*Intellectual's Daily*), November 7, 1981, in *FBIS-Daily Report-China*, November 18, 1981, p. K11.

46. Xing Shugang, Li Yunhua, and Liu Yingua, "Soviet-U.S. Balance of Power and Its Impact on the World Situation in the 1980s," *Guoji Wenti Yanjiu*, (*Journal of International Studies*), No. 1, (January 1983), in *FBIS-Daily Report-China*, April 21, April 21, 1983, pp. A4-5.

47. *FBIS-Daily Report-China*, December 29, 1983, pp. A8.

48. Banning Garrett and Bonnie Glaser, *War and Peace: The Views from Moscow and Peking*, (Berkeley, CA: University of California Press, 1984), p. 71.

49. Jonathan D. Pollack, "China and the Global Strategic Balance," in Harry Harding, ed., *China's Foreign Relations in the 1980s*, (New Haven: Yale University Press, 1984), p. 176.

50. Zhou Jirong, Wang Baoqin, and Gu Guanfu, "Change and Prospects in the Posture of Contention Between the Soviet Union and the United States," *Shijie Zhishi* (*World Knowledge*), No. 23, (December 1, 1983), in *FBIS-Daily Report-China*, January 5, 1984, pp. A4-5.

51. Huang Hua, "Speech by Huang Hua, Chairman of Chinese Delegation, at the U.N. General Assembly," *Peking Review*, Vol. 20, No. 41, (October 7,

1977), p. 35.

52. Samuel S. Kim, ""China and the Third World: In Search of A Peace and Development Line" in Samuel S. Kim, ed., *China and the World: New Directions in Chinese Foreign Relations*, (Boulder, CO: Westview Press, 1989), p. 156.

53. Pei Monong, "A Brief Discussion of the Strategic Relationships Opposing Soviet Hegemonism," *Renmin Ribao (People's Daily)*, July 8, 1981, p. 6.

54. Xing Shugang, Li Yunhua, and Liu Yingua, "Soviet-U.S. Balance of Power and Its Impact on the World Situation in the 1980s," *Guoji Wenti Yanjiu, (Journal of International Studies)*, No. 1, (January 1983), in *FBIS-Daily Report-China*, April 21, April 21, 1983, pp. A4-5, A10.

55. Huan Xiang, "World Prospects for the Years Ahead," *Beijing Review*, Vol. 31, No. 3, (January 18, 1988), p. 20.

56. Huang Xiang, "Adhere to Independent Foreign Policy," *Beijing Review*, Vol. 25, No. 46, (November 15, 1982), p. 23.

57. *Ibid.*

58. Donald Hugh McMillen, "Chinese Perspective on International Security," in Donald Hugh McMillen, ed., *Asian Perspectives on International Security*, (New York, NY: St. Martin's Press, 1984), p. 175.

59. For more accounts regarding the role of the Third World in international relations, see Hu Yaobang, "Create a New Situation in All Fields of Socialist Modernization: Report to the 12th National Congress of the Communist Party of China," *Beijing Review*, Vol. 25, No. 37, September 13, 1982, pp. 31-32.

60. Huan Xiang, "Adhere to Independent Foreign Policy," *Beijing Review*, Vol. 25, No. 46, (November 15, 1982), p. 23.

61. *FBIS-Daily Report-China*, June 12, 1985, pp. K1-2.

62. For example, to lessen tensions with Moscow would help ease pressure from Vietnam in Cambodia. See Thomas W. Robinson, "Choice and Consequence in Sino-American Relations," *Orbis*, Vol. 25, (Spring 1981), p. 38.

63. Xie Yixian, "China's Foreign Policy: A 1980s Tune-Up," *Beijing Review*, Vol. 32, No. 7/8, (February 13, 1989), p. 17.

64. Donald Hugh McMillen, "Chinese Perspective on International Security," in Donald Hugh McMillen, ed., *Asian Perspectives on International Security*, (New York, NY: St. Martin's Press, 1984), p. 168.

65. Michel Oksenberg, "China's Confident Nationalism," *Foreign Affairs*, Vol. 65, No. 3, (1987), p. 501.

66. Carol L. Hamrin, "Emergence of an 'Independent Chinese Foreign Policy' and Shifts in Sino-U.S. Relations," in James Hsiung, ed., *U.S.-Asian Relations*, (New York, NY: Praeger, 1983), pp. 66-67.

67. Hu Yaobang, "Create a New Situation in All Fields of Socialist

Modernization: Report to the 12th National Congress of the Communist Party of China," *Beijing Review*, Vol. 25, No. 37, September 13, 1982, pp. 11-40.

68. *Ibid.*, p. 29.

69. *Ibid.*, p. 20, p. 29.

70. *Ibid.*, pp. 30-31.

71. *Ibid.*

72. *Ibid.*, pp. 31-32.

73. Zhao Ziyang, "Report on the Work of the Government at the First Session of the Sixth National People's Congress, June 6, 1983," *Beijing Review*, Vol. 26, No. 27, (July 4, 1983), p. XXII. (Emphases Added).

74. *Ibid.* (Emphasis Added).

75. *Ibid.*

76. Hu Yaobang, "Create a New Situation in All Fields of Socialist Modernization: Report to the 12th National Congress of the Communist Party of China," *Beijing Review*, Vol. 25, No. 37, September 13, 1982, p. 29.

77. Harry Harding, "China's Changing Roles in the Contemporary World," in Harry Harding, ed., *China's Foreign Relations in the 1980s*, (New Haven, CT: Yale University Press), 1984, p. 200.

78. *Beijing Review*, Vol. 26, No. 32, (August 8, 1983), p. 7.

79. Zhao offered these "three principles" in a meeting with President da Costa of Sao Tome on July 29, 1983, *Ibid.*

80. Robert G. Sutter, *Chinese Foreign Policy: Developments after Mao*, (New York, NY: Praeger Publishers, 1986), p. 148.

81. *FBIS-Daily Report-China*, October 27, 1981, p. A3.

82. *Ibid.*, January 25, 1982, p. K4.

83. "Where Does the Crux of the Sino-U.S. Relationship Lie?" *Beijing Review*, Vol. 25, No. 15, (April 12, 1982), p. 17. Another influential article in *Beijing Review* commented that "Some people wrongly believe that China needs certain countries' help for its socialist [economic] construction and therefore will put up with their threats and interference. But China's socialist economic construction is based on 'self-reliance' while at the same time 'opening to the outside world.' This reflects the spirit of equality and mutual benefit, not dependence on others. In implementing the open policy, our aim is to speed up our economic construction." See Huan Xiang, "Adhere to Independent Foreign Policy," *Beijing Review*, Vol. 25, No. 46, (November 15, 1982), p. 22.

84. *FBIS-Daily Report-China*, August 24, 1981, p. A3.

85. Mei Zhenmin, "U.S. Relationship with the Third World," *Xinhua*, July 8, 1981, in *FBIS-Daily Report-China*, July 9, 1981, pp. B1-2.

86. Ji Liqun, "Soviet-U.S. Contention as Seen from the Situation in El Salvador," *Renmin Ribao (People's Daily)*, February 27, 1981, in *FBIS-Daily Report-China*, March 2, 1981, pp. J1-2; and Yao Chuntao, "The El Salvador Situation Is Evolving," *Renmin Ribao (People's Daily)*, March 28, 1981, in

FBIS-Daily Report-China, April 2, 1981, pp. J1-2.

87. *FBIS-Daily Report-China*, September 2, 1981, p. A3.

88. Qi Ya and Zhou Jirong, "Some Key Issues in the Struggle Against Hegemonism," *Xiandai Guoji Guanxi (The Journal of Contemporary International Relations)*, No. 1, (October 1981), in *China Report-Political, Sociological, and Military Affairs*, No. 312, Joint Publication Research Service, No. 81,165, pp. 1-19; and Li Dai, "Independence and China's External Relations," *Shijie Zhishi (World Knowledge)*, No. 19, (October 1, 1981), in *FBIS-Daily Report-China*, November 19, 1981, pp. A1-5.

89. Cheng Bifan, "U.S.-USSR Contention on the Sea of the Western Pacific," *Renmin Ribao (People's Daily)*, January 19, 1983, in *FBIS-Daily Report-China*, January 20, 1983, pp. A2-6.

90. Sun Dongmin, "The Japanese-U.S. Summit Talks for Strengthening Alliance Relations," *Renmin Ribao (People's Daily)*, January 22, 1983, in *FBIS-Daily Report-China*, January 24, 1983, pp. A8-9.

91. "Be Vigilant Against the Danger of a Revival of Japanese Militarism," *Hongqi*, No. 16, (August 16, 1982), in *FBIS-Daily Report-China*, September 3, 1982, pp. D1, D3.

92. Michael Parks, "China Assails Presence of U.S. Forces in Korea," *Los Angeles Times*, February 2, 1983, p. 7.

93. Chinese Foreign Minister Huang Hua's speech to the 1982 session of the United Nations General Assembly, "China's Position on Current World Issues," *Beijing Review*, Vol. 25, No. 41, (October 11, 1982), pp. 14-18.

94. Thomas P. Bernstein, "China in 1984: The Year of Hong Kong," *Asian Survey*, Vol. XXV, No. 1, (January 1985), p. 48.

95. *FBIS-Daily Report-China*, October 21, 1982, pp. A1-2.

96. *Ibid.*

97. Qizhen Zhu, "Vice Minister of Foreign Affairs, the PRC," *Journal of Northeast Asian Studies*, Vol. III, No. 2, (Summer 1984), pp. 71-75.

98. Parris H. Chang, "Trends and Prospects for U.S.-China Relations," *Asia Pacific Community*, No. 17, (Summer 1982), p. 126.

99. Robert G. Sutter, *Chinese Foreign Policy: Developments after Mao*, (New York: Praeger Publishers, 1986), p. 179.

100. Michael Parks, "Growing U.S.-China Rift Worries Other Nations," *Los Angeles Times*, April 13, 1982, pp. 8-9.

101. Jonathan D. Pollack, *The Lessons of Coalition Politics*, (Santa Monica, CA: Rand Corp., 1984), p. 114.

102. Robert G. Sutter, *Chinese Foreign Policy: Developments after Mao*, (New York, NY: Praeger Publishers, 1986), pp. 197-198.

103. Jonathan D. Pollack, *The Lessons of Coalition Politics*, (Santa Monica, CA: Rand Corp., 1984), pp. 114-115.

104. Ya-chun Chang, "Dilemma in Bush's China Policy under Utopianism," *Central Daily News* (International Edition), January 15, 1992, p.

3.

105. The decision was the attached condition that each sale would still be decided case by case. See Jonathan Pollack, *The Lessons of Coalition Politics*, (Santa Monica, CA: Rand Corp., 1984), p. 108.

106. Licensing procedures for technology export to China were now divided into three zones: a green zone, where licenses would be routinely approved by the Commerce Department without interagency review; an intermediate or yellow zone for "very high technology" that would require case-by-case reviews among all appropriate government agencies, including the Defense Department; and a red zone, consisting of items so advanced that they were generally not shared even with U.S. allies. American officials expected that approximately 75 percent of China's requests would fall within the green zone and could therefore be approved rapidly. Some approvals were also expected for the yellow zone, with only items in the red zone excluded from consideration. See *Ibid.*, p. 117.

107. *FBIS-Daily Report-China*, January 4, 1984, pp. A1-4.

108. Hedrick Smith, "Reagan in U.S. Says China Trip Advanced Ties," *The New York Times*, May 2, 1984, pp. A1, A10.

109. *Ibid.*

110. "China View Mixed on Reagan's Trip," *The New York Times*, May 2, 1984, p. A11.

111. James C. Hsiung, ed., *Beyond China's Independent Foreign Policy: Challenge for the U.S. and Its Asian Allies*, (New York, NY: Praeger Publishers, 1985), p. 1, 170. Also Chi Su, "Sino-Soviet Relations of the 1980s: from Confrontation to Conciliation," in Samuel S.Kim, ed., *China and the World: New Directions in Chinese Foreign Relations*, 2nd ed., (Boulder, CO: Westview Press, 1989), p. 113.

112. Jonathan Pollack, *The Lessons of Coalition Politics*, (Santa Monica, CA: Rand Corp., 1984), .p. 97.

113. *FBIS-Daily Report-USSR*, October 1982, p. B1.

114. Chi Su, "Sino-Soviet Relations of the 1980s: from Confrontation to Conciliation," in Samuel S. Kim, ed., *China and the World: New Directions in Chinese Foreign Relations*, 2nd ed., (Boulder, CO: Westview Press, 1989), p. 112.

115. *FBIS-Daily Report-USSR*, August 29, 1983, p. CC3.

116. *FBIS-Daily Report-China*, September 1, 1983, p. A1.

117. *Ibid.*, September 16, 1983, p. C1.

118. Chi Su, "Sino-Soviet Relations of the 1980s: from Confrontation to Conciliation," in Samuel S. Kim, ed., *China and the World: New Directions in Chinese Foreign Relations*, 2nd ed., (Boulder, CO: Westview Press, 1989), p. 112.

119. Robert G. Sutter, *Chinese Foreign Policy: Developments after Mao*, (New York, NY: Praeger Publishers, 1986), p. 183. Banning Garrett and

Bonnie Glaser, *War and Peace: The Views from Moscow and Peking*, (Berkeley, CA: University of California Press, 1984), p. 78.

120. For detailed accounts, see Chi Su, "Sino-Soviet Relations of the 1980s: from Confrontation to Conciliation," in Samuel S. Kim, ed., *China and the World: New Directions in Chinese Foreign Relations*, 2nd ed., (Boulder, CO: Westview Press, 1989), pp. 112-113; and Robert G. Sutter, *Chinese Foreign Policy: Developments after Mao*, (New York, NY: Praeger Publishers, 1986), pp. 184-186.

121. *Ibid.*

122. Chi Su, "China and the Soviet Union," *Current History*, Vol. 83, No. 494, (September 1984), pp. 246-247.

123. Robert G. Sutter, *Chinese Foreign Policy: Developments after Mao*, (New York: Praeger Publishers, 1986), pp. 185-186; and Chi Su, "Sino-Soviet Relations of the 1980s: from Confrontation to Conciliation," in Samuel S. Kim, ed., *China and the World: New Directions in Chinese Foreign Relations*, 2nd ed., (Boulder, CO: Westview Press, 1989), p. 113.

124. *Beijing Review*, Vol. 28, No. 44, (November 4, 1985), p. 17.

125. Samuel S. Kim, "China and the Third World: In Search of A Neorealist World Policy," in Samuel S. Kim, ed., *China and the World: Chinese Foreign Policy in the Post-Mao Era*, (Boulder, CO: Westview Press, 1984), pp. 190-191.

126. Samuel S. Kim, "China and the Third World: In Search of A Peace and Development Line," in Samuel S. Kim, ed., *China and the World: New Directions in Chinese Foreign Relations*, (Boulder, CO: Westview Press, 1989), pp. 154-155.

127. Samuel S. Kim, "China and the Third World: In Search of A Neorealist World Policy," in Samuel S. Kim, ed., *China and the World: Chinese Foreign Policy in the Post-Mao Era*, (Boulder, CO: Westview Press, 1984), p. 191.

128. For coverage of Zhao's trip, see *FBIS-Daily Report-China* between December-January 1982-83.

129. *Beijing Review*, Vol. 26, No. 4, (January 24, 1983), p. 19.

130. Zhimin Lin, "China's Third World Policy," in Yufan Hao and Guocang Huan, eds., *The Chinese View of the World*, (New York, NY: Pantheon Books, 1989), pp. 227-228.

131. *Ibid.*, p. 241.

132. Robert G. Sutter, *Chinese Foreign Policy: Developments after Mao*, (New York, NY: Praeger Publishers, 1986), p. 158, p. 160.

133. Yitzhak Shichor, "The Middle East," in Gerald Segal and William T. Tow, eds., *Chinese Defense Policy*, (Urbana and Chicago: University of Illinois Press, 1984), p. 267

134. *Ibid.*, p. 268.

135. Michael Weisskopf, "China Plays Both Sides in Persian Gulf War,"

The Washington Post, January 13, 1983, pp. A21, A25.

136. Yitzhak Shichor, "The Middle East," in Gerald Segal and William T. Tow, eds., *Chinese Defense Policy*, (Urbana and Chicago: University of Illinois Press, 1984), p. 269.

Chapter 7

1. Michael B. Yahuda, "The People's Republic of China at 40: Foreign Relations," *The China Quarterly*, No. 119, (September 1989), p. 531.

2. *Wen Wei Po* (Hong Kong), December 1985, 1985, in *FBIS-Daily Report-China*, December 20, 1985, p. W1-2.

3. *Beijing Review*, Vol. 28, No. 42, (October 21, 1985), p. 7. Numbers added.

4. Wan Guang, "U.S.-Soviet Relations in the Present Period," *Liaowang* (*Outlook*), (Overseas Edition), No. 14, (October 12, 1987), in *FBIS-Daily Report-China*, October 16, 1987, pp. 1-2.

5. Peng Di, "Prospects for World Peace as Viewed from the Present International Strategic Posture." *Jiefangjun Bao* (*The People's Liberation Army's Daily*), January 2, 1987, in *FBIS-Daily Report-China*, February 4, 1987, p. A5.

6. Wan Guang, "U.S.-Soviet Relations in the Present Period," *Liaowang* (*Outlook*), (Overseas Edition), No. 14, (October 12, 1987), in *FBIS-Daily Report-China*, October 16, 1987, pp. 1-2.

7. The Chinese argued that with their countervailing military strength, the United States and the Soviet Union stalemated each other's expansionist goals, while their nuclear arsenals denied each the capability of launching a successful nuclear war against the other. The military situation was viewed as one in which neither country "can keep absolute superiority over the other." See Xie Wenqing, "U.S.-Soviet Military Confrontation in the Asian-Pacific Region," *Shijie Zhishi* (*World Knowledge*), No. 6, (March 16, 1987), in *FBIS-Daily Report-China*, March 31, 1987, p. A2.

8. Banning N. Garrett and Bonnie S. Glaser, "Chinese Assessments of Global Trends and the Emerging Era in International Relations," *Asian Survey*, Vol. XXIX, No. 4, (April 1989), p. 349.

9. Li Gang, "Trends of U.S. Post-Reagan Third World Policy," *Liaowang* (*Outlook*), (Overseas Edition), No. 39, (September 26, 1988), in *FBIS-Daily Report-China*, October 4, 1988, pp. 1-2.

10. Steven I. Levine, "Sino-American Relations: Renormalization and Beyond," in Samuel S. Kim, ed., *China and the World: New Directions in Chinese Foreign Relations*, 2nd ed., (Boulder, CO: Westview Press, 1989), p. 92.

11. David T. Jones, "Post-INF Treaty Attitudes in East Asia," *Asian*

Survey, Vol. XXX, No. 5, (May 1990), p. 490.

12. Samuel S. Kim, "China and the Third World: In Search of A Peace and Development Line," in Samuel S. Kim ed., *China and the World: New Directions in Chinese Foreign Relations*, (Boulder, CO: Westview Press, 1989), Note 57, p. 178.

13. Guo Zhenyuan, "Important Changes in U.S.-Soviet Relations and Their Influences," *Renmin Ribao (People's Daily)*, December 18, 1988, in *FBIS-Daily Report-China*, December 23, 1988, pp. 1-2.

14. One Chinese scholar said that it "may even be the beginning of prolonged peaceful competition" between the superpowers as well as among other nations. See He Fang, "The International Situation at Present Is in a Period of Important Changes," *Shijie Zhishi (World Knowledge)*, No. 18, (September 16, 1988), in *FBIS-Daily Report-China*, October 13, 1988, pp. 8-11.

15. Peng Di, "Internationally, We Should Strive for Peace, Domestically for Changes," *Ban Yue Tan (Bi-Monthly)*, No. 18, (September 25, 1988), in *FBIS-Daily Report-China*, October 21, 1988, pp. 2-4.

16. *Beijing Review*, Vol. 35, No. 13, (March 20, 1992), p. 13.

17. Xie Yixian, "China's Foreign Policy: A 1980s Tune-Up," *Beijing Review*, Vol. 32, No. 7/8, (February 13, 1989), pp. 17-18.

18. *Ibid.*, p. 18.

19. For the detailed discussion on China's new security thinking, see Banning N. Garrett and Bonnie S. Glaser, "Chinese Assessments of Global Trends and the Emerging Era in International Relations," *Asian Survey*, Vol. XXIX, No. 4, (April 1989); Michel Oksenberg, "China's Confident Nationalism," *Foreign Affairs*, Vol. 65, No. 3, (1987); and David M. Lampton, "America's China Policy: Developing a Fifth strategy," in Frank J. Macchiarola and Robert B. Oxnam, ed., *The China Challenge: American Policies in East Asia*, (New York, NY: the Academy of Political Science, 1991).

20. Wang Shu, "Three Major Factors Help Bring About Dialogue and Détente," *Shijie Zhishi (World Knowledge)*, No. 18, (September 16, 1988), in *FBIS-Daily Report-China*, October 6, 1988, pp. 1-2.

21. Banning N. Garrett and Bonnie S. Glaser, "Chinese Assessments of Global Trends and the Emerging Era in International Relations," *Asian Survey*, Vol. XXIX, No. 4, (April 1989), p. 348.

22. Song Yimin, "The Relaxation of Soviet-American Tension and Profound Changes in International Relations," *Guoji Wenti Yanjiu (Journal of International Studies)*, No. 1, (January 1988), pp. 1-5.

23. Quoted in Banning N. Garrett and Bonnie S. Glaser, "Chinese Assessments of Global Trends and the Emerging Era in International Relations," *Asian Survey*, Vol. XXIX, No. 4, (April 1989), p. 357.

24. Deng Xiaoping, "Opening Address to the Twelfth Party Congress," in

Harold C. Hinton, eds., *The People's Republic of China 1979-1984: A Documentary Survey*, (Wilmington, DE: Scholarly Resources, Inc., 1986), p. 185.

25. Chao Yang, "A Viewpoint of Keen Insight," *Renmin Ribao (People's Daily)*, November 12, 1986, p. 6.

26. Samuel S. Kim, "China and the Third World: In Search of A Peace and Development Line," in Samuel S. Kim ed., *China and the World: New Directions in Chinese Foreign Relations*, (Boulder, CO: Westview Press, 1989), Note 57, p. 169.

27. *Renmin Ribao (People's Daily)*, June 12, 1986, p. 1.

28. Tai Ming Cheung, "Disarmament and Development in China," *Asian Survey*, Vol. XXVIII, No. 7, (July 1988), p. 765.

29. Paul H.B. Godwin, "Soldiers and Statesmen: Chinese defense and Foreign Policies in the 1990s," in Samuel S. Kim, ed., *China and the World: New Directions in Chinese Foreign Relations*, 2nd ed., (Boulder, CO: Westview Press, 1989), p. 185.

30. The Chinese military possessed substantial resources in airports, naval ports, railways, extensive research and development (R&D) bases, and expertise and facilities to expand communications and energy production. See Tai Ming Cheung, "Disarmament and Development in China," *Asian Survey*, Vol. XXVIII, No. 7, (July 1988), pp. 757-774.

31. Richard Baum, "China in 1985: The Greening of the Revolution," *Asian Survey*, Vol. XXVI, No. 1, (January 1986), p. 38.

32. Quoted in Tai Ming Cheung, "Disarmament and Development in China," *Asian Survey*, Vol. XXVIII, No. 7, (July 1988), p. 766.

33. *Central Daily News* (Taiwan), February 19, 1992, p. 3.

34. *China Daily*, January 3, 1985, p. 1.

35. Richard Baum, "China in 1985: The Greening of the Revolution," *Asian Survey*, Vol. XXVI, No. 1, (January 1986), pp. 36-38.

36. Tai Ming Cheung, "Disarmament and Development in China," *Asian Survey*, Vol. XXVIII, No. 7, (July 1988), p. 767.

37. *Beijing Review*, Vol. 29. NO. 4, (January 27, 1986), pp. 20-27.

38. *The New York Times*, April 21, 1985, p. 3.

39. Tai Ming Cheung, "Disarmament and Development in China," *Asian Survey*, Vol. XXVIII, No. 7, (July 1988), p. 770.

40. *The New York Times*, April 21, 1985, p. 3.

41. *The New York Times*, March 6, 1985, p. A6.

42. *Ibid.*

43. *Xinhua*, June 11, 1985, in *FBIS-Daily Report-China*, June 12, 1985, K1-3.

44. For a detailed discussion on the reshuffle of the PLA officers, see Richard Baum, "China in 1985: The Greening of the Revolution," *Asian Survey*, Vol. XXVI, No. 1, (January 1986); Samuel S. Kim "China and the

Third World: In Search of A Peace and Development Line," in ed., *China and the World: New Directions in Chinese Foreign Relations*, (Boulder, CO: Westview Press, 1989); Paul H.B. Godwin, "Soldiers and Statesmen: Chinese defense and Foreign Policies in the 1990s," in Samuel S. Kim, ed., *China and the World: New Directions in Chinese Foreign Relations*, 2nd ed., (Boulder, CO: Westview Press, 1989); and Stanley Rosen, "China in 1987: The Year of the Thirteenth Party Congress," *Asian Survey*, Vol. XXVIII, No. 1, (January 1988).

45. Zhang Qinsheng, Liang Hunan and Yan Xiaoyin. "A Study and Exploration of Local War Theory," *Liaowang (Outlook)*, (Overseas Edition), No. 37, (September 15, 1986), in *FBIS-Daily Report-China*, September 23, 1986, pp. K3-7.

46. Zong He, "Changes and Developmental Trends in the International Situation," *Shijie Zhishi (World Knowledge)*, No. 11, (1983), in *FBIS-Daily Report-China*, July 21, 1983, pp. A1-5.

47. Hu Xiaoen and Peng Zhonghuai, "'Strengthening Border Buildup' Should Be an Important Content of Military Strategy," *Jiefangjun Bao (The People's Liberation Army's Daily)*, January 22, 1988, in *FBIS-Daily Report-China*, February 4, 1988, pp. 10-11.

48. Zhang Qinsheng, Liang Hunan and Yan Xiaoyin, "A Study and Exploration of Local War Theory," *Liaowang (Outlook)*, (Overseas Edition), No. 37, (September 15, 1986), in *FBIS-Daily Report-China*, September 15, 1986, p. K6.

49. Xiaochuan Zhang, "Chinese Nuclear Strategy," in Yufan Hao and Guocang Huan, eds., *The Chinese View of the World*, (New York, NY: Pantheon Books, 1989), pp. 77-100.

50. Zhang Jianzhi, "Views on Medium-sized Nuclear Powers' Nuclear Strategy," *Jiefangjun Bao (The People's Liberation Army's Daily)*, March 20, 1987, in *FBIS-Daily Report-China*, April 1, 1987, pp. K29-33.

51. Tang Hualiang, "Safeguarding World Peace Is the Primary Objective of Chinese Foreign Policy," *Hongqi*, No. 11, (1984), pp. 16-20.

52. Hu Yaobang, "Create a New Situation in All Fields of Socialist Modernization: Report to the 12th National Congress of the Communist Party of China," *Beijing Review*, Vol. 25, No. 37, September 13, 1982, p. 29.

53. Zhao Ziyang, "Work Together for a Better World," *Beijing Review*, Vol. 28, No. 44, (November 4, 1985), pp. 15-17.

54. "China Advocates Stronger U.N. Role," *Beijing Review*, Vol. 28, No. 40, (October 7, 1985), p. 16.

55. A former Chinese Permanent Representative to the United Nations said in an interview that "China is a unique nation in the Third World. It has the veto right in the Security Council. This ultimately belongs to the Third World. This gives China special influence in the Third World." See Fan Lu and Jung Hong, "China's Influences as Viewed from the U.N.--An Interview with Ling

Qing, Former PRC Permanent Representative to the United Nations," *Ban Yue Tan (Bi-Monthly)*, No. 6, (March 25, 1986), in *FBIS-Daily Report-China*, April 18, 1986, p. A5.

56. Yitzhak Shichor, "China and the Role of the United Nations in the Middle East: Revised Policy," *Asian Survey*, Vol. XXXI, No, 3, (March 1991), p. 264.

57. China avoided participating in numerous Security Council votes and was reluctant to join the other permanent members in these discussions. As the Chinese ambassador Huang Hua said in 1973, "China refuses, and will continue to refuse, to take part in the so-called five-power consultations. The reasons are simple: we have all along been opposed to a big power striking political deals behind the backs of the Palestinians and other Arab peoples." See *Peking Review*, Vol. 16, No. 44, (November 2, 1973), p. 10.

58. Yitzhak Shichor, "China and the Role of the United Nations in the Middle East: Revised Policy," *Asian Survey*, Vol. XXXI, No, 3, (March 1991), pp. 258-259.

59. China did not vote the resolutions on human rights concerning the Islamic Republic of Iran. See Yitzhak Shichor, "China and the Role of the United Nations in the Middle East: Revised Policy," *Asian Survey*, Vol. XXXI, No, 3, (March 1991), pp. 255, 261-262.

60. "China Supports U.N. Peace Forces," *Beijing Review*, Vol. 27, No. 46, (November 12, 1984), p. 12.

61. *Xinhua*, October 18, 1988, in *FBIS-Daily Report-China*, October 18, 1988, p. 2; *Xinhua*, October 28, 1988, in *FBIS-Daily Report-China*, October 31, 1988, p. 1.

62. Yitzhak Shichor, "China and the Role of the United Nations in the Middle East: Revised Policy," *Asian Survey*, Vol. XXXI, No, 3, (March 1991), p. 265.

63. *Ibid.*, p. 266.

64. The Economist Intelligence Unit (London), *Country Report: Vietnam, Laos, Cambodia*, No. 4, (1990), pp. 40-43.

65. *Beijing Review*, Vol. 35, No. 17, (April 27, 1992), p. 11.

66. Xie Yixian, "China's Foreign Policy: A 1980s Tune-Up," *Beijing Review*, Vol. 32, NO. 7/8, (February 13, 1989), p. 18.

67. Samuel S. Kim, "China and the Third World: In Search of A Peace and Development Line," in Samuel S. Kim, ed., *China and the World: New Directions in Chinese Foreign Relations*, (Boulder, CO: Westview Press, 1989), p. 157.

68. Xie Yixian, "China's Foreign Policy: A 1980s Tune-Up," *Beijing Review*, Vol. 32, NO. 7/8, (February 13, 1989), p. 18.

69. Robert G. Sutter, *Chinese Foreign Policy: Developments after Mao*, (New York: Praeger Publishers, 1986), p. 217.

70. Cheung Tai Ming, "Proliferation Is Good, and There's Money in It

Too," *Far Eastern Economic Review*, Vol. 140, No. 22, (June 2, 1988), p. 27.

71. Xiaochuan Zhang, "Chinese Nuclear Strategy," in Yufan Hao and Guocang Huan, eds., *The Chinese View of the World*, (New York, NY: Pantheon Books, 1989), p. 92.

72. *Beijing Review*, Vol. 35, No. 13, (March 30, 1992), p. 16.

73. Xie Yixian, "China's Foreign Policy: A 1980s Tune-Up," *Beijing Review*, Vol. 32, No. 7/8, (February 13, 1989), p. 18.

74. *FBIS-Daily Report-China*, June 3, 1988, pp. 3-4.

75. *Xinhua*, October 26, 1985, in *FBIS-Daily Report-China*, October 28, 1985, p. A1.

76. Quoted in Yitzhak Shichor, "China and the Role of the United Nations in the Middle East: Revised Policy," *Asian Survey*, Vol. XXXI, No, 3, (March 1991), p. 264.

77. State Science and Technology commission, *White Paper on Science and Technology-#2*, (Beijing: Science & Technology Publishing House, 1988).

78. Samuel S. Kim, "China and the Third World: In Search of A Peace and Development Line," in Samuel S. Kim, ed., *China and the World: New Directions in Chinese Foreign Relations*, (Boulder, CO: Westview Press, 1989), p. 172.

79. *Stockholm International Peace Research Institute (SIPRI) Yearbook 1987: World Armaments and Disarmament*, (Oxford: Oxford University Press, 1987), p. 183.

80. Wei-chin Lee, "The Birth of a Salesman: China as an Arms Supplier," *Journal of Northeast Asian Studies*, Vol. VI, No. 4, (Winter 1987/1988), p. 38.

81. For example, the Chinese imitated the U.S. Army's M-16 rifle. The price tag of the Chinese version was $185, while the America's Colt version cost $660. The Chinese homemade version of Soviet MiG-21 (the F-7 in Chinese) was sold at the price of around $2.6 million, while the American F-16 was $15 million. The F-7 sold for just 10 percent of what the French Mirage-2000 costs. *Ibid.*, pp. 37-38.

82. Eden Y. Woon, "Chinese Arms Sales and U.S.-China Military Relations," *Asian Survey*, Vol. XXIX, No. 6, (June 1989), pp. 603-604.

83. R. Bates Gill, "China Looks to Thailand," *Asian Survey*, Vol. XXXI, No. 6, (June 1991), p. 535.

84. Richard F. Grimmett, "Trends in Conventional Arms Transfers to the Third World by Major Supplier, 1980-1987," in *Congressional Research Service Report* 88-352F, Library of Congress, (May 9, 1988), pp. 3, 51, 61.

85. Robert B. Cullen, "Saudi Arabia's Terrier Diplomat," *Newsweek*, Vol. 111, No. 15, (April 11, 1988), p. 42.

86. Paul H.B. Godwin, "Soldiers and Statesmen: Chinese defense and Foreign Policies in the 1990s," in Samuel S. Kim, ed., *China and the World: New Directions in Chinese Foreign Relations*, 2nd ed., (Boulder, CO:

Westview Press, 1989), p. 196.

87. *The Washington Post*, November 12, 1986, p. G3.

88. Fay Willey, Carroll Bogert, and Robert B. Cullen, "Peking Guns for Hard Cash," *Newsweek*, Vol. 109, No. 12, (March 23, 1987), p. 36.

89. On specific descriptions of these corporations, see Eden Y. Woon, "Chinese Arms Sales and U.S.-China Military Relations," *Asian Survey*, Vol. XXIX, No. 6, (June 1989), pp. 606-607.

90. Wei-chin Lee, "The Birth of a Salesman: China as an Arms Supplier," *Journal of Northeast Asian Studies*, Vol. VI, No. 4, (Winter 1987/1988), pp. 36-39.

91. *The Washington Post*, May 29, 1988, p. C7.

92. John Calabrese, "From Flyswatters to Silkworms," *Asian Survey*, Vol. XXX, No. 9, (September 1990), p. 862.

93. John H. Cushman, Jr., "Spread of Ballistic Missiles Troubles U.S.," *The New York Times*, March 19, 1988, p. A3.

94. Paul H.B. Godwin, "Soldiers and Statesmen: Chinese defense and Foreign Policies in the 1990s," in Samuel S. Kim, ed., *China and the World: New Directions in Chinese Foreign Relations*, 2nd ed., (Boulder, CO: Westview Press, 1989), p. 196.

95. David Holley, "China Accuses the U.S. of Rumors on Iran Silkworms," *Los Angeles Times*, November 5, 1987, pp. 1, 7.

96. *The Wall Street Journal*, October 22, 1987, p. 35; and *The New York Times*, October 24, 1987, p. A3.

97. *FBIS-Daily Report-China*, September 8, 1988, p. 1.

98. Samuel S. Kim, "China and the Third World: In Search of A Peace and Development Line," in Samuel S. Kim, ed., *China and the World: New Directions in Chinese Foreign Relations*, 2nd, ed., (Boulder, CO: Westview Press, 1989), p. 159.

99. Robert F. Dernberger, "The Chinese Search for the Path of Self-Sustained Growth in the 1980s: An Assessment," in Joint Economic Committee, U.S. Congress, *China Under the Four Modernizations*, Part 1., (Washington, D.C.: Government Printing Office, 1982), p. 53.

100. "The Communiqué of the Third Plenary Session of the Eleventh Central Committee of the Chinese Communist Party," *Peking Review*, Vol. 21, No. 52, (December 29, 1978), p. 11.

101. Zhao Ziyang, "The Present Economic Situation and the Principles for Future Economic Construction--Report on the Work of the Government Delivered at the Fourth Session of the Fifth National People's Congress, November 30-December 1, 1981," *Beijing Review*, Vol. 24, No. 51, (December 21 1981), p. 23.

102. These four Special Economic Zone were Shenzhen, Xiamen, Zhuhai and Shantou. The location of the four SEZs were well selected. Shenzhen was a border township adjacent to Hong Kong while Xiamen was situated just

across from the Taiwan Strait. Zhuhai was north to Macao and Shantou was the hometown of many overseas Chinese now living in Southeast Asia.

103. More on China's Special Economic Zones, see Joseph Fewsmith, "Special Economic Zones in the PRC," *Problems of Communism*, Vol. 35, (November/December 1986), pp. 78-85; Jici Wang and John Bradbury, "The Changing Industrial Geography of the Chinese Special Economic Zones," *Economic Geography*, Vol. 62, No. 4, (October 1986), pp. 307-320; "Hainan Province--China's Largest SEZ," *Beijing Review*, Vol. 31, No. 18, (May 2, 1988), pp. 18-23; and "Hainan to Adopt More Special Policies," *Ibid.*, Vol. 31, No. 18, (May, 1988), p. 7.

104. The fourteen open cities were: Dalian, Qinhuandao, Tianjin, Yantai, Qingdao, Lianyungang, Nantong, Shanghai, Ningbo, Wenzhou, Fuzhou, Guangzhou, Zhanjiang, and Beihai. See *Beijing Review*, Vol. 27, No. 16, (April 6, 1984), p. 6.

105. They are also called "open economic areas" including the Yangtze River Delta, the Pearl River Delta and the southern part of Fujian.

106. *Beijing Review*, Vol. 31, No. 18, (May 2, 1988), pp. 18-23.

107. "Zhao on Coastal Areas' Development Strategy," *Beijing Review*, Vol. 31, No. 6, (February 8, 1988), p. 19.

108. *FBIS-Daily Report-China*, January 25, 1988, p. 10.

109. *Ibid.*, June 5, 1986, p. K16.

110. Quoted in James M. Ethridge, *China's Unfinished Revolution: Problems and Prospects since Mao*, (San Francisco, CA: China Books & Periodicals, Inc., 1990), p. 130.

111. *The New York Times*, February 21, 1985, p. A7.

112. "Deng Writes on Four modernizations," in *FBIS-Daily Report-China*, February 27, 1979, p. A1.

113. Richard Baum, "China in 1985: The Greening of the Revolution," *Asian Survey*, Vol. XXVI, No. 1, (January 1986), pp. 42-43; James M. Ethridge, *China's Unfinished Revolution: Problems and Prospects since Mao*, (San Francisco, CA: China Books & Periodicals, Inc., 1990), p. 130; and Harry Harding, *China's Second Revolution: Reform after Mao*, (Washington, D.C.: Brookings Institution, 1987), p. 135.

114. *Beijing Review*, Vol. 28, No. 4, (January 28, 1985), p. 15; and *Ibid.*, Vol. 28, No. 13, (April 1, 1985), p. 15.

115. Gan Feng, "'Opening a Window' and 'Installing a Window Screen,'" *Hongqi*, No. 8, (April 16, 1985), in *China Report: Red Flag*, Joint Publication Research Service, June 26, 1985, pp. 83-84.

116. Bruce Cumings, "The Political Economy of China's Turn Outward," in Samuel S. Kim, ed., *China and the World: New Directions in Chinese Foreign Relations*, 2nd ed., (Boulder, CO: Westview Press, 1989), p. 215.

117. *Beijing Review*, Vol. 32, No. 40, (October 2, 1989), p. 32 and Vol. 33, No. 44, (October 29, 1990), p. 26.

118. Shu-yun Ma, "Recent Changes in China's Pure Trade Theory," *The China Quarterly*, No. 106, (June 1986), pp. 291-305.

119. On China's foreign trade reforms, see Zheng Tuobin, "The Problem of Reforming China's Trade System," *Chinese Economic Studies*, Vol. XX, No. 4, (Summer 1987), pp. 27-49.

120. *Beijing Review*, Vol. 33, No. 17, (April 23, 1989), p. III and *Beijing Review*, Vol. 33, No. 44, (October 29, 1990), p. 26.

121 China's foreign trade relative to its GNP was 27.3 percent in 1988, 26.1 percent in 1989, 31.4 percent in 1990, and 36.7 percent in 1991 respectively. See Thomas R. Gottschang, "The Economy's Continued Growth," *Current History*, Vol. 91, No. 566, (September 1992), pp. 268-269.

122. *Beijing Review*, Vol. 34, No. 10, (March 11, 1991), p. VI. and Vol. 35, No. 16, (April 20, 1992), p. II.

123. Mechele Ledic, "Foreign Economic Relations," in Gerald Segal, ed., *Chinese Politics and Foreign Policy Reform*, (London: Kegan Paul International Ltd., 1990), pp. 237-238.

124. *Beijing Review*, Vol. 32, No. 23, (June 5, 1989), pp. 39-40.

125. Gerald Segal, ed., *Chinese Politics and Foreign Policy Reform*, (London: Kegan Paul International, 1990), p. 239.

126. Mechele Ledic, "Foreign Economic Relations," in Gerald Segal, ed., *Chinese Politics and Foreign Policy Reform*, (London: Kegan Paul International Ltd., 1990), pp. 236-238.

127. In 1990, the value of China's exports was $62.06 billion and the value of its imports was $53.35 billion. See *Beijing Review*, Vol. 34, No. 10, (March 11, 1991), p. VI. In 1991, the volume of China's exports was $71.96 billion while the volume of its imports was $63.8 billion. See *Ibid.*, Vol. 35, No. 19, (May 11, 1992), p. 15.

128. *Beijing Review*, Vol. 32, No. 10, (March 6, 1989), pp. 21-22 and p. 26.

129. James M. Ethridge, *China's Unfinished Revolution: Problems and Prospects since Mao*, (San Francisco, CA: China Books & Periodicals, Inc., 1990), p. 134.

130. For example, Taiwanese direct investment on the mainland was approximately $2 billion-3 billion by the end of 1990. There is a tendency that Taiwan is likely to surpass Hong Kong and becomes the largest investor in China in the 1990s. See "The South China Miracle: A Great Leap Forward," *The Economist*, Vol. 321, No. 7727, (October 5, 1991), pp. 19-22. Also see Pamela Baldinger, "The Birth of Greater China," *The China Business Review*, Vol. 19, No. 3, (May/June 1992), p. 15.

131. *Beijing Review*, Vol. 32, No. 10, (March 6, 1989), pp. 26-27.

132. James M. Ethridge, *China's Unfinished Revolution: Problems and Prospects since Mao*, (San Francisco, CA: China Books & Periodicals, Inc., 1990), pp. 138-139; and *Beijing Review*, Vol. 32, No. 10, (March 6, 1989),

p. 22.

133. *Beijing Review*, Vol. 32, No. 10, (March 6, 1989), p. 22.

134. James M. Ethridge, *China's Unfinished Revolution: Problems and Prospects since Mao*, (San Francisco, CA: China Books & Periodicals, Inc., 1990), pp. 138-139.

135. *FBIS-Daily Report-China*, February 29, 1984, p. I2.

136. *Beijing Review*, Vol. 32, No. 10, (March 6, 1989), p. 22.

137. *Beijing Review*, Vol. 33, No. 50, (December 10, 1990), p. 40.

138. Mechele Ledic, "Foreign Economic Relations," in Gerald Segal, ed., *Chinese Politics and Foreign Policy Reform*, (London: Kegan Paul International Ltd., 1990), pp. 248-250.

139. For the overview of China's participation in international economic organizations, see William R. Feeney, "Chinese Policy Toward Multilateral Economic Institutions," in Samuel S. Kim, ed., *China and the World: New Directions in Chinese Foreign Relations*, 2nd ed., (Boulder, CO: Westview Press, 1989), pp. 237-263.

140. *Beijing Review*, Vol. 32, No. 10, (March 6, 1989), p. VI; Vol. 34, No. 15, (April 15, 1991), p. 18; Vol. 34, No. 10, (March 11, 1991), p. VI. Vol. 35, No. 16, (April 20, 1992), p. II.

141. Harry G. Gelber, "China's New Economic and Strategic Uncertainties and the Security Prospects," *Asian Survey*, Vol. XXX, No. 7, (July 1990), p. 653.

142. David M. Lampton, "America's China Policy: Developing a Fifth strategy," in Frank J. Macchiarola and Robert B. Oxnam, ed., *The China Challenge: American Policies in East Asia*, (New York, NY: the Academy of Political Science, 1991), p. 159.

Chapter 8

1. *Beijing Review*, Vol. 32, No. 7/8, (February 13, 1989), p. 21.

2. Steven I. Levine, "Sino-American Relations: Renormalization and Beyond," in Samuel S. Kim, ed., *China and the World: New Directions in Chinese Foreign Relations*, 2nd ed., (Boulder, CO: Westview Press, 1989), pp. 89-94.

3. Li Peng, "Report on the Work of the Government Delivered at the First Session of the Seventh National People's Congress, March 25, 1988," *Beijing Review*, Vol. 31, No. 17, (April 25, 1988), p. 45.

4. *FBIS-Daily Report-China*, February 22, 1989, p. 1.

5. Huan Xiang, "Sino-US Relations Over the Past Year," *Beijing Review*, Vol. 31, No. 7/8, (February 15, 1988), p. 31.

6. Michael Armacost, "China and the U.S.: Present and Future," a speech to the National Council for U.S.-China Trade, June 1, 1988. U.S. Department

of State, Bureau of Public Affairs, *Current Policy*, No. 1079, p. 3.

7. Quoted in Donald S. Zagoria, "The End of the Cold War in Asia: Its Impact on China," in Frank J. Macchiarola and Robert B. Oxnam, eds., *The China Challenge: American Policies in East Asia*, (New York, NY: the Academy of Political Science, 1991), p. 7.

8. Guocang Huan, "China's Policy Toward the United States," in Yufan Hao and Guocang Huan, eds., *The Chinese View of the World*, (New York, NY: Pantheon Books, 1989), p. 153.

9. *The New York Times*, April 4, 1987, pp. A1, A4.

10. *The New York Times* , November 6, 1986, p. A3.

11. Eden Y. Woon, "Chinese Arms Sales and U.S.-China Military Relations," *Asian Survey*, Vol. XXIX, No. 6, (June 1989), pp. 602-603 and John W. Garver, "The 'New Type' of Sino-Soviet Relations," *Asian Survey*, Vol. XXIX, No. 12, (December 1989), p. 1144.

12. Steven I. Levine, "Sino-American Relations: Renormalization and Beyond," in Samuel S. Kim, ed., *China and the World: New Directions in Chinese Foreign Relations*, 2nd ed., (Boulder, CO: Westview Press, 1989), p. 97.

13. Molly Moore and David Ottaway, "U.S. Reacts to China's Silkworm Sale; Technology Transfer Delayed," *The Washington Post*, (October 23, 1987), p. A32. Also see Eden Y. Woon, "Chinese Arms Sales and U.S.-China Military Relations," *Asian Survey*, Vol. XXIX, No. 6, (June 1989), p. 613.

14. *Beijing Review*, Vol. 32, No. 10, (March 6, 1989), p. 21.

15. *The China Business Review*, Vol. 15, No. 3, (May/June 1988), p. 57; David M. Lampton, "America's China Policy: Developing a Fifth strategy," in Frank J. Macchiarola and Robert B. Oxnam, ed., *The China Challenge: American Policies in East Asia*, (New York, NY: the Academy of Political Science, 1991), p. 159; and Harry Harding, "The US and Greater China," *The China Business Review*, Vol. 19, No. 3, (May/June 1992), pp. 18-23.

16. Steven I. Levine, "Sino-American Relations: Renormalization and Beyond," in Samuel S. Kim, ed., *China and the World: New Directions in Chinese Foreign Relations*, 2nd ed., (Boulder, CO: Westview Press, 1989), p. 100.

17. *Renmin Ribao*, (*People's Daily*), October 19, 1988, p. 1.

18. Harry Harding, "The US and Greater China," *The China Business Review*, Vol. 19, No. 3, (May/June 1992), p. 20.)

19. David M. Lampton, "America's China Policy: Developing a Fifth strategy," in Frank J. Macchiarola and Robert B. Oxnam, ed., *The China Challenge: American Policies in East Asia*, (New York, NY: the Academy of Political Science, 1991), p. 159.

20. Steven I. Levine, "Sino-American Relations: Renormalization and Beyond," in Samuel S. Kim, ed., *China and the World: New Directions in Chinese Foreign Relations*, 2nd ed., (Boulder, CO: Westview Press, 1989), pp.

101-102.

21. *The New York Times*, February 10, 1985, p. 3 and March 31, 1985, p. 19.

22. *Beijing Review*, Vol. 28, No. 24, (June 17, 1985), p. 7; and *The New York Times*, April 4, 1985, p. A5.

23. Huan Xiang, "Sino-US Relations Over the Past Year," *Beijing Review*, Vol. 31, No. 7/8, (February 15, 1988), pp. 29-31.

24. *Ibid.*, p. 31.

25. Guocang Huan, "China's Policy Toward the United States," in Yufan Hao and Guocang Huan, eds., *The Chinese View of the World*, (New York, NY: Pantheon Books, 1989), p. 153.

26. *Ibid.*, p. 145.

27. Donald S. Zagoria, "The End of the Cold War in Asia: Its Impact on China," in Frank J. Macchiarola and Robert B. Oxnam, eds., *The China Challenge: American Policies in East Asia*, (New York, NY: the Academy of Political Science, 1991), p. 7.

28. Guocang Huan, "China's Policy Toward the United States," in Yufan Hao and Guocang Huan, eds., *The Chinese View of the World*, (New York, NY: Pantheon Books, 1989), p. 144.

29. *Beijing Review*, Vol. 28, No. 44, (November 4, 1985), pp. 10-11.

30. Richard Baum, "China in 1985: The Greening of the Revolution," *Asian Survey*, Vol. XXVI, No. 1, (January 1986), p. 47 and Carolyn McGiffert Ekedahl and Melvin A. Goodman, "Gorbachev's 'New Directions' in Asia," *Journal of Northeast Asian Studies*, Vol. VIII, No. 3, (Fall 1989), p. 7.

31. Stanley Rosen, "China in 1986: A Year of Consolidation," *Asian Survey*, Vol. XXVII, No. 1, (January 1987), p. 49.

32. *The New York Times*, July 29, 1986, p. A6.

33. Daniel Southerland, "Moscow, Beijing Set Border Talks," *The Washington Post*, January 22, 1987, p. A26.

34. *The New York Times*, July 29, 1986, p. A6.

35. Ivan Arkhipov was a senior deputy primer minister, for whom the Chinese had high regards for he used to serve during the 1950s as the chief for the Soviet economic aid mission to China.

36. James C.F. Wang, *Contemporary Chinese Politics: An Introduction*, 3rd ed., (Englewood Cliffs, NJ: Prentice-Hall, Inc., 1989), p. 328.

37. During the second round of talks held in August 1987, Soviets officially accepted the principle that the middle line of the navigable channel was the border line on the Amur and Ussuri Rivers. A working group of specialists was established to study the issue. In May 1988, it was reported that Chinese and Soviet military officials met for the first time since 1969 as part of the working groups on border demarcation. See *Ibid.*, p. 329.

38. Stanley Rosen, "China in 1986: A Year of Consolidation," *Asian Survey*, Vol. XXVII, No. 1, (January 1987), pp. 49-50.

39. *Beijing Review*, Vol. 30, No. 15, (April 13, 1987), p. 14.
40. *Ibid.*, Vol. 29, No. 38, (September 22, 1986), pp. 4-5.
41. *Ibid.*, Vol. 30, No. 15, (April 13, 1987), p. 14.
42. Dao Huy Ngoc, "The Struggle for Peace in Cambodia," in Frank J. Macchiarola and Robert B. Oxnam, eds., *The China Challenge: American Policies in East Asia*, (New York, NY: the Academy of Political Science, 1991), p. 134.
43. Carolyn McGiffert Ekedahl and Melvin A. Goodman, "Gorbachev's 'New Directions' in Asia," *Journal of Northeast Asian Studies*, Vol. VIII, No. 3, (Fall 1989), p. 8.
44. John W. Garver, "The 'New Type' of Sino-Soviet Relations," *Asian Survey*, Vol. XXIX, No. 12, (December 1989), p. 1138.
45. Chi Su, "Sino-Soviet Relations of the 1980s: from Confrontation to Conciliation," in Samuel S.Kim., ed., *China and the World: New Directions in Chinese Foreign Relations*, 2nd ed., (Boulder, CO: Westview Press, 1989), p. 115.
46. John W. Garver, "The 'New Type' of Sino-Soviet Relations," *Asian Survey*, Vol. XXIX, No. 12, (December 1989), p. 1138.
47. Stanley Rosen, "China in 1987: The Year of the Thirteenth Party Congress," *Asian Survey*, Vol. XXVIII, No. 1, (January 1988), p. 46.
48. Back in August 1985 Hanoi conditionally committed itself to having all its forces out of Cambodia by 1990. See Stanley Rosen, "China in 1987: The Year of the Thirteenth Party Congress," *Asian Survey*, Vol. XXVIII, No. 1, (January 1988), p. 46; and Dao Huy Ngoc, "The Struggle for Peace in Cambodia," in Frank J. Macchiarola and Robert B. Oxnam, eds., *The China Challenge: American Policies in East Asia*, (New York, NY: the Academy of Political Science, 1991), p. 134.
49. *Ibid.*
50. Nayan Chanda, "Taking a Soft Line: Vietnam Signals China that It Wants Improved Relations," *Far Eastern Economic Review*, Vol. 142, No. 49, (December 8, 1988), p. 27 and Robert A. Scalapino, "China's Relations with Its Neighbors," in Frank J. Macchiarola and Robert B. Oxnam, eds., *The China Challenge: American Policies in East Asia.*, (New York, NY: the Academy of Political Science, 1991), p. 66.
51. *FBIS-Daily Report-USSR*, September 19, 1988, p. 21; and *The Washington Post*, September 17, 1988, p. A1.
52. John W. Garver, "The 'New Type' of Sino-Soviet Relations," *Asian Survey*, Vol. XXIX, No. 12, (December 1989), p. 1139.
53. But Vietnam sidestepped China's demands for international supervision of the withdrawal and for establishment of a quadripartite Cambodian government in tandem with the withdrawal. *Ibid.*, p. 1140.
54. *FBIS-Daily Report-China*, January 12, 1989, p. 9.
55. "Sino-Soviet Summit in Sight," *Beijing Review*, Vol. 32, No. 7/8,

rity Pact) since 1980; sharing the cost of maintaining the American forces
pan; transfers of advanced Japanese technology related to defense to the
deployment of 48 F-16 fighter-bombers in Northern Japan since 1985;
ncrease in defense spending. See Reinhard Drifte, *Arms Production in
: The Military Applications of Civilian Technology*, (Boulder, CO:
iew Press, 1986); and Hiroshi Kimura, "The Soviet Military buildup: Its
t on Japan and its Aims," in Richard Solomon and Masataka Kosaka,
*The Soviet Far East Military Buildup: Nuclear dilemmas and Asia
ty*, (London: Croom Helm, 1986, pp. 111-113.

)6. *Renmin Ribao (People's Daily)*, (Overseas Edition), June 12, 1992,

7. Robert A. Scalapino, "China's Relations with Its Neighbors," in
J. Macchiarola and Robert B. Oxnam, eds., *The China Challenge:
an Policies in East Asia*, (New York, NY: the Academy of Political
, 1991), p. 63.
3. Paul H. Kreisberg, "China's Asia Policies," in Frank J. Macchiarola
ert B. Oxnam, ed., *The China Challenge: American Policies in East
Vew York, NY: the Academy of Political Science, 1991), p. 76.
. *Beijing Review*, Vol. 32, No. 7/8, (February 13, 1989), p. 21.
. Paul H. Kreisberg, "China's Asia Policies," in Frank J. Macchiarola
ert B. Oxnam, ed., *The China Challenge: American Policies in East
ew York, NY: the Academy of Political Science, 1991), p. 77.
Stanley Rosen, "China in 1987: The Year of the Thirteenth Party
," *Asian Survey*, Vol. XXVIII, No. 1, (January 1988), p. 47.
Robert Delfs, "Seoul's Hi-Tech Lure across the Yellow Sea," *Far
nomic Review*, Vol. 142, No. 49, (December 8, 1988), pp. 20-21.
statistics showed that the two-way trade with South Korea increased
58 billion in 1987 to $3.087 billion in 1988 and to $3.143 billion in
e Gerrit W. Gong, "China and the Dynamics of Unification in
Asia," in Frank J. Macchiarola and Robert B. Oxnam, ed., *The
allenge: American Policies in East Asia*, (New York, NY: the
of Political Science, 1991), p. 98.
Jae Ho Chung, "South Korea-China Economic Relations," *Asian
ol. XXVIII, No. 10, (October 1988), p. 1042; and David Dollar,
rea-China Trade Relations," *Asian Survey*, Vol. XXIX, No. 12,
1989), pp. 1174-1175.
Renmin Ribao (People's Daily), September 19, 1986, p. 1; and *The
Post*, September 2, 1986, p. F2.
tanley Rosen, "China in 1987: The Year of the Thirteenth Party
Asian Survey, Vol. XXVIII, No. 1, (January 1988), p. 47.
i Haibo, "Tumen River Delta: Far East's Future Rotterdam,"
iew*, Vol. 35, No. 16, (April 20, 1992), pp. 5-6.
hina Daily*, August 25, 1992, p. 1.

(February 13, 1989), pp. 11-12.

56. In fact, Vietnam announced in September 1989 that the withdrawal had been completed. The Chinese were quite satisfied with that. See Carolyn McGiffert Ekedahl and Melvin A. Goodman, "Gorbachev's 'New Directions' in Asia," *Journal of Northeast Asian Studies*, Vol. VIII, No. 3, (Fall 1989), p. 9 and Michael B. Yahuda, "The People's Republic of China at 40: Foreign Relations," *The China Quarterly*, No. 119, (September 1989), p. 527.

57. "Sino-Soviet Summit in Sight," *Beijing Review*, Vol. 32, No. 7/8, (February 13, 1989), p. 12.

58. *Ibid.*, p. 7.

59. Stanley Rosen, "China in 1987: The Year of the Thirteenth Party Congress," *Asian Survey*, Vol. XXVIII, No. 1, (January 1988), p. 46.

60. "Sino-Soviet Summit in Sight," *Beijing Review*, Vol. 32, No. 7/8, (February 13, 1989), pp. 11-12.

61. "Sino-Soviet Joint Communiqué, Beijing, May 18, 1989," *Beijing Review*, Vol. 32, No. 22, (May 29, 1989), p. 15.

62. *Ibid.*, p. 7.

63. Hu Yaobang was demoted from his post as General Secretary of the Chinese Communist Party in January 1987. He was criticized by the conservative faction of the party for not resolutely opposing "bourgeois liberalization" and for his reluctance to suppress student demonstration in late December 1986. Zhao Ziyang was chosen as acting General Secretary. He officially became General Secretary of the Party in November 1987. Li Peng succeeded Zhao as premier in March 1988. Zhao Ziyang stepped down from his post as the party chief in the wake of the Tiananmen Square Incident in June 1989. He was succeeded by Jiang Zemin.

64. "Sino-Soviet Joint Communiqué, Beijing, May 18, 1989," *Beijing Review*, Vol. 32, No. 22, (May 29, 1989), pp. 15-17.

65. The figures were obtained from Chi Su, "Sino-Soviet Relations of the 1980s: from Confrontation to Conciliation," in Samuel S.Kim., ed., *China and the World: New Directions in Chinese Foreign Relations*, 2nd ed., (Boulder, CO: Westview Press, 1989), p. 115; James C.F. Wang, *Contemporary Chinese Politics: An Introduction*, 3rd ed., (Englewood Cliffs, NJ: Prentice-Hall, Inc., 1989), p. 329; Michel Oksenberg, "China's Confident Nationalism," *Foreign Affairs*, Vol. 65, No. 3, (1987), p. 510; Stanley Rosen, "China in 1986: A Year of Consolidation," *Asian Survey*, Vol. XXVII, No. 1, (January 1987), p. 50; Guocang Huan, "Sino-Soviet Relations," in Yufan Hao and Guocang Huan, eds., *The Chinese View of the World*, (New York, NY: Pantheon Books, 1989), p. 104; *The New York Times*, July 9, 1985, p. A5; and *Beijing Review*, Vol. 32, No. 10, (March 6, 1989), p. 21.

66. James C.F. Wang, *Contemporary Chinese Politics: An Introduction*, 3rd ed., (Englewood Cliffs, NJ: Prentice-Hall, Inc., 1989), p. 329.

67. Guocang Huan, "Sino-Soviet Relations," in Yufan Hao and Guocang

Huan, eds., *The Chinese View of the World*, (New York, NY: Pantheon Books, 1989), p. 104.

68. Robert A. Scalapino, "China's Relations with Its Neighbors," in Frank J. Macchiarola and Robert B. Oxnam, eds., *The China Challenge: American Policies in East Asia.*, (New York, NY: the Academy of Political Science, 1991), p. 66.

69. *Christian Science Monitor*, July 9, 1985, p. 1.

70. Ming Chen, "Sino-East European Relations," in Yufan Hao and Guocang Huan, eds., *The Chinese View of the World*, (New York, NY: Pantheon Books, 1989), pp. 266-267 and Stanley Rosen, "China in 1987: The Year of the Thirteenth Party Congress," *Asian Survey*, Vol. XXVIII, No. 1, (January 1988), p. 47.

71. Hu Yaobang, "Create a New Situation in All Fields of Socialist Modernization: Report to the 12th National Congress of the Communist Party of China," *Beijing Review*, Vol. 25, No. 37, September 13, 1982, p. 31.

72. Laura Newby, "Sino-Japanese Relations," in Gerald Segal, ed., *Chinese Politics and Foreign Policy Reform*, (London: Kegan Paul International Ltd., 1990), pp. 196-201.

73. Donald W. Klein, "China and the Second World," in Samuel S. Kim, ed., *China and the World: New Directions in Chinese Foreign Relations*, 2nd ed., (Boulder, CO: Westview Press, 1989), p. 140.

74. "Three Principles for Sino-Japanese Economic Relations, *Beijing Review*, Vol. 25, No. 24, (June 14, 1982), p. 6.

75. Allen S. Whiting, *China Eyes Japan*, (Berkeley, CA: University of California Press, 1989), p. 100.

76. *Beijing Review*, Vol. 32, No. 10, (March 6, 1989), p. 21.

77. Tomozo Morino, "China-Japan Trade and Investment Relations," in Frank J. Macchiarola and Robert B. Oxnam, ed., *The China Challenge: American Policies in East Asia*, (New York, NY: the Academy of Political Science, 1991), p. 90.

78. Charles Smith, "The Ties that Bind: Sino-Japanese Dependence," *Far Eastern Economic Review*, Vol. 132, No. 17, (April 24, 1986), pp. 73-80.

79. *Beijing Review*, Vol. 31, No. 5, (February 1, 1988), p. 18.

80. Michael B. Yahuda, "The People's Republic of China at 40: Foreign Relations," *The China Quarterly*, No. 119, (September 1989), p. 532.

81. James C.F. Wang, *Contemporary Chinese Politics: An Introduction*, 3rd ed., (Englewood Cliffs, NJ: Prentice-Hall, Inc., 1989), p. 346.

82. Michel Oksenberg, "China's Confident Nationalism," *Foreign Affairs*, Vol. 65, No. 3, (1987), p. 512.

83. John W. Garver, "Chinese Foreign Policy: The Diplomacy of Damage Control," *Current History*, Vol. 90, No. 557, (September 1991), pp. 241-246.

84. Tomozo Morino, "China-Japan Trade and Investment Relations," in Frank J. Macchiarola and Robert B. Oxnam, ed., *The China Challenge:*

American Policies in East Asia, (New York, NY: Science, 1991), p. 93.

85. Laura Newby, "Sino-Japanese Relations, *Chinese Politics and Foreign Policy Reform*, (London Ltd., 1990), p. 201.

86. Allen S. Whiting, *China Eyes Japan*, (Be California Press, 1989), p. 120.

87. *Beijing Review*, Vol. 30, No. 2, (January

88. Allen S. Whiting, *China Eyes Japan*, (B California Press, 1989), p. 116.

89. *FBIS-Daily Report-China*, June 30, 1987

90. Michel Oksenberg, "China's Confident N Vol. 65, No. 3, (1987), p. 513.

91. Donald W. Klein, "China and the Second ed., *China and the World: New Directions in Ch ed., (Boulder, CO: Westview Press, 1989), pp.

92. *Renmin Ribao (People's Daily)*, Octob

93. *Chengming* (Hong Kong), No. 97, (No

94. Charles Smith, "Sanity Returns after *Eastern Economic Review*, Vol. 135, No. 12, (

95. *The Asian Wall Street Journal*, Decem

96. *Beijing Review*, Vol. 30, No. 15, (Ap

97. *Renmin Ribao (People's Daily)*, (Over 1.

98. James C.F. Wang, *Contemporary Ch 3rd ed., (Englewood Cliffs, NJ: Prentice-Hal

99. "An Interview with Teng Hsiao-P (February 5, 1979), p. 34.

100. Jonathan D. Pollack, *The Lesso Monica, CA: Rand Corp., 1984), p. 57.

101. *FBIS-Daily Report-China*, August

102. *FBIS-Daily Report-Asia*, January

103. James C.F. Wang, *Contemporary 3rd ed., (Englewood Cliffs, NJ: Prentice-H

104. Steven I. Levine, "China in Asia Harry Harding, ed., *China's Foreign Relati Yale University Press, 1984), pp. 177-22

105. Under Nakasone and his predec military capabilities expanded. Japan bec military nature, such as defense of an exp nautical miles off its shores and 1,000 mil Defense Forces; participation in the joi member states (i.e., the Australia, New

118. Robert A. Scalapino, "China's Relations with Its Neighbors," in Frank J. Macchiarola and Robert B. Oxnam, eds., *The China Challenge: American Policies in East Asia*, (New York, NY: the Academy of Political Science, 1991), p. 69.

119. Paul H. Kreisberg, "China's Asia Policies," in Frank J. Macchiarola and Robert B. Oxnam, ed., *The China Challenge: American Policies in East Asia*, (New York, NY: the Academy of Political Science, 1991), p. 85.

120. In the 1980s, Vietnam's economy was largely dependent upon Soviet aid. The Russians got involved in 250 projects and the Soviet Union accounted for 64 percent of Vietnam's foreign trade. Under the 1985-1990 Soviet five-year plan, aid to Vietnam was around $12.8-14.4 billion. See Sophie Ouinn-Judge, "Ten Year Itch: Soviets Admit Much of Economic Aid to Hanoi Was Wasted," *Far East Economic Review*, Vol. 142, No. 45, (November 10, 1988), p. 23.

121. For example, Moscow would give only a quarter of the amount of strategic commodities provided annually during the 1986-1990 plan period to Vietnam in 1991. Only about 20 projects would receive assistance compared with as many as 100 in the past. See the Economist Intelligence Unit (London), *Country Report: Vietnam, Laos, Cambodia*, No. 1, (1991), pp. 20-21.

122. With a population of 63 million, Vietnam had a regular army of more than one million plus nearly three million in reserve and quasi-military units, making it, per capita, the world's largest national military force. See Xiaobo Lu, "China and Southeast Asia," in Yufan Hao and Guocang Huan, eds., *The Chinese View of the World*, (New York, NY: Pantheon Books, 1989), p. 209.

123. The Economist Intelligence Unit (London), *Country Report: Vietnam, Laos, Cambodia*, No. 1, (1990), p. 17; and No. 1 (1991), p. 14.

124. The Economist Intelligence Unit (London), *Country Report: Vietnam, Laos, Cambodia*, No. 2, (1990), p. 5; and No. 3, (1990), p. 14.

125. Steven J. Hood, "Beijing's Cambodia Gamble and the Prospects for Peace in Indochina," *Asian Survey*, Vol. XXX, No. 10, (October 1990), p. 987.

126. The Economist Intelligence Unit (London), *Country Report: Vietnam, Laos, Cambodia*, No. 1, (1991), p. 13.

127. Douglas Pike, "Vietnam in 1990: The Last Picture Show," *Asian Survey*, Vol. XXXI, No. 1, (January 1991), p. 43.

128. Steven J. Hood, "Beijing's Cambodia Gamble and the Prospects for Peace in Indochina," *Asian Survey*, Vol. XXX, No. 10, (October 1990), p. 978.

129. Paul H. Kreisberg, "China's Asia Policies," in Frank J. Macchiarola and Robert B. Oxnam, ed., *The China Challenge: American Policies in East Asia*, (New York, NY: the Academy of Political Science, 1991), p. 85.

130. Zhang Zhinian, "Cambodia Ushers in Peace," *Beijing Review*, Vol. 34, No. 44, (November 4, 1991), p. 7.

296   *Foreign Policy Restructuring As Adaptive Behavior*

131. Chen Jiabao, "A New Era Begins in Sino-Vietnamese Relations" and "Sino-Vietnamese Joint Communiqué," *Beijing Review*, Vol. 34, No. 46, (November 11, 1991), pp. 7-9; and pp. 13-14.

132. *The Straits Times*, November 26, 1990, p. 3.

133. Paul H. Kreisberg, "China's Asia Policies," in Frank J. Macchiarola and Robert B. Oxnam, ed., *The China Challenge: American Policies in East Asia*, (New York, NY: the Academy of Political Science, 1991), pp. 76-84.

134. *Renmin Ribao*, November 12, 1988, p. 1.

135. Xiaobo Lu, "China and Southeast Asia," in Yufan Hao and Guocang Huan, eds., *The Chinese View of the World*, (New York, NY: Pantheon Books, 1989), pp. 222-223; and *Central Daily News* (International Edition), July 29, 1992, p. 1.

136. Denis Fred Simon, "China in the World Economic System," and Frederick Z. Brown, "Security Issues in South East Asia," in Frank J. Macchiarola and Robert B. Oxnam, ed., *The China Challenge: American Policies in East Asia*, (New York, NY: the Academy of Political Science, 1991), p. 21, p. 121; and Xiaobo Lu, "China and Southeast Asia," in Yufan Hao and Guocang Huan, eds., *The Chinese View of the World*, (New York, NY: Pantheon Books, 1989), pp. 215-216.

137. Tatyana L. Shaumian, "India's Foreign Policy," *Asian Survey*, Vol. XXVIII, No. 11, (November 1988), p. 1168.

138. *Ibid.*

139. Sumit Ganguly, "The Sino-Indian Border Talks, 1981-1090," *Asian Survey*, Vol. XXIX, No. 12, (December 1989), pp. 1129-1131 and Stanley Rosen, "China in 1987: The Year of the Thirteenth Party Congress," *Asian Survey*, Vol. XXVIII, No. 1, (January 1988), p. 51.

140. Sumit Ganguly, "The Sino-Indian Border Talks, 1981-1090," *Asian Survey*, Vol. XXIX, No. 12, (December 1989), p. 1123.

141. Du Zhenfeng, "A New Chapter in Sino-Indian Relations," *Beijing Review*, Vol. 34, No. 50, (December 16, 1991), p. 7.

142. Robert A. Scalapino, "China's Relations with Its Neighbors," in Frank J. Macchiarola and Robert B. Oxnam, eds., *The China Challenge: American Policies in East Asia*, (New York, NY: the Academy of Political Science, 1991),p. 70.

143. Stanley Rosen, "China in 1986: A Year of Consolidation," *Asian Survey*, Vol. XXVII, No. 1, (January 1987), p. 50.

144. Carolyn McGiffert Ekedahl and Melvin A. Goodman, "Gorbachev's 'New Directions' in Asia," *Journal of Northeast Asian Studies*, Vol. VIII, No. 3, (Fall 1989), p. 11.

145. Jean-Pierre Cabestan, "Sino-European Relations," in Gerald Segal, ed. *Chinese Politics and Foreign Policy Reform*, (London: Kegan Paul International Ltd., 1990), p. 215.

146. Donald W. Klein, "China and the Second World," in Samuel S. Kim,

ed., *China and the World: New Directions in Chinese Foreign Relations*, 2nd ed., (Boulder, CO: Westview Press, 1989), pp. 134-142.

147. Donald W. Klein, "China and the Second World," in Samuel S. Kim, ed., *China and the World: New Directions in Chinese Foreign Relations*, 2nd ed., (Boulder, CO: Westview Press, 1989), p. 134.

148. Hu Yaobang, "Create a New Situation in All Fields of Socialist Modernization: Report to the 12th National Congress of the Communist Party of China," *Beijing Review*, Vol. 25, No. 37, September 13, 1982, pp. 29-32.

149. Li Peng, "Resolutely Carry Out the Principles of Improvement, Rectification and Deepened Reform--Report on the Work of the Government Delivered at the Second Session of the Seventh National People's Congress, March 20, 1989," *Beijing Review*, Vol. 32, No. 16, (April 17, 1989), pp. XXI-XXIV.

150. Jean-Pierre Cabestan, "Sino-European Relations," in Gerald Segal, ed. *Chinese Politics and Foreign Policy Reform*, (London: Kegan Paul International Ltd., 1990), pp. 218-219.

151. "Economic Parley, Developing Trust," *Beijing Review*, Vol. 31, No. 45, (November 7, 1988), pp. 15-16.

152. Shen Shouyuan, "Sino-European Relations in the Global Context," *Asian Survey*, Vol. XXVI, No. 11, (November 1986), p. 1173.

153. Jean-Pierre Cabestan, "Sino-European Relations," in Gerald Segal, ed. *Chinese Politics and Foreign Policy Reform*, (London: Kegan Paul International Ltd., 1990), p. 225.

154. *FBIS-Daily Report-China*, April 7, 1989, pp. 11-12.

155. *Beijing Review*, Vol. 32, No. 10, (March 6, 1989), p. 27.

156. *Wenhuibao* (Shanghai), July 26, 1990, p. 1.

157. *Beijing Review*, Vol. 32, No. 10, (March 6, 1989), p. 21.

158. Jean-Pierre Cabestan, "Sino-European Relations," in Gerald Segal, ed. *Chinese Politics and Foreign Policy Reform*, (London: Kegan Paul International Ltd., 1990), p. 225-6.

159. *Ibid.*, p. 222.

160. John W. Garver, "Chinese Foreign Policy: The Diplomacy of Damage Control," *Current History*, Vol. 90, No. 557, (September 1991), pp. 241-246.

161. Xin Hua, "China's Successful Diplomacy," *Beijing Review*, Vol. 35, No. 19, (Mary 11, 1992), p. 14.

162. Deng Xiaoping, "On the Current Situation and Tasks," in Harold C. Hinton, *The People's Republic of China 1979-1984: A Documentary Survey*, (Wilmington, DE: Scholarly Resources Inc., 1986), p. 3.

163. "A Significant Concept," *Beijing Review*, Vol. 27, No. 44, October 29, 1984, pp. 16-17.

164. Robert G. Sutter, *Chinese Foreign Policy: Developments after Mao*, (New York: Praeger Publishers, 1986), p. 205.

165. Zhiduan Deng, "Beijing's Policy on Hong Kong," in Yufan Hao and Guocang Huan, eds., *The Chinese View of the World*, (New York, NY: Pantheon Books, 1989), p. 293.

166. Andrew Scobell, "Hong Kong's Influence on China," *Asian Survey*, Vol. XXVIII, No. 6, (June 1988), p. 608; and William H. Overholt, "Hong Kong and China after 1997: The Real Issues," in Frank J. Macchiarola and Robert B. Oxnam, ed., *The China Challenge: American Policies in East Asia*, (New York, NY: the Academy of Political Science, 1991), p. 34.

167. Zhiduan Deng, "Beijing's Policy on Hong Kong," in Yufan Hao and Guocang Huan, eds., *The Chinese View of the World*, (New York, NY: Pantheon Books, 1989), p. 293.

167. William H. Overholt, "Hong Kong and China after 1997: The Real Issues," in Frank J. Macchiarola and Robert B. Oxnam, ed., *The China Challenge: American Policies in East Asia*, (New York, NY: the Academy of Political Science, 1991), p. 34.

168. K.C. Mun and T.S. Chan, "The Role of Hong Kong in United States-China Trade," *Columbia Journal of World Business*, Vol. XXI, No. 1, (Spring 1986), pp. 70-71.

169. Zhiduan Deng, "Beijing's Policy on Hong Kong," in Yufan Hao and Guocang Huan, eds., *The Chinese View of the World*, (New York, NY: Pantheon Books, 1989), pp. 293-294.

170. Robert G. Sutter, *Chinese Foreign Policy: Developments after Mao*, (New York: Praeger Publishers, 1986), p. 208.

171. Zhiduan Deng, "Beijing's Policy on Hong Kong," in Yufan Hao and Guocang Huan, eds., *The Chinese View of the World*, (New York, NY: Pantheon Books, 1989), p. 288.

172. For the text of the Convention, see "Convention between Great Britain and China Respecting an Extension of Hong Kong Territory (Signed at Peking, June 9th, 1898)," in Michael Hurst, ed., *Key Treaties for the Great Powers, 1814-1914*, (Newton Abbott, England: David & Charles, 1972), pp. 688-689.

173. Quoted in Robert G. Sutter, *Chinese Foreign Policy: Developments after Mao*, (New York, NY: Praeger Publishers, 1986), p. 208.

174. T.L. Tsim, "1997: Peking's Strategy for Hong Kong," *The World Today*, January 1984, p. 38.

175. More on the negotiations between London and Beijing on the future of Hong Kong, see Ian Scott, *Political Change and the Crisis of Legitimacy in Hong Kong*, (Honolulu, HI: University of Hawaii Press, 1989).

176. Robert G. Sutter, *Chinese Foreign Policy: Developments after Mao*, (New York, NY: Praeger Publishers, 1986), p. 210.

177. "Joint Declaration of the Government of the People's Republic of China and the Government of the United Kingdom of Great Britain and Northern Ireland on the Question of Hong Kong," *Beijing Review*, Vol. 27,

No. 40, (October 1, 1984), pp. I-XX. Also see "China, Britain Sign Historic Hong Kong Pact," *Beijing Review*, Vol. 27, No. 52, (December 24, 1984), pp. 6-8.

178. Thomas P. Bernstein, "China in 1984: The Year of Hong Kong," *Asian Survey*, Vol. XXV, No. 1, (January 1985), p. 33.

179. The Basic Law for Hong Kong was announced on April 28, 1988. The text of the law is in *Beijing Review*, Vol. 31, No. 19, (May 9, 1988), pp. 23-51.

180. Quoted in William H. Overholt, "Hong Kong and China after 1997: The Real Issues," in Frank J. Macchiarola and Robert B. Oxnam, ed., *The China Challenge: American Policies in East Asia*, (New York, NY: the Academy of Political Science, 1991), p. 34.

181. *Beijing Review*, Vol. 30, No. 13, (March 30, 1987), p. 4 and "Joint Declaration of the Government of the People's Republic of China and the Government of the Republic of Portugal on the Question of Macao," *Beijing Review*, Vol. 30, No. 14, (April 6, 1987), (Supplement).

182. *China Times*, interview with President Yang Shangkun, September 24, 1990, p. 1.

183. "Talks Over Jet Break Icy Silence," *Beijing Review* Vol. 29, No. 22, (June 2, 1986), pp. 5-7.

184. Allen S. Whiting, "Chinese Foreign Policy Options in the 1990s," in Samuel S. Kim, ed., *China and the World: New Directions in Chinese Foreign Relations*, (Boulder, CO: Westview Press, 1989), p. 306.

185. *Renmin Ribao*, July 14, 1988, p. 1 and *Beijing Review*, Vol. 33, No. 39, (September 24, 1990), pp. 21-22. *Central Daily News* (International Edition), September 23, 1990, p. 1.)

186. Fang Sheng, "Prospects for Mainland-Taiwan Relations," *Beijing Review*, Vol. 35, No. 17, (April 27, 1992), pp. 30-32; and Qingguo Jia, "Changing Relations Across the Taiwan Strait," *Asian Survey*, Vol. XXXII, No. 3, (March 1992), pp. 277-289..

187. Li Shuiwang, "Review on a Year of Change & Preview," *Beijing Review*, Vol. 31, No. 45, (November 7, 1988), pp. 22-27.

188. Fang Sheng, "Prospects for Mainland-Taiwan Relations," *Beijing Review*, Vol. 35, No. 17, (April 27, 1992), pp. 30-32; and David Shambaugh, "China in 1990: The Year of Damage Control," *Asian Survey*, Vol. XXXI, No. 1, (January 1991), p. 47.

189. Gerrit W. Gong, "China and the Dynamics of Unification in Northeast Asia," in Frank J. Macchiarola and Robert B. Oxnam, ed., *The China Challenge: American Policies in East Asia*, (New York, NY: the Academy of Political Science, 1991), p. 101.

190. Robert A. Scalapino, "China's Relations with Its Neighbors," in Frank J. Macchiarola and Robert B. Oxnam, eds., *The China Challenge: American Policies in East Asia*, (New York, NY: the Academy of Political

Science, 1991), p. 72.

191. Robert A. Scalapino, "China's Relations with Its Neighbors," in Frank J. Macchiarola and Robert B. Oxnam, eds., *The China Challenge: American Policies in East Asia*, (New York, NY: the Academy of Political Science, 1991), p. 72.

192. Gerrit W. Gong, "China and the Dynamics of Unification in Northeast Asia," in Frank J. Macchiarola and Robert B. Oxnam, ed., *The China Challenge: American Policies in East Asia*, (New York, NY: the Academy of Political Science, 1991), p. 101.

193. *Beijing Review*, Vol. 34, No. 52, (December 30, 1991), p. 5.

194. Gerrit W. Gong, "China and the Dynamics of Unification in Northeast Asia," in Frank J. Macchiarola and Robert B. Oxnam, ed., *The China Challenge: American Policies in East Asia*, (New York, NY: the Academy of Political Science, 1991), p. 101.

195. Michael B. Yahuda, "The People's Republic of China at 40: Foreign Relations," *The China Quarterly*, No. 119, (September 1989), p. 533.

196. Li Jiaquan, "'Taiwan Independence'--A Blind Alley," *Beijing Review*, Vol.35, No. 23, (June 8, 1992), pp. 24-27.

Chapter 9

1. Gerald Segal, "Sino-Soviet Relations," in Gerald Segal, ed., *Chinese Politics and Foreign Policy Reform*, (London: Kegan Paul International Ltd., 1990), p. 161.

2. Jean-Pierre Cabestan, "Sino-European Relations," in Gerald Segal, ed. *Chinese Politics and Foreign Policy Reform*, (London: Kegan Paul International Ltd., 1990), p. 219.

3. Robert L. Worden, Andrea Matles Savada, and Ronald E. Dolan, eds., *China: a country study*, (Washington, D.C: Headquarters, Department of the Army, 1988), p. 473.

4. Xie Yixian, "China's Foreign Policy: A 1980s Tune-Up," *Beijing Review*, Vol. 32, No. 7/8, (February 13, 1989), p. 17.

5. Robert G. Sutter, *Chinese Foreign Policy: Developments after Mao*, (New York, NY: Praeger Publishers, 1986), p. 61.

6. Deng Xiaoping, "A New Approach towards Stabilizing the World Situation," February 1984, in Deng Xiaoping, *Build Socialism with Chinese Characteristics*, (Beijing: Foreign Languages Press, 1985), pp. 23-24.

7. Harry Harding, *China's Second Revolution: Reform after Mao*, (Washington, D.C.: Brookings Institution, 1987), p. 246.

8. Michael B. Yahuda, "Sino-American Relations," in Gerald Segal, ed., *Chinese Politics and Foreign Policy Reform*, (London: Kegan Paul International Ltd., 1990), p. 184.

9. Gavin Boyd, "China," in Gavin Boyd and Gerald W. Hopple, eds., *Political Change and Foreign Policies*, (New York, NY: St Martin's Press, 1987), p. 127.

10. David Bachman, "Varieties of Chinese Conservatism and the Fall of Hu Yaobang," *Journal of Northeast Asian Studies*, Vol. VII, No. 1, (Spring 1988), p. 34.

11. *Ibid.*, p. 35.

12. Quansheng Zhao, "Domestic Sources of Chinese Foreign Policy: from Vertical to Horizontal Authoritarianism." A research paper presented at the 1991 Annual Meeting of the American Political Science Association, Washington, D.C., (August 29/September 1, 1991), p. 9.

13. Tang Tsou, *The Cultural Revolution and Post-Mao Reforms: A Historical Perspective*, (Chicago: The University of Chicago Press, 1986), pp. 219-258.

14. On the economic issues, Deng was in favor of fundamental economic changes and opening up. But on political issues, Deng's ideas were not very provocative and he was not a political liberal. He supported the party rule even though he might be willing to tolerate somewhat more pluralism within the party and a more rapid turnover of power to younger leaders than some vested interest conservatives. Deng did discuss political reform at various times, most clearly in August 1980, but the themes he emphasized were eliminating a "feudal, patriarchal style of rule," opposition to bureaucratism, developing the legal system, and separating the work of the government from the work of the party. He wanted the party to cultivate outstanding younger party members so that they could quickly rise to top leadership positions. He favored greater autonomy for scientific and technical experts, and expanded the definition of the academic. This allowed the intellectuals to enjoy a relatively more freedom than they had had under Mao. All these efforts, in essence, were aimed only at rationalizing the political system under the party's rule rather than introducing political democratization. Deng, in fact, never accepted the adoption of multi-party system as the basis of political reform. See David Bachman, "Varieties of Chinese Conservatism and the Fall of Hu Yaobang," *Journal of Northeast Asian Studies*, Vol. VII, No. 1, (Spring 1988), p. 35.

15. Yufan Hao and Guocang Huan, eds. *The Chinese View of the World*, (New York, NY: Pantheon Books, 1989), p. xxviii.

16. Harry Harding, *China's Second Revolution: Reform after Mao*, (Washington, D.C.: Brookings Institution, 1987), p. 244.

17. Zhao Ziyang, "Report on the Seventh Five-Year Plan," March 25, 1986, *Beijing Review*, Vol. 29, No. 16, (April 21, 1986), pp. I-XX.

18. Michel Oksenberg, "China's Confident Nationalism," *Foreign Affairs*, Vol. 65, No. 3, (1987), p. 520.

19. *Ibid.* pp. 504-505.

20. Michael B. Yahuda, "Sino-American Relations," in Gerald Segal, ed.,

Chinese Politics and Foreign Policy Reform, (London: Kegan Paul International Ltd., 1990), p. 182.

21. Harry Harding, *China's Second Revolution: Reform after Mao*, (Washington, D.C.: Brookings Institution, 1987), pp. 245-246.

22. Michel Oksenberg, "China's Confident Nationalism," *Foreign Affairs*, Vol. 65, No. 3, (1987), p. 505.

23. *Ibid.*, p. 502.

24. *Ibid.*

25. Beijing made some efforts in order to coordinate different institutional interests in conducting China's foreign policy. For example, on July 27-31, 1991, the PLA's foreign affairs working conference was held in Beijing, right after the State Council's foreign affairs working conference. See *Renmin Ribao* (*People's Daily*), August 1, 1991, p. 1.

26. Michael B. Yahuda, "The People's Republic of China at 40: Foreign Relations," *The China Quarterly*, No. 119, (September 1989), p. 536.

27. Under the State Council there are the Center for International studies and the Institute of Contemporary International Relations. Every foreign-policy-related ministry, such as the Ministry of Foreign Affairs and the Ministry of Foreign Economic Relations and Trade, has its own research institute. At the Academy of Social Sciences there are also several internationally oriented research institutions concentrating not only on world political and economic relations but also on regional studies, such as concentrations on the Soviet Union and Eastern Europe, the United States, Japan, Latin America, South Asia, Middle East and Western Europe. These are also research institutions of international studies at major universities located in Beijing. The military also set up its strategic study groups.

28. Michel Oksenberg, "China's Confident Nationalism," *Foreign Affairs*, Vol. 65, No. 3, (1987), p. 519.

29. Gilbert Rozman, *The Chinese Debate About Soviet Socialism,*, (Princeton, NJ: Princeton University Press, 1987).

30. Quansheng Zhao, "Domestic Sources of Chinese Foreign Policy: from Vertical to Horizontal Authoritarianism." A research paper presented at the 1991 Annual Meeting of the American Political Science Association, Washington, D.C., (August 29/September 1, 1991), p. 18.

31. Gavin Boyd, "China," in Gavin Boyd and Gerald W. Hopple, eds., *Political Change and Foreign Policies*, (New York, NY: St Martin's Press, 1987), p. 134.

32. James N. Rosenau, "Toward Single-Country Theories of Foreign Policy: the Case of the USSR," in Charles F. Hermann, Charles W. Kegley, Jr. and James N. Rosenau, eds., *New Directions in the Study of Foreign Policy*, (Boston: Allen & Unwin, 1987), p. 64.

33. Charles F. Hermann, "Changing Course: When Governments Choose to Redirect Foreign Policy," *International Studies Quarterly*, Vol. 34, No. 1,

(March 1990), p. 11.

34. Takestrugu Tsurutani, "Japan," in Gavin Boyd and Gerald W. Hopple, eds., *Political Change and Foreign Policies*, (New York, NY: St Martin's Press, 1987), p. 105.

35. Michael Haas, *International Conflict*, (Indianapolis, IN: The Bobbs-Merrill Company, Inc., 1974), p. 487.

36. Samuel S. Kim, "China and the Third World: In Search of A Peace and Development Line," in Samuel S. Kim, ed., *China and the World: New Directions in Chinese Foreign Relations*, (Boulder, CO: Westview Press, 1989), p. 174.

37. Orville Schell, *Discos and Democracy*, (New York, NY: Pantheon Books, 1988), pp. 71-116.

38. Michael B. Yahuda, "The People's Republic of China at 40: Foreign Relations," *The China Quarterly*, No. 119, (September 1989), p. 539.

39. *Central Daily News* (International Edition), April 15, 1992, p. 4.

40. Hwei-ling Huo, "Patterns of Behavior in China's Foreign Policy," *Asian Survey*, Vol. XXXII, No. 3, (March 1992), p. 274.

41. Donald S. Zagoria, "The End of the Cold War in Asia: Its Impact on China," in Frank J. Macchiarola and Robert B. Oxnam, eds., *The China Challenge: American Policies in East Asia*, (New York, NY: the Academy of Political Science, 1991), p. 7.

42. Zhong Shiyou, "Fresh Impetus from Deng's Message," *Beijing Review*, Vol. 35, No. 15, (April 13, 1992), pp. 4-6.

43. Hwei-ling Huo, "Patterns of Behavior in China's Foreign Policy," *Asian Survey*, Vol. XXXII, No. 3, (March 1992), p. 267.

44. The central task refers to economic construction. One basic point means reform and opening-up. The other is the upholding of the four cardinal principles of socialism, the people's democratic dictatorship, the leadership of the Communist Party, and Marxism-Leninism and Mao Zedong thought. *Renmin Ribao (People's Daily)*, (Overseas Edition), March 12, 1992, p. 1.

45. "The South China Miracle: A Great Leap Forward," *The Economist*, Vol. 321, No. 7727, (October 5, 1991), pp. 19-20, 22.

46. *Ibid.*

47. Frank Gibney, Jr., "China's Renegade Province: Guangdong does find without either Marx or Mao," *Newsweek*, Vol. 119, No. 7, (February 17, 1992), p. 35.

48. Hwei-ling Huo, "Patterns of Behavior in China's Foreign Policy," *Asian Survey*, Vol. XXXII, No. 3, (March 1992), pp. 263-276.

49. Donald S. Zagoria, "The End of the Cold War in Asia: Its Impact on China," in Frank J. Macchiarola and Robert B. Oxnam, eds., *The China Challenge: American Policies in East Asia*, (New York, NY: the Academy of Political Science, 1991), p. 8.

50. John W. Garver, "Chinese Foreign Policy: The Diplomacy of

Damage Control," *Current History*, Vol. 90, No. 557, (September 1991), pp. 241-246.

51. *Beijing Review*, Vol. 34, No. 35, (September 2, 1991), p. 7.

INDEX

(February 13, 1989), pp. 11-12.

56. In fact, Vietnam announced in September 1989 that the withdrawal had been completed. The Chinese were quite satisfied with that. See Carolyn McGiffert Ekedahl and Melvin A. Goodman, "Gorbachev's 'New Directions' in Asia," *Journal of Northeast Asian Studies*, Vol. VIII, No. 3, (Fall 1989), p. 9 and Michael B. Yahuda, "The People's Republic of China at 40: Foreign Relations," *The China Quarterly*, No. 119, (September 1989), p. 527.

57. "Sino-Soviet Summit in Sight," *Beijing Review*, Vol. 32, No. 7/8, (February 13, 1989), p. 12.

58. *Ibid.*, p. 7.

59. Stanley Rosen, "China in 1987: The Year of the Thirteenth Party Congress," *Asian Survey*, Vol. XXVIII, No. 1, (January 1988), p. 46.

60. "Sino-Soviet Summit in Sight," *Beijing Review*, Vol. 32, No. 7/8, (February 13, 1989), pp. 11-12.

61. "Sino-Soviet Joint Communiqué, Beijing, May 18, 1989," *Beijing Review*, Vol. 32, No. 22, (May 29, 1989), p. 15.

62. *Ibid.*, p. 7.

63. Hu Yaobang was demoted from his post as General Secretary of the Chinese Communist Party in January 1987. He was criticized by the conservative faction of the party for not resolutely opposing "bourgeois liberalization" and for his reluctance to suppress student demonstration in late December 1986. Zhao Ziyang was chosen as acting General Secretary. He officially became General Secretary of the Party in November 1987. Li Peng succeeded Zhao as premier in March 1988. Zhao Ziyang stepped down from his post as the party chief in the wake of the Tiananmen Square Incident in June 1989. He was succeeded by Jiang Zemin.

64. "Sino-Soviet Joint Communiqué, Beijing, May 18, 1989," *Beijing Review*, Vol. 32, No. 22, (May 29, 1989), pp. 15-17.

65. The figures were obtained from Chi Su, "Sino-Soviet Relations of the 1980s: from Confrontation to Conciliation," in Samuel S.Kim., ed., *China and the World: New Directions in Chinese Foreign Relations*, 2nd ed., (Boulder, CO: Westview Press, 1989), p. 115; James C.F. Wang, *Contemporary Chinese Politics: An Introduction*, 3rd ed., (Englewood Cliffs, NJ: Prentice-Hall, Inc., 1989), p. 329; Michel Oksenberg, "China's Confident Nationalism," *Foreign Affairs*, Vol. 65, No. 3, (1987), p. 510; Stanley Rosen, "China in 1986: A Year of Consolidation," *Asian Survey*, Vol. XXVII, No. 1, (January 1987), p. 50; Guocang Huan, "Sino-Soviet Relations," in Yufan Hao and Guocang Huan, eds., *The Chinese View of the World*, (New York, NY: Pantheon Books, 1989), p. 104; *The New York Times*, July 9, 1985, p. A5; and *Beijing Review*, Vol. 32, No. 10, (March 6, 1989), p. 21.

66. James C.F. Wang, *Contemporary Chinese Politics: An Introduction*, 3rd ed., (Englewood Cliffs, NJ: Prentice-Hall, Inc., 1989), p. 329.

67. Guocang Huan, "Sino-Soviet Relations," in Yufan Hao and Guocang

Huan, eds., *The Chinese View of the World*, (New York, NY: Pantheon Books, 1989), p. 104.

68. Robert A. Scalapino, "China's Relations with Its Neighbors," in Frank J. Macchiarola and Robert B. Oxnam, eds., *The China Challenge: American Policies in East Asia.*, (New York, NY: the Academy of Political Science, 1991), p. 66.

69. *Christian Science Monitor*, July 9, 1985, p. 1.

70. Ming Chen, "Sino-East European Relations," in Yufan Hao and Guocang Huan, eds., *The Chinese View of the World*, (New York, NY: Pantheon Books, 1989), pp. 266-267 and Stanley Rosen, "China in 1987: The Year of the Thirteenth Party Congress," *Asian Survey*, Vol. XXVIII, No. 1, (January 1988), p. 47.

71. Hu Yaobang, "Create a New Situation in All Fields of Socialist Modernization: Report to the 12th National Congress of the Communist Party of China," *Beijing Review*, Vol. 25, No. 37, September 13, 1982, p. 31.

72. Laura Newby, "Sino-Japanese Relations," in Gerald Segal, ed., *Chinese Politics and Foreign Policy Reform*, (London: Kegan Paul International Ltd., 1990), pp. 196-201.

73. Donald W. Klein, "China and the Second World," in Samuel S. Kim, ed., *China and the World: New Directions in Chinese Foreign Relations*, 2nd ed., (Boulder, CO: Westview Press, 1989), p. 140.

74. "Three Principles for Sino-Japanese Economic Relations, *Beijing Review*, Vol. 25, No. 24, (June 14, 1982), p. 6.

75. Allen S. Whiting, *China Eyes Japan*, (Berkeley, CA: University of California Press, 1989), p. 100.

76. *Beijing Review*, Vol. 32, No. 10, (March 6, 1989), p. 21.

77. Tomozo Morino, "China-Japan Trade and Investment Relations," in Frank J. Macchiarola and Robert B. Oxnam, ed., *The China Challenge: American Policies in East Asia*, (New York, NY: the Academy of Political Science, 1991), p. 90.

78. Charles Smith, "The Ties that Bind: Sino-Japanese Dependence," *Far Eastern Economic Review*, Vol. 132, No. 17, (April 24, 1986), pp. 73-80.

79. *Beijing Review*, Vol. 31, No. 5, (February 1, 1988), p. 18.

80. Michael B. Yahuda, "The People's Republic of China at 40: Foreign Relations," *The China Quarterly*, No. 119, (September 1989), p. 532.

81. James C.F. Wang, *Contemporary Chinese Politics: An Introduction*, 3rd ed., (Englewood Cliffs, NJ: Prentice-Hall, Inc., 1989), p. 346.

82. Michel Oksenberg, "China's Confident Nationalism," *Foreign Affairs*, Vol. 65, No. 3, (1987), p. 512.

83. John W. Garver, "Chinese Foreign Policy: The Diplomacy of Damage Control," *Current History*, Vol. 90, No. 557, (September 1991), pp. 241-246.

84. Tomozo Morino, "China-Japan Trade and Investment Relations," in Frank J. Macchiarola and Robert B. Oxnam, ed., *The China Challenge:*

American Policies in East Asia, (New York, NY: the Academy of Political Science, 1991), p. 93.

85. Laura Newby, "Sino-Japanese Relations," in Gerald Segal, ed., *Chinese Politics and Foreign Policy Reform*, (London: Kegan Paul International Ltd., 1990), p. 201.

86. Allen S. Whiting, *China Eyes Japan*, (Berkeley, CA: University of California Press, 1989), p. 120.

87. *Beijing Review*, Vol. 30, No. 2, (January 12, 1987), pp. 26-27.

88. Allen S. Whiting, *China Eyes Japan*, (Berkeley, CA: University of California Press, 1989), p. 116.

89. *FBIS-Daily Report-China*, June 30, 1987, D4-5.

90. Michel Oksenberg, "China's Confident Nationalism," *Foreign Affairs*, Vol. 65, No. 3, (1987), p. 513.

91. Donald W. Klein, "China and the Second World," in Samuel S. Kim, ed., *China and the World: New Directions in Chinese Foreign Relations*, 2nd ed., (Boulder, CO: Westview Press, 1989), pp. 140-141.

92. *Renmin Ribao (People's Daily)*, October 2, 1984, p. 1.

93. *Chengming* (Hong Kong), No. 97, (November 1985), pp. 6-7.

94. Charles Smith, "Sanity Returns after the Big Buying Spree," *Far Eastern Economic Review*, Vol. 135, No. 12, (March 19, 1987), p. 68.

95. *The Asian Wall Street Journal*, December 4, 1985, p. 16.

96. *Beijing Review*, Vol. 30, No. 15, (April 13, 1987), p. 15.

97. *Renmin Ribao (People's Daily)*, (Overseas Edition), June 11, 1987, p. 1.

98. James C.F. Wang, *Contemporary Chinese Politics: An Introduction*, 3rd ed., (Englewood Cliffs, NJ: Prentice-Hall, Inc., 1989), p. 347.

99. "An Interview with Teng Hsiao-P'ing," *Time*, Vol. 113, No. 6, (February 5, 1979), p. 34.

100. Jonathan D. Pollack, *The Lessons of Coalition Politics*, (Santa Monica, CA: Rand Corp., 1984), p. 57.

101. *FBIS-Daily Report-China*, August 12, 1986, p. D1.

102. *FBIS-Daily Report-Asia*, January 12, 1987, C4.

103. James C.F. Wang, *Contemporary Chinese Politics: An Introduction*, 3rd ed., (Englewood Cliffs, NJ: Prentice-Hall, Inc., 1989), p. 348.

104. Steven I. Levine, "China in Asia: the PRC as a regional power," in Harry Harding, ed., *China's Foreign Relations in the 1980s*, (New Haven, CT: Yale University Press, 1984), pp. 177-224.

105. Under Nakasone and his predecessors Ohira and Suzuki, Japanese military capabilities expanded. Japan became more involved in activities of military nature, such as defense of an expanded perimeter of "several hundred nautical miles off its shores and 1,000 miles of sea lanes" by the Maritime Self Defense Forces; participation in the joint naval exercises with the ANZUS member states (i.e., the Australia, New Zealand and the United States Mutual

Security Pact) since 1980; sharing the cost of maintaining the American forces in Japan; transfers of advanced Japanese technology related to defense to the U.S.; deployment of 48 F-16 fighter-bombers in Northern Japan since 1985; and increase in defense spending. See Reinhard Drifte, *Arms Production in Japan: The Military Applications of Civilian Technology*, (Boulder, CO: Westview Press, 1986); and Hiroshi Kimura, "The Soviet Military buildup: Its Impact on Japan and its Aims," in Richard Solomon and Masataka Kosaka, eds., *The Soviet Far East Military Buildup: Nuclear dilemmas and Asia Security*, (London: Croom Helm, 1986, pp. 111-113.

106. *Renmin Ribao (People's Daily)*, (Overseas Edition), June 12, 1992, p. 6.

107. Robert A. Scalapino, "China's Relations with Its Neighbors," in Frank J. Macchiarola and Robert B. Oxnam, eds., *The China Challenge: American Policies in East Asia*, (New York, NY: the Academy of Political Science, 1991), p. 63.

108. Paul H. Kreisberg, "China's Asia Policies," in Frank J. Macchiarola and Robert B. Oxnam, ed., *The China Challenge: American Policies in East Asia*, (New York, NY: the Academy of Political Science, 1991), p. 76.

109. *Beijing Review*, Vol. 32, No. 7/8, (February 13, 1989), p. 21.

110. Paul H. Kreisberg, "China's Asia Policies," in Frank J. Macchiarola and Robert B. Oxnam, ed., *The China Challenge: American Policies in East Asia*, (New York, NY: the Academy of Political Science, 1991), p. 77.

111. Stanley Rosen, "China in 1987: The Year of the Thirteenth Party Congress," *Asian Survey*, Vol. XXVIII, No. 1, (January 1988), p. 47.

112. Robert Delfs, "Seoul's Hi-Tech Lure across the Yellow Sea," *Far East Economic Review*, Vol. 142, No. 49, (December 8, 1988), pp. 20-21. Another statistics showed that the two-way trade with South Korea increased from $1.68 billion in 1987 to $3.087 billion in 1988 and to $3.143 billion in 1989. See Gerrit W. Gong, "China and the Dynamics of Unification in Northeast Asia," in Frank J. Macchiarola and Robert B. Oxnam, ed., *The China Challenge: American Policies in East Asia*, (New York, NY: the Academy of Political Science, 1991), p. 98.

113. Jae Ho Chung, "South Korea-China Economic Relations," *Asian Survey*, Vol. XXVIII, No. 10, (October 1988), p. 1042; and David Dollar, "South Korea-China Trade Relations," *Asian Survey*, Vol. XXIX, No. 12, (December 1989), pp. 1174-1175.

114. *Renmin Ribao (People's Daily)*, September 19, 1986, p. 1; and *The Washington Post*, September 2, 1986, p. F2.

115. Stanley Rosen, "China in 1987: The Year of the Thirteenth Party Congress," *Asian Survey*, Vol. XXVIII, No. 1, (January 1988), p. 47.

116. Li Haibo, "Tumen River Delta: Far East's Future Rotterdam," *Beijing Review*, Vol. 35, No. 16, (April 20, 1992), pp. 5-6.

117. *China Daily*, August 25, 1992, p. 1.